taste of home
Bakeshop *favorites*

taste of home

B O O K S

taste of home Reader's Digest

EDITORIAL

Editor-in-Chief: **CATHERINE CASSIDY**

Executive Editor, Print and Digital Books: **STEPHEN C. GEORGE**
Creative Director: **HOWARD GREENBERG**
Editorial Services Manager: **KERRI BALLIET**

Editor: **CHRISTINE RUKAVENA**
Associate Creative Director: **EDWIN ROBLES JR.**
Art Director: **RUDY KROCHALK**
Content Production Manager: **JULIE WAGNER**
Layout Designer: **CATHERINE FLETCHER**
Copy Chief: **DEB WARLAUMONT MULVEY**
Copy Editor: **ALYSSE GEAR**
Recipe Editor: **MARY KING**
Contributing Layout Designers: **HOLLY PATCH, MATT FUKUDA**
Recipe Content Manager: **COLLEEN KING**
Recipe Testing: **TASTE OF HOME TEST KITCHEN**
Food Photography: **TASTE OF HOME PHOTO STUDIO**
Executive Assistant: **MARIE BRANNON**
Editorial Assistant: **MARILYN ICZKOWSKI**

BUSINESS

Vice President, Publisher: **JAN STUDIN, JAN_STUDIN@RD.COM**
Regional Account Director: **DONNA LINDSKOG, DONNA_LINDSKOG@RD.COM**
Eastern Account Director: **JOANNE CARRARA**
Eastern Account Manager: **KARI NESTOR**
Account Manager: **GINA MINERBI**
Midwest & Western Account Director: **JACKIE FALLON**
Midwest Account Manager: **LORNA PHILLIPS**
Michigan Sales Representative: **LINDA C. DONALDSON**
Southwestern Account Representative: **SUMMER NILSSON**

Corporate Digital and Integrated Sales Director, N.A.: **STEVE SOTTILE**
Associate Marketing Director, Integrated Solutions: **KATIE GAON WILSON**
Digital Sales Planner: **TIM BAARDA**

General Manager, Taste of Home Cooking Schools: **ERIN PUARIEA**

Direct Response Advertising: **KATHERINE ZITO, DAVID GELLER ASSOCIATES**

Vice President, Creative Director: **PAUL LIVORNESE**
Executive Director, Brand Marketing: **LEAH WEST**
Senior Marketing Manager: **VANESSA BAILEY**
Associate Marketing Manager: **BETSY CONNORS**

Vice President, Magazine Marketing: **DAVE FIEGEL**

READER'S DIGEST NORTH AMERICA

Vice President, Business Development: **JONATHAN BIGHAM**
President, Books and Home Entertaining: **HAROLD CLARKE**
Chief Financial Officer: **HOWARD HALLIGAN**
VP, General Manager, Reader's Digest Media: **MARILYNN JACOBS**
Chief Marketing Officer: **RENEE JORDAN**
Vice President, Chief Sales Officer: **MARK JOSEPHSON**
General Manager, Milwaukee: **FRANK QUIGLEY**
Vice President, Chief Content Officer: **LIZ VACCARIELLO**

THE READER'S DIGEST ASSOCIATION, INC.

President and Chief Executive Officer: **ROBERT E. GUTH**

For other **TASTE OF HOME BOOKS** and products, visit us at **TASTEOFHOME.COM.**

For more **READER'S DIGEST** products and information, visit **RD.COM** (in the United States) or **RD.CA** (in Canada).

International Standard Book Number: **978-1-61765-093-2**
Library of Congress Control Number: **2012932605**

COVER PHOTOGRAPHY
Photographer: **DAN ROBERTS**
Food Styling Manager: **SARAH THOMPSON**
Food Stylist: **SHANNON ROUM**
Set Styling Manager: **STEPHANIE MARCHESE**
Set Stylist: **GRACE NATOLI SHELDON**

PICTURED ON FRONT COVER: (clockwise from top left):
Strawberry Tuile Cannoli, page 114; Fudgy Brownies, page 42; Magnolia Dream Cheesecake, page 129; Chocolate Cupcakes, page 61; Lemon Coconut Squares, page 9; Sugar Cookie Tarts, page 127; Almond Petits Fours, page 235.

PICTURED ON BACK COVER: (clockwise from top left):
Peach Blueberry Pie, page 94; Raspberry Truffle Cake Pops, page 54; Amaretto Dream Cupcakes, page 51; Cranberry Orange Bagels, page 291.

PICTURED ON SPINE:
Almond Venetian Dessert, page 111.

Table *of* Contents

10 Baking tips for Success

Are you ready to create gorgeous bakery-quality treats at home?

Follow these pointers to ensure baking success every time. Review the common baking terms, pan information and measurement guides on the following pages. Then grab an apron and get started!

1. Read—It's Fundamental

Read the entire recipe before you begin. If you are not familiar with a technique or term, refer to a cooking reference or search for information on the Internet. Visit *tasteofhome.com* for how-to videos, articles and tips on baking.

2. Check Out Ingredients

Assemble all of the ingredients for the recipe.

Gather all of the ingredients before you begin to make sure you have everything that is needed.

3. Prep Ingredients Before Mixing

Prepare all the ingredients. Let butter soften, separate eggs, chop nuts, etc.

Too firm—butter is too hard to cream.

Butter is softened just right.

4. Get The Oven Ready

Position oven rack before preheating the oven.

Position the oven rack so the baking pan will be in center of the oven, or position the oven rack as the recipe directs. Preheat the oven. For yeast breads, preheat the oven during the final rise time.

5. Select And Prep Pans

Use the type of pan and the size of pan stated in the recipe. Generally, pans are filled two-thirds to three-fourths full.

This pan is too full.

Use an 8-in. x 4-in. loaf pan filled two-thirds full, plus a muffin pan for extra batter; a larger 9-in. x 5-in. loaf pan; or several 5-3/4-in. x 3-in. loaf pans.

Grease the pan as the recipe directs with shortening or cooking spray.

Grease and flour the pan if the recipe directs. For yeast breads, prepare pans before shaping the dough.

6. Measure with Precision

Accurately measure the ingredients. Use a liquid measuring cup for wet ingredients, such as milk, honey, molasses, corn syrup, water, juice or oil. Before measuring sticky ingredients like molasses or corn syrup, coat the inside of the measuring tool with cooking spray. This will make cleanup easier.

Check level of liquid at your eye level.

Fill dry ingredients to the rim and sweep off excess with the flat edge of a metal spatula or knife.

Dry measuring cups allow ingredients to be measured right to the rim of the cup. They are used to measure dry and packable ingredients like flour, sugar, chocolate chips, nuts, shortening and sour cream.

Wet and dry ingredients should be filled to the rim of the spoon.

Measuring spoons are used to measure both liquid and dry ingredients. It's nice to have two sets when baking. Use one set for measuring the liquid ingredients and the other for dry.

7. Mix It Up

Follow the mixing directions as they are written. Altering the method may affect how the final baked good looks and/or tastes.

Cream until light and fluffy.

Fold lighter-weight ingredients into heavier ones with a rubber spatula.

Use a sturdy wooden spoon to stir chips, nuts and dried fruit into heavy batters.

8. Start the Timer

Most recipes give a range for the baking time. Set a kitchen timer for the low end of the time range immediately after the food has been placed in the oven.

Set the timer for the shortest time given in the recipe.

9. Check Doneness

Check for doneness at the shortest time given in the recipe using the stated doneness test. If the baked good does not test done, continue baking and check again.

The toothpick is clean; the cake is done.

The toothpick has crumbs on it; the cake needs more baking time.

10. Take Time To Cool

A wire rack is used for cooling baked goods because it allows air to circulate around the food, which prevents moist, soggy spots. Many cookies can be immediately removed from the baking pan to a wire rack.

Carefully transfer to wire rack to cool.

Cool most baked goods for 10 minutes before removing from the pan.

Other foods like cakes and quick breads need to rest for 10 minutes in their pans. The resting time helps prevent these items from crumbling when they are removed. Still other items—angel food cakes and chiffon cakes baked in tube pans—are cooled completely in their pans. Some baked goods are delicious warm, but others should cool completely for frosting or easy slicing.

Common Baking Terms

Bake—To cook in an oven surrounded by dry heat. When baking, it is important to preheat the oven before placing the food inside.

Beat—To rapidly mix with a spoon, fork, wire whisk or electric mixer.

Blend—To combine several ingredients with a spoon, electric mixer, blender or food processor.

Caramelize—To heat sugar in a skillet or saucepan over low heat until melted and golden brown in color.

Coats Spoon—To leave a thin, even, smooth film on the back of a spoon. This is one of the doneness tests for stirred custards.

Combine—To place several ingredients in a single bowl or container and thoroughly mix.

Cream—To beat softened butter, margarine or shortening alone or with sugar using a spoon or mixer until light and fluffy.

Cube—To cut foods into 1/2-inch to 1-inch square pieces.

Cut In—To break down and distribute cold butter, margarine or shortening into a flour mixture using a pastry blender or two knives.

Dash—A measurement less than 1/8 teaspoon that is used for herbs, spices or hot pepper sauce. This is not a precise measurement.

Dice—To cut foods into 1/8-inch to 1/4-inch cubes.

Dissolve—To stir a solid food with a liquid until none of the solid remains, such as

yeast with warm water or gelatin in boiling water.

Dot—To break up small pieces of butter and distribute evenly over the top of pie filling or dough.

Drizzle—To slowly spoon or pour a thin stream of icing, melted butter or other liquid.

Flute—To make a "V" shape or scalloped edge on a pie crust with your thumb and fingers.

Fold—To combine light or delicate ingredients such as whipped cream or egg whites with other ingredients without beating. A rubber spatula is used to gently cut down through the ingredients, move across the bottom of the bowl and bring up part of the mixture.

Frost—To cover a cake, cupcake or cookie with a spreadable frosting.

Glaze—To coat the exterior of sweet or savory foods with a thin, glossy mixture.

Grease—To rub the inside of a baking dish or pan with shortening, butter or oil or to coat with cooking spray.

Grease and Flour—To rub a thin layer of shortening, butter or oil over the inside of a baking pan or dish and then dust with flour. The excess flour is shaken out of the pan. Cakes baked in round baking pans or fluted tube pans generally require that the pan be greased and floured.

Knead—To work dough by using a pressing and folding action to make it smooth and elastic.

Line—To cover a baking sheet with a piece of parchment paper, waxed paper or foil to prevent sticking.

Marble—To swirl light and dark batters for a cake, bar, pie or cheesecake. The batters should not be combined into one color; there should still be two distinctive batters after marbling.

Mince—To cut foods into very fine pieces no larger than 1/8 inch.

Mix—To stir or beat ingredients together with a spoon or a fork until well combined.

Moisten—To add enough liquid to dry ingredients while gently stirring to make a wet but not runny mixture. Often used in the preparation of muffins.

Pinch—A small amount (less than 1/8 teaspoon) of a seasoning or spice that is easily held between the thumb and index finger. This is not a precise measurement.

Pipe—To force a soft mixture, such as whipped cream, frosting or meringue, through a pastry bag and/or tip for a fancy shape or design.

Prick—To pierce food or pastry with the tines of a fork to prevent it from bursting or rising during baking.

Separate—To remove the egg white from the egg yolk.

Sift—To pass dry ingredients, such as confectioners' sugar or flour, through a fine-mesh strainer to remove lumps, add air and combine several dry ingredients.

Soft Peaks—The stage of beating egg whites or heavy whipping cream when the beater is lifted from the mixture and points of the peaks curl over.

Soften—To bring butter or cream cheese to a soft consistency by letting it stand at room temperature for a short time.

Stiff Peaks—The stage of beating egg whites or heavy whipping cream when the beater is lifted from the mixture and points of the peaks stand straight up.

Stir—To blend a combination of ingredients by hand using a spoon in a circular motion.

Whip—To beat rapidly by hand or with an electric mixer to add air and increase volume.

Choosing Bakeware

Baking pans are made of metal. Aluminum pans with dull finishes give the best overall results. Pans with dark finishes often cook and brown foods more quickly. If you use pans with dark finishes, you may need to adjust the baking time and cover tops of baked goods with foil to prevent overbrowning. Insulated pans and pans with shiny finishes generally take longer to bake and brown foods.

Baking dishes are made of ovenproof glass or ceramic. If you substitute a glass baking dish in a recipe calling for a metal pan, reduce the oven temperature by 25° to avoid overbaking.

To determine your bakeware's measurements, use a ruler to measure from one inside top edge to the opposite inside top edge. To measure height, place a ruler on the outside of the dish and measure from the bottom to a top edge. For volume, fill the pan or dish to the rim with measured water.

For best results, use the pan size called for in the recipe. However, the chart below offers some practical substitutions.

If you don't have this pan(s):	use this pan(s) instead:
One 9-in. x 5-in. loaf pan	Three 5¾-in. x 3-in. x 2-in. loaf pans
One 8-in. x 4-in. loaf pan	Two 5¾-in. x 3-in. x 2-in. loaf pans
One 9-in. round baking pan	One 8-in. square baking dish
Two 9-in. round baking pans	One 13-in. x 9-in. baking pan
One 10-in. fluted tube pan	One 10-in. tube pan or two 9-in. x 5-in. loaf pans
One 13-in. x 9-in. baking pan	Two 9-in. round baking pans or two 8-in. square baking dishes

Weight & Measurement Equivalents

Teaspoon and Tablespoon Measures

Dash or pinch	= less than ⅛ teaspoon
1½ teaspoons	= ½ tablespoon
3 teaspoons	= 1 tablespoon; ½ fluid ounce
4½ teaspoons	= 1½ tablespoons
2 tablespoons	= ⅛ cup; 1 fluid ounce
4 tablespoons	= ¼ cup; 2 fluid ounces
5⅓ tablespoons	= ⅓ cup; 5 tablespoons plus 1 teaspoon
8 tablespoons	= ½ cup; 4 fluid ounces
10⅔ tablespoons	= ⅔ cup; 10 tablespoons plus 2 teaspoons
12 tablespoons	= ¾ cup; 6 fluid ounces
16 tablespoons	= 1 cup; 8 fluid ounces; ½ pint

Cup Measures

⅛ cup	= 2 tablespoons; 1 fluid ounce
¼ cup	= 4 tablespoons; 2 fluid ounces
⅓ cup	= 5⅓ tablespoons
½ cup	= 8 tablespoons; 4 fluid ounces
⅔ cup	= 10⅔ tablespoons
¾ cup	= 12 tablespoons; 6 fluid ounces
⅞ cup	= ¾ cup plus 2 tablespoons
1 cup	= 16 tablespoons; 8 fluid ounces; ½ pint
2 cups	= 1 pint; 16 fluid ounces
4 cups	= 2 pints; 1 quart; 32 fluid ounces

Pints, Quarts, Gallons and Pounds

½ pint	= 1 cup; 8 fluid ounces
1 pint	= 2 cups; 16 fluid ounces
1 quart	= 4 cups; 32 fluid ounces
4 quarts	= 16 cups; 1 gallon
16 ounces	= 1 pound

Cookies,
Brownies & Bars

Lemon Coconut Squares

The tangy citrus flavor of these no-fuss squares is especially yummy on warm days. It reminds me of selling lemonade on the sidewalk as a little girl.

DONNA BIDDLE, ELMIRA, NEW YORK

PREP: 25 MIN. • **BAKE:** 20 MIN. + COOLING • **MAKES:** 4 DOZEN

- 1½ cups all-purpose flour
- ½ cup confectioners' sugar
- ¾ cup cold butter, cubed
- 4 eggs
- 1½ cups sugar
- ½ cup lemon juice
- 1 teaspoon baking powder
- ¾ cup flaked coconut

1. In a small bowl, combine flour and confectioners' sugar; cut in the butter until crumbly. Press into a lightly greased 13-in. x 9-in. baking pan. Bake at 350° for 15 minutes.

2. Meanwhile, in another small bowl, beat the eggs, sugar, lemon juice and baking powder until combined. Pour over crust; sprinkle with coconut.

3. Bake at 350° for 20-25 minutes or until golden brown. Cool on a wire rack. Cut into squares.

Coffee 'n' Cream Brownies

A friend gave me the recipe for these rich cake-like brownies topped with a creamy coffee filling and chocolate glaze. I like to garnish each square with a chocolate-covered coffee bean.

MICHELLE TIEMSTRA, LACOMBE, ALBERTA

PREP: 35 MIN. • **BAKE:** 25 MIN. + STANDING • **MAKES:** 16 SERVINGS

- ½ cup butter, cubed
- 3 ounces unsweetened chocolate, chopped
- 2 eggs
- 1 cup sugar
- 1 teaspoon vanilla extract
- ⅔ cup all-purpose flour
- ¼ teaspoon baking soda

FILLING:
- 1 tablespoon heavy whipping cream
- 1 teaspoon instant coffee granules
- 2 tablespoons butter, softened
- 1 cup confectioners' sugar

GLAZE:
- 1 cup (6 ounces) semisweet chocolate chips
- ⅓ cup heavy whipping cream

1. In a microwave, melt the butter and chocolate; stir until smooth. Cool slightly. In a small bowl, beat the eggs, sugar and vanilla; stir in chocolate mixture. Combine flour and baking soda; stir into chocolate mixture.

2. Spread into a greased 8-in. square baking pan. Bake at 350° for 25-30 minutes or until a toothpick inserted near the center comes out clean (do not overbake). Cool on a wire rack.

3. For filling, combine cream and coffee granules in a small bowl; stir until coffee is dissolved. In another small bowl, cream butter and confectioners' sugar until light and fluffy; beat in coffee mixture. Spread over brownies.

4. In a small saucepan, combine chips and cream. Cook and stir over low heat until chocolate is melted and mixture is thickened. Cool slightly. Carefully spread over filling. Let stand for 30 minutes or until glaze is set. Cut into squares. Store in the refrigerator.

Maple Pecan Cookies

When I bake cookies for the annual youth ski trip, I try at least one new recipe. When I received recipe requests for these frosted goodies, I knew I had a keeper.

NANCY JOHNSON, LAVERNE, OKLAHOMA

PREP: 20 MIN. • **BAKE:** 10 MIN./BATCH + COOLING • **MAKES:** 7 DOZEN

- 1 **cup shortening**
- ½ **cup butter, softened**
- 2 **cups packed brown sugar**
- 2 **eggs**
- 1 **teaspoon vanilla extract**
- 1 **teaspoon maple flavoring**
- 3 **cups all-purpose flour**
- 2 **teaspoons baking soda**
- 1 **package (10 to 12 ounces) white baking chips**
- ½ **cup chopped pecans**

FROSTING:

- ¼ **cup butter, softened**
- 4 **cups confectioners' sugar**
- 1 **teaspoon maple flavoring**
- 3 **to 5 tablespoons 2% milk**
- 1½ **cups pecan halves**

1. In a large bowl, cream the shortening, butter and brown sugar until light and fluffy. Add eggs, one at a time, beating well after each addition. Beat in vanilla and maple flavoring. Combine flour and baking soda; gradually add to the creamed mixture and mix well. Stir in white chips and pecans.

2. Drop by tablespoonfuls 2 in. apart onto ungreased baking sheets. Bake at 350° for 9-11 minutes or until golden brown. Cool for 2 minutes before removing to wire racks.

3. In a large bowl, cream the butter, confectioners' sugar, maple flavoring and enough milk to achieve spreading consistency. Frost each cookie with 1 teaspoon frosting; top with a pecan half.

Cinnamon Snaps

Since I'm a longtime cinnamon fan, I decided to give traditional gingersnaps a different twist. My husband and son agree I spiced them up just right.

CATHY CAIN, CARMEL, CALIFORNIA

PREP: 20 MIN. • **BAKE:** 10 MIN./BATCH • **MAKES:** 4½ DOZEN

- ¾ **cup shortening**
- 1 **cup packed brown sugar**
- 1 **egg**
- ¼ **cup molasses**
- 2¼ **cups all-purpose flour**
- 2 **teaspoons baking soda**
- 2 **teaspoons ground cinnamon**
- ½ **teaspoon salt**
- **Granulated sugar**

1. In a large bowl, cream shortening and brown sugar until light and fluffy. Beat in egg and molasses. Combine flour, baking soda, cinnamon and salt; gradually beat into creamed mixture. Roll into 1-in. balls, then roll in granulated sugar.

2. Place 2 in. apart on ungreased baking sheets. Bake at 350° for 10-12 minutes or until cookies are set and tops are cracked. Remove to wire racks to cool.

White Chocolate Cranberry Cookies

The red and white coloring in these sweet cookies makes them a festive addition to any cookie tray. The pairing of tart cranberry and rich, buttery white chocolate is a real classic.

DONNA BECK, SCOTTDALE, PENNSYLVANIA

PREP: 20 MIN. • **BAKE:** 10 MIN./BATCH • **MAKES:** 2 DOZEN

- ⅓ cup butter, softened
- ½ cup packed brown sugar
- ⅓ cup sugar
- 1 egg
- 1 teaspoon vanilla extract
- 1½ cups all-purpose flour
- ½ teaspoon salt
- ½ teaspoon baking soda
- ¾ cup dried cranberries
- ½ cup white baking chips

1. In a large bowl, beat butter and sugars until crumbly, about 2 minutes. Beat in egg and vanilla. Combine the flour, salt and baking soda; gradually add to butter mixture and mix well. Stir in cranberries and chips.

2. Drop by heaping tablespoonfuls 2 in. apart onto baking sheets coated with cooking spray. Bake at 375° for 8-10 minutes or until lightly browned. Cool for 1 minute before removing to wire racks.

Caramel Cookie Pops

My fun little chocolate chip cookies will be a hit with kids and adults alike. You can coat the caramel with your favorite type of nuts, sprinkles or mini chips.

TAMMY DANIELS, BATAVIA, OHIO

PREP: 40 MIN. **BAKE:** 10 MIN./BATCH + STANDING • **MAKES:** 4 DOZEN

- ½ **cup butter, softened**
- ¼ **cup confectioners' sugar**
- ¼ **cup packed brown sugar**
- ¼ **teaspoon salt**
- 1 **egg**
- ½ **teaspoon vanilla extract**
- 2 **cups all-purpose flour**
- ½ **cup miniature semisweet chocolate chips**
- 48 **round toothpicks**
- 1 **package (11 ounces) Kraft caramel bits**
- 2 **tablespoons water**
- 1 **cup finely chopped pecans**

1. In a bowl, cream butter, sugars and salt until fluffy. Beat in egg and vanilla. Gradually add flour and mix well. Stir in chips.

2. Shape dough into 1-in. balls; place 2 in. apart on greased baking sheets. Bake at 350° for 10-12 minutes or until set. Immediately insert a round toothpick in center of each cookie. Remove to wire racks to cool completely.

3. In a small saucepan, combine caramels and water. Cook and stir over medium-low heat until smooth. Holding a cookie by the toothpick, dip in caramel mixture, turning to coat. Allow excess to drip off. Immediately dip the bottom and sides in pecans.

4. Place on waxed paper. Repeat. Let stand until set.

Linzer Cookies

This specialty cookie takes a little extra effort, but the results are sweet! They really help to make the holidays feel special.

JANE PEARCY, VERONA, WISCONSIN

PREP: 30 MIN. + CHILLING • **BAKE:** 10 MIN./BATCH + COOLING
MAKES: 3 DOZEN

- 1¼ **cups butter, softened**
- 1 **cup sugar**

- 2 **eggs**
- 3 **cups all-purpose flour**
- 1 **tablespoon baking cocoa**
- ½ **teaspoon salt**
- ¼ **teaspoon ground cinnamon**
- ¼ **teaspoon ground nutmeg**
- ⅛ **teaspoon ground cloves**
- 2 **cups ground almonds**
- 6 **tablespoons seedless raspberry jam**
- 3 **tablespoons confectioners' sugar**

1. In a large bowl, cream butter and sugar until light and fluffy. Add eggs, one at a time, beating well after each addition. Combine the flour, cocoa, salt and spices; gradually add to creamed mixture and mix well. Stir in almonds. Refrigerate for 1 hour or until easy to handle.

2. On a lightly floured surface, roll out dough to ⅛-in. thickness. Cut with a floured 2½-in. round cookie cutter. From the center of half of the cookies, cut out a 1½-in. shape.

3. Place on ungreased baking sheets. Bake at 350° for 10-12 minutes or until edges are golden brown. Remove to wire racks to cool.

4. Spread the bottom of each solid cookie with ½ teaspoon jam. Sprinkle cutout cookies with confectioners' sugar; carefully place over jam.

White Chocolate Raspberry Thumbprints

When I pass around the cookie tray, all eyes land on these fancy thumbprints. The white chocolate filling and dab of jewel-toned jam will satisfy the most discriminating sweet tooth.

AGNES WARD, STRATFORD, ONTARIO

PREP: 25 MIN. + CHILLING • **BAKE:** 10 MIN./BATCH + COOLING
MAKES: ABOUT 3 DOZEN

- ¾ **cup butter, softened**
- ½ **cup packed brown sugar**
- 2 **eggs, separated**
- 1¼ **cups all-purpose flour**
- ¼ **cup baking cocoa**
- 1¼ **cups finely chopped pecans or walnuts**

FILLING:
- 4 **ounces white baking chocolate, coarsely chopped**
- 2 **tablespoons butter**
- ¼ **cup seedless raspberry jam**

1. In a large bowl, cream the butter and brown sugar until light and fluffy. Beat in egg yolks. Combine flour and cocoa; gradually add to creamed mixture and mix well. Cover and refrigerate for 1-2 hours or until easy to handle.

2. In a shallow bowl, whisk egg whites until foamy. Place nuts in another shallow bowl. Shape dough into 1-in. balls. Dip in egg whites, then roll in nuts.

3. Using a wooden spoon handle, make an indentation in center of each cookie. Place 1 in. apart on greased baking sheets. Bake at 350° for 8-10 minutes. Remove to wire racks to cool.

4. In a microwave, melt white chocolate and butter; stir until smooth. Spoon about ½ teaspoon into each cookie. Top each with about ¼ teaspoon jam. Store in an airtight container.

Old-Fashioned Gingersnaps

I discovered this recipe many years ago, and it's been a favorite among our family and friends since. We especially love them during the holidays.

FRANCIS STOOPS, STONEBORO, PENNSYLVANIA

PREP: 15 MIN. + CHILLING • **BAKE:** 10 MIN./BATCH + COOLING
MAKES: ABOUT 4 DOZEN

- 1 **cup butter, softened**
- 1 **cup sugar**
- 1 **egg**
- ¼ **cup molasses**
- 2 **cups all-purpose flour**
- 2 **teaspoons baking soda**
- 1 **teaspoon ground cinnamon**
- 1 **teaspoon ground cloves**
- 1 **teaspoon ground ginger**
- ¼ **teaspoon salt**
  Additional sugar

1. In a bowl, cream the butter and sugar. Beat in egg and molasses. Combine the flour, baking soda, cinnamon, cloves, ginger and salt; gradually add to creamed mixture. Chill.

2. Roll into 1¼-in. balls and dip into sugar. Place 2 in. apart on ungreased baking sheets. Bake at 375° for about 10 minutes or until set and surface cracks. Cool on wire racks.

Macaroon Bars

Guests will never recognize the refrigerated crescent roll dough that goes into these almond-flavored bars. You can assemble these chewy coconut treats in no time.

CAROLYN KYZER, ALEXANDER, ARKANSAS

PREP: 10 MIN. • **BAKE:** 30 MIN. + COOLING • **MAKES:** 3 DOZEN

3¼ cups flaked coconut, divided
1 can (14 ounces) sweetened condensed milk
1 teaspoon almond extract
1 tube (8 ounces) refrigerated crescent rolls

SHORT & SWEET

1. Sprinkle 1½ cups coconut into a well-greased 13-in. x 9-in. baking pan. Combine milk and extract; drizzle half over the coconut. Unroll crescent dough into one long rectangle; seal seams and perforations. Place in pan. Drizzle with remaining milk mixture; sprinkle with remaining coconut.

2. Bake at 350° for 30-35 minutes or until golden brown. Cool completely on a wire rack before cutting. Store in the refrigerator.

Cheesecake Brownies

Brownies are my grandson's favorite, so we always make some when he comes to visit. These cheesecake ones are creamy and scrumptious.

BARBARA BANZHOF, MUNCY, PENNSYLVANIA

PREP: 30 MIN. • **BAKE:** 30 MIN. + COOLING • **MAKES:** 3 DOZEN

- 1 **package fudge brownie mix (13-inch x 9-inch pan size)**
- 2 **packages (3 ounces each) cream cheese, softened**
- 6 **tablespoons butter, softened**
- ½ **cup sugar**
- 2 **tablespoons all-purpose flour**
- 1 **teaspoon vanilla extract**
- 2 **eggs, lightly beaten**
- 1 **can (16 ounces) chocolate frosting**

1. Prepare brownie mix batter according to the package directions. Spread 2 cups into a greased 13-in. x 9-in. baking dish; set aside.

2. In a small bowl, beat the cream cheese, butter, sugar, flour and vanilla until smooth. Add eggs; beat on low speed just until combined. Spread evenly over brownie batter. Top with remaining brownie batter. Cut through batter with a knife to swirl.

3. Bake at 350° for 28-32 minutes or until a toothpick inserted near the center comes out with moist crumbs (brownies may appear moist). Cool completely on a wire rack. Spread frosting over brownies.

Neapolitan Crispy Bars

These festive goodies will have your friends and family members buzzing over the multicolored layers as well as the tempting chocolate and strawberry flavors.

TASTE OF HOME TEST KITCHEN

PREP: 15 MIN. • **COOK:** 30 MIN. + COOLING • **MAKES:** 1 DOZEN

    1   package (10 ounces) large marshmallows, divided
    3   tablespoons butter, divided
    2   cups Cocoa Krispies
    ½   cup miniature semisweet chocolate chips
    4   cups Rice Krispies, divided
    ½   cup strawberry preserves
    5   drops red food coloring, optional

1. In a large saucepan, combine a third of the marshmallows (about 2 cups) and 1 tablespoon butter. Cook and stir over medium-low heat until melted. Remove from the heat; stir in Cocoa Krispies and chocolate chips. Press into a greased 11-in. x 7-in. dish.

2. In a large saucepan, combine a third of the marshmallows and 1 tablespoon butter. Cook and stir over medium-low heat until melted. Remove from the heat; stir in 2 cups Rice Krispies. Press into dish over chocolate layer.

3. In a large saucepan, combine remaining marshmallows and butter. Cook and stir over medium-low heat until melted. Remove from the heat; stir in preserves and food coloring if desired. Stir in remaining Rice Krispies. Press into the dish. Cool. Cut into bars.

Lemon-Lime Bars

I baked these bars for a luncheon on a hot summer day. A gentleman made his way to the kitchen to compliment the cook who made them.

HOLLY WILKINS, LAKE ELMORE, VERMONT

PREP: 20 MIN. • **BAKE:** 20 MIN. + COOLING • **MAKES:** 4 DOZEN

    1   cup butter, softened
    ½   cup confectioners' sugar
    2   teaspoons grated lime peel
    1¾ cups all-purpose flour
    ¼   teaspoon salt

FILLING:

    4   eggs
    1½ cups sugar
    ¼   cup all-purpose flour
    ½   teaspoon baking powder
    ⅓   cup lemon juice
    2   teaspoons grated lemon peel
        Confectioners' sugar

1. In a large bowl, cream the butter and confectioners' sugar until light and fluffy. Beat in lime peel. Combine flour and salt; gradually add to creamed mixture and mix well.

2. Press into a greased 13-in. x 9-in. baking dish. Bake at 350° for 13-15 minutes or just until edges are lightly browned.

3. Meanwhile, in another large bowl, beat eggs and sugar. Combine the flour and baking powder. Gradually add to egg mixture. Stir in lemon juice and peel; beat until frothy. Pour over hot crust.

4. Bake for 20-25 minutes or until light golden brown. Cool on a wire rack. Dust with the confectioners' sugar. Cut into squares. Store in the refrigerator.

Jumbo Chocolate Chip Cookies

These huge cookies are a family favorite. No one can resist their sweet chocolaty taste.

LORI SPORER, OAKLEY, KANSAS

PREP: 15 MIN. + CHILLING • **BAKE:** 15 MIN./BATCH • **MAKES:** 2 DOZEN

- ⅔ **cup shortening**
- ⅔ **cup butter, softened**
- 1 **cup sugar**
- 1 **cup packed brown sugar**
- 2 **eggs**
- 2 **teaspoons vanilla extract**
- 3½ **cups all-purpose flour**
- 1 **teaspoon baking soda**
- 1 **teaspoon salt**
- 2 **cups (12 ounces) semisweet chocolate chips**
- 1 **cup chopped pecans**

1. In a large bowl, cream shortening, butter and sugars until light and fluffy. Beat in eggs and vanilla. Combine the flour, baking soda and salt; add to creamed mixture and mix well. Fold in the chocolate chips and pecans. Chill for at least 1 hour.

2. Drop by ¼ cupfuls 2 in. apart onto greased baking sheets. Bake at 375° for 13-15 minutes or until golden brown. Cool for 5 minutes before removing to wire racks.

Cranberry Swirl Biscotti

A friend of mine who is known for her excellent cookies shared this recipe with me. The mix of cranberries and cherry preserves is so fun and unexpected.

LISA KILCUP, GIG HARBOR, WASHINGTON

PREP: 20 MIN. • **BAKE:** 40 MIN. + COOLING
MAKES: ABOUT 2½ DOZEN

- ⅔ **cup dried cranberries**
- ½ **cup cherry preserves**
- ½ **teaspoon ground cinnamon**
- ½ **cup butter, softened**
- ⅔ **cup sugar**
- 2 **eggs**
- 1 **teaspoon vanilla extract**
- 2¼ **cups all-purpose flour**
- ¾ **teaspoon baking powder**
- ¼ **teaspoon salt**
- **GLAZE:**
- ¾ **cup confectioners' sugar**
- 1 **tablespoon 2% milk**
- 2 **teaspoons butter, melted**
- 1 **teaspoon almond extract**

1. In a food processor, combine the cranberries, preserves and cinnamon. Cover and process until smooth; set aside.

2. In a large bowl, cream butter and sugar until light and fluffy. Beat in eggs and vanilla. Combine the flour, baking powder and salt; gradually add to creamed mixture and mix well.

3. Divide dough in half. On a lightly floured surface, roll each portion into a 12-in. x 8-in. rectangle. Spread each with cranberry filling; roll up jelly-roll style, starting with a short side.

4. Place seam side down 4 in. apart on a lightly greased baking sheet. Bake at 325° for 25-30 minutes or until lightly browned.

5. Carefully transfer the logs to a cutting board; cool for 5 minutes. With a serrated knife, cut into ½-in. slices. Place on lightly greased baking sheets. Bake 15 minutes longer or until centers are firm and dry. Remove to wire racks.

6. In a small bowl, combine glaze ingredients; drizzle over warm biscotti. Cool completely. Store in an airtight container.

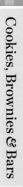

Blueberry Lattice Bars

Since our area has an annual blueberry festival, my daughters and I are always looking for great new berry recipes to enter in the cooking contest. These lovely bars won a blue ribbon one year.

DEBBIE AYERS, BAILEYVILLE, MAINE

PREP: 25 MIN. + CHILLING • **BAKE:** 30 MIN. + COOLING • **MAKES:** 2 DOZEN

   1 **cup butter, softened**
   ½ **cup sugar**
   1 **egg**
   ½ **teaspoon vanilla extract**
   2¾ **cups all-purpose flour**
   ¼ **teaspoon salt**
FILLING:
   3 **cups fresh or frozen blueberries**
   1 **cup sugar**
   3 **tablespoons cornstarch**

1. In a large bowl, cream butter and sugar until light and fluffy. Beat in egg and vanilla. Combine the flour and salt; gradually add to creamed mixture and mix well. Cover and refrigerate for 2 hours.

2. Meanwhile, in a small saucepan, bring the blueberries, sugar and cornstarch to a boil. Cook and stir for 2 minutes or until thickened.

3. Roll two-thirds of the dough into a 14-in. x 10-in. rectangle. Place in a greased 13-in. x 9-in. baking dish. Top with filling. Roll out remaining dough to ¼-in. thickness. Cut into ½-in.-wide strips; make a lattice crust over filling.

4. Bake at 375° for 30-35 minutes or until top is golden brown. Cool on a wire rack. Cut into bars.

Pumpkin Bars

What could be more appropriate for a Halloween treat than a pan of pumpkin-flavored bars? Actually, they're a hit with my family throughout the year.

BRENDA KELLER, ANDALUSIA, ALABAMA

PREP: 15 MIN. • **BAKE:** 25 MIN. + COOLING • **MAKES:** 2 DOZEN

    4 eggs
1⅔ cups sugar
    1 cup canola oil
    1 can (15 ounces) solid-pack pumpkin
    2 cups all-purpose flour
    2 teaspoons ground cinnamon
    2 teaspoons baking powder
    1 teaspoon baking soda
    1 teaspoon salt
ICING:
    1 package (3 ounces) cream cheese, softened
    2 cups confectioners' sugar
¼ cup butter, softened
    1 teaspoon vanilla extract
    1 to 2 tablespoons milk

1. In a bowl, beat eggs, sugar, oil and pumpkin. Combine flour, cinnamon, baking powder, baking soda and salt; gradually add to pumpkin mixture and mix well. Pour into an ungreased 15-in. x 10-in. x 1-in. baking pan. Bake at 350° for 25-30 minutes or until set. Cool completely.

2. For icing, beat cream cheese, confectioners' sugar, butter and vanilla in a small bowl. Add enough of the milk to achieve desired spreading consistency. Spread icing over bars. Store in the refrigerator.

Citrus Biscotti

Often, I'll package some of my home-baked biscotti with a mug and a special blend of coffee to give as a gift.

CLAIRE BROGREN, WINSIDE, NEW YORK

PREP: 20 MIN. • **BAKE:** 40 MIN. + COOLING

MAKES: ABOUT 4 DOZEN

½ cup butter, softened
1½ cups sugar
    4 eggs
    1 tablespoon grated lemon peel
    2 teaspoons grated orange peel
    1 teaspoon vanilla extract
3¾ cups all-purpose flour
    2 teaspoons baking powder
        Dash salt
    2 tablespoons coarsely ground almonds

1. In a large bowl, cream butter and sugar. Add 3 eggs, one at a time, beating well after each. Beat in lemon peel, orange peel and vanilla.

2. Combine the flour, baking powder and salt; gradually add to creamed mixture. Divide dough into four portions; shape each into an 8-in. x 2-in. rectangle on ungreased baking sheets.

3. In a small bowl, lightly beat remaining egg; brush evenly over dough. Sprinkle with almonds.

4. Bake at 350° for 25-30 minutes or until lightly browned. Cool for 5 minutes.

5. Transfer to a cutting board; cut diagonally with a serrated knife into ¾-in. slices. Place cut side down on ungreased baking sheets.

6. Bake for 12-14 minutes or until golden brown, turning once. Cool on wire racks. Store in an airtight container.

Bakeshop HOW-TO

Cutting Biscotti

After the rectangular biscotti dough is baked, it needs to be cut into slices and returned to the oven.

With a serrated knife, cut the cookie into ½- or ¾-in.-thick slices.

Place the sliced cookies cut side down on a baking sheet and bake as directed.

Orange Nanaimo Bars

I originally created these rich bars for my co-workers. Everyone raved over the orange and chocolate flavor combination, which makes them different from most. They're now a staple for many gatherings.

DEL MASON, MARTENSVILLE, SASKATCHEWAN

PREP: 40 MIN. + CHILLING • **MAKES:** 3 DOZEN

- ⅓ cup butter, cubed
- ¼ cup sugar
- 1 dark chocolate candy bar (3¼ ounces), chopped
- 1 egg, beaten
- 17 shortbread cookies, crushed
- ½ cup flaked coconut
- ½ cup finely chopped pecans
- 1 teaspoon grated orange peel

FILLING:
- ½ cup butter, softened
- 2 tablespoons instant vanilla pudding mix
- 2 cups confectioners' sugar
- 2 tablespoons orange juice
- 1 teaspoon grated orange peel
- 1 to 2 drops orange paste food coloring, optional

GLAZE:
- 1 dark chocolate candy bar (3¼ ounces), chopped
- 1 teaspoon butter

1. In a large heavy saucepan, combine the butter, sugar and candy bar. Cook and stir over medium-low heat until melted. Whisk a small amount of hot mixture into egg. Return all to the pan, whisking constantly. Cook and stir over medium-low heat until mixture reaches 160°.

2. In a large bowl, combine the cookie crumbs, coconut, pecans and orange peel. Stir in chocolate mixture until blended. Press into a greased 9-in. square baking pan. Refrigerate for 30 minutes or until set.

3. For filling, in a large bowl, cream butter and pudding mix. Beat in the confectioners' sugar, orange juice, peel and food coloring if desired. Spread over crust.

4. For glaze, melt candy bar and butter in a microwave; stir until smooth. Spread over top. Refrigerate until set. Cut into bars.

Peanut Butter Cookie Pops

A miniature candy bar is the hidden treat inside these fun pops. My sons brought these cookies home from school after their teacher made a bunch for her class. The kids loved nibbling them on a stick. Of course, the taste was also a hit!

MARTHA HOOVER, COATESVILLE, PENNSYLVANIA

PREP: 20 MIN. • **BAKE:** 15 MIN. + COOLING • **MAKES:** 1 DOZEN

- ½ cup butter, softened
- ½ cup creamy peanut butter
- ½ cup sugar
- ½ cup packed brown sugar
- 1 egg
- 1 teaspoon vanilla extract
- 1½ cups all-purpose flour
- ½ teaspoon baking powder
- ½ teaspoon baking soda
- ¼ teaspoon salt
- 12 wooden craft sticks
- 12 fun-size Snickers or Milky Way candy bars

1. In a small bowl, cream butter, peanut butter and sugars until light and fluffy. Beat in egg and vanilla until light and fluffy. Combine flour, baking powder, baking soda and salt; gradually add to creamed mixture and mix well.

2. Insert a wooden stick into the small end of each candy bar. Divide dough into 12 pieces; wrap one piece around each candy bar. Place 4 in. apart on ungreased baking sheets.

3. Bake at 375° for 14-16 minutes or until golden brown. Cool for 10 minutes; remove from pans to wire racks to cool completely.

2. Turn dough onto a floured surface; knead in almonds. On a baking sheet coated with cooking spray, shape the dough into a 12-in. x 3-in. rectangle. Bake at 350° for 28-30 minutes or until lightly browned. Cool for 10 minutes.

3. Transfer to a cutting board; cut diagonally with a serrated knife into 13 slices. Place cut side down on a baking sheet coated with cooking spray. Bake for 20-25 minutes or until firm and crisp, turning once. Remove to a wire rack to cool.

4. Drizzle white chocolate over biscotti; let stand until set. Store in an airtight container.

Little-Batch Rocky Road Brownies

Years ago, my girlfriend and I combined our favorite brownie recipes. With the addition of miniature marshmallows and chocolate chips, we created a chocoholic's dream—and it's so easy to double for company.

DONNA SAWATZKY, PIEDMONT, OKLAHOMA

PREP: 10 MIN. • **BAKE:** 30 MIN. + COOLING • **MAKES:** 6 SERVINGS

- ¼ cup butter, cubed
- 1 ounce unsweetened chocolate, chopped
- ½ cup sugar
- 1 egg, lightly beaten
- ½ teaspoon vanilla extract
- ⅛ teaspoon salt
- ¼ cup all-purpose flour
- ½ cup miniature marshmallows
- ⅓ cup miniature semisweet chocolate chips
- ⅓ cup chopped pecans

1. In a small heavy saucepan, melt butter and chocolate; stir until smooth.

2. Remove from the heat; stir in sugar. Stir in the egg, vanilla and salt until well blended. Stir in flour just until blended. Fold in the marshmallows, chips and pecans.

3. Spread into a greased 8-in. x 4-in. loaf pan. Bake at 350° for 30-35 minutes or until a toothpick inserted near the center comes out clean. Cool on a wire rack.

Chocolate Almond Biscotti

During college, I came across a chocolate biscotti recipe and played around with it until I came up with something I truly love. It's great for dunking into tea or coffee.

LORI HINZE, MCCOOK, NEBRASKA

PREP: 30 MIN. • **BAKE:** 50 MIN. + COOLING • **MAKES:** 13 COOKIES

- ¼ cup butter, softened
- ⅔ cup sugar
- 1 egg
- 2 tablespoons beaten egg
- 1 ounce semisweet chocolate, melted and cooled
- ½ teaspoon instant coffee granules
- ½ teaspoon hot water
- 1¼ cups all-purpose flour
- 2 tablespoons baking cocoa
- 1½ teaspoons baking powder
- ¼ teaspoon salt
- ⅓ cup slivered almonds, toasted
- 3 ounces white baking chocolate, melted

1. In a small bowl, cream butter and sugar until light and fluffy. Beat in eggs and semisweet chocolate until blended. Dissolve coffee granules in hot water; beat into chocolate mixture. Combine the flour, cocoa, baking powder and salt; gradually add to chocolate mixture and mix well.

Salted Peanut Bars

You'll never look at Rice Krispies Treats the same way again after trying these nutty three-tiered cookie, marshmallow and cereal bars.

DENISE KIRSCH, MCLEANSBORO, ILLINOIS

PREP: 20 MIN. • **BAKE:** 15 MIN. + CHILLING • **MAKES:** 2 DOZEN

- 1 package (17½ ounces) peanut butter cookie mix
- 3 tablespoons canola oil
- 1 tablespoon water
- 1 egg
- 1 package (10 ounces) peanut butter chips
- ⅔ cup corn syrup
- ¼ cup butter, cubed
- 2 cups Rice Krispies
- 2 cups salted peanuts
- 2 teaspoons vanilla extract
- 3 cups miniature marshmallows

1. In a large bowl, combine the cookie mix, oil, water and egg. Press onto the bottom of a greased 13-in. x 9-in. pan.

2. Bake at 350° for 12-15 minutes or until set. Meanwhile, in a large saucepan, combine the chips, corn syrup and butter. Cook and stir over medium-low heat until smooth. Remove from the heat. Stir in the Rice Krispies, peanuts and vanilla.

3. Sprinkle marshmallows over crust. Bake 1-2 minutes longer or until marshmallows begin to puff. Spread cereal mixture over top. Cool completely on a wire rack. Refrigerate until firm. Cut into bars.

Fudge Puddles

I was inspired to make these cookies after enjoying them on a little break from my Christmas shopping. I changed a few things when I got home, and my Fudge Puddles became a favorite with my husband's family.

KIMARIE MAASSEN, AVOCA, IOWA

PREP: 25 MIN. + CHILLING • **BAKE:** 20 MIN./BATCH + COOLING
MAKES: 4 DOZEN

- ½ cup butter, softened
- ½ cup creamy peanut butter
- ½ cup sugar
- ½ cup packed light brown sugar
- 1 egg
- ½ teaspoon vanilla extract
- 1¼ cups all-purpose flour
- ¾ teaspoon baking soda
- ½ teaspoon salt

FUDGE FILLING:
- 1 cup milk chocolate chips
- 1 cup (6 ounces) semisweet chocolate chips
- 1 can (14 ounces) sweetened condensed milk
- 1 teaspoon vanilla extract
  Chopped peanuts

1. In a large bowl, cream the butter, peanut butter and sugars. Beat in egg and vanilla. Combine the flour, baking soda and salt; gradually add to creamed mixture and mix well. Chill for 1 hour.

2. Shape into 48 balls, 1 in. each. Place in lightly greased mini-muffin tins. Bake at 325° for 14-16 minutes or until lightly browned. Using the end of a wooden spoon handle, make a ⅜- to ½-in.-deep indentation in the center of each. Cool in pans for 5 minutes before removing to wire racks to cool completely.

3. For filling, in a microwave, melt chocolate chips. Stir in milk and vanilla until smooth. Fill each shell with filling. Sprinkle with peanuts. (Leftover filling can be stored in the refrigerator and served warm over ice cream.)

Dreamy Chocolate Chip Bars

This recipe is my children's favorite (and mine!). For even more sweet flavor, they always ask me to dust the bars with confectioners' sugar.

KATHARINE FLY, FARWELL, TEXAS

PREP: 25 MIN. • **BAKE:** 20 MIN. + COOLING • **MAKES:** 4 DOZEN

- 1 cup plus 2 tablespoons all-purpose flour, divided
- 1 cup quick-cooking oats
- 1½ cups packed brown sugar, divided
- ½ cup cold butter, cubed
- 2 eggs
- 2 teaspoons vanilla extract
- 1½ cups flaked coconut
- 1 cup chopped walnuts
- 1 teaspoon baking powder
- ¼ teaspoon salt
- 1 cup (6 ounces) semisweet chocolate chips

1. In a large bowl, combine 1 cup flour, oats and ½ cup brown sugar; cut in butter until crumbly. Press into a greased 13-in. x 9-in. baking pan. Bake at 375° for 8-10 minutes or until golden brown. Cool on a wire rack.

2. In a large bowl, beat eggs, vanilla and remaining brown sugar. Combine the coconut, walnuts, baking powder, salt and remaining flour; gradually add to egg mixture and mix well. Stir in chocolate chips.

3. Spread evenly over crust. Bake for 18-20 minutes or until golden brown. Cut into bars while warm. Cool on a wire rack.

Cranberry Lemon Sandwiches

I bake cookies all year long, so my friends and family call me the Cookie Lady! Whenever I bake these for Christmas, I make three batches–one to keep at home for my husband and two to give as gifts.

PATRICIA MICHALSKI, OSWEGO, NEW YORK

PREP: 20 MIN. + CHILLING • **BAKE:** 15 MIN./BATCH
MAKES: ABOUT 4½ DOZEN

- 1 cup butter, softened
- 1 cup shortening
- 1 cup sugar
- 1 cup confectioners' sugar
- 2 eggs
- 2 teaspoons vanilla extract
- 4 cups all-purpose flour
- 1 teaspoon cream of tartar
- 1 teaspoon grated lemon peel
- ½ teaspoon salt
- ¾ cup dried cranberries

FILLING:
- ⅔ cup butter, softened
- 2¾ cups confectioners' sugar
- ¼ cup 2% milk
- 1¼ teaspoons grated lemon peel

1. In a large bowl, cream the butter, shortening and sugars until light and fluffy. Add eggs, one at a time, beating well after each addition. Beat in vanilla. Combine the flour, cream of tartar, lemon peel and salt; gradually add to the creamed mixture and mix well. Stir in cranberries. Cover and refrigerate for 2 hours or until easy to handle.

2. Roll into 1-in. balls. Place 2 in. apart on ungreased baking sheets. Flatten with a glass dipped in sugar. Bake at 350° for 12-14 minutes or until edges are lightly browned. Remove to wire racks to cool.

3. In a small bowl, combine the filling ingredients; beat until smooth. Spread on the bottoms of half of the cookies; top with remaining cookies.

Red Velvet Whoopie Pies

These cookies are a delightful twist on the classic cake. Sometimes I substitute canned cream cheese frosting for the filling.

JUDI DEXHEIMER, STURGEON BAY, WISCONSIN

PREP: 40 MIN. • **BAKE:** 10 MIN./BATCH + COOLING • **MAKES:** 2 DOZEN

- 2 **ounces semisweet chocolate, chopped**
- ¾ **cup butter, softened**
- 1 **cup sugar**
- 2 **eggs**
- ½ **cup sour cream**
- 1 **tablespoon red food coloring**
- 1½ **teaspoons white vinegar**
- 1 **teaspoon clear vanilla extract**
- 2¼ **cups all-purpose flour**
- ¼ **cup baking cocoa**
- 2 **teaspoons baking powder**
- ½ **teaspoon salt**
- ¼ **teaspoon baking soda**

FILLING:
- 1 **package (8 ounces) cream cheese, softened**
- ½ **cup butter, softened**
- 2½ **cups confectioners' sugar**
- 2 **teaspoons clear vanilla extract**

TOPPINGS:
- **White baking chips, melted**
- **Finely chopped pecans**

1. In a microwave, melt the chocolate; stir until smooth. Set aside.

2. In a large bowl, cream the butter and sugar until light and fluffy. Beat in the eggs, sour cream, food coloring, vinegar and vanilla. Combine the flour, cocoa, baking powder, salt and baking soda; gradually add to creamed mixture and mix well. Stir in melted chocolate.

3. Drop by tablespoonfuls 2 in. apart onto parchment paper-lined baking sheets. Bake at 375° for 8-10 minutes or until edges are set. Cool for 2 minutes before removing from pans to wire racks to cool completely.

4. For filling, in a large bowl, beat cream cheese and butter until fluffy. Beat in confectioners' sugar and vanilla until smooth. Spread filling on the bottoms of half of the cookies, about 1 tablespoon on each. Top with remaining cookies. Drizzle with melted baking chips; sprinkle with nuts. Store in an airtight container in the refrigerator.

Polka-Dot Macaroons

These chewy cookies are really easy to mix up in a hurry, and they're a favorite with both adults and kids. I've been baking for a long time and, believe me, these never last long.

JANICE LASS, DORR, MICHIGAN

PREP: 15 MIN. • **BAKE:** 10 MIN./BATCH • **MAKES:** ABOUT 4½ DOZEN

- 5 **cups flaked coconut**
- 1 **can (14 ounces) sweetened condensed milk**
- ½ **cup all-purpose flour**
- 1½ **cups M&M's minis**

SHORT & SWEET

1. In a large bowl, combine the coconut, milk and flour. Stir in M&M's.

2. Drop by rounded tablespoonfuls 2 in. apart onto baking sheets coated with cooking spray. Bake at 350° for 8-10 minutes or until edges are lightly browned. Remove to wire racks.

Papa's Sugar Cookies

My grandchildren love my crisp sugar cookies. Their subtle macadamia nut, cinnamon and orange peel flavors go perfectly together.

LEE DOVERSPIKE, NORTH RIDGEVILLE, OHIO

PREP: 20 MIN. + CHILLING • **BAKE:** 10 MIN./BATCH • **MAKES:** 8 DOZEN

- 1 **cup butter, softened**
- 1 **cup canola oil**
- 1 **cup sugar**
- 1 **cup confectioners' sugar**
- 2 **eggs**
- 2 **tablespoons butter flavoring**
- 1 **tablespoon grated orange peel**
- 1 **tablespoon vanilla extract**
- 5½ **cups all-purpose flour**
- ¼ **cup ground macadamia nuts**
- 1½ **teaspoons baking soda**
- 1 **teaspoon salt**
- 1 **teaspoon cream of tartar**
- 1 **teaspoon ground cinnamon**
  Additional granulated sugar

1. In a large bowl, beat the butter, oil and sugars until well blended. Add eggs, one at a time, beating well after each addition. Beat in the butter flavoring, orange peel and vanilla.

2. Combine the flour, nuts, baking soda, salt, cream of tartar and cinnamon; gradually add to butter mixture and mix well. Cover and refrigerate for 1 hour or until easy to handle.

3. Roll into 1-in. balls, then roll in additional sugar. Place 2 in. apart on ungreased baking sheets. Flatten with a glass dipped in additional sugar.

4. Bake at 350° for 10-12 minutes or until edges begin to brown. Remove to wire racks.

Cappuccino Cake Brownies

If you like your sweets with a cup of coffee, this recipe is for you! These no-nut brownies combine a mild coffee flavor with the richness of semisweet chocolate chips. They're a quick anytime treat at our house.

MARY HOUCHIN, LEBANON, ILLINOIS

PREP: 15 MIN. • **BAKE:** 25 MIN. + COOLING • **MAKES:** 16 BROWNIES

- 1 tablespoon instant coffee granules
- 2 teaspoons boiling water
- 1 cup (6 ounces) semisweet chocolate chips
- ¼ cup butter, softened
- ½ cup sugar
- 2 eggs
- ½ cup all-purpose flour
- ¼ teaspoon ground cinnamon

SHORT & SWEET

1. In a small bowl, dissolve coffee in water; set aside. In a microwave, melt chocolate chips; stir until smooth. In a small bowl, cream butter and sugar until light and fluffy. Beat in eggs, melted chocolate and coffee mixture. Combine flour and cinnamon; gradually add to creamed mixture until blended.

2. Pour into a greased 8-in. square baking pan. Bake at 350° for 25-30 minutes or until a toothpick inserted near the center comes out clean. Cool on a wire rack. Cut into squares.

Chocolate Mint Brownies

One of the best things about this recipe is that the brownies get moister if you leave them in the refrigerator for a day or two. The problem at our house is no one can leave them alone for that long!

HELEN BAINES, ELKTON, MARYLAND

PREP: 20 MIN. • **BAKE:** 30 MIN. + CHILLING • **MAKES:** 5-6 DOZEN

- ½ cup butter, softened
- 1 cup sugar
- 4 eggs
- 1 can (16 ounces) chocolate syrup
- 1 teaspoon vanilla extract
- 1 cup all-purpose flour
- ½ teaspoon salt

FILLING:
- ½ cup butter, softened
- 2 cups confectioners' sugar
- 1 tablespoon water
- ½ teaspoon mint extract
- 3 drops green food coloring

TOPPING:
- 1 package (10 ounces) mint chocolate chips
- ½ cup plus 1 tablespoon butter, cubed

1. In a large bowl, cream butter and sugar until light and fluffy. Add eggs, one at a time, beating well after each addition. Beat in syrup and vanilla. Add flour and salt; mix well.

2. Pour into a greased 13-in. x 9-in. baking pan. Bake at 350° for 30 minutes (top of brownie will still appear wet). Cool on a wire rack.

3. For filling, in a small bowl, cream butter and confectioners' sugar; add the water, extract and food coloring until blended. Spread over cooled brownies. Refrigerate until set.

4. For topping, melt chocolate chips and butter. Cool for 30 minutes, stirring occasionally. Spread over filling. Chill. Cut into bars. Store in the refrigerator.

Editor's Note: *If mint chocolate chips are not available, place 2 cups (12 ounces) semisweet chocolate chips and ¼ teaspoon peppermint extract in a plastic bag; seal and toss to coat. Allow chips to stand for 24-48 hours.*

Chocolate Gingersnaps

When my daughter, Jennifer, was 15 years old, she created this recipe as a way to combine two of her favorite flavors. They're great with a glass of milk.

PAULA ZSIRAY, LOGAN, UTAH

PREP: 45 MIN. + CHILLING • **BAKE:** 10 MIN./BATCH • **MAKES:** 3 DOZEN

- ½ cup butter, softened
- ½ cup packed dark brown sugar
- ¼ cup molasses
- 1 tablespoon water
- 2 teaspoons minced fresh gingerroot
- 1½ cups all-purpose flour
- 1 tablespoon baking cocoa
- 1¼ teaspoons ground ginger
- 1 teaspoon baking soda
- 1 teaspoon ground cinnamon
- ¼ teaspoon ground nutmeg
- ¼ teaspoon ground cloves
- 7 ounces semisweet chocolate, chopped
- ¼ cup sugar

1. In a large bowl, cream the butter and brown sugar until light and fluffy. Beat in the molasses, water and gingerroot. Combine the flour, cocoa, ginger, baking soda, cinnamon, nutmeg and cloves; gradually add to creamed mixture and mix well. Stir in chocolate. Cover and refrigerate for 2 hours or until easy to handle.

2. Shape dough into 1-in. balls; roll in sugar. Place 2 in. apart on greased baking sheets.

3. Bake at 350° for 10-12 minutes or until tops begin to crack. Cool for 2 minutes before removing to wire racks.

Butterscotch Cashew Bars

I knew these nutty bars were a success when I took them on our annual family vacation. My husband couldn't stop eating them... and my sister-in-law, who is a great cook, asked for the recipe. It makes a big batch, which is good, because they go quickly!

LORI BERG, WENTZVILLE, MISSOURI

PREP: 20 MIN. • **BAKE:** 15 MIN. + COOLING • **MAKES:** 3½ DOZEN

- 1 cup plus 2 tablespoons butter, softened
- ¾ cup plus 2 tablespoons packed brown sugar
- 2½ cups all-purpose flour
- 1¾ teaspoons salt
- **TOPPING:**
- 1 package (10 to 11 ounces) butterscotch chips
- ½ cup plus 2 tablespoons light corn syrup
- 3 tablespoons butter
- 2 teaspoons water
- 2½ cups salted cashew halves

1. In a large bowl, cream the butter and brown sugar until light and fluffy. Combine flour and salt; add to creamed mixture just until combined.

2. Press into a greased 15-in. x 10-in. x 1-in. baking pan. Bake at 350° for 10-12 minutes or until lightly browned.

3. Meanwhile, in a small saucepan, combine the butterscotch chips, corn syrup, butter and water. Cook and stir over medium heat until smooth.

4. Spread over crust. Sprinkle with cashews; press down lightly. Bake for 11-13 minutes or until topping is bubbly and lightly browned. Cool on a wire rack. Cut into bars.

1. In a large bowl, cream butter and sugar until light and fluffy. Combine the flour, baking powder and salt. Combine the eggs, milk and vanilla.

2. Add dry ingredients to the creamed mixture alternately with egg mixture, beating well after each addition. Divide dough in half; chill for 2 hours or until firm.

3. Roll out one portion of the dough into a 15-in. x 10-in. rectangle; carefully transfer to a greased 15-in. x 10-in. x 1-in. baking pan. Spread with raspberry filling.

4. Roll out remaining dough to ¼-in. thickness. Cut into ½-in.-wide strips; make a lattice crust over filling. Bake at 350° for 30 minutes or until golden brown. Cool on a wire rack.

5. In a small bowl, beat the butter, shortening, cream cheese and marshmallow creme until smooth. Gradually add the confectioners' sugar and milk until smooth. Drizzle over bars. Chill until set. Cut into bars.

Frosted Raspberry Bars

While visiting a friend, I tried one of these tempting treats that her daughter made. After one bite, I knew I had to have the recipe. These cake-like bars with fruity filling are perfect for any potluck or party.

ESTHER HORST, AUGUSTA, WISCONSIN

PREP: 25 MIN. + CHILLING • **BAKE:** 30 MIN. + COOLING
MAKES: 2 DOZEN

- 1 **cup butter, softened**
- ¼ **cup sugar**
- 3 **cups all-purpose flour**
- 3 **teaspoons baking powder**
- 1 **teaspoon salt**
- 2 **eggs**
- ½ **cup milk**
- 1 **teaspoon vanilla extract**
- 1 **can (21 ounces) raspberry pie filling**
FROSTING:
- 1 **tablespoon butter, softened**
- 1 **tablespoon shortening**
- 1 **ounce cream cheese, softened**
- 2 **tablespoons marshmallow creme**
- ½ **cup plus 1 tablespoon confectioners' sugar**
- 1 **tablespoon milk**

Chewy Pecan Pie Bars

This is one of my husband's favorite recipes, and I've been making it for many years. If you like pecan pie, you'll love the flavor of these bars.

JUDY TAYLOR, SHREVEPORT, LOUISIANA

PREP: 10 MIN. • **BAKE:** 30 MIN. + COOLING • **MAKES:** 2 DOZEN

- ¼ **cup butter, melted**
- 2 **cups packed brown sugar**
- ⅔ **cup all-purpose flour**
- 4 **eggs**
- 2 **teaspoons vanilla extract**
- ¼ **teaspoon baking soda**
- ¼ **teaspoon salt**
- 2 **cups chopped pecans**
  Confectioners' sugar

1. Pour butter into an ungreased 13-in. x 9-in. baking pan; set aside. In a large bowl, beat the brown sugar, flour, eggs, vanilla, baking soda and salt until well blended. Stir in pecans. Spread over butter.

2. Bake at 350° for 30-35 minutes or until set. Remove from the oven; immediately dust with confectioners' sugar. Cool before cutting.

Deluxe Chocolate Marshmallow Bars

I've been asked to share this chocolaty layered recipe more than any other in my collection. It's a longtime favorite of our three daughters and I can't even begin to count how many times I have made them!

ESTHER SHANK, HARRISONBURG, VIRGINIA

PREP: 25 MIN. • **BAKE:** 15 MIN. + COOLING • **MAKES:** 3 DOZEN

- ¾ cup butter, softened
- 1½ cups sugar
- 3 eggs
- 1 teaspoon vanilla extract
- 1⅓ cups all-purpose flour
- 3 tablespoons baking cocoa
- ½ teaspoon baking powder
- ½ teaspoon salt
- ½ cup chopped nuts, optional
- 4 cups miniature marshmallows

TOPPING:
- 1⅓ cups semisweet chocolate chips
- 1 cup peanut butter
- 3 tablespoons butter
- 2 cups Rice Krispies

1. In a small bowl, cream butter and sugar until light and fluffy. Add eggs, one at a time, beating well after each addition. Beat in vanilla.

2. Combine the flour, cocoa, baking powder and salt; gradually add to creamed mixture. Stir in nuts if desired. Spread in a greased 15-in. x 10-in. x 1-in. baking pan.

3. Bake at 350° for 15-18 minutes or until set. Sprinkle with marshmallows; bake 2-3 minutes longer or until melted. Place pan on a wire rack. Using a knife dipped in water, spread marshmallows evenly over the top. Cool completely.

4. For topping, combine the chocolate chips, peanut butter and butter in a small saucepan. Cook and stir over low heat until blended. Remove from the heat; stir in Rice Krispies. Immediately spread over bars. Chill until set.

Pecan Logs

Folks always expect to find these tender treats on the cookie trays I give out at Christmas. They're not overly sweet and go great with a steaming cup of coffee or tea.

JOYCE BECK, GADSDEN, ALABAMA

PREP: 15 MIN. + CHILLING • **BAKE:** 15 MIN./BATCH + COOLING
MAKES: ABOUT 2½ DOZEN

- 1 **cup butter, softened**
- 5 **tablespoons confectioners' sugar**
- 2 **teaspoons vanilla extract**
- 2 **cups all-purpose flour**
- 1 **cup finely chopped pecans**
  Confectioners' sugar

1. In a small bowl, cream butter and sugar until light and fluffy. Beat in vanilla. Add the flour, beating on low speed just until combined. Stir in pecans. Cover and refrigerate for 30 minutes or until easy to handle.

2. Shape ½ cupfuls into ½-in.-thick logs. Cut logs into 2-in. pieces. Place 2 in. apart on greased baking sheets. Bake at 350° for 15-18 minutes or until lightly browned. Roll warm cookies in confectioners' sugar; cool on wire racks.

White Chip Cranberry Blondies

We created these delicious blondies sure to satisfy the sweet tooth of any health-conscious cook. Applesauce moistens the batter while making these treats lighter than most.

TASTE OF HOME TEST KITCHEN

PREP: 15 MIN. • **BAKE:** 15 MIN. + COOLING • **MAKES:** 20 BARS

- 2 eggs
- ¼ cup canola oil
- ¼ cup unsweetened applesauce
- 1½ teaspoons vanilla extract
- 1⅓ cups all-purpose flour
- ⅔ cup packed brown sugar
- 1 teaspoon baking powder
- ½ teaspoon salt
- 1 cup dried cranberries, divided
- ½ cup white baking chips
- ½ cup chopped pecans

1. In a large bowl, beat the eggs, oil, applesauce and vanilla. Combine the flour, brown sugar, baking powder and salt; stir into egg mixture until blended. Stir in ½ cup cranberries (batter will be thick).

2. Spread into a 13-in. x 9-in. baking pan coated with cooking spray. Top with chips, pecans and remaining cranberries; gently press toppings down.

3. Bake at 350° for 15-20 minutes or until a toothpick inserted near the center comes out clean. Cool on a wire rack. Cut into bars.

Gingerbread Whoopie Pies

These spiced-just-right whoopie pies combine two popular flavors in one fun treat. The moist cookies are rolled in sugar before baking for a bit of crunch.

JAMIE JONES, MADISON, GEORGIA

PREP: 25 MIN. + CHILLING • **BAKE:** 10 MIN./BATCH + COOLING
MAKES: ABOUT 2 DOZEN

- ¾ cup butter, softened
- ¾ cup packed brown sugar
- ½ cup molasses
- 1 egg
- 3 cups all-purpose flour
- 2 teaspoons ground ginger
- 1 teaspoon ground cinnamon
- 1 teaspoon baking soda
- ¼ teaspoon salt
- ½ cup sugar

FILLING:
- ¾ cup butter, softened
- ¾ cup marshmallow creme
- 1½ cups confectioners' sugar
- ¾ teaspoon lemon extract

1. In a large bowl, cream butter and brown sugar until light and fluffy. Beat in molasses and egg. Combine the flour, ginger, cinnamon, baking soda and salt; gradually add to creamed mixture and mix well. Cover and refrigerate for at least 3 hours.

2. Shape into 1-in. balls; roll in sugar. Place 3 in. apart on ungreased baking sheets. Flatten to ½-in. thickness with a glass dipped in sugar. Bake at 350° for 8-10 minutes or until set. Cool for 2 minutes before removing from pans to wire racks to cool completely.

3. For filling, in a small bowl, beat butter and marshmallow creme until light and fluffy. Gradually beat in confectioners' sugar and extract.

4. Spread filling on the bottoms of half of the cookies, about 1 tablespoon on each; top with remaining cookies.

LEMON POPPY SEED COOKIES

Lemon Poppy Seed Cookies

My family of lemon lovers has a weakness for these refreshing cookies. The poppy seeds and hint of ginger make them even more delicious.

CAROL OWEN, SALINA, KANSAS

PREP: 35 MIN. + CHILLING • **BAKE:** 10 MIN./BATCH
MAKES: ABOUT 4½ DOZEN

- 1¼ cups sugar
- 1 cup butter-flavored shortening
- 2 eggs
- ¼ cup light corn syrup
- 1 tablespoon grated lemon peel
- 1½ teaspoons lemon extract
- 1 teaspoon vanilla extract
- 3 cups all-purpose flour
- 2 tablespoons poppy seeds
- 1 teaspoon ground ginger
- ¾ teaspoon baking powder
- ½ teaspoon salt
- ½ teaspoon baking soda

1. In a large bowl, cream sugar and shortening until light and fluffy. Beat in the eggs, corn syrup, lemon peel and extracts. Combine the remaining ingredients; gradually add to the creamed mixture and mix well.

2. Shape into three balls, then flatten into disks. Wrap in plastic wrap and refrigerate for 1 hour or until firm.

3. Roll each portion of dough between two sheets of waxed paper to ⅛-in. thickness. Cut with a floured 2½-in. fluted round cookie cutter. Using a floured spatula, place 1 in. apart on greased baking sheets. Reroll scraps if desired.

4. Bake at 375° for 6-8 minutes or until edges are golden brown. Cool for 2 minutes before removing from pans to wire racks.

Pistachio Chocolate Macarons

These light and airy pistachio cookies feature a devilishly luscious chocolate filling.

TASTE OF HOME TEST KITCHEN

PREP: 35 MIN. • **BAKE:** 10 MIN./BATCH + COOLING • **MAKES:** 16 COOKIES

- 3 egg whites
- 1¼ cups confectioners' sugar
- ¾ cup pistachios
- Dash salt
- ¼ cup sugar
- **CHOCOLATE FILLING:**
- 4 ounces bittersweet chocolate, chopped
- ½ cup heavy whipping cream
- 2 teaspoons corn syrup
- 1 tablespoon butter

1. Place egg whites in a small bowl; let stand at room temperature for 30 minutes. Place confectioners' sugar and pistachios in a food processor. Cover and process until pistachios become a fine powder.

2. Add salt to egg whites; beat on medium speed until soft peaks form. Gradually add sugar, 1 tablespoon at a time, beating on high until stiff peaks form. Fold in pistachio mixture.

3. Place mixture in a heavy-duty resealable plastic bag; cut a small hole in a corner of bag. Pipe 1-in.-diameter cookies 1 in. apart onto parchment paper-lined baking sheets. Bake at 350° for 10-12 minutes or until lightly browned and firm to the touch. Cool completely on pans on wire racks.

4. Place chocolate in a small bowl. In a small saucepan, bring cream and corn syrup just to a boil. Pour over chocolate; whisk until smooth. Whisk in butter. Cool, stirring occasionally, to room temperature or until filling reaches a spreading consistency, about 45 minutes. Spread on the bottoms of half of the cookies; top with remaining cookies.

White Chocolate Cherry Shortbread

Our children and grandchildren declared this festive, flavorful cookie a keeper. We gave a batch to our mail carrier to thank her for trudging through so much snow, and she requested the recipe.

RUTH ANNE DALE, TITUSVILLE, PENNSYLVANIA

PREP: 30 MIN. • **BAKE:** 10 MIN./BATCH + STANDING
MAKES: ABOUT 4 DOZEN

- 2½ **cups all-purpose flour**
- ¾ **cup sugar, divided**
- 1 **cup cold butter, cubed**
- ½ **cup finely chopped maraschino cherries, patted dry**
- 12 **ounces white baking chocolate, finely chopped, divided**
- ½ **teaspoon almond extract**
- 2 **teaspoons shortening**
  Coarse sugar and red edible glitter

1. In a large bowl, combine flour and ½ cup sugar; cut in butter until crumbly. Knead in the cherries, ⅔ cup white chocolate and extract until dough forms a ball.

2. Shape into ¾-in. balls. Place 2 in. apart on ungreased baking sheets. Flatten slightly with a glass dipped in remaining sugar. Bake at 325° for 10-12 minutes or until edges are lightly browned. Remove to wire racks to cool completely.

3. In a microwave, melt shortening and remaining white chocolate; stir until smooth.

4. Dip half of each cookie into chocolate; allow excess to drip off. Place on waxed paper; sprinkle with the coarse sugar and edible glitter.

5. Let stand until set. Store in an airtight container.

Editor's Note: *Edible glitter is available from Wilton Industries. Call 800-794-5866 or visit wilton.com.*

Bakeshop TIP

About Shortbread

Shortbread gets its fine crumb from the way it is mixed. Cutting butter into dry ingredients results in tiny bits of flour-coated butter throughout the dough and a cookie that is tender and crumbly at the same time. If you don't have a pastry blender, use two knives to cut in the cold butter.

Cappuccino Flats

These coffee-flavored cookies are so delicious most people can't believe they're made in my own kitchen instead of a gourmet bakery!

JACQUELINE CLINE, DRUMMOND, WISCONSIN

PREP: 20 MIN. + CHILLING • **BAKE:** 10 MIN./BATCH + STANDING
MAKES: 4½ DOZEN

- ½ **cup butter, softened**
- ½ **cup shortening**
- ½ **cup sugar**
- ½ **cup packed brown sugar**
- 1 **tablespoon instant coffee granules**
- 1 **teaspoon warm water**
- 1 **egg**
- 2 **ounces unsweetened chocolate, melted and cooled**
- 2 **cups all-purpose flour**
- 1 **teaspoon ground cinnamon**
- ¼ **teaspoon salt**

GLAZE:
- 1½ **cups semisweet chocolate chips**
- 3 **tablespoons shortening**

1. In a large bowl, cream butter, shortening and sugars until light and fluffy. Dissolve coffee in water; add to creamed mixture with egg and melted chocolate until blended. Combine the flour, cinnamon and salt; gradually add to creamed mixture and mix well (dough will be sticky). Shape into two 6½-in. rolls; wrap each in plastic wrap. Refrigerate for 4 hours or until firm.

2. Unwrap and cut into ¼-in. slices. Place 2 in. apart on ungreased baking sheets. Bake at 350° for 10-12 minutes or until firm. Remove to wire racks to cool completely.

3. In a microwave, melt chocolate chips and shortening; stir until smooth. Dip each cookie halfway in the chocolate; allow excess to drip off. Place on waxed paper; let stand until set.

Iced Anise Cookies

It was a family tradition to have these cookies on Thanksgiving, Christmas and Easter. My grandmother always kept some on hand for her grandchildren.

LINDA HARRINGTON, WINDHAM, NEW HAMPSHIRE

PREP: 40 MIN. • **BAKE:** 10 MIN./BATCH + COOLING • **MAKES:** 6 DOZEN

    2⅔ cups all-purpose flour
    ½ cup sugar
    3 teaspoons baking powder
    3 eggs
    ½ cup butter, melted
    ¼ cup 2% milk
    2 teaspoons anise extract
ICING:
    ¼ cup butter, softened
    2 cups confectioners' sugar
    3 tablespoons 2% milk
    ½ teaspoon lemon extract
       Coarse and colored sugars, optional

1. In a large bowl, combine 2 cups flour, sugar and baking powder. In a small bowl, whisk the eggs, butter, milk and extract. Stir into dry ingredients until blended. Stir in the remaining flour until dough forms a ball. Turn onto a floured surface; knead until smooth.

2. Shape dough by rounded teaspoonfuls into thin 6-in. ropes; twist each rope into a "Q" shape. Place on ungreased baking sheets. Bake at 350° for 8-10 minutes or until set. Remove from pans to wire racks to cool completely.

3. For icing, in a small bowl, beat butter until fluffy. Add the confectioners' sugar, milk and extract; beat until smooth. Spread over tops of cookies; decorate with sugars if desired.

Raspberry Walnut Shortbread

A sweet raspberry filling is sandwiched between a crispy crust and a crunchy brown sugar topping in these satisfying bars.

PAT HABIGER, SPEARVILLE, KANSAS

PREP: 15 MIN. • **BAKE:** 20 MIN. + COOLING • **MAKES:** 16 SERVINGS

    1¼ cups plus 2 tablespoons all-purpose flour, divided
    ½ cup sugar
    ½ cup cold butter
    ½ cup raspberry jam
    2 eggs
    ½ cup packed brown sugar
    1 teaspoon vanilla extract
    ⅛ teaspoon baking soda
    1 cup finely chopped walnuts

1. In a bowl, combine 1¼ cups flour and sugar; cut in butter until crumbly. Press into a greased 9-in. square baking pan. Bake at 350° for 20-25 minutes or until edges are lightly browned. Place on a wire rack. Spread jam over hot crust.

2. In a bowl, beat eggs, brown sugar and vanilla. Combine baking soda and remaining flour; stir into the egg mixture just until combined. Fold in the walnuts. Spoon over jam; spread evenly.

3. Bake for 17-20 minutes or until golden brown and set. Cool completely on a wire rack before cutting.

Fudgy Brownies

Rich brownies are topped with a peanut butter pudding frosting, making this a recipe the whole family will love. These are perfect for a potluck, bake sale or yummy after-dinner treat.

AMY CROOK, SYRACUSE, UTAH

PREP: 20 MIN. • **BAKE:** 25 MIN. + CHILLING • **MAKES:** 2½ DOZEN

- 1 **package fudge brownie mix (13-inch x 9-inch pan size)**
- 1½ **cups confectioners' sugar**
- ½ **cup butter, softened**
- 2 **to 3 tablespoons peanut butter**
- 2 **tablespoons cold 2% milk**
- 4½ **teaspoons instant vanilla pudding mix**
- 1 **can (16 ounces) chocolate fudge frosting**

1. Prepare and bake brownies according to the package directions. Cool on a wire rack.

2. Meanwhile, in a small bowl, beat the confectioners' sugar, butter, peanut butter, milk and pudding mix until smooth. Spread over brownies. Refrigerate for 30 minutes or until firm. Frost with chocolate fudge frosting just before cutting.

Carrot Cookie Bites

These soft and delicious cookies are an all-time family favorite. Their aroma while baking is absolutely irresistible! I'm always asked for the recipe.

JEANIE PETRIK, GREENSBURG, KENTUCKY

PREP: 15 MIN. • **BAKE:** 10 MIN./BATCH • **MAKES:** 7 DOZEN

- ⅔ **cup shortening**
- 1 **cup packed brown sugar**
- 2 **eggs**
- ½ **cup buttermilk**
- 1 **teaspoon vanilla extract**
- 2 **cups all-purpose flour**
- 1 **teaspoon ground cinnamon**
- ½ **teaspoon salt**
- ¼ **teaspoon baking powder**
- ¼ **teaspoon baking soda**
- ¼ **teaspoon ground nutmeg**
- ¼ **teaspoon ground cloves**
- 2 **cups quick-cooking oats**
- 1 **cup shredded carrots**
- ½ **cup chopped pecans**

1. In a large bowl, cream shortening and brown sugar until light and fluffy. Beat in the eggs, buttermilk and vanilla. Combine the flour, cinnamon, salt, baking powder, baking soda, nutmeg and cloves; gradually add to creamed mixture. Stir in the oats, carrots, and pecans.

2. To freeze cookie dough, drop desired amount of dough by rounded teaspoonfuls onto baking sheets; freeze until firm. Transfer frozen cookie dough balls into a resealable plastic freezer bag. May be frozen for up to 3 months.

3. Drop remaining cookie dough by rounded teaspoonfuls 2 in. apart onto ungreased baking sheets. Bake at 375° for 6-8 minutes or until lightly browned. Remove to wire racks to cool.

To use frozen cookie dough: Place frozen dough balls 2 in. apart on ungreased baking sheets. Bake at 375° for 10-15 minutes or until lightly browned. Remove to wire racks to cool.

Frosted Cashew Cookies

We enjoy these cookies every Christmas, but they're special year-round with coffee or even tucked into a lunch box. My sister's sister-in-law discovered the recipe. I won a blue ribbon with these cookies at my county fair.

SHEILA WYUM, RUTLAND, NORTH DAKOTA

PREP: 20 MIN. • **BAKE:** 10 MIN./BATCH + COOLING
MAKES: ABOUT 3 DOZEN

- ½ cup butter, softened
- 1 cup packed brown sugar
- 1 egg
- ⅓ cup sour cream
- ½ teaspoon vanilla extract
- 2 cups all-purpose flour
- ¾ teaspoon each baking powder, baking soda and salt
- 1¾ cups salted cashew halves

BROWNED BUTTER FROSTING:
- ½ cup butter, cubed
- 3 tablespoons half-and-half cream
- ¼ teaspoon vanilla extract
- 2 cups confectioners' sugar
  Additional cashew halves, optional

1. In a bowl, cream the butter and brown sugar until light and fluffy. Beat in egg, sour cream and vanilla; mix well. Combine the flour, baking powder, baking soda and salt; add to creamed mixture and mix well. Stir in cashews.

2. Drop by rounded teaspoonfuls 2 in. apart onto greased baking sheets. Bake at 375° for 8-10 minutes or until lightly browned. Cool on a wire rack.

3. For the frosting, lightly brown butter in a small saucepan. Remove from the heat; add cream and vanilla. Beat in the confectioners' sugar until thick and smooth. Frost cookies. Top each with a cashew half if desired.

Chocolate Cherry Cupcakes

Inside each of these little cakes is a fruity surprise! At kids' parties, adult soirees or anything in between, guests will adore them.

BERTILLE COOPER, CALIFORNIA, MARYLAND

PREP: 15 MIN. • **BAKE:** 20 MIN. • **MAKES:** 2 DOZEN

- 1 package (18¼ ounces) chocolate cake mix
- 1⅓ cups water
- ½ cup canola oil
- 3 eggs
- 1 can (21 ounces) cherry pie filling
- 1 can (16 ounces) vanilla frosting
  Chocolate curls, optional

SHORT & SWEET

1. In a large bowl, combine the cake mix, water, oil and eggs; beat on low speed for 30 seconds. Beat on medium for 2 minutes.

2. Spoon batter by ¼ cupfuls into paper-lined muffin cups. Spoon a rounded teaspoon of pie filling onto the center of each cupcake. Set remaining pie filling aside.

3. Bake at 350° for 20-25 minutes or until a toothpick inserted near the center comes out clean. Remove from pans to wire racks to cool completely.

4. Frost cupcakes; top each with one cherry from pie filling. Refrigerate remaining pie filling for another use. Garnish with chocolate curls if desired.

Chocolate Hazelnut Torte

Most cake recipes feed a crowd. So we came up with this elegant little cake that serves six. That's plenty for two, with enough leftovers to sneak bites and midnight snacks for a few days after!

TASTE OF HOME TEST KITCHEN

PREP: 30 MIN. + CHILLING • **BAKE:** 25 MIN. + COOLING
MAKES: 6 SERVINGS

- ⅓ cup butter, softened
- 1 cup packed brown sugar
- 1 egg
- 1 teaspoon vanilla extract
- 1 cup all-purpose flour
- ¼ cup baking cocoa
- 1 teaspoon baking soda
- ⅛ teaspoon salt
- ½ cup sour cream
- ½ cup brewed coffee, room temperature

FROSTING:
- 7 ounces semisweet chocolate, chopped
- 1 cup heavy whipping cream
- 2 tablespoons sugar
- ⅓ cup Nutella
  Chocolate curls and hazelnuts, optional

1. In a small bowl, cream butter and brown sugar until light and fluffy. Beat in egg and vanilla. Combine the flour, cocoa, baking soda and salt; gradually beat into creamed mixture alternately with sour cream and coffee.

2. Pour into two greased and floured 6-in. round baking pans. Bake at 350° for 25-30 minutes or until a knife inserted near the center comes out clean. Cool for 10 minutes before removing from pans to wire racks to cool completely.

3. For frosting, in a small saucepan, melt chocolate with cream and sugar over low heat; stir until smooth. Remove from the heat; whisk in Nutella. Transfer to a small bowl; cover and refrigerate until frosting reaches spreading consistency, stirring occasionally.

4. Spread frosting between layers and over top and sides of cake. Garnish with chocolate curls and hazelnuts if desired.

2. Bake at 350° for 40-45 minutes or until a toothpick inserted near the center comes out clean. Cool for 10 minutes before removing from pan to a wire rack to cool completely.

3. In a small bowl, combine glaze ingredients until smooth; drizzle over cake.

Low-Fat Carrot Cake

Loaded with spice and carrot flavor, this moist and luscious cake is guaranteed to impress.

REBECCA BAIRD, SALT LAKE CITY, UTAH

PREP: 30 MIN. • **BAKE:** 30 MIN. + COOLING • **MAKES:** 16 SERVINGS

  2 **cups packed brown sugar**
  ½ **cup buttermilk**
  2 **egg whites**
  1 **egg**
  2 **tablespoons canola oil**
  1 **teaspoon vanilla extract**
2½ **cups cake flour**
  1 **teaspoon baking soda**
  1 **teaspoon ground cinnamon**
  ½ **teaspoon ground allspice**
  ¼ **teaspoon ground nutmeg**
  ¼ **teaspoon ground cloves**
  ⅛ **teaspoon salt**
  3 **cups grated carrots**
  1 **can (8 ounces) unsweetened crushed pineapple, drained**
  2 **ounces reduced-fat cream cheese**
  1 **cup confectioners' sugar**
  ½ **teaspoon lemon juice**
  ⅛ **teaspoon vanilla extract**

1. In a large bowl, beat the brown sugar, buttermilk, egg whites, egg, oil and vanilla until well blended. Combine the flour, baking soda, spices and salt; gradually beat into sugar mixture until blended. Fold in carrots and pineapple. Pour into a 13-in. x 9-in. baking dish coated with cooking spray.

2. Bake at 350° for 30-35 minutes or until a toothpick inserted near the center comes out clean. Cool completely on a wire rack.

3. In a small bowl, beat cream cheese until fluffy. Add the confectioners' sugar, lemon juice and vanilla; beat until smooth. Drizzle over cake.

Lemon-Lime Poppy Seed Cake

There's plenty of lemon-lime flavor in this tender cake to please any citrus lover. Plus, it's a breeze to make.

VICTORIA HAHN, NORTHAMPTON, PENNSYLVANIA

PREP: 20 MIN. • **BAKE:** 40 MIN. + COOLING • **MAKES:** 12 SERVINGS

  1 **package (18¼ ounces) yellow cake mix**
  1 **package (3.4 ounces) instant vanilla pudding mix**
  ¼ **cup poppy seeds**
  4 **eggs**
  ½ **cup water**
  ½ **cup canola oil**
  ¼ **cup lemon juice**
  ¼ **cup lime juice**
GLAZE:
1¾ **cups confectioners' sugar**
  2 **tablespoons lemon juice**
  2 **tablespoons lime juice**

SHORT & SWEET

1. In a large bowl, combine the first eight ingredients. Beat on low speed for 30 seconds; beat on medium for 2 minutes. Pour into a greased and floured 10-in. fluted tube pan.

Caramel Cashew Cake Pops

Nothing beats the pairing of buttery caramel and rich cashews; add it to a chocolaty cake pop and you have one irresistible little treat.

TASTE OF HOME TEST KITCHEN

PREP: 1½ HOURS + CHILLING • **MAKES:** 4 DOZEN

    1   **package (18¼ ounces) chocolate cake mix**
    ¾   **cup canned dulce de leche**
   48   **lollipop sticks**
   2½   **pounds milk chocolate candy coating, coarsely chopped**
        Chopped cashews

1. Prepare and bake cake mix according to package directions, using a greased 13-in. x 9-in. baking pan. Cool completely on a wire rack.

2. Crumble cake into a large bowl. Add dulce de leche and mix well. Shape into 1-in. balls. Place on baking sheets; insert sticks. Freeze for at least 2 hours or refrigerate for at least 3 hours or until cake balls are firm.

3. In a microwave, melt candy coating. Dip each cake ball in coating; allow excess to drip off. Coat with cashews. Insert cake pops into a foam block to stand. Let stand until set.

Raspberry Fudge Torte

People are surprised to hear this impressive torte starts with a simple cake mix—they're sure I bought it at a bakery.

JULIE HEIN, YORK, PENNSYLVANIA

PREP: 30 MIN. + CHILLING • **BAKE:** 25 MIN. + COOLING
MAKES: 12 SERVINGS

- 1 package (18¼ ounces) devil's food cake mix
- 1 cup (8 ounces) sour cream
- ¾ cup water
- 3 eggs
- ⅓ cup canola oil
- 1 teaspoon vanilla extract
- 1 cup miniature semisweet chocolate chips

GANACHE:
- 1 cup (6 ounces) semisweet chocolate chips
- ½ cup heavy whipping cream
- 1 tablespoon butter

RASPBERRY CREAM:
- 1 package (10 ounces) frozen sweetened raspberries, thawed
- 3 tablespoons sugar
- 4 teaspoons cornstarch
- ½ cup heavy whipping cream, whipped

1. In a large bowl, combine the cake mix, sour cream, water, eggs, oil and vanilla; beat on low speed for 30 seconds. Beat on medium for 2 minutes. Fold in miniature chips.

2. Pour into three greased and floured 9-in. round baking pans. Bake at 350° for 25-30 minutes or until a toothpick inserted near the center comes out clean. Cool for 10 minutes before removing from pans to wire racks to cool completely.

3. For ganache, place chocolate chips in a small bowl. In a small saucepan, bring cream just to a boil. Pour over chocolate; whisk until smooth. Whisk in butter. Chill until mixture reaches spreading consistency, stirring occasionally.

4. For raspberry cream, mash and strain raspberries, reserving juice; discard seeds. In a small saucepan, combine sugar and cornstarch; stir in raspberry juice. Bring to a boil, cook and stir over low heat for 1-2 minutes or until thickened. Place in a bowl; chill for 30 minutes. Fold in whipped cream.

5. Place one cake layer on a serving plate; spread with half of the ganache. Top with second cake layer and the raspberry cream. Top with remaining cake layer; spread with remaining ganache. Store in the refrigerator.

Sweet Potato Pound Cake

Since we are originally from Texas, we naturally love sweet potatoes. But this rich and buttery pound cake deserves to be a tradition in any home, whether you're from the South, East, North or West.

DIANE MANNIX, HELMVILLE, MONTANA

PREP: 25 MIN. • **BAKE:** 50 MIN. + COOLING • **MAKES:** 12 SERVINGS

- 1 cup butter, softened
- 2 cups sugar
- 4 eggs
- 1 teaspoon vanilla extract
- 3 cups all-purpose flour
- 2 teaspoons baking powder
- 1 teaspoon ground cinnamon
- ½ teaspoon baking soda
- ¼ teaspoon salt
- ¼ teaspoon ground nutmeg
- 2 cups cold mashed sweet potatoes

GLAZE:
- 1 cup confectioners' sugar
- 1 teaspoon grated orange peel
- 3 to 5 teaspoons orange juice

1. In a large bowl, cream butter and sugar until light and fluffy. Add eggs, one at a time, beating well after each addition. Beat in vanilla.

2. Combine the flour, baking powder, cinnamon, baking soda, salt and nutmeg; beat into the creamed mixture alternately with the sweet potatoes. Beat just until combined (batter will be stiff).

3. Pour into a greased and floured 10-in. fluted tube pan. Bake at 350° for 50-60 minutes or until a toothpick inserted near the center comes out clean.

4. Cool for 10 minutes before removing from pan to a wire rack to cool completely.

5. For glaze, in a small bowl, combine the confectioners' sugar, orange peel and enough orange juice to achieve desired consistency. Drizzle over cake.

1. Prepare and bake cake according to package directions. Cool completely. Crumble cake into a large bowl.

2. In a small bowl, combine hot water and coffee granules; stir until dissolved. Add the frosting, cocoa and chocolate syrup; stir until combined. Add to cake; beat on low speed until blended. Stir in chocolate chips. Shape into 1-in. balls.

3. In a microwave, melt candy coating; stir until smooth. Dip balls in coating mixture; allow excess to drip off. Place on waxed paper; sprinkle with toppings of your choice. Let stand until set. Store in airtight containers.

Heavenly Chocolate-Fudge Cake Balls

My special treat is similar to the popular cake pops—but without the stick! They're guaranteed to calm any chocolate craving and jazz up holiday goodie trays all at the same time. Best of all, their pretty appearance doesn't give away their simple prep.

LYNN DAVIS, MORENO VALLEY, CALIFORNIA

PREP: 1¾ HOURS + STANDING • **BAKE:** 30 MIN. + COOLING
MAKES: 95 CAKE BALLS

- 1 **package (18¼ ounces) devil's food cake mix**
- 2 **tablespoons hot water**
- 1 **teaspoon instant coffee granules**
- 1 **cup chocolate fudge frosting**
- ⅓ **cup baking cocoa**
- ¼ **cup chocolate syrup**
- 1⅓ **cups miniature semisweet chocolate chips**
- 2 **pounds white candy coating, chopped**
  Optional toppings: milk chocolate English toffee bits, toasted flaked coconut and crushed candy canes

Pistachio Cake

Mom is well-known for her holiday cookies, candies and cakes. This delicious dessert starts conveniently with a cake mix and instant pudding. You're sure to get requests for second helpings when you serve it.

BECKY BRUNETTE, MINNEAPOLIS, MINNESOTA

PREP: 15 MIN. • **BAKE:** 45 MIN. + CHILLING • **MAKES:** 12-15 SERVINGS

- 1 **package (18¼ ounces) white cake mix**
- 1 **package (3.4 ounces) instant pistachio pudding mix**
- 1 **cup lemon-lime soda**
- 1 **cup canola oil**
- 3 **eggs**
- 1 **cup chopped walnuts**

FROSTING:
- 1½ **cups cold milk**
- 1 **package (3.4 ounces) instant pistachio pudding mix**
- 1 **carton (8 ounces) frozen whipped topping, thawed**
- ½ **cup pistachios, toasted**

1. In a large bowl, combine the first five ingredients; beat on low speed for 30 seconds. Beat on medium for 2 minutes; stir in walnuts.

2. Pour into a greased 13-in. x 9-in. baking pan. Bake at 350° for 45-50 minutes or until a toothpick inserted near the center comes out clean. Cool on a wire rack.

3. For frosting, in a large bowl, beat milk and pudding mix on low speed for 2 minutes. Fold in whipped topping. Spread over cake. Sprinkle with pistachios. Refrigerate for at least 1 hour before cutting.

Amaretto Dream Cupcakes

Treat yourself to these indulgent little cupcakes laced with the irresistible flavor of amaretto and slivered almonds.

ANETTE STEVENS, OLDS, ALBERTA

PREP: 20 MIN. • **BAKE:** 15 MIN. + COOLING • **MAKES:** 2 DOZEN

- ¾ **cup butter, softened**
- 1½ **cups packed brown sugar**
- 2 **eggs**
- 2 **cups all-purpose flour**
- 1½ **teaspoons baking powder**
- ½ **teaspoon baking soda**
- ¼ **teaspoon salt**
- ½ **cup buttermilk**
- ¼ **cup amaretto**
- ⅓ **cup slivered almonds**
  Amaretto Butter Frosting (recipe at right)

1. In a large bowl, cream butter and brown sugar until light and fluffy. Add eggs, one at a time, beating well after each.

2. Combine the flour, baking powder, baking soda and salt. Add to the creamed mixture alternately with buttermilk and amaretto, beating well after each addition. Stir in almonds.

3. Fill paper-lined muffins cups two-thirds full. Bake at 375° for 14-16 minutes or until a toothpick comes out clean. Cool for 5 minutes before removing from pans to wire racks to cool completely. Frost cupcakes.

Amaretto Butter Frosting

Put the crowning touch on amaretto cupcakes with this rich and buttery topper.

ANETTE STEVENS, OLDS, ALBERTA

PREP/TOTAL TIME: 15 MIN. • **MAKES:** 2¼ CUPS

- 3 **cups confectioners' sugar**
- ¼ **cup butter, melted**
- 3 **to 4 tablespoons heavy whipping cream**
- 2 **to 3 tablespoons amaretto**

1. In a small bowl, beat confectioners' sugar and butter. Add 3 tablespoons cream and 2 tablespoons amaretto; beat until smooth. Add remaining cream and amaretto if needed to achieve spreading consistency.

Pound Cake

I'm happy to share a third-generation family recipe with you. This cake is rich and buttery with a lovely golden brown crust. Seasonal fresh fruit is perfect with this one.

MARGIE DALTON, CHICAGO, ILLINOIS

PREP: 20 MIN. • **BAKE:** 1 HOUR + COOLING
MAKES: 2 CAKES (12 SERVINGS EACH)

- 2 **cups butter, softened**
- 4 **cups confectioners' sugar**
- 6 **eggs**
- 1 **teaspoon almond extract**
- 3 **cups all-purpose flour**
- ½ **teaspoon salt**
    Fresh raspberries and whipped cream, optional

1. In a large bowl, cream butter and confectioners' sugar until light and fluffy, about 5 minutes. Add eggs, one at a time, beating well after each addition. Beat in extract. Combine flour and salt; gradually add to creamed mixture. Beat just until combined.

2. Transfer to two greased 8-in. x 4-in. loaf pans. Bake at 325° for 60-70 minutes or until a toothpick inserted near the center comes out clean. Cool for 10 minutes before removing from pans to wire racks. Serve with raspberries and whipped cream if desired.

Chocolate Angel Cake

When I first got married, I could barely boil water. My dear mother-in-law taught me how to make the lightest angel food cakes ever. This chocolate version is an easy yet impressive treat. For many years, it was our son's birthday cake.

JOYCE SHIFFLER, COLORADO SPRINGS, COLORADO

PREP: 25 MIN. • **BAKE:** 35 MIN. + COOLING • **MAKES:** 16 SERVINGS

- 1½ cups egg whites (about 10)
- 1½ cups confectioners' sugar
- 1 cup cake flour
- ¼ cup baking cocoa
- 1½ teaspoons cream of tartar
- ½ teaspoon salt
- 1 cup sugar

FROSTING:
- 1½ cups heavy whipping cream
- ½ cup sugar
- ¼ cup baking cocoa
- ½ teaspoon salt
- ½ teaspoon vanilla extract
    Chocolate leaves, optional

1. Place egg whites in a large bowl; let stand at room temperature for 30 minutes. Sift together confectioners' sugar, flour and cocoa three times; set aside.

2. Add cream of tartar and salt to egg whites; beat on medium speed until soft peaks form. Gradually add sugar, about 2 tablespoons at a time, beating on high until stiff glossy peaks form and sugar is dissolved. Gradually fold in flour mixture, about ½ cup at a time.

3. Spoon into an ungreased 10-in. tube pan. Cut through batter with a knife to remove air pockets. Bake on the lowest oven rack at 375° for 35-40 minutes or until lightly browned and entire top appears dry. Immediately invert pan; cool completely, about 1 hour. Run a knife around side and center tube of pan. Remove cake to a serving plate.

4. In a large bowl, combine the first five frosting ingredients; cover and chill for 1 hour. Beat until stiff peaks form.

5. Spread over the top and sides of cake. Store in the refrigerator. Garnish with chocolate leaves if desired.

Bakeshop HOW-TO

Beating Meringue to Stiff Peaks

In a large bowl, beat egg whites, cream of tartar, vanilla and salt on medium speed until egg whites begin to increase in volume and soft peaks form. To test for soft peaks, lift the beaters from the whites; the peaks should curl down. Gradually add sugar on high speed as you beat meringue to stiff peaks. Whites should stand straight up and cling to the beaters as shown. Avoid overbeating.

2. Pour into prepared pans. Bake at 350° for 25-30 minutes or until a toothpick inserted near the center comes out clean. Cool for 10 minutes before removing to wire racks to cool.

3. For frosting, in a large bowl, beat cream cheese and sugar until smooth. Beat in chocolate syrup and vanilla. Add the whipping cream. Beat on high speed until light and fluffy, about 5 minutes.

4. Cut each cake horizontally into two layers. Place bottom layer on a serving plate; drizzle with 2 tablespoons coffee. Spread with ¾ cup frosting. Repeat layers twice. Top with the remaining cake layer; frost cake with remaining frosting. Refrigerate overnight. Garnish with chopped candy bar.

Raspberry Truffle Cake Pops

Rich chocolate with a hint of raspberry liqueur...it doesn't get more enticing than this!

TASTE OF HOME TEST KITCHEN

PREP: 1½ HOURS + CHILLING • **MAKES:** 4 DOZEN

- 1 **package (18¼ ounces) white cake mix**
- ½ **cup canned vanilla frosting**
- ⅓ **cup seedless raspberry jam, melted**
- 2 **to 3 tablespoons raspberry liqueur**
  Red food coloring, optional
- 48 **lollipop sticks**
- 2½ **pounds dark chocolate candy coating, chopped**
  Pink candy coating, chopped
  Pink sprinkles and decorative sugar, optional

1. Prepare and bake cake mix according to package directions, using a greased 13-in. x 9-in. baking pan. Cool completely on a wire rack.

2. Crumble cake into a large bowl. Add the frosting, jam, liqueur and food coloring if desired; mix well. Shape into 1-in. balls. Place on baking sheets; insert sticks. Freeze for at least 2 hours or refrigerate for at least 3 hours or until firm.

3. In a microwave, melt dark candy coating. Dip each cake pop in coating; allow excess to drip off. Insert cake pops into a foam block to stand. Melt pink candy coating; drizzle over cake pops. Decorate some cake pops with sprinkles and sugar if desired. Let stand until set.

Tiramisu Toffee Torte

Tiramisu is Italian for "pick-me-up," and this treat truly lives up to its name. It's worth every bit of effort to see my husband's eyes light up when I put a piece of this delicious torte in front of him.
DONNA GONDA, NORTH CANTON, OHIO

PREP: 25 MIN. • **BAKE:** 25 MIN. + CHILLING • **MAKES:** 12 SERVINGS

- 1 **package (18¼ ounces) white cake mix**
- 1 **cup strong brewed coffee, room temperature**
- 4 **egg whites**
- 4 **Heath candy bars (1.4 ounces each), chopped**

FROSTING:
- 4 **ounces cream cheese, softened**
- ⅔ **cup sugar**
- ⅓ **cup chocolate syrup**
- 2 **teaspoons vanilla extract**
- 2 **cups heavy whipping cream**
- 6 **tablespoons strong brewed coffee, room temperature**
- 1 **Heath candy bar (1.4 ounces), chopped**

1. Line two greased 9-in. round baking pans with waxed paper and grease the paper; set aside. In a large bowl, combine the cake mix, coffee and egg whites; beat on low speed for 30 seconds. Beat on medium for 2 minutes. Fold in chopped candy bars.

Orange-Lemon Cake

Family and friends will love this moist cake's refreshing citrus taste and its pretty presentation.

ANN ROBINSON, BLOOMINGTON, INDIANA

PREP: 15 MIN. • **BAKE:** 35 MIN. + COOLING • **MAKES:** 12 SERVINGS

1 package (18¼ ounces) lemon cake mix
1 package (3 ounces) orange gelatin
⅔ cup water
⅔ cup canola oil
4 eggs

SHORT & SWEET

ICING:
1 cup confectioners' sugar
3 to 4 teaspoons orange juice

1. In a large bowl, combine the cake mix, gelatin, water, oil and eggs; beat on low speed for 30 seconds. Beat on medium for 2 minutes. Pour into a greased and floured 10-in. fluted tube pan.

2. Bake at 350° for 35-40 minutes or until a toothpick inserted near the center comes out clean. Cool for 10 minutes before removing from pan to a wire rack to cool completely.

3. Combine confectioners' sugar and enough orange juice to achieve desired consistency. Drizzle over cake.

Cherry Vanilla Cake Pops

Pop goes the party! No worries about who's cutting the cake; just serve and pop.

TASTE OF HOME TEST KITCHEN

PREP: 1½ HOURS + CHILLING • **MAKES:** 4 DOZEN

- 1 package (18¼ ounces) white cake mix
- 1 cup cream cheese frosting
- 2 to 3 tablespoons maraschino cherry juice
- 48 lollipop sticks
- 48 maraschino cherries, stems removed, drained
- 2½ pounds white candy coating, chopped
  Red pearl sugar

1. Prepare and bake cake mix according to package directions, using a greased 13-in. x 9-in. baking pan. Cool completely on a wire rack.

2. Crumble cake into a large bowl. Add frosting and cherry juice; mix well. Shape mixture by tablespoonfuls around cherries. Place on baking sheets; insert sticks. Freeze for at least 2 hours or refrigerate for at least 3 hours or until cake balls are firm.

3. In a microwave, melt the candy coating; stir until smooth. Dip each cake pop in coating; allow excess to drip off. Sprinkle with red pearl sugar. Insert cake pops into a foam block to let stand until set.

Strawberry Poke Cake

Strawberry shortcake takes on a wonderful new twist with this super-simple recipe. Strawberry gelatin and strawberries liven up each pretty slice of this lovely layered cake that's made from a handy boxed mix.

MARY JO GRIGGS, WEST BEND, WISCONSIN

PREP: 25 MIN. • **BAKE:** 25 MIN. + CHILLING • **MAKES:** 12 SERVINGS

- 1 package (18¼ ounces) white cake mix
- 1¼ cups water
- 2 eggs
- ¼ cup canola oil
- 2 packages (10 ounces each) frozen sweetened sliced strawberries, thawed
- 2 packages (3 ounces each) strawberry gelatin

SHORT & SWEET

- 1 carton (12 ounces) frozen whipped topping, thawed, divided
  Fresh strawberries, optional

1. In a large bowl, beat the cake mix, water, eggs and oil on low speed for 30 seconds. Beat on medium for 2 minutes.

2. Pour into two greased and floured 9-in. round baking pans. Bake at 350° for 25-35 minutes or until a toothpick inserted near the center comes out clean. Cool for 10 minutes; remove from pans to wire racks to cool completely.

3. Using a serrated knife, level tops of cakes if necessary. Return layers, top side up, to two clean 9-in. round baking pans. Pierce cakes with a meat fork or wooden skewer at ½-in. intervals.

4. Drain juice from strawberries into a 2-cup measuring cup; refrigerate berries. Add water to juice to measure 2 cups; pour into a small saucepan. Bring to a boil; stir in gelatin until dissolved. Chill for 30 minutes. Gently spoon over each cake layer. Chill for 2-3 hours.

5. Dip bottom of one pan in warm water for 10 seconds. Invert cake onto a serving platter. Top with reserved strawberries and 1 cup whipped topping. Place second cake layer over topping.

6. Frost cake with remaining whipped topping. Chill for at least 1 hour. Serve with fresh berries if desired. Refrigerate leftovers.

Chocolate Mint Layer Cake

With its rich chocolate icing and minty whipped cream filling, this cake is the perfect finale to a special meal.

JEAN PORTWINE, RECLUSE, WYOMING

PREP: 35 MIN. • **BAKE:** 25 MIN. + CHILLING • **MAKES:** 12 SERVINGS

- ½ cup butter, softened
- 1¾ cups sugar
- 3 eggs
- 4 ounces unsweetened chocolate, melted and cooled
- 1 teaspoon vanilla extract
- 1¾ cups all-purpose flour
- ¾ teaspoon baking soda
- ½ teaspoon salt
- ¾ cup 2% milk
- ½ cup water

FILLING:
- 1 cup heavy whipping cream
- 3 tablespoons confectioners' sugar
- ⅛ teaspoon peppermint extract
- 3 to 4 drops green food coloring, optional

ICING:
- 1 cup (6 ounces) semisweet chocolate chips
- ¼ cup butter, cubed
- ⅓ cup evaporated milk
- 1 teaspoon vanilla extract
- 1½ cups confectioners' sugar

1. Line two greased 9-in. round baking pans with waxed paper. Grease and flour the paper; set aside.

2. In a large bowl, cream the butter and sugar until light and fluffy. Add eggs, one at a time, beating well after each addition. Beat in chocolate and vanilla. Combine the flour, baking soda and salt; add to creamed mixture alternately with milk and water, beating well after each addition.

3. Pour into prepared pans. Bake at 350° for 24-28 minutes or until a toothpick inserted near the center comes out clean. Cool for 10 minutes before removing from pans to wire racks.

4. For filling, in a small bowl, beat the cream until it begins to thicken. Add confectioners' sugar and extract; beat until stiff peaks form. Beat in food coloring if desired. Place one cake layer on a serving plate; spread with filling. Top with second layer.

5. For icing, in a microwave-safe bowl, melt chips and butter; stir until smooth. Cool slightly. Beat in evaporated milk and vanilla. Gradually beat in confectioners' sugar until smooth. Frost and decorate cake. Chill 2 hours before slicing.

Brownie Cupcakes

I grew up in my parents' bakery, which might explain why I don't like frosting! These cupcakes are just my style. They come out shiny on top and are great without frosting.

CINDY LANG, HAYS, KANSAS

PREP: 15 MIN. • **BAKE:** 20 MIN. + COOLING • **MAKES:** 4 SERVINGS

- ¼ cup semisweet chocolate chips
- ¼ cup butter, cubed
- 1 egg
- ¼ cup sugar
- ¼ teaspoon vanilla extract
- ¼ cup all-purpose flour
- ¼ cup chopped pecans

1. In a microwave, melt chocolate chips and butter; stir until smooth. Cool slightly. In a small bowl, beat egg and sugar. Stir in vanilla and chocolate mixture. Gradually add flour; fold in pecans.

2. Fill paper-lined muffin cups two-thirds full. Bake at 325° for 20-25 minutes or until tops begin to crack. Cool for 10 minutes before removing from pan to a wire rack.

Applesauce Spice Cupcakes

I began making these moist cupcakes in grade school and I still bake them today!

EDNA HOFFMAN, HEBRON, INDIANA

PREP: 15 MIN. • **BAKE:** 25 MIN. + COOLING • **MAKES:** 1 DOZEN

- ⅓ cup butter, softened
- ¾ cup sugar
- 2 eggs
- 1 teaspoon vanilla extract
- 1⅓ cups all-purpose flour
- 1 teaspoon baking powder
- ½ teaspoon baking soda
- ½ teaspoon salt
- 1 teaspoon ground cinnamon
- ½ teaspoon ground nutmeg
- ⅛ teaspoon ground cloves
- ¾ cup applesauce
  Cream cheese frosting

1. In a large bowl, cream butter and sugar until light and fluffy. Add eggs, one at a time, beating well after each addition. Beat in vanilla. Combine the dry ingredients; add to creamed mixture alternately with applesauce.

2. Fill greased or paper-lined muffin cups two-thirds full. Bake at 350° for 25 minutes or until a toothpick inserted near the center comes out clean. Cool for 10 minutes before removing to a wire rack to cool completely. Frost cupcakes.

Lemon Chiffon Cake

This moist, airy cake was my dad's favorite. Mom revamped the original recipe to include lemons. I'm not much of a baker, so I don't make it very often. But when I do, my family is thrilled!

TRISHA KAMMERS, CLARKSTON, WASHINGTON

PREP: 25 MIN. • **BAKE:** 50 MIN. + COOLING • **MAKES:** 16 SERVINGS

- 7 eggs, separated
- 2 cups all-purpose flour
- 1½ cups sugar
- 3 teaspoons baking powder
- 1 teaspoon salt
- ¾ cup water
- ½ cup canola oil
- 4 teaspoons grated lemon peel
- 2 teaspoons vanilla extract
- ½ teaspoon cream of tartar

LEMON FROSTING:
- ⅓ cup butter, softened
- 3 cups confectioners' sugar
- ¼ cup lemon juice
- 4½ teaspoons grated lemon peel
  Dash salt

1. Place egg whites in a large bowl; let stand at room temperature for 30 minutes.

2. In a large bowl, combine the flour, sugar, baking powder and salt. In another bowl, whisk the egg yolks, water, oil, lemon peel and vanilla; add to dry ingredients and beat until well blended. Add cream of tartar to egg whites; beat on medium speed until stiff peaks form. Fold into batter.

3. Gently spoon into an ungreased 10-in. tube pan. Cut through batter with a knife to remove air pockets. Bake on the lowest oven rack at 325° for 50-55 minutes or until cake springs back when lightly touched. Immediately invert pan; cool completely, about 1 hour.

4. Run a knife around side and center tube of pan. Remove cake to a serving plate. In a small bowl, combine frosting ingredients; beat until smooth. Spread over top of cake, allowing frosting to drape down the sides.

Chocolate Cupcakes

This classic recipe is simply amazing! Try sitting down with a glass of cold milk and see if you can eat just one!

MARLENE MARTIN, COUNTRY HARBOUR MINES, NOVA SCOTIA

PREP: 20 MIN. • **BAKE:** 15 MIN. + COOLING • **MAKES:** 16 CUPCAKES

- ½ cup butter, softened
- 1 cup sugar
- 1 egg
- 1 teaspoon vanilla extract
- 1½ cups all-purpose flour
- ½ cup baking cocoa
- 1 teaspoon baking soda
- ¼ teaspoon salt
- ½ cup water
- ½ cup buttermilk
  Frosting of your choice

1. In a small bowl, cream butter and sugar until light and fluffy. Beat in egg and vanilla. Combine the flour, cocoa, baking soda and salt; gradually add to creamed mixture alternately with water and buttermilk, beating well after each addition.

2. Fill paper-lined muffin cups two-thirds full. Bake at 375° for 12-15 minutes or until a toothpick inserted near the center comes out clean. Cool for 10 minutes before removing from pans to wire racks to cool completely. Frost cupcakes.

Cream-Filled Pumpkin Cupcakes

Here's a deliciously different use for pumpkin. Bursting with flavor and plenty of eye-catching appeal, these sweet and spicy filled cupcakes are bound to dazzle your family.

ALI JOHNSON, PETERSBURG, PENNSYLVANIA

PREP: 35 MIN. • **BAKE:** 20 MIN. + COOLING • **MAKES:** ABOUT 1½ DOZEN

- 2 cups sugar
- ¾ cup canola oil
- 1 can (15 ounces) solid-pack pumpkin
- 4 eggs
- 2 cups all-purpose flour
- 2 teaspoons baking soda
- 1 teaspoon salt
- 1 teaspoon baking powder
- 1 teaspoon ground cinnamon

FILLING:
- 1 tablespoon cornstarch
- 1 cup milk
- ½ cup shortening
- ¼ cup butter, softened
- 2 cups confectioners' sugar
- ½ teaspoon vanilla extract, optional
  Whole cloves, optional

1. In a large bowl, beat the sugar, oil, pumpkin and eggs until well blended. Combine the flour, baking soda, salt, baking powder and cinnamon; gradually beat into pumpkin mixture until well blended.

2. Fill paper-lined muffin cups two-thirds full. Bake at 350° for 18-22 minutes or until a toothpick inserted near the center comes out clean. Cool for 10 minutes before removing from pans to wire racks to cool completely.

3. For filling, combine cornstarch and milk in a small saucepan until smooth. Bring to a boil, stirring constantly. Remove from the heat; cool to room temperature.

4. In a large bowl, cream the shortening, butter and confectioners' sugar until light and fluffy. Beat in vanilla if desired. Gradually add the cornstarch mixture, beating until smooth.

5. Using a sharp knife, cut a 1-in. circle 1 in. deep in the top of each cupcake. Carefully remove tops and set aside. Spoon or pipe filling into cupcakes. Replace tops. If desired, add a clove "pumpkin stem" to each top.

Pineapple Upside-Down Cake

Try this traditional dessert, which has been updated with packaged items for convenience. It has the same fabulous flavor as any from-scratch version.

KAREN ANN BLAND, GOVE, KANSAS

PREP: 10 MIN. • **BAKE:** 45 MIN. • **MAKES:** 12-15 SERVINGS

- ¼ cup butter, melted
- 1 can (20 ounces) sliced pineapple
- 10 pecan halves
- 1 jar (12 ounces) apricot preserves
- 1 package (18¼ ounces) yellow cake mix

SHORT & SWEET

1. Pour butter into a well-greased 13-in. x 9-in. baking dish. Drain pineapple, reserving ¼ cup juice. Arrange pineapple slices in prepared pan; place a pecan half in the center of each slice. Combine the apricot preserves and reserved pineapple juice; spoon over pineapple slices.

2. Prepare cake batter according to package directions; pour over pineapple.

3. Bake at 350° for 45-50 minutes or until a toothpick inserted near the center comes out clean. Immediately invert onto a large serving platter. Cool slightly; serve warm.

Cherry Pound Cake

Nothing beats this rich, classic pound cake, with the pretty surprise of bright red cherries tucked inside and dotting the creamy icing. This one's perfect for the holidays.

EVVA FOLTZ HANES, CLEMMONS, NORTH CAROLINA

PREP: 25 MIN. • **BAKE:** 1¼ HOURS + COOLING • **MAKES:** 12 SERVINGS

- 1 jar (10 ounces) maraschino cherries, divided
- 1 cup butter, softened
- ½ cup shortening
- 3 cups sugar
- 6 eggs
- 1 teaspoon vanilla extract
- ¾ cup 2% milk
- 3¾ cups all-purpose flour

FROSTING:
- 1 package (3 ounces) cream cheese, softened
- ¼ cup butter, softened
- 3¾ cups confectioners' sugar
- ½ teaspoon vanilla extract
- ½ cup flaked coconut
- ¼ cup chopped walnuts
  Additional coconut, optional

1. Drain and chop cherries, reserving juice; set aside.

2. In a large bowl, cream the butter, shortening and sugar until light and fluffy. Add eggs, one at a time, beating well after each addition. Beat in vanilla. Combine milk and ¼ cup reserved cherry juice; add to creamed mixture alternately with flour, beating well after each addition. Fold in ½ cup cherries.

3. Transfer to a greased and floured 10-in. tube pan. Bake at 325° for 1¼ to 1½ hours or until a toothpick inserted near the center comes out clean. Cool for 10 minutes before removing from pan to a wire rack to cool completely.

4. In a large bowl, beat cream cheese and butter until fluffy. Add the confectioners' sugar, vanilla and enough reserved cherry juice to achieve spreading consistency. Fold in coconut and remaining chopped cherries. Frost cake. Sprinkle with walnuts and additional coconut if desired.

Black Forest Cake

When my daughter went to Germany on a backpacking trip, she said the streets were lined with pastry shops. Here's an easy take on one of the country's most popular desserts.

PATRICIA RUTHERFORD, WINCHESTER, ILLINOIS

PREP: 10 MIN. • **BAKE:** 25 MIN. + CHILLING • **MAKES:** 6-8 SERVINGS

- 1 **package (9 ounces) chocolate cake mix**
- ½ **cup water**
- 1 **egg**
- 1 **package (3 ounces) cream cheese, softened**

SHORT & SWEET

- 2 **tablespoons sugar**
- 1 **carton (8 ounces) frozen whipped topping, thawed**
- 1 **can (21 ounces) cherry pie filling**

1. In a small bowl, beat the cake mix, water and egg on medium speed for 3-4 minutes. Pour into a greased 9-in. springform pan; place pan on a baking sheet.

2. Bake at 350° for 23-25 minutes or until cake springs back when lightly touched. Cool on a wire rack.

3. In a small bowl, beat cream cheese and sugar until fluffy; fold in whipped topping. Spread pie filling over cake; top with cream cheese mixture. Cover and refrigerate for 4 hours. Remove sides of pan.

Heavenly Surprise Mini Cupcakes

My grandmother was an accomplished baker, and this was one of the many special desserts she enjoyed making. It's fun to bite into these dense chocolate goodies and discover an extra treat inside.

JORUN MEIERDING, MANKATO, MINNESOTA

PREP: 35 MIN. • **BAKE:** 15 MIN./BATCH + COOLING • **MAKES:** 6 DOZEN

FILLING:
- 1 package (8 ounces) cream cheese, softened
- ⅓ cup sugar
- 1 egg
- ⅛ teaspoon salt
- 1 cup flaked coconut
- 1 cup finely chopped walnuts
- 1 cup (6 ounces) miniature semisweet chocolate chips

BATTER:
- 2 cups sugar
- 1½ cups water
- ¾ cup canola oil
- 2 eggs
- 2 teaspoons vanilla extract
- 1 teaspoon white vinegar
- 3 cups all-purpose flour
- ½ cup baking cocoa
- 1 teaspoon baking soda
- 1 teaspoon salt

FROSTING:
- ½ cup heavy whipping cream
- 1⅓ cups semisweet chocolate chips

1. For filling, in a small bowl, beat cream cheese and sugar until light and fluffy. Add egg and salt; mix well. Stir in the coconut, walnuts and chocolate chips. Set aside.

2. For batter, in a large bowl, beat the sugar, water, oil, eggs, vanilla and vinegar until well blended. Combine the flour, cocoa, baking soda and salt; gradually beat into oil mixture until blended.

3. Fill paper-lined miniature muffin cups one-third full with batter. Drop filling by teaspoonfuls into the center of each. Top with additional batter, filling cups three-fourths full.

4. Bake at 350° for 12-15 minutes or until a toothpick inserted in the cake portion of a cupcake comes out clean. Cool for 10 minutes before removing from pans to wire racks to cool completely.

5. For frosting, in a small saucepan, melt chocolate with cream over low heat; stir until blended. Remove from the heat. Cool to room temperature. Frost cupcakes. Refrigerate leftovers.

Editor's Note: *Cupcakes may also be baked in 30 paper-lined muffin cups for 20-25 minutes.*

Bakeshop TIP

Cupcake Baking Success

To allow good air circulation while baking cupcakes, leave at least 1 inch of space between the pans and between the sides of the oven. If using two oven racks, stagger the pans so that they are not direcly over one another. Switch pan positions and rotate them 180° halfway through baking. Cool in the pans for 10 minutes before cooling completely on wire racks.

1. Place a layer of ladyfingers on the bottom and around the sides of an ungreased 9-in. springform pan. In a large bowl, beat the cream cheese, 1 cup sugar and 1 teaspoon vanilla until smooth. Beat in lemon juice and peel.

2. In a small bowl, beat cream until it begins to thicken. Add remaining sugar and vanilla; beat until stiff peaks form. Fold into cream cheese mixture. Spread half over crust.

3. Arrange remaining ladyfingers in a spoke pattern over top. Evenly spread with the remaining cream cheese mixture. Top with pie filling. Refrigerate overnight.

Jelly Gem Cupcakes

My mother taught me this simple way to fill cupcakes with fruit jelly. Take these tender treats to your next get-together and watch faces light up after just one bite.

EDITH HOLLIDAY, FLUSHING, MICHIGAN

PREP: 20 MIN. • **BAKE:** 15 MIN. + COOLING • **MAKES:** 3 DOZEN

- 1 cup shortening
- 2 cups sugar
- 2 eggs
- 2 teaspoons vanilla extract
- 3½ cups all-purpose flour
- 5 teaspoons baking powder
- 1 teaspoon salt
- 1½ cups 2% milk
- ¾ cup strawberry or grape jelly
- Frosting of your choice
- Colored sprinkles, optional

1. In a large bowl, cream shortening and sugar until light and fluffy. Add eggs, one at a time, beating well after each addition. Beat in vanilla. Combine the flour, baking powder and salt; add to creamed mixture alternately with milk, beating well after each addition.

2. Fill 36 paper-lined muffin cups half full. Drop jelly by teaspoonfuls into the center of each.

3. Bake at 375° for 15-20 minutes or until a toothpick inserted in cupcake comes out clean. Cool for 10 minutes; remove from pans to wire racks to cool completely. Frost cupcakes; decorate with sprinkles if desired.

Cherry Cheese Torte

You can't help but impress people when you set out this lovely torte. It makes any occasion feel a bit more special. No one will guess how straightforward it really was!

LISA RADELET, BOULDER, COLORADO

PREP: 20 MIN. + CHILLING • **MAKES:** 12 SERVINGS

- 2 packages (3 ounces each) ladyfingers
- 1 package (8 ounces) cream cheese, softened
- 1 cup plus 1 teaspoon sugar, divided
- 2 teaspoon vanilla extract, divided
- 2 teaspoons lemon juice
- 1 teaspoon grated lemon peel
- 2 cups heavy whipping cream
- 1 can (21 ounces) cherry or blueberry pie filling

Cherry Cordial Cake Balls

Brandy and coffee add mild flavor to these scrumptious cherry cake balls.

SUSAN WESTERFIELD, ALBUQUERQUE, NEW MEXICO

PREP: 1 HOUR • **BAKE:** 35 MIN. + STANDING • **MAKES:** 6 DOZEN

 1 package (18¼ ounces) fudge marble cake mix
1¼ cups plus 3 tablespoons strong brewed coffee, divided
 ¼ cup canola oil
 3 eggs
 1 jar (10 ounces) maraschino cherries without stems, well drained
 ⅓ cup brandy
 ¼ cup cherry preserves
 1 cup canned chocolate frosting
 4 pounds milk chocolate candy coating, chopped
 2 tablespoons shortening

1. In a large bowl, combine the cake mix, 1¼ cups coffee, oil and eggs; beat on low speed for 30 seconds. Beat on medium for 2 minutes.

2. Pour batter into a greased and floured 13-in. x 9-in. baking pan. Bake at 350° for 30-35 minutes or until a toothpick inserted near the center comes out clean. Cool completely. Place cherries in a food processor; cover and process until coarsely chopped. Transfer to a small bowl; stir in the brandy, preserves and remaining coffee. Crumble cake into a large bowl. Add frosting and cherry mixture; beat well. Shape into 1-in. balls.

3. In a microwave, melt candy coating and shortening; stir until smooth. Dip balls in chocolate mixture; allow excess to drip off. Place on waxed paper; let stand until set. Store in an airtight container overnight before serving.

Hummingbird Cake

This impressive cake is my dad's favorite, so I always make it for his birthday. It also makes a great Easter dessert and is lovely with a summer meal.

NANCY ZIMMERMAN, CAPE MAY COURT HOUSE, NEW JERSEY

PREP: 40 MIN. • **BAKE:** 25 MIN. + COOLING • **MAKES:** 12 SERVINGS

- 2 cups mashed ripe bananas
- 1½ cups canola oil
- 3 eggs
- 1 can (8 ounces) unsweetened crushed pineapple, undrained
- 1½ teaspoons vanilla extract
- 3 cups all-purpose flour
- 2 cups sugar
- 1 teaspoon salt
- 1 teaspoon baking soda
- 1 teaspoon ground cinnamon
- 1 cup chopped walnuts

PINEAPPLE FROSTING:
- ¼ cup shortening
- 2 tablespoons butter, softened
- 1 teaspoon grated lemon peel
- ¼ teaspoon salt
- 6 cups confectioners' sugar
- ½ cup unsweetened pineapple juice
- 2 teaspoons half-and-half cream
  Chopped walnuts, optional

1. In a large bowl, beat the bananas, oil, eggs, pineapple and vanilla until well blended. Combine the flour, sugar, salt, baking soda and cinnamon; gradually beat into banana mixture until blended. Stir in walnuts.

2. Pour into three greased and floured 9-in. round baking pans. Bake at 350° for 25-30 minutes or until a toothpick inserted near the center comes out clean. Cool for 10 minutes before removing from pans to wire racks to cool completely.

3. For frosting, in a large bowl, beat the shortening, butter, lemon peel and salt until fluffy. Add confectioners' sugar alternately with pineapple juice. Beat in cream. Spread between layers and over top and sides of cake. Sprinkle with walnuts if desired.

Bakeshop HOW-TO

Easily Finishing a Cake

Peaks: Press the flat side of a tablespoon or teaspoon into the frosting and pull straight up, forming a peak. Repeat over top and sides of cake.

Zigzags: Run the tines of a table fork through the frosting in a wavy motion.

Waves: Use the back of a tablespoon or teaspoon to make a small twisting motion in one direction. Then move the spoon over a little and make another twist in the opposite direction. Repeat until entire cake is covered.

Chocolate Cream Cheese Cupcakes

I got the recipe for these filled cupcakes from a dear friend many years ago. I have made them many times for my family and for church functions. They're irresistible.

VIVIAN MORRIS, CLEBURNE, TEXAS

PREP: 30 MIN. • **BAKE:** 25 MIN. + COOLING • **MAKES:** 20 CUPCAKES

- 1   **package (8 ounces) cream cheese, softened**
- 1½ **cups sugar, divided**
- 1   **egg**
- 1   **teaspoon salt, divided**
- 1   **cup (6 ounces) semisweet chocolate chips**
- 1½ **cups all-purpose flour**
- ¼   **cup baking cocoa**
- 1   **teaspoon baking soda**
- 1   **cup water**
- ⅓   **cup canola oil**
- 1   **tablespoon white vinegar**

FROSTING:
- 3¾ **cups confectioners' sugar**
- 3   **tablespoons baking cocoa**
- ½   **cup butter, melted**
- 6   **tablespoons milk**
- 1   **teaspoon vanilla extract**
- ⅓   **cup chopped pecans**

1. For filling, in a small mixing bowl, beat cream cheese and ½ cup sugar until smooth. Beat in egg and ½ teaspoon salt until combined. Fold in chocolate chips; set aside.

2. In a bowl, combine the flour, cocoa, baking soda, and remaining sugar and salt. In another bowl, whisk the water, oil and vinegar; stir into dry ingredients just until moistened.

3. Fill paper-lined muffin cups half full with batter. Drop filling by heaping tablespoonfuls into the center of each. Bake at 350° for 24-26 minutes or until a toothpick inserted in cake comes out clean. Cool for 10 minutes before removing from pans to wire racks to cool completely.

4. For frosting, in a large mixing bowl, combine confectioners' sugar, cocoa, butter, milk and vanilla; beat until blended. Frost cupcakes; sprinkle with pecans. Store in the refrigerator.

Coconut-Rum Cake Pops

Plan your own tropical escape with these surprisingly light-tasting pops. Angel food cake is a nice change of pace.

TASTE OF HOME TEST KITCHEN

PREP: 1½ HOURS + CHILLING • **MAKES:** 4 DOZEN

- 1   **package (16 ounces) angel food cake mix**
- ¾   **cup canned vanilla frosting**
- 1   **cup flaked coconut**
- 1   **teaspoon coconut extract**
- ½   **teaspoon rum extract**
- 48 **lollipop sticks**
- 2½ **pounds white candy coating, chopped**
     Lightly toasted flaked coconut

1. Prepare and bake cake mix according to package directions. Cool completely on a wire rack.

2. Crumble cake into a large bowl. In a small bowl, combine the frosting, coconut and extracts; stir into cake until blended. Shape into 1-in. balls. Place on baking sheets; insert sticks. Freeze for at least 2 hours or refrigerate for at least 3 hours or until cake balls are firm.

3. In a microwave, melt candy coating; stir until smooth. Dip each cake pop in coating; allow excess to drip off. Roll in toasted coconut. Insert cake pops into a foam block to stand. Let stand until set.

Cinnamon Mocha Cupcakes

Like to end a meal with a little something sweet? These chocolaty cupcakes will do the trick. They don't make a huge batch, so you can share a few and enjoy the rest yourself!

EDNA HOFFMAN, HEBRON, INDIANA

PREP: 15 MIN. • **BAKE:** 20 MIN. + COOLING • **MAKES:** 8 CUPCAKES

¼ **cup butter, softened**
⅔ **cup sugar**
1 **egg**
½ **teaspoon vanilla extract**
¾ **cup plus 2 tablespoons all-purpose flour**
¼ **cup baking cocoa**
½ **teaspoon baking soda**
½ **teaspoon salt**
¼ **teaspoon baking powder**
¼ **teaspoon ground cinnamon**
¼ **cup strong brewed coffee, room temperature**
3 **tablespoons buttermilk**
1 **cup chocolate frosting**
¾ **teaspoon instant coffee granules**
1 **teaspoon hot water**

1. In a small bowl, cream the butter and sugar until light and fluffy. Beat in egg and vanilla. Combine the flour, cocoa, baking soda, salt, baking powder and cinnamon; add to creamed mixture alternately with coffee and buttermilk, beating well after each addition.

2. Fill paper-lined muffin cups half full with batter. Bake at 350° for 18-20 minutes or until a toothpick comes out clean. Cool for 5 minutes before removing from pan to a wire rack to cool completely.

3. Place the frosting in a bowl. Dissolve coffee granules in hot water; stir into frosting until smooth. Frost cupcakes.

Sachertorte

Guests will be surprised to hear this dessert starts with a basic cake mix. Each bite features the delightful flavors of chocolate, almonds and apricots.

TASTE OF HOME TEST KITCHEN

PREP: 30 MIN. • **BAKE:** 25 MIN. + CHILLING • **MAKES:** 16 SERVINGS

- ½ cup chopped dried apricots
- ½ cup amaretto
- 1 package (18¼ ounces) devil's food cake mix
- ¾ cup water
- ⅓ cup canola oil
- 3 eggs

APRICOT FILLING:
- ⅔ cup apricot preserves
- 1 tablespoon amaretto

FROSTING:
- ½ cup butter, softened
- 4½ cups confectioners' sugar
- ¾ cup baking cocoa
- ⅓ cup boiling water
- 1 tablespoon amaretto
- 1 cup sliced almonds, toasted

1. In a small bowl, combine apricots and amaretto; let stand for 15 minutes. In a large bowl, combine the cake mix, water, oil, eggs and apricot mixture. Beat on low speed for 30 seconds; beat on medium for 2 minutes.

2. Pour into two greased and floured 9-in. round baking pans. Bake at 350° for 25-30 minutes or until a toothpick inserted near the center comes out clean. Cool for 10 minutes before removing from pans to wire racks to cool completely.

3. For filling, in a small saucepan, heat apricot preserves and amaretto on low until preserves are melted, stirring occasionally; set aside.

4. For frosting, in a large bowl, cream the butter, confectioners' sugar and cocoa until light and fluffy. Add water and amaretto. Beat on low speed until combined. Beat on medium for 1 minute or until frosting achieves spreading consistency.

5. Cut each cake horizontally into two layers. Place a bottom layer on a serving plate; spread with half of the filling. Top with another cake layer; spread with ⅔ cup frosting. Top with third layer and remaining filling. Top with remaining cake layer.

6. Frost top and sides of cake with remaining frosting. Gently press almonds into the sides. Refrigerate for several hours before slicing.

Cream Cheese Sheet Cake

This tender, buttery sheet cake with a thin layer of fudge frosting is perfect for a crowd. It's always popular at potlucks and parties. It's not uncommon to see folks going back for second and even third slices.

GAYE MANN, ROCKY MOUNT, NORTH CAROLINA

PREP: 20 MIN. + COOLING • **BAKE:** 30 MIN. + COOLING
MAKES: 24-30 SERVINGS

- 1 cup plus 2 tablespoons butter, softened
- 2 packages (3 ounces each) cream cheese, softened
- 2¼ cups sugar
- 6 eggs
- ¾ teaspoon vanilla extract
- 2¼ cups cake flour

FROSTING:
- 1 cup sugar
- ⅓ cup evaporated milk
- ½ cup butter, cubed
- ½ cup semisweet chocolate chips

1. In a large bowl, cream the butter, cream cheese and sugar until light and fluffy. Add eggs, one at a time, beating well after each addition. Beat in vanilla. Add flour until well blended.

2. Pour into a greased 15-in. x 10-in. x 1-in. baking pan. Bake at 325° for 30-35 minutes or until a toothpick inserted near the center comes out clean. Cool completely on a wire rack.

3. For frosting, in a small saucepan, combine sugar and milk; bring to a boil over medium heat. Cover and cook for 3 minutes (do not stir). Stir in butter and chocolate chips until melted. Cool slightly. Stir frosting; spread over top of cake.

Mini Blueberry Bundt Cakes

These pretty little blueberry cakes are topped with a yummy lemon-flavored glaze. The recipe makes three tiny cakes so you might want to bake up a couple of batches if you plan to serve more people.

CATHY ISAAK, RIVERS, MANITOBA

PREP: 20 MIN. • **BAKE:** 25 MIN. + COOLING • **MAKES:** 3 SERVINGS

- ¼ **cup butter, softened**
- ½ **cup sugar**
- 1 **egg**
- ¼ **cup 2% milk**
- ½ **teaspoon vanilla extract**
- 1 **cup all-purpose flour**
- 1 **teaspoon baking powder**
- ¼ **teaspoon salt**
- 1½ **cups fresh or frozen blueberries**

LEMON ICING:
- ½ **cup confectioners' sugar**
- 1½ **teaspoons 2% milk**
- 1 **teaspoon lemon juice**
  Additional blueberries, optional

1. In a small bowl, cream butter and sugar. Beat in the egg, milk and vanilla. Combine the flour, baking powder and salt; beat into creamed mixture. Fold in blueberries.

2. Pour into three 4-in. fluted tube pans coated with cooking spray. Bake at 350° for 25-30 minutes or until a toothpick inserted near the center comes out clean. Cool for 10 minutes before removing from pans to wire racks to cool completely.

3. For icing, in a small bowl, combine the confectioners' sugar, milk and lemon juice; drizzle over cakes. Garnish with additional berries if desired.

Editor's Note: *If using frozen blueberries, use without thawing to avoid discoloring the batter.*

Caramel Apple Cupcakes

Bring these extra-special cupcakes to your next bake sale and watch how quickly they disappear! Kids will go for the fun appearance and tasty toppings, while adults will appreciate the moist spiced cake underneath.

DIANE HALFERTY, CORPUS CHRISTI, TEXAS

PREP: 25 MIN. • **BAKE:** 20 MIN. + COOLING • **MAKES:** 1 DOZEN

- 1 **package (18¼ ounces) spice cake mix or 1 package (18 ounces) carrot cake mix**
- 2 **cups chopped peeled tart apples**
- 20 **caramels**
- 3 **tablespoons 2% milk**
- 1 **cup finely chopped pecans, toasted**
- 12 **Popsicle sticks**

1. Prepare cake batter according to package directions; fold in apples.

2. Fill 12 greased or paper-lined jumbo muffin cups three-fourths full. Bake at 350° for 20 minutes or until a toothpick inserted near the center comes out clean. Cool for 10 minutes before removing from pans to wire racks to cool completely.

3. In a small saucepan, cook the caramels and milk over low heat until smooth. Spread over cupcakes. Sprinkle with pecans. Insert a wooden stick into the center of each cupcake.

Chai Cupcakes

You'll get a double dose of the the spicy blend that's frequently used to flavor tea in these tender single-size cakes. Both the cupcake and frosting use the sweet blend of spices.

TASTE OF HOME TEST KITCHEN

PREP: 25 MIN. • **BAKE:** 25 MIN. + COOLING • **MAKES:** 1 DOZEN

- ½ teaspoon each ground ginger, cinnamon, cardamom and cloves
- ⅛ teaspoon pepper
- ½ cup butter, softened
- 1 cup sugar
- 1 egg
- ½ teaspoon vanilla extract
- 1½ cups cake flour
- 1½ teaspoons baking powder
- ¼ teaspoon salt
- ⅔ cup 2% milk

FROSTING:
- 6 tablespoons butter, softened
- 3 cups confectioners' sugar
- ¾ teaspoon vanilla extract
- 3 to 4 tablespoons 2% milk
  Ground cinnamon

1. In a small bowl, combine the ginger, cinnamon, cardamom, cloves and pepper; set aside.

2. In a large bowl, cream butter and sugar until light and fluffy. Beat in egg and vanilla. Combine the flour, baking powder, salt and 1½ teaspoons spice mixture. Gradually add to creamed mixture alternately with milk, beating well after each addition.

3. Fill paper-lined muffin cups two-thirds full. Bake at 350° for 24-28 minutes or until a toothpick inserted near the center comes out clean. Cool for 10 minutes before removing from pans to wire racks to cool completely.

4. In a large bowl, beat butter until fluffy; beat in the confectioners' sugar, vanilla and remaining spice mixture until smooth. Add enough milk to reach desired consistency. Pipe frosting over cupcakes; sprinkle with cinnamon.

Pumpkin Spice Layer Cake

No one will guess this stunning dessert with yummy cinnamon frosting started with a mix. It's a perfect treat year-round.

LINDA MURRAY, ALLENSTOWN, NEW HAMPSHIRE

PREP: 25 MIN. • **BAKE:** 25 MIN. + COOLING • **MAKES:** 10-12 SERVINGS

- 1 **package (18¼ ounces) yellow cake mix**
- 3 **eggs**
- 1 **cup water**
- 1 **cup canned pumpkin**
- 1¾ **teaspoons ground cinnamon, divided**
- ¼ **teaspoon ground ginger**
- ¼ **teaspoon ground nutmeg**
- 2½ **cups vanilla frosting**
- 1¼ **cups chopped walnuts**

1. In a large bowl, combine the cake mix, eggs, water, pumpkin, 1 teaspoon cinnamon, ginger and nutmeg; beat on low speed for 30 seconds. Beat on medium for 2 minutes.

2. Pour into two well-greased and floured 9-in. round baking pans. Bake at 375° for 25-30 minutes or until a toothpick inserted near the center comes out clean. Cool for 10 minutes before removing from pans to wire racks to cool completely.

3. Combine frosting and remaining cinnamon; spread between layers and over top and sides of cake. Press walnuts lightly into frosting on sides of cake.

Orange Grove Cake

A few years ago, I won Best in Show at the Western Idaho State Fair for this citrusy cake with its luscious filling and creamy frosting. It's bursting with orange flavor.

AMANDA BOWYER, CALDWELL, IDAHO

PREP: 55 MIN. + CHILLING • **BAKE:** 20 MIN. + COOLING
MAKES: 16 SERVINGS

- 1 cup butter, softened
- 1¾ cups sugar
- 4 eggs
- ⅓ cup orange juice
- 2 teaspoons grated orange peel
- 3 cups cake flour
- 2½ teaspoons baking powder
- ½ teaspoon salt
- ⅔ cup 2% milk

FILLING:
- ½ cup sugar
- 1 tablespoon plus 2 teaspoons cornstarch
- ⅔ cup orange juice
- 2 tablespoons water
- 3 egg yolks, beaten
- 2 tablespoons lemon juice
- 1 teaspoon grated orange peel
- ⅛ teaspoon salt

SYRUP:
- ½ cup sugar
- ⅓ cup water
- ¼ cup orange juice
- 1 teaspoon orange extract

FROSTING:
- 1 cup butter, softened
- 4 cups confectioners' sugar
- 3 tablespoons heavy whipping cream
- 1 teaspoon grated orange peel
- 1 teaspoon orange extract
- ¼ teaspoon salt

1. In a large bowl, cream butter and sugar until light and fluffy. Add eggs, one at a time, beating well after each addition. Beat in orange juice and peel. Combine the flour, baking powder and salt; add to the creamed mixture alternately with milk, beating well after each addition.

2. Transfer to two greased and floured 9-in. round baking pans. Bake at 350° for 20-25 minutes or until a toothpick inserted near the center comes out clean. Cool for 10 minutes before removing from pans to wire racks to cool completely.

3. For filling, in a small saucepan, combine sugar and cornstarch. Stir in orange juice and water until smooth. Bring to a boil; cook and stir for 1 minute or until thickened. Remove from the heat.

4. Stir a small amount of hot mixture into egg yolks; return all to the pan, stirring constantly. Bring to a gentle boil; cook and stir 1 minute longer. Remove from the heat; gently stir in the lemon juice, orange peel and salt. Cool to room temperature without stirring. Refrigerate for 1 hour.

5. For syrup, in a small saucepan, bring the sugar, water and orange juice to a boil. Reduce heat; simmer, uncovered, for 10 minutes or until reduced to about ½ cup. Remove from the heat; stir in extract. Cool.

6. For frosting, in a large bowl, beat butter until light and fluffy. Add the remaining ingredients; beat until smooth.

7. Cut each cake horizontally into two layers. Place bottom layer on a serving plate; brush with 2 tablespoons syrup and spread with ⅓ cup filling. Repeat layers twice. Top with remaining cake layer; brush with remaining syrup. Frost top and sides of cake.

Hawaiian Sunset Cake

This three-layer orange cake is lovely enough to share—though you may not want to!—yet it's so simple to fix that you'll find yourself making it all the time. A boxed mix keeps it convenient while the pineapple-coconut filling makes it feel extra special.

KARA DE LA VEGA, SANTA ROSA, CALIFORNIA

PREP: 20 MIN. + CHILLING • **BAKE:** 25 MIN. + COOLING

MAKES: 16 SERVINGS

- 1 **package (18¼ ounces) white or orange cake mix**
- 1½ **cups milk**
- 1 **package (3.4 ounces) instant vanilla pudding mix**
- 1 **package (3 ounces) orange gelatin**
- 4 **eggs**
- ½ **cup canola oil**

FILLING:
- 1 **can (20 ounces) crushed pineapple, drained**
- 2 **cups sugar**
- 1 **package (10 ounces) flaked coconut**
- 1 **cup (8 ounces) sour cream**
- 1 **carton (8 ounces) frozen whipped topping, thawed**
  Toasted coconut, optional

1. In a large bowl, combine the first six ingredients; beat on low speed for 30 seconds. Beat on medium for 2 minutes.

2. Pour into three greased and floured 9-in. round baking pans. Bake at 350° for 25-30 minutes or until a toothpick inserted near the center comes out clean. Cool for 10 minutes before removing from pans to wire racks to cool completely.

3. In a large bowl, combine the pineapple, sugar, coconut and sour cream. Set aside 1 cup for frosting. Place one cake on a serving plate; top with a third of the remaining pineapple mixture. Repeat layers twice.

4. Fold whipped topping into the reserved pineapple mixture. Spread over top and sides of cake. Sprinkle with toasted coconut if desired. Refrigerate until serving.

Cannoli Cupcakes

These jumbo cupcakes feature a fluffy cannoli-like filling. White chocolate curls on top are the crowning touch.

TASTE OF HOME TEST KITCHEN

PREP: 50 MIN. • **BAKE:** 25 MIN. + COOLING • **MAKES:** 8 CUPCAKES

- 1 **package (18¼ ounces) white cake mix**
- ¾ **cup heavy whipping cream, divided**
- 1 **cup ricotta cheese**
- 1 **cup confectioners' sugar**
- ½ **cup Mascarpone cheese**
- ¼ **teaspoon almond extract**
- ½ **cup chopped pistachios**
- 4 **ounces white baking chocolate, chopped**
  White chocolate curls

1. Prepare cake mix batter according to package directions. Fill paper-lined jumbo muffin cups three-fourths full. Bake according to package directions for 24-28 minutes or until a toothpick inserted near the center comes out clean. Cool for 10 minutes before removing from pans to wire racks to cool completely.

2. In a small bowl, beat ½ cup cream until stiff peaks form; set aside. In a large bowl, combine the ricotta cheese, confectioners' sugar, Mascarpone cheese and extract until smooth. Fold in pistachios and the whipped cream.

3. Cut the top off of each cupcake. Spread or pipe cupcakes with cheese mixture; replace tops. In a small saucepan, melt white baking chocolate with remaining cream over low heat; stir until smooth. Remove from the heat. Cool to room temperature. Spoon over cupcakes; sprinkle with chocolate curls. Refrigerate leftovers.

Blueberry Angel Cupcakes

Like angel food cake, these yummy cupcakes don't last long at my house. They're so light and airy that they melt in your mouth.

KATHY KITTELL, LENEXA, KANSAS

PREP: 25 MIN. • **BAKE:** 15 MIN. + COOLING • **MAKES:** 2½ DOZEN

11 **egg whites**
 1 **cup plus 2 tablespoons cake flour**
1½ **cups sugar, divided**
1¼ **teaspoons cream of tartar**
 1 **teaspoon vanilla extract**
½ **teaspoon salt**
1½ **cups fresh or frozen blueberries**
 1 **teaspoon grated lemon peel**
GLAZE:
 1 **cup confectioners' sugar**
 3 **tablespoons lemon juice**

1. Place egg whites in a large bowl; let stand at room temperature for 30 minutes. Sift together flour and ½ cup sugar three times; set aside.

2. Add cream of tartar, vanilla and salt to egg whites; beat on medium speed until soft peaks form. Gradually add remaining sugar, about 2 tablespoons at a time, beating on high until stiff glossy peaks form and sugar is dissolved. Gradually fold in flour mixture, about ½ cup at a time. Fold in blueberries and lemon peel.

3. Fill paper-lined muffin cups three-fourths full. Bake at 375° for 14-17 minutes or until cupcakes spring back when lightly touched. Immediately remove from pans to wire racks to cool completely.

4. In a small bowl, whisk confectioners' sugar and lemon juice until smooth. Brush over cupcakes. Let stand until set.

Editor's Note: *If using frozen blueberries, use without thawing to avoid discoloring the batter.*

Boston Cream Pie

This classic dessert can be made for a crowd without much fuss. It's pretty, tasty and always popular at picnics and potlucks.

CLARA HONEYAGER, NORTH PRAIRIE, WISCONSIN

PREP: 20 MIN. + CHILLING • **BAKE:** 25 MIN. + COOLING
MAKES: 24 SERVINGS

- 1 package (18¼ ounces) yellow cake mix
- 2¾ cups cold milk
- 1 package (5.1 ounces) instant vanilla pudding mix
- 1 jar (16 ounces) hot fudge ice cream topping, warmed
- 24 maraschino cherries with stems, optional

1. Prepare and bake cake according to package directions, using a greased 13-in. x 9-in. baking pan. Cool completely on a wire rack.

2. Meanwhile, in a large bowl, beat milk and pudding mix on low for 2-3 minutes. Cover and chill for at least 30 minutes. Cut cake into 24 pieces; split each piece horizontally. Place about 1 heaping tablespoon of pudding between layers. Spread each with 1 tablespoon fudge topping and garnish with a cherry if desired.

Poppy Seed Chiffon Cake

This attractive cake never fails to please. It's a great choice for that special birthday celebration.

MARILYN BECK, MEDICINE HAT, ALBERTA

PREP: 70 MIN. & STANDING • **BAKE:** 50 MIN. + COOLING
MAKES: 16 SERVINGS

- ½ cup poppy seeds
- 1 cup water
- 8 eggs
- 2 cups all-purpose flour
- 1½ cups sugar
- 3 teaspoons baking powder
- 1 teaspoon salt
- ¼ teaspoon baking soda
- ½ cup canola oil
- 2 teaspoons vanilla extract
- ½ teaspoon cream of tartar

GLAZE:
- 1 cup confectioners' sugar
- ¼ cup milk
- 2 tablespoons butter, melted
- ¼ teaspoon vanilla extract
  Edible flowers, optional

1. In a small bowl, soak poppy seeds in water for 1 hour. Separate eggs; let stand at room temperature for 30 minutes.

2. In a large bowl, combine the flour, sugar, baking powder, salt and baking soda. In another bowl, whisk the egg yolks, oil, vanilla and poppy seed mixture. Add to dry ingredients; beat until well blended. In another large bowl, beat egg whites and cream of tartar until stiff peaks form. Fold into batter.

3. Pour into an ungreased 10-in. tube pan. Cut through batter with a knife to remove air pockets. Bake at 325° for 50-55 minutes or until cake springs back when lightly touched. Immediately invert pan; cool completely, about 1 hour. Run a knife around side and center tube of pan. Remove cake to a serving plate.

4. In a small bowl, combine glaze ingredients. Pour over cake; garnish with flowers if desired.

Editor's Note: *Verify that flowers are edible and have not been treated with chemicals.*

Pies & Tarts

Chocolate Berry Tarts

I sometimes use a ready-made graham tart shells if I'm short on time. Either way, this rich berry dessert is an elegant treat.

LOUISE GILBERT, QUESNEL, BRITISH COLUMBIA

PREP: 20 MIN. + CHILLING • **MAKES:** 2 SERVINGS

- 5 tablespoons butter, divided
- 1 cup chocolate graham cracker crumbs (about 5 whole crackers)
- 2 teaspoons sugar
- 3 tablespoons heavy whipping cream
- ⅛ teaspoon ground cinnamon
- ⅔ cup semisweet chocolate chips
- ⅓ cup fresh blackberries
- ⅓ cup fresh raspberries
   Confectioners' sugar

1. In a small microwave-safe bowl, melt 4 tablespoons butter; stir in cracker crumbs and sugar. Press onto the bottom and up the sides of two 4-in. fluted tart pans with removable bottoms. Freeze for 1 hour or until firm.

2. In a small saucepan, combine the cream, cinnamon and remaining butter. Bring to a boil over medium heat, stirring constantly. Remove from the heat; stir in chocolate chips until melted. Pour into crusts. Refrigerate until firm, about 1 hour.

3. Just before serving, arrange berries over filling; sprinkle with confectioners' sugar.

Apple Pie in a Goblet

This dish is not only easy but very elegant. I got the recipe from a church cooking class and now make it often. You can serve it in bowls, but I always get more oohs and aahs when I put it in pretty goblets.

RENEE ZIMMER, GIG HARBOR, WASHINGTON

PREP: 10 MIN. • **COOK:** 25 MIN. • **MAKES:** 4 SERVINGS

- 3 large tart apples, peeled and chopped
- ¼ cup sugar
- ¼ cup water
- ¾ teaspoon ground cinnamon
- ¼ teaspoon ground nutmeg
- 12 shortbread cookies, crushed
- 2 cups vanilla ice cream
   Whipped cream

1. In a large saucepan, combine the apples, sugar, water, cinnamon and nutmeg. Bring to a boil. Reduce heat; cover and simmer for 10 minutes or until apples are tender. Uncover; cook 9-11 minutes longer or until most of the liquid has evaporated. Remove from the heat.

2. In each of four goblets or parfait glasses, layer 1 tablespoon cookie crumbs, the ice cream and the apple mixture. Top with remaining cookie crumbs and whipped cream. Serve immediately.

Key Lime Mousse Cups

Light and lovely, these little key lime phyllo tarts are so refreshing served as an after-dinner treat—and they take just minutes to whip up!

SUZANNE PAULEY, RENTON, WASHINGTON

PREP/TOTAL TIME: 20 MIN. • **MAKES:** 2½ DOZEN

4   ounces cream cheese, softened
⅔   cup sweetened condensed milk
¼   cup key lime juice

½   cup heavy whipping cream, whipped
2   packages (1.9 ounces each) frozen miniature phyllo tart shells
    Fresh raspberries and lime wedges, optional

1. In a large bowl, beat the cream cheese, milk and juice until smooth; fold in whipped cream.

2. Spoon or pipe into tart shells. Garnish with raspberries and lime wedges if desired. Serve immediately.

Lemon Meringue Pie

My father loves lemon meringue pie and always wants one for his birthday. I rely on this recipe, which won first place at our county fair. It has a flaky crust, refreshing lemon filling and soft meringue with pretty golden peaks.

SUSAN JONES, BRADFORD, OHIO

PREP: 30 MIN. • **BAKE:** 30 MIN. + CHILLING • **MAKES:** 6-8 SERVINGS

- 1½ cups all-purpose flour
- ½ teaspoon salt
- ½ cup shortening
- ¼ cup cold water

FILLING:
- 1½ cups sugar
- ¼ cup cornstarch
- 3 tablespoons all-purpose flour
- ¼ teaspoon salt
- 1½ cups water
- 3 egg yolks, lightly beaten
- 2 tablespoons butter
- ⅓ cup lemon juice
- 1 teaspoon grated lemon peel
- 1 teaspoon lemon extract

MERINGUE:
- 3 egg whites
- ¼ teaspoon cream of tartar
- 6 tablespoons sugar

1. In a small bowl, combine flour and salt; cut in the shortening until crumbly. Gradually add water, tossing with a fork until dough forms a ball. Roll out pastry to fit a 9-in. pie plate. Transfer pastry to pie plate. Trim pastry to ½ in. beyond edge of pie plate; flute edges.

2. Line with a double thickness of heavy-duty foil. Bake at 450° for 8 minutes or until lightly browned. Remove foil; cool on a wire rack.

3. For filling, in a small saucepan, combine the sugar, cornstarch, flour and salt. Gradually stir in water until smooth. Cook and stir over medium-high heat until thickened and bubbly. Reduce heat; cook and stir 2 minutes longer. Remove from the heat. Stir a small amount of mixture into egg yolks; return all to the pan, stirring constantly. Bring to a gentle boil; cook and stir for 2 minutes. Remove from the heat. Gently stir in the butter, lemon juice, peel and extract until butter is melted. Pour hot filling into crust.

4. In a small bowl, beat egg whites and cream of tartar on medium speed until soft peaks form. Gradually beat in sugar, 1 tablespoon at a time, on high until stiff glossy peaks form and sugar is dissolved. Spread evenly over hot filling, sealing edges to crust.

5. Bake at 350° for 12-15 minutes or until the meringue is golden brown. Cool on a wire rack for 1 hour. Refrigerate for at least 3 hours before serving. Store leftovers in the refrigerator.

Bakeshop HOW-TO

Topping a Pie with Meringue

Spread meringue over hot filling to minimize "weeping" (the watery layer between the meringue and pie filling). Use a small spatula or butter knife to create attractive peaks. Seal meringue to the pie's edges to keep it from shrinking in the oven. Cool the pie away from drafts, then chill well before serving.

Cranberry Custard Meringue Pie

I love to serve this pie when my family is here. My grandchildren call it the red-colored pie with the fluff topping.

LEE BREMSON, KANSAS CITY, MISSOURI

PREP: 35 MIN. • **BAKE:** 15 MIN. + CHILLING
MAKES: 8 SERVINGS

- 3 **eggs, separated**
  Pastry for single-crust pie (9 inches)
- 1¾ **cups fresh or frozen cranberries**
- 1 **tablespoon grated orange peel**
- 1¼ **cups plus 6 tablespoons sugar, divided**
- 1 **cup water**
  Dash salt
  Dash ground cinnamon
- 4 **teaspoons plus ¼ cup cornstarch, divided**
- ¼ **cup orange juice**
- 2 **cups 2% milk, divided**
- 1 **tablespoon butter**
- 1 **teaspoon vanilla extract**
- ¼ **teaspoon cream of tartar**

1. Place egg whites in a small bowl; let stand at room temperature for 30 minutes.

2. Meanwhile, line a 9-in. pie plate with pastry; trim and flute edges. Line pastry shell with a double thickness of heavy-duty foil. Bake at 450° for 8 minutes. Remove foil; bake 5 minutes longer. Cool on a wire rack.

3. In a small saucepan, combine the cranberries, orange peel, ½ cup sugar, water, salt and cinnamon. Cook over medium heat until berries pop, about 15 minutes. Combine 4 teaspoons cornstarch and orange juice until smooth; stir into cranberry mixture. Bring to a boil; cook and stir for 1-2 minutes or until thickened. Remove from the heat; set aside.

4. In another small saucepan, heat ¾ cup sugar and 1¾ cups milk until bubbles form around sides of pan. In a small bowl, combine the remaining cornstarch and milk. Whisk in egg yolks until blended. Add a small amount of hot milk mixture; return all to the pan, whisking constantly.

5. Whisk vigorously over medium heat as mixture begins to thicken (mixture will become very thick). Bring to a boil; whisk 2 minutes longer. Remove from the heat; whisk in butter and vanilla. Transfer custard to crust; spread evenly with reserved cranberry mixture.

6. Add cream of tartar to egg whites; beat on medium speed until soft peaks form. Gradually beat in remaining sugar, 1 tablespoon at a time, on high until stiff glossy peaks form and sugar is dissolved. Spread meringue over hot filling, sealing edges to crust.

7. Bake at 350° for 12-15 minutes or until meringue is golden brown. Cool on a wire rack for 1 hour. Refrigerate overnight.

Fresh Blueberry Pie

I've been making this dessert for decades. It represents our state well because Michigan is the leader in blueberry production. Nothing says summer like a piece of fresh blueberry pie!

LINDA KERNAN, MASON, MICHIGAN

PREP: 15 MIN. + COOLING • **MAKES:** 6-8 SERVINGS

- ¾ **cup sugar**
- 3 **tablespoons cornstarch**
- ⅛ **teaspoon salt**
- ¼ **cup cold water**
- 5 **cups fresh blueberries, divided**
- 1 **tablespoon butter**
- 1 **tablespoon lemon juice**
  1 pastry shell (9 inches), baked

1. In a large saucepan, combine sugar, cornstarch, salt and water over medium heat until smooth. Add 3 cups blueberries. Bring to a boil; cook and stir for 2 minutes or until thickened and bubbly.

2. Remove from the heat. Add butter, lemon juice and remaining berries; stir until butter is melted. Cool.

3. Pour pie filling into prepared pastry shell. Refrigerate until serving.

Cranberry Pear Crisp Pie

Filled with a bubbling combination of cranberries and pears, this oat- and cinnamon-topped pie is a wonderful change of pace from the traditional.

PRISCILLA GILBERT, INDIAN HARBOUR BEACH, FLORIDA

PREP: 25 MIN. • **BAKE:** 55 MIN. + COOLING • **MAKES:** 8 SERVINGS

- 5 cups sliced peeled fresh pears
- 1 tablespoon lemon juice
- 1 teaspoon vanilla extract
- 1⅔ cups fresh or frozen cranberries
- ½ cup packed brown sugar
- ⅓ cup all-purpose flour
  Pastry for single-crust pie (9 inches)

TOPPING:
- ¼ cup all-purpose flour
- ¼ cup quick-cooking oats
- 3 tablespoons packed brown sugar
- ¾ teaspoon ground cinnamon
- 2 tablespoons cold butter

1. Place the pears in a large bowl; sprinkle with lemon juice and vanilla. Add cranberries. Combine the brown sugar and flour; sprinkle over fruit and gently toss to coat.

2. Roll out pastry to fit a 9-in. pie plate. Transfer pastry to pie plate. Trim pastry to ½ in. beyond edge of plate; flute edges. Add filling.

3. In a small bowl, combine the flour, oats, brown sugar and cinnamon. Cut in butter until crumbly. Sprinkle over filling.

4. Cover edges of pastry loosely with foil. Bake at 375° for 30 minutes. Remove foil; bake 25-30 minutes longer or until filling is bubbly. Cool on a wire rack.

Cran-Orange Pie in a Jar

These individual pudding pies in a jar are simply irresistible! Be prepared for compliments when you serve these.

TASTE OF HOME TEST KITCHEN

PREP: 20 MIN. + CHILLING • **MAKES:** 4 SERVINGS

- 1 cup graham cracker crumbs
- 2 tablespoons butter, melted
- 2 cups cold milk
- 1 package (3.3 ounces) instant white chocolate pudding mix
- ½ teaspoon grated orange peel
- ½ cup whole-berry cranberry sauce

1. In a small bowl, combine cracker crumbs and butter. Press into the bottoms of four half-pint canning jars.

2. In another bowl, whisk milk and pudding mix for 2 minutes. Stir in orange peel. Let stand for 2 minutes or until soft-set. Spoon over crusts. Top with cranberry sauce. Cover and refrigerate for at least 1 hour.

Macaroon Cherry Pie

In summer, I use homegrown cherries in this amazing pie with a crunchy coconut topping. But canned tart cherries yield a dessert that's almost as delicious. I always bake this pie around Presidents' Day or Valentine's Day, but it's popular with my family the whole year through.

LORI DANIELS, BEVERLY, WEST VIRGINIA

PREP: 25 MIN. • **BAKE:** 40 MIN. + CHILLING • **MAKES:** 6-8 SERVINGS

- Pastry for single-crust pie (9 inches)
- 3 cans (14½ ounces each) pitted tart cherries
- 1 cup sugar
- ⅓ cup cornstarch
- ½ teaspoon ground cinnamon
- ¼ teaspoon red food coloring, optional

TOPPING:
- 1 egg, lightly beaten
- 2 tablespoons milk
- 1 tablespoon butter
- ¼ teaspoon almond extract
- ¼ cup sugar
- ⅛ teaspoon salt
- 1 cup flaked coconut
- ½ cup sliced almonds

1. Line a 9-in. deep-dish pie plate with pastry. Trim to ½-in. beyond edge of plate; flute edges. Bake at 400° for 6 minutes; set aside.

2. Drain cherries, reserving 1 cup juice. Set cherries aside. In a large saucepan, combine sugar and cornstarch; gradually stir in cherry juice until blended. Bring to a boil over medium heat; cook and stir for 2 minutes or until thickened.

3. Remove from the heat; stir in cinnamon and food coloring if desired. Gently fold in cherries. Pour into crust. Cover edges loosely with foil. Bake at 400° for 20 minutes.

4. Meanwhile, in a large bowl, combine the first six topping ingredients. Stir in coconut and almonds.

5. Remove foil from pie; spoon topping over pie. Bake at 350° for 20 minutes or until topping is lightly browned. Cool on a wire rack for 1 hour. Chill for 4 hours or overnight before cutting.

Strawberry Tart

Looking for the perfect ending to any summertime meal? Here's a creamy swift-to-fix tart that boasts a surprise chocolate layer just next to the crust. You could also make individual tartlets instead of one big one.

DAWN TRINGALI, HAMILTON SQUARE, NEW JERSEY

PREP: 30 MIN. + CHILLING • **YIELD:** 6-8 SERVINGS

- 1 **sheet refrigerated pie pastry**
- 3 **ounces German sweet chocolate, melted**
- 2 **packages (8 ounces each) cream cheese, softened**
- 3 **tablespoons heavy whipping cream**
- 2 **teaspoons vanilla extract**
- 1-¾ **cups confectioners' sugar**
- 2-½ **cups sliced fresh strawberries**
- ¼ **cup red currant jelly**

1. Press pastry onto the bottom and up the sides of an ungreased 9-in. fluted tart pan with a removable bottom. Place on a baking sheet. Bake at 450° for 10-12 minutes or until golden brown. Cool on a wire rack.

2. Spread melted chocolate over bottom of crust. Refrigerate for 5-10 minutes or until almost set. Meanwhile, in a large bowl, beat the cream cheese, cream and vanilla until smooth. Gradually beat in confectioners' sugar. Spread filling over chocolate layer.

3. Arrange strawberries over filling; brush with jelly. Refrigerate for at least 2 hours. Remove sides of pan before serving.

Easy Pumpkin Pie

Pumpkin pie does not have to be difficult to make. This recipe has wonderful flavor and is sure to be a hit at your holiday meal.

MARTY RUMMEL, TROUT LAKE, WASHINGTON

PREP: 10 MIN. • **BAKE:** 50 MIN. + COOLING • **MAKES:** 8 SERVINGS

- 3 **eggs**
- 1 **cup canned pumpkin**
- 1 **cup evaporated milk**
- ½ **cup sugar**
- ¼ **cup maple syrup**
- 1 **teaspoon ground cinnamon**
- ½ **teaspoon salt**
- ½ **teaspoon ground nutmeg**
- ½ **teaspoon maple flavoring**
- ½ **teaspoon vanilla extract**
- 1 **frozen pie shell (9 inches)**
  Additional pie pastry, optional
  Whipped cream, optional

1. In a large bowl, beat the first 10 ingredients until smooth; pour into pastry shell. Cover edges loosely with foil.

2. Bake at 400° for 10 minutes. Reduce heat to 350°; bake 40-45 minutes longer or until a knife inserted near the center comes out clean. Remove foil. Cool on a wire rack.

3. If decorative cutouts are desired, roll additional pastry to ⅛-in. thickness; cut out with 1-in. to 1½-in. leaf-shaped cookie cutters. With a sharp knife, score leaf veins on cutouts.

4. Place on an ungreased baking sheet. Bake at 400° for 6-8 minutes or until golden brown. Remove to a wire rack to cool. Arrange around edge of pie. Garnish with whipped cream if desired.

Bumbleberry Pie

This pie recipe makes one of the flakiest crusts ever and is sure to impress! The filling is delicious with the different berries, tart apple and rhubarb.

SUZANNE ALBERTS, ONALASKA, WISCONSIN

PREP: 20 MIN. + CHILLING • **BAKE:** 1 HOUR + COOLING
MAKES: 6-8 SERVINGS

1½ cups all-purpose flour
1 teaspoon salt
1 teaspoon sugar
1 cup cold butter
¼ cup cold water
FILLING:
1 medium tart apple, peeled and diced
1 cup diced fresh or frozen rhubarb, thawed
1 cup fresh or frozen raspberries, thawed and drained
1 cup fresh or frozen blueberries, thawed and drained
1 cup sliced fresh or frozen strawberries, thawed and drained
1 cup sugar
½ cup all-purpose flour
1 tablespoon lemon juice

1. In a small bowl, combine the flour, salt and sugar. Cut in butter until mixture ensembles coarse crumbs. Gradually add water, tossing with a fork until a ball forms. Cover and refrigerate for 1 hour.

2. On a lightly floured surface, roll out half of the dough to fit a 9-in. pie plate. Transfer pastry to pie plate. Trim pastry to ½ in. beyond edge of plate.

3. In a large bowl, combine the filling ingredients; pour into crust. Roll out the remaining pastry; make a lattice crust. Seal and flute edges. Cover edges loosely with foil.

4. Bake at 400° for 20 minutes. Reduce heat to 350°; remove foil. Bake 40-45 minutes longer or until crust is golden brown and filling is bubbly. Cool on a wire rack.

Berry Shortbread Pizza

This beautiful berry-topped pizza tastes as good as it looks! It's impossible to resist the pecan shortbread crust, rich cheesecake-like layer, glossy berry topping and sprinkling of luscious fresh fruit. It's an ideal summertime dessert or take-along treat for a brunch buffet.

MARIA SCHUSTER, WOLF POINT, MONTANA

PREP: 30 MIN. • **BAKE:** 10 MIN. + CHILLING • **MAKES:** 10-12 SERVINGS

- 1 cup all-purpose flour
- ¼ cup confectioners' sugar
- ½ cup cold butter, cubed
- ½ cup chopped pecans
- 1 package (8 ounces) cream cheese, softened
- 1 egg
- ⅓ cup sugar

TOPPING:
- 1¾ cups frozen mixed berries, thawed
- ½ cup sugar
- 2 tablespoons cornstarch
- ¼ cup water
- 2½ cups fresh strawberries, sliced
- 2 cups fresh blackberries
- 2 cups fresh raspberries
- 1 cup fresh blueberries

1. In a bowl, combine flour and confectioners' sugar. Cut in butter until crumbly. Stir in pecans. Press into an ungreased 12-in. pizza pan.

2. Bake at 350° for 12-14 minutes or until crust is set and edges are lightly browned.

3. Meanwhile, in a bowl, beat cream cheese, egg and sugar until smooth. Spread over crust. Bake 8-10 minutes longer or until set. Cool to room temperature.

4. For topping, process mixed berries and sugar in a food processor until blended. In a small saucepan, combine cornstarch and water until smooth. Stir in mixed berry mixture until blended. Bring to a boil; cook and stir for 2 minutes or until thickened. Set mixture aside to cool, stirring frequently.

5. Spread berry mixture over the cream cheese layer. Arrange fresh berries on top. Refrigerate for at least 2 hours before slicing.

Mini Apple Tarts

These cute tarts have a golden crust brimming with a sweet-tart apple and cherry filling. They look and taste delicious!

TASTE OF HOME TEST KITCHEN

PREP: 20 MIN. • **BAKE:** 20 MIN. + COOLING • **MAKES:** 4 SERVINGS

- Pastry for single-crust pie (9 inches)
- 1 cup apple pie filling
- 2 tablespoons dried cherries
- 1 teaspoon finely chopped crystallized ginger
- ¼ teaspoon ground cinnamon
- 1 egg white
- 1 tablespoon water
- 1 teaspoon coarse sugar

1. Divide pastry in half. On a lightly floured surface, roll each half into a 9-in. circle. Transfer to a parchment paper-lined baking sheet.

2. In a small bowl, combine the pie filling, cherries, ginger and cinnamon. Spoon over each pastry to within 2 in. of edges. Fold up edges of pastry over filling, leaving center uncovered. Beat egg white and water; brush over folded pastry. Sprinkle with sugar.

3. Bake at 400° for 20-25 minutes or until crusts are lightly browned. Using parchment paper, slide tarts onto a wire rack to cool.

Cherry Tarts

At our house, we celebrate George Washington's birthday with these tasty little cherry pies.

VERNA BURKHOLDER, DORCHESTER, WISCONSIN

PREP: 30 MIN. + CHILLING • **BAKE:** 10 MIN. + COOLING
MAKES: 8 SERVINGS

- 1½ **cups all-purpose flour**
- ½ **teaspoon salt**
- ½ **cup shortening**
- 4 **to 5 tablespoons cold water**
- ¾ **cup sugar**
- 3 **tablespoons cornstarch**
- 2 **cans (14½ ounces each) pitted tart cherries**
- 1 **tablespoon butter**
- ¼ **teaspoon almond extract**
- 4 **to 5 drops red food coloring, optional**

1. In a small bowl, combine flour and salt. Cut in shortening until mixture resembles coarse crumbs. Add enough water until dough forms a ball. Refrigerate for 30 minutes.

2. On a lightly floured surface, roll out dough to ⅛-in. thickness. Cut out eight 5-in. circles. Place each over an inverted custard cup on an ungreased 15-in. x 10-in. x 1-in. baking pan; flute edges.

3. Bake at 450° for 10-11 minutes or until golden brown. Cool for 5 minutes before removing tart shells from custard cups; cool completely on wire racks.

4. For filling, in a large saucepan, combine sugar and cornstarch. Drain cherries, reserving 1 cup juice. Set cherries aside. Stir reserved juice into sugar mixture until smooth. Bring to a boil; cook and stir for 2 minutes or until thickened. Remove from the heat; stir in the cherries, butter, extract and food coloring if desired. Cool to room temperature. Spoon about ¼ cup filling into each tart shell.

Peach Blueberry Pie

What a flavor! That's what I hear most often after folks try this pie I invented one day when I was short of peaches for a full crust.

SUE THUMMA, SHEPHERD, MICHIGAN

PREP: 15 MIN. • **BAKE:** 40 MIN. + COOLING • **MAKES:** 6-8 SERVINGS

- 1 **cup sugar**
- ⅓ **cup all-purpose flour**
- ½ **teaspoon ground cinnamon**
- ⅛ **teaspoon ground allspice**
- 3 **cups sliced peeled fresh peaches**
- 1 **cup fresh or frozen unsweetened blueberries**
  Pastry for double-crust pie (9 inches)
- 1 **tablespoon butter**
  Milk
  Cinnamon-sugar

1. In a large bowl, combine sugar, flour, cinnamon and allspice. Add the peaches and blueberries; toss gently.

2. Line pie plate with bottom crust; add the filling. Dot with butter. Top with a lattice crust. Brush crust with milk; sprinkle with cinnamon-sugar.

3. Bake at 400° for 40-45 minutes or until crust is golden brown and filling is bubbly. Cool completely on a wire rack.

Editor's Note: *Frozen fruit may be used if it is thawed and well drained.*

Caramel Peanut Fantasy

Packed with peanuts and gooey with caramel, this do-ahead treat is one sweet dream of a dessert to serve company. With an easy cookie crust and scrumptious candy bar layers, it goes together quickly and will disappear just as fast!

TASTE OF HOME TEST KITCHEN

PREP: 30 MIN. + CHILLING • **MAKES:** 12 SERVINGS

2 **cups crushed vanilla wafers (about 60 wafers)**
⅓ **cup butter, melted**
20 **caramels**
15 **miniature Snickers candy bars**
½ **cup caramel ice cream topping**
½ **cup heavy whipping cream, divided**
2 **cups salted peanuts, chopped**
¾ **cup semisweet chocolate chips**

1. In a small bowl, combine wafer crumbs and butter. Press onto the bottom of a greased 9-in. springform pan. Place on a baking sheet. Bake at 350° for 8-10 minutes. Cool on a wire rack.

2. In a heavy saucepan, combine the caramels, candy bars, caramel topping and ¼ cup cream; cook and stir over low heat until smooth and blended. Remove from the heat; stir in peanuts. Spread over crust. Cover and refrigerate for 1 hour.

3. In a microwave, melt chocolate chips and remaining cream; stir until smooth. Spread over caramel layer. Cover and refrigerate for 1 hour or until serving.

Cherry-Berry Streusel Pie

I entered this delicious pie in the Oklahoma State Fair and won a ribbon. It's very pretty and tastes great, especially served with a scoop of vanilla ice cream.

ROSALIE SEEBECK, BETHANY, OKLAHOMA

PREP: 1 HOUR + CHILLING • **BAKE:** 55 MIN. + COOLING
MAKES: 8 SERVINGS

- 2½ **cups all-purpose flour**
- 1 **tablespoon sugar**
- 1 **teaspoon salt**
- 1 **cup cold butter, cubed**
- 7 **to 8 tablespoons cold water**

FILLING:
- 2 **cans (21 ounces each) cherry pie filling**
- 1 **cup fresh or frozen raspberries**
- ¼ **cup packed brown sugar**
- ¼ **teaspoon ground cinnamon**

TOPPING:
- 1 **cup yellow cake mix**
- ½ **cup chopped pecans, toasted**
- ½ **cup flaked coconut**
- ¼ **cup butter, melted**
- 2 **tablespoons 2% milk**
- 2 **tablespoons sugar**

1. Place the flour, sugar and salt in a food processor; cover and pulse until blended. Add butter; cover and pulse until mixture resembles coarse crumbs. While processing, gradually add water until dough forms a ball.

2. Divide dough in half so that one portion is slightly larger than the other; wrap each in plastic wrap. Refrigerate for 30 minutes or until easy to handle.

3. On a lightly floured surface, roll out larger portion of dough to fit a 9-in. deep-dish pie plate. Transfer pastry to pie plate; trim pastry to ½ in. beyond edge of plate. Combine the filling ingredients; spoon into crust. Sprinkle with dry cake mix, pecans and coconut. Drizzle with butter.

4. Roll out remaining pastry to a 13-inch circle; cut into strips for a lattice top. While creating the lattice top, twist the pastry strips for a decorative effect. Seal and flute edges of pie.

5. Brush lattice top with milk; sprinkle with sugar. Cover edges loosely with foil. Bake at 375° for 55-65 minutes or until crust is golden brown and filling is bubbly. Cool on a wire rack.

Bakeshop TIP

Pretty Flower Pie

Try a flower-topped pie instead of a lattice crust. To make, use a paring knife to cut the pie dough into strips of various size. Use a 2- or 3-in. round cookie cutter to make the center of the flower. Lay the strips on top of the pie, overlapping them at random. Top with the round center in the middle. Adhere strips together by dabbing with water as you go, or brush egg wash over the finished pie. Sprinkle with coarse sugar and bake.

Classic Cherry Pie

My dad loves all kinds of fruit pies, especially this one, so I make it for his birthday every year.

JOHANNA GEROW, RAYTOWN, MISSOURI

PREP: 40 MIN. • **BAKE:** 35 MIN. + COOLING • **MAKES:** 6-8 SERVINGS

- 2 **cans (14 ounces each) pitted tart cherries**
- 1 **cup sugar**
- ¼ **cup cornstarch**
- ⅛ **teaspoon salt**
- 2 **tablespoons butter**
- ½ **teaspoon almond extract**
- ½ **teaspoon vanilla extract**
- ¼ **teaspoon red food coloring, optional**
  Pastry for double-crust pie (9 inches)
- 1 **egg yolk, lightly beaten**
  Additional sugar

1. Drain cherries, reserving 1 cup juice. Set cherries aside. In a large saucepan, combine the sugar, cornstarch and salt; gradually stir in reserved cherry juice until smooth. Bring to a boil; cook and stir for 2 minutes or until thickened. Remove from the heat; stir in the butter, extracts and food coloring if desired. Fold in cherries. Cool slightly.

2. Line a 9-in. pie plate with bottom crust; trim pastry even with edge. Pour filling into crust. Roll out remaining pastry; make a lattice crust. Trim, seal and flute edges. Brush lattice top with egg yolk. Sprinkle with additional sugar.

3. Cover edges loosely with foil. Bake at 425° for 15 minutes. Remove foil. Bake 20-25 minutes longer or until crust is golden brown and filling is bubbly. Cool on wire rack.

Bakeshop **HOW-TO**

Creating a Lattice-Topped Pie

Make a pastry for a double-crust pie. Line a 9-in. pie plate with the bottom pastry and trim to 1 in. beyond the edge of plate. Roll out remaining pastry to a 12-in. circle. With a fluted pastry wheel, pizza cutter or a sharp knife, cut pastry into ½-in.- to 1-in.-wide strips. Lay strips in rows about ½ in. to ¾ in. apart. (Use longer strips for the center of the pie and shorter strips for the sides.)

Fold every other strip halfway back. Starting at the center, add strips at right angles, lifting every other strip as the cross strips are put down.

Continue to add strips, lifting and weaving until lattice top is complete.

Trim strips even with pastry edge. Fold bottom pastry up and over ends of strips and seal. Flute edges.

Pear Frangipane Tart

Pears and almonds make a pleasing match in this classic dessert. It looks lovely with the sliced fruit arranged on top. How can something so simple taste this wonderful?

LILY JULOW, GAINESVILLE, FLORIDA

PREP: 25 MIN. • **BAKE:** 40 MIN. • **MAKES:** 6-8 SERVINGS

- 1¼ cups blanched almonds
- ½ cup plus 4½ teaspoons sugar, divided
- ⅓ cup all-purpose flour
- ¼ teaspoon salt
- 5 tablespoons cold butter, divided
- 2 eggs
- ¼ cup milk
- 1 can (15¼ ounces) pear halves, drained and thinly sliced

1. In a food processor, combine almonds and ½ cup sugar. Cover and process until blended; transfer to a bowl. Stir in flour and salt. In a microwave-safe bowl, melt 4 tablespoons butter; whisk in eggs and milk. Stir into almond mixture.

2. Pour into a greased 9-in. fluted tart pan with a removable bottom. Arrange pear slices over batter. Sprinkle with remaining sugar; dot with remaining butter.

3. Place on a baking sheet. Bake at 350° for 40-45 minutes or until crust is golden brown. Serve warm or at room temperature. Refrigerate leftovers.

German Apple Pie

I first tasted this pie many years ago when my children's baby sitter made it. I asked for the recipe and have prepared it many times since.

MRS. WOODROW TAYLOR, ADAMS CENTER, NEW YORK

PREP: 20 MIN. • **BAKE:** 65 MIN. + COOLING • **MAKES:** 8 SERVINGS

- 1½ cups all-purpose flour
- ½ teaspoon salt
- ½ cup shortening
- 1 teaspoon vanilla extract
- 2 to 3 tablespoons ice water
FILLING:
- 1 cup sugar
- ¼ cup all-purpose flour
- 2 teaspoons ground cinnamon
- 6 cups sliced peeled tart apples
- 1 cup heavy whipping cream
  Whipped cream, optional

1. In a small bowl, combine flour and salt; cut in the shortening until crumbly. Add vanilla. Gradually add water, tossing with a fork until dough forms a ball. Roll out pastry to fit a 9-in. pie plate. Transfer pastry to pie plate. Trim pastry to ½ in. beyond edge of pie plate; flute edges.

2. For filling, combine the sugar, flour and cinnamon; sprinkle 3 tablespoons into crust. Layer with half of the apples; sprinkle with half of the remaining sugar mixture. Repeat layers. Pour cream over all.

3. Bake at 450° for 10 minutes. Reduce heat to 350° bake for 55-60 minutes or until apples are tender. Cool on a wire rack. Store in the refrigerator. Serve with whipped cream if desired.

Spiced Winter Fruit Pie

This flavorful pie makes any gathering a celebration. It's a delightful choice for Thanksgiving or Christmas.

MARIAN PLATT, SEQUIM, WASHINGTON

PREP: 25 MIN. • **BAKE:** 55 MIN. + COOLING • **MAKES:** 6-8 SERVINGS

- Pastry for double-crust pie (9 inches)
- ¾ cup sugar
- 3 tablespoons cornstarch
- 1 teaspoon ground cinnamon
- ¼ teaspoon ground allspice
- 5 cups sliced peeled fresh pears
- 2 cups fresh or frozen cranberries, thawed
- 2 tablespoons butter
- 1 egg
- 1 tablespoon whole milk
  Additional sugar

1. Line a 9-in. pie plate with bottom pastry; set aside. In a large bowl, combine the sugar, cornstarch, cinnamon and allspice. Add pears and cranberries; toss to coat. Spoon into crust; dot with butter.

2. Roll out remaining pastry; make a lattice crust. Trim, seal and flute edges.

3. In a small bowl, whisk egg and milk; brush over pastry. Sprinkle with additional sugar. Cover pie loosely with foil to prevent overbrowning.

4. Bake at 450° for 15 minutes. Reduce heat to 350° and remove foil; bake for 40-45 minutes or until crust is golden brown and filling is bubbly. Cool on a wire rack.

Candy Apple Pie

This is the only apple pie my husband will eat, but that's all right since he makes it as often as I do. Like a combination of apple and pecan pie, it's a sweet treat that usually tops off our holiday meals from New Year's all the way through to Christmas!

CINDY KLEWENO, BURLINGTON, COLORADO

PREP: 20 MIN. • **BAKE:** 45 MIN. • **MAKES:** 8 SERVINGS

- 6 **cups sliced peeled tart apples**
- 2 **tablespoons lime juice**
- ¾ **cup sugar**
- ¼ **cup all-purpose flour**
- ½ **teaspoon ground cinnamon**
- ¼ **teaspoon salt**
  Pastry for double-crust pie (9 inches)
- 2 **tablespoons butter**

TOPPING:
- 2 **tablespoons butter**
- ¼ **cup packed brown sugar**
- 1 **tablespoon heavy whipping cream**
- ¼ **cup chopped pecans**

1. In a large bowl, toss apples with lime juice. Combine the sugar, flour, cinnamon and salt; add to apples and toss lightly.

2. Line a 9-in. pie plate with bottom crust and trim even with edge; fill with apple mixture. Dot with butter. Roll out remaining pastry to fit top of pie. Place over filling. Trim, seal and flute edges; cut slits in pastry.

3. Bake at 400° for 40-45 minutes or until golden brown and apples are tender.

4. For topping, melt butter in a small saucepan. Stir in brown sugar and cream; bring to a boil, stirring constantly. Remove from the heat and stir in pecans.

5. Pour over top crust. Bake 3-4 minutes longer or until bubbly. Place on a wire rack. Serve warm.

White Chocolate Berry Pie

When strawberries are in season, I love to make this pretty pie. It's so easy and doesn't require any baking!

CONNIE LAUX, ENGLEWOOD, OHIO

PREP: 20 MIN. + CHILLING • **MAKES:** 8 SERVINGS

- 5 **ounces white baking chocolate, chopped, divided**
- 2 **tablespoons milk**
- 1 **package (3 ounces) cream cheese, softened**
- ⅓ **cup confectioners' sugar**
- 1 **teaspoon grated orange peel**
- 1 **cup heavy whipping cream, whipped**
- 1 **graham cracker crust (9 inches)**
- 2 **cups sliced fresh strawberries**

1. In a microwave, melt four ounces of white chocolate with milk; stir until smooth. Cool to room temperature.

2. Meanwhile, in a large bowl, beat cream cheese and sugar until smooth. Beat in orange peel and melted chocolate. Fold in whipped cream.

3. Spread into crust. Arrange strawberries on top. Melt remaining white chocolate; drizzle over berries. Refrigerate for at least 1 hour. Store in the refrigerator.

Lemon Burst Tartlets

You'll love the taste of lemon and raspberry in these quick and easy bites. Their little size makes them perfect for a party.

PAM JAVOR, NORTH HUNTINGDON, PENNSYLVANIA

PREP/TOTAL TIME: 20 MIN. • **MAKES:** 2½ DOZEN

- 1   **jar (10 ounces) lemon curd**
- 1   **carton (8 ounces) frozen whipped topping, thawed**
- 5   **to 6 drops yellow food coloring, optional**
- ⅔   **cup raspberry cake and pastry filling**

SHORT & SWEET

- 2   **packages (1.9 ounces each) frozen miniature phyllo tart shells**
- 30 **fresh raspberries**

1. In a large bowl, combine the lemon curd, whipped topping and food coloring if desired until smooth.

2. Spoon 1 teaspoon raspberry filling into each tart shell. Pipe or spoon lemon mixture over filling. Garnish each with a raspberry. Refrigerate leftovers.

Editor's Note: *This recipe was tested with Solo brand cake and pastry filling. Look for it in the baking aisle.*

Creamy Peanut Butter Pie

Quartered peanut butter cups top this rich, smooth pie. It's always a hit at gatherings. It saves time, too, because it can be made in advance and frozen until needed.

RHONDA MCDANIEL ROSSVILLE, GEORGIA

PREP: 15 MIN. + CHILLING • **YIELD:** 6-8 SERVINGS

- 2 **packages (8 ounces each) cream cheese, softened**
- 1 **cup sugar**
- ⅔ **cup creamy peanut butter**
- ⅔ **cup whipped topping**
- 14 **peanut butter cups, divided**
- 1 **chocolate crumb crust (9 inches)**

1. In a small bowl, beat the cream cheese, sugar and peanut butter until light and fluffy. Fold in whipped topping. Coarsely chop half of the peanut butter cups; stir into cream cheese mixture.

2. Spoon into crust. Quarter remaining peanut butter cups; arrange over the top. Refrigerate for at least 4 hours before serving.

SHORT & SWEET

Peach Streusel Pie

A delightful summertime pie, this dessert is overflowing with fresh peach flavor. Each slice is like a sweet trip down memory lane. The streusel topping makes this pie a little different than the ordinary and adds homemade flair.

SALLY HOLBROOK, PASADENA, CALIFORNIA

PREP: 15 MIN. • **BAKE:** 40 MIN. + COOLING • **MAKES:** 8 SERVINGS

- 1 egg white, lightly beaten
- 1 unbaked pastry shell (9 inches)
- ¾ cup all-purpose flour
- ½ cup packed brown sugar
- ⅓ cup sugar
- ¼ cup cold butter, cubed
- 6 cups sliced peeled fresh peaches

1. Brush egg white over pastry shell; set aside.

2. In a small bowl, combine flour and sugars; cut in butter until mixture resembles fine crumbs. Sprinkle two-thirds into pastry; top with peaches. Sprinkle with remaining crumb mixture.

3. Bake at 375° for 40-45 minutes or until filling is bubbly and peaches are tender.

Chocolate Chip Banana Cream Pie

This rich treat is a hit every time I serve it. The creamy filling, brimming with bananas, is refreshing, and the cookie crust provides a chocolaty crunch. Even a small sliver will satisfy the biggest sweet tooth.

TAYLOR CARROLL, PARKESBURG, PENNSYLVANIA

PREP: 35 MIN. + CHILLING • **MAKES:** 6-8 SERVINGS

- 1 tube (16½ ounces) refrigerated chocolate chip cookie dough
- ⅓ cup sugar
- ¼ cup cornstarch
- ⅛ teaspoon salt
- 2⅓ cups 2% milk
- 5 egg yolks, lightly beaten
- 2 tablespoons butter
- 2 teaspoons vanilla extract, divided
- 3 medium firm bananas
- 1½ cups heavy whipping cream
- 3 tablespoons confectioners' sugar

1. Cut cookie dough in half widthwise. Let one portion stand at room temperature for 5-10 minutes to soften (return the other half to the refrigerator for another use).

2. Press dough onto the bottom and up the sides of an ungreased 9-in. pie plate. Bake at 375° for 11-12 minutes or until lightly browned. Cool on a wire rack.

3. In a large saucepan, combine the sugar, cornstarch and salt. Stir in milk until smooth. Cook and stir over medium-high heat until thickened and bubbly. Reduce heat; cook and stir 2 minutes longer. Remove from the heat. Stir a small amount of hot filling into egg yolks; return all to the pan, stirring constantly. Bring to a gentle boil; cook and stir 2 minutes longer. Remove from the heat; stir in butter and 1 teaspoon vanilla.

4. Spread 1 cup filling into prepared crust. Slice bananas; arrange over filling. Pour remaining filling over bananas. Refrigerate for 2 hours or until set.

5. In a large bowl, beat cream until it begins to thicken. Add confectioners' sugar and remaining vanilla; beat until stiff peaks form. Spread over pie. Refrigerate for 1 hour or until chilled.

Maple Butter Tarts

These individual tarts are so scrumptious and syrupy that I often double the recipe so I have enough for guests to take home. They're a little slice of heaven alongside a cup of coffee.

LORRAINE CALAND, SHUNIAH, ONTARIO

PREP: 20 MIN. • **BAKE:** 20 MIN. + COOLING • **MAKES:** 8 TARTS

- 1 package (15 ounces) refrigerated pie pastry
- 1½ cups raisins
- 2 cups boiling water
- 1¾ cups packed brown sugar
- 3 eggs
- ½ cup butter, melted
- ¼ cup maple syrup
- 1 teaspoon maple flavoring
  Butter pecan or vanilla ice cream, optional

1. Cut each pastry sheet into quarters; roll each quarter into a 6-in. circle. Transfer pastry to eight ungreased 4-in. fluted tart pans with removable bottoms. Trim pastry even with edges. Place on baking sheets. Bake at 450° for 5-6 minutes or until golden brown. Cool on wire racks. Reduce heat to 350°.

2. Place raisins in a large bowl. Cover with boiling water; let stand for 5 minutes. Drain. In another bowl, beat the brown sugar, eggs, butter, syrup and flavoring; stir in raisins. Divide filling among tart shells.

3. Bake for 16-20 minutes or until centers are just set (mixture will jiggle). Cool on a wire rack. Serve with ice cream if desired.

Lemon Tart with Almond Crust

Arizona produces an abundance of lemons, and everyone is always looking for new ways to use them. This beautiful tart is my delicious solution to the excess-lemon problem!

LOIS KINNEBERG, PHOENIX, ARIZONA

PREP: 40 MIN. • **BAKE:** 10 MIN. + COOLING • **MAKES:** 6-8 SERVINGS

- 1 cup all-purpose flour
- ½ cup sliced almonds, toasted
- ¼ cup sugar
- 6 tablespoons cold butter
- ½ teaspoon almond extract
- ¼ teaspoon salt
- 2 to 3 tablespoons cold water

FILLING:
- 3 eggs
- 3 egg yolks
- 1 cup sugar
- ¾ cup lemon juice
- 2 tablespoons grated lemon peel
  Dash salt
- 6 tablespoons butter, cubed

1. Place the flour, almonds, sugar, butter, extract and salt in a food processor. Cover and pulse until blended. Gradually add water, 1 tablespoon at a time, pulsing until mixture forms a soft dough.

2. Press onto the bottom and up the sides of a greased 9-in. fluted tart pan with a removable bottom. Bake at 400° for 15-20 minutes or until golden brown. Cool on a wire rack. Reduce heat to 325°.

3. In a small heavy saucepan over medium heat, whisk the eggs, egg yolks, sugar, lemon juice, peel and salt until blended. Add butter; cook, whisking constantly, until mixture is thickened and coats the back of a spoon. Pour into crust. Bake for 8-10 minutes or until set. Cool on a wire rack. Refrigerate leftovers.

Rustic Caramel Apple Tart

Like an apple pie without the pan, this scrumptious tart has a crispy crust that cuts nicely under a yummy caramel topping.

BETTY FULKS, ONIA, ARKANSAS

PREP: 20 MIN. + CHILLING • **BAKE:** 25 MIN. • **MAKES:** 4 SERVINGS

- ⅔ **cup all-purpose flour**
- 1 **tablespoon sugar**
- ⅛ **teaspoon salt**
- ¼ **cup cold butter, cubed**
- 6½ **teaspoons cold water**
- ⅛ **teaspoon vanilla extract**

FILLING:
- 1½ **cups chopped peeled tart apples**
- 3 **tablespoons sugar**
- 1 **tablespoon all-purpose flour**

TOPPING:
- 1 **teaspoon sugar**
- ¼ **teaspoon ground cinnamon**
- 2 **tablespoons caramel ice cream topping, warmed**

1. In a large bowl, combine the flour, sugar and salt; cut in butter until crumbly. Gradually add water and vanilla, tossing with a fork until dough forms a ball. Cover and refrigerate for at least 30 minutes.

2. On a lightly floured surface, roll dough into a 10-in. circle. Transfer to a parchment paper-lined baking sheet. Combine the filling ingredients; spoon over pastry to within 2 in. of edges. Fold up edges of pastry over filling, leaving center uncovered. Combine sugar and cinnamon; sprinkle over filling.

3. Bake at 400° for 25-30 minutes or until crust is golden and filling is bubbly. Using parchment paper, slide tart onto a wire rack. Drizzle with caramel topping. Serve warm.

Caramel Pecan Pie

This is hands down the best pecan pie—it's so good, it's scary! I make it for Thanksgiving because there will be others around to share it with me. Toss the bag of caramels to your kid or spouse and promise they can eat whatever is left after they unwrap your 36 caramels.

DOROTHY REINHOLD, MALIBU, CALIFORNIA

PREP: 25 MIN. • **BAKE:** 35 MIN. + COOLING • **MAKES:** 6-8 SERVINGS

- 36 caramels
- ¼ cup water
- ¼ cup butter, cubed
- 3 eggs
- ¾ cup sugar
- 1 teaspoon vanilla extract
- ⅛ teaspoon salt
- 1⅓ cups chopped pecans, toasted
  Frozen deep-dish pie shell
  Pecan halves, optional

1. In a small heavy saucepan, combine the caramels, water and butter. Cook and stir over low heat until caramels are melted. Remove from the heat and set aside.

2. In a small bowl, beat the eggs, sugar, vanilla and salt until smooth. Gradually add caramel mixture. Stir in chopped pecans. Pour into pie shell. If desired, arrange pecan halves over filling.

3. Bake at 350° for 35-40 minutes or until set. Cool on a wire rack. Refrigerate leftovers.

German Plum Tart

The buttery crust of this fruit-filled treat will simply melt in your mouth. You can substitute sliced apples or peaches for the plums with tasty results. I've also used fresh blueberries.

HELGA SCHLAPE, FLORHAM PARK, NEW JERSEY

PREP: 10 MIN. • **BAKE:** 35 MIN. • **MAKES:** 6-8 SERVINGS

- ½ cup butter, softened
- 4 tablespoons sugar, divided
- 1 egg yolk
- ¾ to 1 cup all-purpose flour
- 2 pounds plums, quartered (about 4 cups)

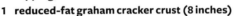

1. In a small bowl, cream butter and 3 tablespoons sugar until light and fluffy. Beat in egg yolk. Gradually add flour, ¼ cup at a time, until mixture forms a soft dough. Press onto the bottom and up the sides of a 10-in. pie plate.

2. Arrange plums, skin side up with edges overlapping, in crust; sprinkle with remaining sugar. Bake at 350° for 35-45 minutes or until crust is golden brown and fruit is tender.

Low-Fat Key Lime Pie

For a taste of paradise, try this light and creamy confection. It's low in fat, sugar and fuss. Dessert doesn't get any better than that!

FRANCES VANFOSSAN, WARREN, MICHIGAN

PREP: 20 MIN. + CHILLING • **MAKES:** 8 SERVINGS

- 1 package (.3 ounce) sugar-free lime gelatin
- ¼ cup boiling water
- 2 cartons (6 ounces each) key lime yogurt
- 1 carton (8 ounces) frozen fat-free whipped topping, thawed
- 1 reduced-fat graham cracker crust (8 inches)

1. In a large bowl, dissolve gelatin in boiling water. Whisk in yogurt. Fold in whipped topping. Pour into crust. Refrigerate for at least 2 hours or until set.

Pastries

Almond Venetian Dessert

These beautiful bars feature three colorful cake-like layers, an apricot filling and a chocolate topping.

REVA BECKER, FARMINGTON HILLS, MICHIGAN

PREP: 35 MIN. • **BAKE:** 15 MIN. + CHILLING • **MAKES:** ABOUT 2 DOZEN

- ½ cup almond paste
- ¾ cup butter, softened
- ½ cup sugar
- 2 eggs, separated
- ¼ teaspoon almond extract
- 1 cup all-purpose flour
- ⅛ teaspoon salt
- 5 drops green food coloring
- 4 drops red food coloring
- ⅔ cup apricot preserves
- 3 ounces semisweet chocolate, chopped

1. Grease the bottoms of three 8-in. square baking dishes. Line with waxed paper and grease the paper; set aside.

2. Place almond paste in a large bowl; break up with a fork. Add the butter, sugar, egg yolks and extract; beat until smooth and fluffy. Stir in flour and salt. In another bowl, beat egg whites until soft peaks form. Stir a fourth of the whites into the dough, then fold in the remaining whites (dough will be stiff).

3. Divide dough evenly into three portions, about ⅔ cup each. Tint one portion green and one portion pink; leave the remaining portion white. Spread each portion into a prepared pan. Bake at 350° for 13-15 minutes or until edges are golden brown. Immediately invert onto wire racks; remove waxed paper. Place another wire rack on top and turn over. Cool completely.

4. Place green layer on a large piece of plastic wrap. Spread evenly with ⅓ cup apricot preserves. Top with white layer and spread with remaining preserves. Top with pink layer. Bring plastic over layers. Slide onto a baking sheet and set a cutting board on top to compress layers. Refrigerate overnight.

5. In a microwave-safe bowl, melt chocolate. Remove cutting board and unwrap dessert. Spread melted chocolate over top; let stand until set. With a sharp knife, trim edges. Cut into 2-in. x ⅝-in. bars. Store in an airtight container.

Presto Peach Napoleons

When your family has a taste for pie but time is ticking away, make this fast and fruity dessert. For a tasty twist, use cherry pie filling instead.

TASTE OF HOME TEST KITCHEN

PREP: 20 MIN. + COOLING • **MAKES:** 6 SERVINGS

- 1 sheet frozen puff pastry, thawed
- 1 egg white
- 1 tablespoon water
- 1½ teaspoons sugar
- 1 can (21 ounces) peach or cherry pie filling
- ¼ teaspoon almond extract
- 2 cups whipped topping

SHORT & SWEET

1. On a lightly floured surface, unfold pastry and roll to ⅜-in. thickness. Cut along fold lines into three pieces. Cut each piece in half widthwise; place on an ungreased baking sheet.

2. Beat egg white and water; brush over pastry. Sprinkle with sugar. Bake at 400° for 9-11 minutes or until golden brown. Cool on a wire rack.

3. Split each pastry in half horizontally. Combine pie filling and extract; spoon over bottom halves of pastries. Top with whipped topping and pastry tops.

Mini Cherry Tarts

I use refrigerated crescent dough to bake up these little tarts in no time flat. No one can resist the cherry cheesecake-like flavors tucked inside.

FRANCES POSTE, WALL, SOUTH DAKOTA

PREP: 20 MIN. • **BAKE:** 15 MIN. + COOLING • **MAKES:** 2 DOZEN

- 1　**tube (8 ounces) refrigerated crescent rolls**
- 1　**package (3 ounces) cream cheese, softened**
- ¼　**cup confectioners' sugar**
- 1　**cup canned cherry pie filling**
- ¼　**teaspoon almond extract**

1. Place crescent dough on a lightly floured surface; seal seams and perforations. Cut into 24 pieces; press onto the bottoms and up the sides of greased miniature muffin cups. In a small bowl, beat cream cheese and confectioners' sugar until smooth. Place about ½ teaspoon in each cup. Combine pie filling and extract; place about 2 teaspoons in each cup.

2. Bake at 375° for 12-14 minutes or until edges are lightly browned. Remove to wire racks to cool. Refrigerate until serving.

Apple Dumplings for Two

I watch a lot of cooking shows and like to dabble when I can. Sometimes it's nice to have a dessert without any leftovers.

ROGER SLIVON, GENESEE DEPOT, WISCONSIN

PREP: 15 MIN. • **BAKE:** 40 MIN. • **MAKES:** 2 SERVINGS

- 1　**sheet frozen puff pastry**
- 2　**small tart apples, peeled and cored**
- 4　**teaspoons brown sugar**
- 1　**tablespoon chopped walnuts**
- ⅛　**teaspoon ground cinnamon**
- 4　**teaspoons butter, divided**

GLAZE:
- 3　**tablespoons confectioners' sugar**
- ½　**teaspoon 2% milk**
- ½　**teaspoon lemon juice**
- ⅛　**teaspoon vanilla extract**

1. Using a sharp knife, cut pastry sheet in half. Return half to the freezer. Thaw remaining pastry. On a lightly floured surface, roll pastry into a 14-in. x 7-in. rectangle. Cut into two 7-in. squares.

2. Place an apple on each square. In a small bowl, combine the brown sugar, walnuts and cinnamon. Spoon into center of each apple; top each with 1 teaspoon butter. Gently bring up corners of pastry to center; pinch edges to seal. Place in a shallow 3-cup baking dish coated with cooking spray. Melt remaining butter; brush over pastry.

3. Bake at 375° for 40-45 minutes or until apples are tender and pastry is golden brown. In a small bowl, combine glaze ingredients. Drizzle over dumplings. Serve warm.

Bakeshop HOW-TO

Tart Tampers Make It Easy

Place a portion of dough in each mini muffin cup. Using firm pressure, push the dough down and up the sides of the cup. If the dough has not moved up the sides of the cup as far as you want, try rocking the tamper back and forth.

Banana Cream Eclairs

To surprise my banana-loving family, I made this dessert for a reunion, where it stood out among the usual fare. These special treats look and taste delicious.

RUBY WILLIAMS, BOGALUSA, LOUISIANA

PREP: 40 MIN. • **BAKE:** 25 MIN. + COOLING • **MAKES:** 16 SERVINGS

- 1 **cup water**
- ½ **cup butter, cubed**
- ¼ **cup sugar**
- ½ **teaspoon salt**
- 1 **cup all-purpose flour**
- 4 **eggs**

FILLING:
- 2½ **cups heavy whipping cream**
- 3 **tablespoons sugar**
- 1 **teaspoon vanilla extract**
- 3 **to 4 medium firm bananas**

GLAZE:
- ½ **cup confectioners' sugar**
- 2 **tablespoons baking cocoa**
- 2 **tablespoons butter, melted**
- 1 **teaspoon vanilla extract**
- 1 **to 2 tablespoons boiling water**
- ½ **cup finely chopped pecans**

1. In a large saucepan, bring the water, butter, sugar and salt to a boil. Add flour all at once and stir until a smooth ball forms. Remove from the heat; let stand for 5 minutes. Add eggs, one at a time, beating well after each addition. Continue beating until dough is smooth and shiny.

2. Insert a ¾-in. round tip into a pastry bag; add dough. Pipe 3-in. strips about 3 in. apart on a greased baking sheet. Bake at 400° for 25-30 minutes or until golden brown. Remove to wire racks. Immediately split puffs open; remove tops and set aside. Discard soft dough from inside. Cool puffs.

3. In a large bowl, beat cream until it begins to thicken. Add sugar and vanilla; beat until stiff peaks form. In another bowl, mash bananas; gently fold in whipped cream. Spoon into eclairs; replace tops.

4. In a small bowl, combine the confectioners' sugar, cocoa, butter and vanilla. Add enough water to make a thin glaze. Spread over eclairs. Sprinkle with pecans. Refrigerate leftovers.

Strawberry Tuile Cannoli

My mom and I created this recipe by combining two different ones. The cute cookies are crispy on the outside yet light and fluffy inside. You could also bake them flat and serve the filling as a cookie dip.

CRYSTAL BRIDDICK, COLFAX, ILLINOIS

PREP: 40 MIN. • **BAKE:** 5 MIN./BATCH • **MAKES:** ABOUT 2 DOZEN

- 4 ounces cream cheese, softened
- ¼ cup sugar
- 2 tablespoons seedless strawberry jam
- ¼ cup heavy whipping cream, whipped
- 1 to 3 drops red food coloring, optional

BATTER:
- ½ cup sugar
- ⅓ cup all-purpose flour
- 2 egg whites
- ¼ teaspoon vanilla extract
- ⅛ teaspoon salt
- ¼ cup butter, melted and cooled
  Chopped fresh strawberries, optional

1. For filling, in a small bowl, beat the cream cheese, sugar and jam until blended. Fold in whipped cream and food coloring if desired. Chill.

2. In a small bowl, whisk the sugar, flour, egg whites, vanilla and salt until smooth. Whisk in butter until blended. Line baking sheets with parchment paper. Preparing four cookies at a time, drop batter by 1½ teaspoonfuls 4 in. apart onto prepared pans. Bake at 400° for 5-8 minutes or until edges are lightly browned.

3. Loosen each cookie and curl around a wooden spoon handle. Press lightly to seal; hold until set, about 20 seconds. Remove and place on waxed paper to cool. Continue with remaining cookies. If cookies become too cool to shape, return to oven for 1 minute to soften.

4. Just before serving, pipe or spoon filling into cookie shells. Dip ends of cookies into chopped strawberries if desired. Refrigerate leftovers.

Funnel Cakes

These are much simpler to make than doughnuts but taste just as good. They have been a regular treat of ours since we came across them when we lived in the Ozarks.

MARY FAITH YODER, UNITY, WISCONSIN

PREP: 15 MIN. • **COOK:** 5 MIN./BATCH • **MAKES:** 8 CAKES

- 2 **eggs**
- 1 **cup milk**
- 1 **cup water**
- ½ **teaspoon vanilla extract**
- 3 **cups all-purpose flour**
- ¼ **cup sugar**
- 1 **tablespoon baking powder**
- ¼ **teaspoon salt**
  Oil for deep-fat frying
  Confectioners' sugar

1. In a large bowl, beat eggs. Add milk, water and vanilla until well blended. Combine flour, sugar, baking powder and salt; beat into egg mixture until smooth. In an electric skillet or deep-fat fryer, heat oil to 375°.

2. Cover the bottom of a funnel spout with your finger; ladle ½ cup of batter into the funnel. Holding the funnel several inches above the oil, release your finger and move the funnel in a spiral motion until all the batter is released (scraping with a rubber spatula if needed).

3. Fry for 2 minutes on each side or until golden brown. Drain on paper towels. Dust with confectioners' sugar and serve warm.

Editor's Note: *The batter can be poured from a liquid measuring cup instead of a funnel.*

Apple Pie Pastries

My co-worker Debbie treated the office to these spectacular mini apple pies. Everyone fell in love with the warm filling and flaky, buttery crust.

GINNY ALFANO, CANASTOTA, NEW YORK

PREP: 40 MIN. + CHILLING • **BAKE:** 30 MIN. • **MAKES:** 16 SERVINGS

- 2 **cups all-purpose flour**
- 1 **teaspoon salt**
- 1 **cup cold butter, cubed**
- 1 **tablespoon cider vinegar**
- ½ **cup milk**

FILLING:
- ¾ **cup packed brown sugar**
- 1 **tablespoon all-purpose flour**
- 1 **teaspoon ground cinnamon**
- 5 **tablespoons cold butter, divided**
- 5-6 **small tart apples, peeled and cored**
- ¼ **cup sugar**

1. In a large bowl, combine flour and salt. Cut in butter until crumbly. Sprinkle with vinegar. Gradually add milk, tossing with a fork until dough forms a ball. Cover and refrigerate for 20 minutes or until easy to handle.

2. Meanwhile, in another bowl, combine the brown sugar, flour and cinnamon. Cut in 2 tablespoons butter until crumbly; set aside. Melt the remaining butter. Cut apples into ½-in.-thick rings.

3. Shape dough into sixteen 1½-in. balls; roll into 5-in. circles. Brush with 2 tablespoons melted butter.

4. Place one apple ring in the center of each circle. Top each with 2 teaspoons brown sugar mixture. Fold edges of dough over apple rings, leaving centers uncovered; crimp edges. Brush dough with remaining melted butter; sprinkle with sugar.

5. Place 1 in. apart on ungreased baking sheets. Bake at 375° for 30-35 minutes or until golden brown and apples are tender. Serve warm.

Caramel Apple Dumplings

When our apples become ripe, it's not unusual for me to make as many as 30 of these fruity dumplings! I've relied on the recipe for more than 50 years.

OMAHA PETERSON, KINTA, OKLAHOMA

PREP: 30 MIN. • **BAKE:** 50 MIN. • **MAKES:** 7 SERVINGS

2¼ cups all-purpose flour
2 teaspoons plus ¼ cup sugar, divided
1 teaspoon salt
1 cup shortening
2 eggs
¼ cup water
2 teaspoons white vinegar
7 medium tart apples, peeled and cored
7 tablespoons butter
¼ teaspoon ground cinnamon
CARAMEL SAUCE:
1 jar (12¼ ounces) caramel ice cream topping
1½ cups packed brown sugar
1 cup water
¼ cup butter, cubed

1. In a large bowl, combine the flour, 2 teaspoons sugar and salt; cut in shortening until crumbly. In a small bowl, combine 1 egg, water and vinegar; gradually add to crumb mixture, tossing with a fork until dough forms a ball. Divide into seven portions.

2. On a lightly floured surface, roll each portion into a 7-in. square. Place an apple on each pastry square; place 1 tablespoon butter in the center of each. Combine cinnamon and remaining sugar; sprinkle over apples.

3. Bring up corners of pastry to center; pinch edges to seal. Beat remaining egg; brush over pastry. Place in a greased 13-in. x 9-in. baking dish. Bake at 350° for 15 minutes.

4. Meanwhile, in a large saucepan, combine the sauce ingredients. Bring to a boil; cook and stir until smooth and blended. Pour over apples. Bake 35-40 minutes longer or until apples are tender and pastry is golden brown, basting occasionally with sauce. Serve warm.

Easy Cherry Strudels

The original recipe for these strudels called for phyllo dough sheets and was very time-consuming. Once, by mistake, I bought puff pastry sheets and found that they were much faster.

SUSAN DANCY, TALLAHASSEE, FLORIDA

PREP: 15 MIN. • **BAKE:** 20 MIN. • **MAKES:** 2 STRUDELS (5 SLICES EACH)

1 can (14½ ounces) pitted tart cherries
1 cup sugar
½ cup dried cranberries or raisins
1 tablespoon butter
3 tablespoons cornstarch
1½ cups chopped walnuts
1 package (17.3 ounces) frozen puff pastry, thawed
1 egg, lightly beaten

1. Drain cherries, reserving ⅓ cup juice. In a large saucepan, combine the cherries, sugar, cranberries and butter. Cook and stir over medium heat until heated through. Combine cornstarch and reserved juice and add to the pan. Bring to a boil. Cook and stir 1-2 minutes longer or until thickened. Remove from the heat; stir in walnuts.

2. Unfold one pastry sheet and cut in half. Mound half of the cherry mixture on one pastry half to within ½ in. of edges. Top with remaining pastry half; pinch edges to seal. Repeat with remaining pastry and filling.

3. Place on a greased foil-lined baking sheet. With a sharp knife, cut diagonal slits into tops of strudels; brush with egg. Bake at 400° for 20-25 minutes or until golden brown.

Easy Elephant Ears

You'll love the classic cinnamon-sugar flavor of these crispy bite-size treats. Even more, you'll love that they call for just three ingredients and are so simple to assemble.

BOB ROSE, WAUKESHA, WISCONSIN

PREP: 20 MIN. • **BAKE:** 15 MIN./BATCH • **MAKES:** ABOUT 2½ DOZEN

- 1 **package (17.3 ounces) frozen puff pastry, thawed**
- ½ **cup sugar**
- 2 **teaspoons ground cinnamon**

SHORT & SWEET

1. On a lightly floured surface, roll one sheet of puff pastry into an 11-in. x 8-in. rectangle. Combine sugar and cinnamon; sprinkle half of mixture over pastry.

2. Working from the short sides, roll up dough jelly-roll style toward the center. With a sharp knife, cut roll into ½-in. slices. Place on parchment paper-lined baking sheets. Repeat with remaining pastry and sugar mixture.

3. Bake at 375° for 12-15 minutes or until crisp and golden brown. Remove from pans to wire racks.

Lemon Cream Puffs

The fluffy filling for these cream puffs has an unexpected citrus flavor. It's a refreshing change from other cream puffs.

DOREEN MARTIN, KITIMAT, BRITISH COLUMBIA

PREP: 20 MIN. + CHILLING • **BAKE:** 30 MIN. + COOLING
MAKES: 10 SERVINGS

  ½ cup water
  ¼ cup butter, cubed
  ½ cup all-purpose flour
  2 eggs
LEMON FILLING:
  1 egg, beaten
  ⅓ cup sugar
  3 tablespoons lemon juice
  2 tablespoons butter, cubed
  1 cup heavy whipping cream
  2 teaspoons sugar
    Confectioners' sugar

1. In a large saucepan, bring water and butter to a boil. Add flour all at once, stirring until a smooth ball forms. Remove from the heat; let stand for 5 minutes. Add eggs, one at a time, beating well after each addition. Continue beating until mixture is smooth.

2. Drop by rounded tablespoonfuls 3 in. apart onto greased baking sheets.

3. Bake at 400° for 30-35 minutes or until golden brown. Remove to wire racks. Immediately split puffs and remove tops; discard soft dough from inside. Set puffs and tops aside to cool.

4. For filling, in a small heavy saucepan, combine the egg, sugar, lemon juice and butter. Cook and stir over medium heat until mixture is thick enough to coat the back of a spoon. Transfer the mixture to a small bowl; refrigerate until partially set.

5. In a large bowl, beat cream and sugar until stiff peaks form; fold into lemon mixture. Fill cream puffs; replace tops. Dust with confectioners' sugar.

Thelma's Chocolate Eclair

I love eclairs but making the actual pastry is difficult so I came up with this recipe as a substitute. It still satisfies my cravings with the same wonderful flavors.

THELMA BEAM, ESBON, KANSAS

PREP: 20 MIN. + CHILLING • **MAKES:** 12-15 SERVINGS

  18 whole graham crackers
  3½ cups cold milk
  2 packages (3.4 ounces each) instant vanilla pudding mix
  1 carton (8 ounces) frozen whipped topping, thawed
  2 ounces semisweet chocolate
  2 tablespoons butter
  1½ cups confectioners' sugar
  3 tablespoons milk
  1 teaspoon vanilla extract
  1 teaspoon light corn syrup

1. Line a 13-in. x 9-in. dish with nine whole graham crackers; set aside.

2. In a large bowl, whisk milk and pudding mixes for 2 minutes. Let stand for 2 minutes or until soft-set; fold in whipped topping. Spread over graham crackers. Top with remaining crackers.

3. In a microwave-safe bowl, melt chocolate and butter. Stir in the remaining ingredients. Spread over graham cracker layer. Cover and refrigerate for 8 hours or overnight.

Java Cream Puffs

These fun and fancy goodies have chopped pecans in the puffs and mouthwatering mocha cream filling.

IOLA EGLE, BELLA VISTA, ARKANSAS

PREP: 25 MIN. + CHILLING • **BAKE:** 30 MIN. + COOLING
MAKES: 8 SERVINGS

- ½ cup water
- ¼ cup butter, cubed
- ⅛ teaspoon salt
- ½ cup all-purpose flour
- 2 eggs
- ¼ cup finely chopped pecans

MOCHA CREAM FILLING:
- ½ cup strong brewed coffee
- 24 large marshmallows
- 1½ cups heavy whipping cream
- ¼ cup hot fudge ice cream topping, warmed

1. In a large saucepan, bring water, butter and salt to a boil. Add flour all at once and stir until a smooth ball forms. Remove from the heat; let stand for 5 minutes. Add eggs, one at a time, beating well after each addition. Continue beating until mixture is smooth and shiny. Stir in pecans.

2. Drop by rounded tablespoonfuls 3 in. apart onto a greased baking sheet. Bake at 400° for 30-35 minutes or until golden brown. Remove to a wire rack. Immediately split puffs open; remove tops and set aside. Discard soft dough from inside. Cool puffs.

3. For filling, in a large saucepan, combine coffee and marshmallows. Cook over low heat until marshmallows are melted. Transfer to a large bowl; cover and chill just until thickened.

4. In a large bowl, beat cream until soft peaks form. Whisk chilled coffee mixture until light in color; fold in whipped cream. Just before serving, fill each puff with about ⅓ cup filling. Replace tops and drizzle with fudge topping.

Bakeshop HOW-TO

Making Cream Puffs

Bring water, butter and salt to a boil in a saucepan. Add the flour all at once; stir briskly until the mixture leaves the sides of the pan and forms a ball.

Remove from heat; let stand for 5 minutes to allow mixture to cool before adding the eggs. Beat well after adding each egg. Continue beating until mixture is smooth and shiny.

Drop dough 3 in. apart onto a greased baking sheet. Bake as directed.

Remove puffs from pan to a wire rack. Immediately split puffs and set tops aside; remove soft dough from inside with a fork and discard. Fill as directed.

Apple Strudels

This is one of my favorite recipes to make during autumn. The aroma of homemade strudel baking on a cool, crisp day is absolutely wonderful.

HELEN LESH, FORSYTH, MISSOURI

PREP: 20 MIN. + CHILLING • **BAKE:** 55 MIN. + COOLING

MAKES: 3 STRUDELS (12 SLICES EACH)

- 1 **cup cold butter, cubed**
- 2 **cups all-purpose flour**
- 1 **cup (8 ounces) sour cream**
- ¼ **teaspoon salt**

FILLING:

- 2 **cups dry bread crumbs**
- ¼ **cup butter, melted**
- 4 **medium tart apples, peeled and chopped**
- 2 **cups sugar**
- 1 **cup golden raisins**
- ½ **cup chopped pecans**
- 2 **teaspoons ground cinnamon**
  Confectioners' sugar, optional

1. In a large bowl, cut butter into flour until mixture resembles coarse crumbs. Stir in sour cream and salt. Shape the dough into a ball; cover and refrigerate overnight.

2. For filling, combine bread crumbs and butter. Add the apples, sugar, raisins, pecans and cinnamon, set aside. Divide dough into thirds; turn onto a floured surface. Roll each into a 15-in. x 12-in. rectangle. Spoon filling evenly onto dough; spread to within 1 in. of edges. Roll up from a long side; pinch seams and ends to seal.

3. Carefully place each loaf seam side down on an ungreased baking sheet. Bake at 350° for 55-60 minutes or until lightly browned. Cool completely on wire racks. Dust with confectioners' sugar if desired.

tasteofhome.com

Baby Boston Cream Pies

A vanilla custard is sandwiched between tender, cake-like cookies.

EVANGELINE BRADFORD, ERLANGER, KENTUCKY

PREP: 70 MIN. + CHILLING • **BAKE:** 5 MIN./BATCH + COOLING
MAKES: 4 DOZEN

- 6 tablespoons sugar
- 3 tablespoons cornstarch
- ¼ teaspoon salt
- 1 cup 2% milk
- 6 tablespoons heavy whipping cream
- 1 egg yolk, beaten
- 2 teaspoons vanilla extract

COOKIES:
- 9 tablespoons butter, softened
- 1 cup sugar
- 2 egg yolks
- 1 egg
- 2 teaspoons vanilla extract
- ½ teaspoon grated lemon peel
- 1 cup plus 2 tablespoons cake flour
- 1 cup all-purpose flour
- ¾ teaspoon baking soda
- ½ teaspoon salt
- ½ cup plus 2 tablespoons buttermilk

GLAZE:
- 2 ounces unsweetened chocolate, chopped
- 4 teaspoons butter
- ½ cup whipping cream
- 1 cup confectioners' sugar

1. In a small heavy saucepan, combine the sugar, cornstarch and salt. Stir in milk and cream until smooth. Cook and stir over medium-high heat until thickened and bubbly. Reduce heat to low; cook and stir 2 minutes longer.

2. Remove from the heat. Stir a small amount of hot mixture into egg yolk; return all to the pan, stirring constantly. Bring to a gentle boil; cook and stir 2 minutes longer. Remove from the heat. Stir in vanilla. Cool for 15 minutes, stirring occasionally. Transfer to a small bowl. Press waxed paper onto surface of custard. Refrigerate for 2-3 hours.

3. In a large bowl, cream butter and sugar until light and fluffy. Beat in the egg yolks, egg, vanilla and lemon peel. Combine the cake flour, all-purpose flour, baking soda and salt; gradually add to creamed mixture alternately with buttermilk and mix well.

4. Drop by rounded teaspoonfuls 2 in. apart onto greased baking sheets. Bake at 400° for 5-7 minutes or until firm to the touch. Remove to wire racks to cool completely.

5. Spread custard over the bottoms of half of the cookies; top with remaining cookies.

6. For glaze, place chocolate and butter in a small bowl. In a small saucepan, bring cream just to a boil. Pour over chocolate and butter; whisk until smooth. Stir in confectioners' sugar. Spread over cookies; let dry completely. Store in the refrigerator.

Baklava

Here's my recipe for the traditional sweet and nutty Greek pastry. It's a tasty end to any meal.

JOSIE BOCHEK, STURGEON BAY, WISCONSIN

PREP: 1¼ HOURS • **BAKE:** 45 MIN. + COOLING • **MAKES:** 3 DOZEN

- 4 cups finely chopped walnuts
- ¼ cup sugar
- 1 tablespoon ground cinnamon
- 1 cup butter, melted
- 1 package (16 ounces) frozen phyllo dough, thawed

SYRUP:
- 1 cup sugar
- ½ cup water
- ¼ cup honey
- 1 teaspoon lemon juice
- 1 teaspoon vanilla extract

1. In a small bowl, combine the walnuts, sugar and cinnamon; set aside. Grease a 13-in. x 9-in. baking dish with some of the melted butter. Unroll phyllo dough sheets (keep dough covered with plastic wrap while assembling).

2. Place one sheet of phyllo in baking dish; brush with butter. Top with a second sheet; brush with butter. Fold long ends under to fit the dish. Sprinkle with about ¼ cup nut mixture. Repeat 18 times, layering two sheets, brushing with butter and sprinkling with nut mixture. Top with remaining dough; brush with butter. Cut into 2-in. diamonds with a sharp knife.

3. Bake at 350° for 45-55 minutes or until golden brown. Meanwhile, in a saucepan, combine the syrup ingredients; bring to a boil. Reduce heat; simmer, uncovered, for 10 minutes. Pour over warm baklava. Cool on a wire rack.

Instant Chocolate Pastries

My sister and I became addicted to Nutella while traveling in Europe. Now we're always thinking of ways to incorporate it into recipes. This one came about after making puff pastries with apple filling. We thought, "Why not try chocolate?"

DEE WOLF, SYRACUSE, UTAH

PREP/TOTAL TIME: 20 MIN. • **MAKES:** 6 SERVINGS

1 **sheet frozen puff pastry, thawed**
6 **tablespoons Nutella**
1 **egg, beaten**
    Confectioners' sugar, optional

1. Unfold puff pastry; cut into six rectangles. Place on a greased baking sheet. Spread 1 tablespoon Nutella over half of a rectangle; fold dough over filling. Press edges with a fork to seal. Repeat for remaining pastries. Brush with egg; prick tops with a fork.

2. Bake at 400° for 10-14 minutes or until puffy and golden brown. Sprinkle with confectioners' sugar if desired. Serve warm.

Pizzelle Cannoli

We made two Italian treats into one with beautiful pizzelle cookies wrapped around a rich, chocolaty cannoli filling. If you don't have a pizzelle iron, try the filling in the simple baked cannoli shells on page 114.

TASTE OF HOME TEST KITCHEN

PREP: 45 MIN. + COOLING • **COOK:** 5 MIN./BATCH
MAKES: 12 FILLED PIZZELLE

---

1 **egg**
¼ **cup sugar**
¼ **cup butter, melted**
½ **teaspoon vanilla extract**
¼ **teaspoon grated lemon peel**
⅛ **teaspoon almond extract**
½ **cup all-purpose flour**
¼ **teaspoon baking powder**
FILLING:
¾ **cup sugar**
3 **tablespoons cornstarch**
1 **cup milk**
1⅛ **teaspoons vanilla extract**
1 **drop cinnamon oil, optional**
1¾ **cups ricotta cheese**
1 **milk chocolate candy bar with almonds**
    (4¼ ounces), chopped
½ **cup chopped pistachios**

1. In a large bowl, beat the egg, sugar, butter, vanilla, lemon peel and almond extract until blended. Combine flour and baking powder; stir into egg mixture and mix well.

2. Bake in a preheated pizzelle iron according to manufacturer's directions until golden brown. Remove cookies and immediately shape into tubes. Place on wire racks to cool.

3. In a small saucepan, combine sugar and cornstarch. Stir in milk until smooth. Bring to a boil; cook and stir for 2 minutes or until thickened. Stir in vanilla and cinnamon oil if desired. Cool completely.

4. In a large bowl, beat ricotta cheese until smooth. Gradually beat in custard mixture. Fold in chocolate. Spoon or pipe into shells. Dip each side in pistachios. Serve immediately. Refrigerate leftovers.

Crisscross Apple Crowns

Wake 'em up on chilly mornings with the tempting aroma of apples and cinnamon filling the house. I love making these for breakfast. They're different and so easy.

TERESA MORRIS, LAUREL, DELAWARE

PREP: 30 MIN. • **BAKE:** 20 MIN. • **MAKES:** 8 SERVINGS

1⅓ cups chopped peeled tart apples
⅓ cup chopped walnuts
⅓ cup raisins
½ cup sugar, divided
2 tablespoons all-purpose flour
2 teaspoons ground cinnamon, divided
    Dash salt

1 package (16.3 ounces) large refrigerated flaky biscuits
2 teaspoons butter, melted

1. In a large microwave-safe bowl, combine the apples, walnuts, raisins, 3 tablespoons sugar, flour, ¾ teaspoon cinnamon and salt. Microwave on high for 2-3 minutes or until almost tender.

2. Flatten each biscuit into a 5-in. circle. Combine remaining sugar and cinnamon; sprinkle a rounded teaspoonful of sugar mixture over each. Top each with ¼ cup apple mixture. Bring up edges to enclose mixture; pinch edges to seal.

3. Place seam side down in ungreased muffin cups. Brush tops with butter; sprinkle with remaining sugar mixture. With a sharp knife, cut an X in the top of each.

4. Bake at 350° for 18-22 minutes or until golden brown. Cool for 5 minutes before removing from pan to a wire rack.

Chocolate Eclairs

With creamy filling and fudgy frosting, homemade eclairs are extra special. Family and friends will love these.

JESSICA CAMPBELL, VIOLA, WISCONSIN

PREP: 45 MIN. • **BAKE:** 35 MIN. + COOLING • **MAKES:** 9 SERVINGS

- 1 **cup water**
- ½ **cup butter, cubed**
- ¼ **teaspoon salt**
- 1 **cup all-purpose flour**
- 4 **eggs**

FILLING:
- 2½ **cups cold milk**
- 1 **package (5.1 ounces) instant vanilla pudding mix**
- 1 **cup heavy whipping cream**
- ¼ **cup confectioners' sugar**
- 1 **teaspoon vanilla extract**

FROSTING:
- 2 **ounces semisweet chocolate**
- 2 **tablespoons butter**
- 1¼ **cups confectioners' sugar**
- 2 **to 3 tablespoons hot water**

1. In a large saucepan, bring the water, butter and salt to a boil. Add flour all at once and stir until a smooth ball forms. Remove from the heat; let stand for 5 minutes. Add eggs, one at a time, beating well after each addition. Continue beating until mixture is smooth and shiny.

2. Using a tablespoon or a pastry tube with a No. 10 or larger tip, form dough into 4-in. x 1½-in. strips on a greased baking sheet. Bake at 400° for 35-40 minutes or until puffed and golden. Remove to a wire rack. Immediately split eclairs open; remove tops and set aside. Discard soft dough from inside. Cool eclairs.

3. In a large bowl, beat milk and pudding mix according to package directions. In another bowl, whip cream until soft peaks form. Beat in sugar and vanilla; fold into pudding. Fill eclairs (chill any remaining filling for another use).

4. For frosting, in a microwave, melt chocolate and butter; stir until smooth. Stir in sugar and enough hot water to achieve a smooth consistency. Cool slightly. Frost eclairs. Store in refrigerator.

Sugar Cookie Tarts

These little tarts are pretty enough for an elegant occasion, but are super easy to make. For a nice look, arrange the fruits in a circular pattern. Fresh fruit tastes the best, but you can substitute canned for a darling treat in a snap.

BARB WHITE, LIGONIER, PENNSYLVANIA

PREP: 20 MIN. + CHILLING • **MAKES:** 4 SERVINGS

- 5 **tablespoons sugar, divided**
- 1 **teaspoon cornstarch**
  Dash salt
- 3 **tablespoons water**
- 2 **tablespoons orange juice**
- 1 **tablespoon lemon juice**
- 1 **package (3 ounces) cream cheese, softened**
- 4 **large sugar cookies (3 inches)**
  Assorted fresh fruit

1. For glaze, in a small saucepan, combine 3 tablespoons sugar, cornstarch and salt. Gradually stir in the water, orange juice and lemon juice. Bring to a boil over medium heat; cook and stir for 2 minutes or until thickened. Remove from the heat; cool.

2. In a small bowl, beat cream cheese and remaining sugar until smooth. Spread over each cookie; arrange fruit on top. Drizzle with glaze. Refrigerate until chilled.

Cranberry-Pear Strudel

This stylish dessert is sure to please everyone. It's delicious served warm with a scoop of reduced-fat ice cream or whipped topping.

LEAH BEATTY, COBOURG, ONTARIO

PREP: 35 MIN. + COOLING • **BAKE:** 20 MIN. + COOLING
MAKES: 10 SERVINGS

- ½ **cup sugar**
- 1 **tablespoon cornstarch**
- 3 **large pears, peeled and finely chopped**
- ½ **cup fresh or frozen cranberries, thawed**
- 2 **tablespoons butter**
- ½ **cup dried cranberries**
- 1 **teaspoon ground ginger**
- 1 **teaspoon grated orange peel**
- ½ **teaspoon ground cinnamon**
- 6 **sheets phyllo dough (14 inches x 9 inches)**
  Cooking spray
- 1 **teaspoon confectioners' sugar**

1. In a large bowl, combine sugar and cornstarch. Add pears and cranberries; toss gently to coat. In a large nonstick skillet, melt butter over medium-high heat. Add fruit mixture; cook and stir for 7-8 minutes or until cranberries pop. Stir in the dried cranberries, ginger, orange peel and cinnamon. Cool.

2. Line a baking sheet with foil and coat the foil with cooking spray; set aside. Place one sheet of phyllo dough on a work surface; coat with cooking spray. Repeat layers five times. (Keep phyllo dough covered with plastic wrap and a damp towel until ready to use each sheet.)

3. Spread cranberry mixture over dough to within 1 in. of edges. Fold in sides. Roll up, starting at a long side. Place seam side down on prepared baking sheet.

4. Bake at 400° for 20-23 minutes or until golden brown. Remove from pan to a wire rack to cool. Dust with confectioners' sugar before serving.

Cheesecakes

Magnolia Dream Cheesecake

Your guests will be amazed when they learn that you made this gorgeous cheesecake at home! The Italian-style dessert is flavored with a delightful combination of hazelnut and peach.

CHARLENE CHAMBERS, ORMOND BEACH, FLORIDA

PREP: 50 MIN. • **BAKE:** 1½ HOURS + CHILLING • **MAKES:** 16 SERVINGS

- 1 cup hazelnuts, toasted, divided
- 12 whole graham crackers
- ¼ cup sugar
- 6 tablespoons unsalted butter, melted

FILLING:
- 1½ pounds ricotta cheese
- 2 packages (8 ounces each) cream cheese, softened
- 2 cups (16 ounces) sour cream
- 1½ cups sugar
- 6 tablespoons all-purpose flour
- 4 tablespoons hazelnut liqueur, divided
- 6 eggs, lightly beaten
- 3 medium peaches, sliced

1. Place a greased 10-in. springform pan on a double thickness of heavy-duty foil (about 18 in. square). Securely wrap foil around pan.

2. Place hazelnuts in a food processor; cover and pulse until coarsely chopped. Set aside ¼ cup for garnish. Add graham crackers and sugar to food processor; cover and process until finely chopped. Add butter; process until blended. Press onto the bottom and 1 in. up the sides of prepared pan. Place pan on a baking sheet. Bake at 325° for 10 minutes. Cool on a wire rack.

3. In a large bowl, beat the ricotta, cream cheese, sour cream and sugar until well blended. Beat in flour and 2 tablespoons liqueur. Add eggs; beat on low speed just until combined. Pour into crust. Place springform pan in a large baking pan; add 1 in. of hot water to larger pan.

4. Bake at 325° for 1½ hours or until center is just set and top appears dull. Remove springform pan from water bath. Cool on a wire rack for 10 minutes. Carefully run a knife around edge of pan to loosen; cool 1 hour longer. Refrigerate overnight.

5. Toss peaches with remaining liqueur; arrange over top of cheesecake. Sprinkle reserved hazelnuts in the center. Remove sides of pan.

Raspberry Cheesecake Pie

This creamy cheesecake pie with a raspberry layer is refreshing and light. It's perfect after a heavy meal.

STEVE JOSSERAND, DECATUR, ILLINOIS

PREP: 50 MIN. + CHILLING • **MAKES:** 6-8 SERVINGS

- 2 packages (8 ounces each) cream cheese, softened
- ½ cup sugar
- ½ teaspoon vanilla extract
- 2 eggs, lightly beaten
- 1 chocolate crumb crust (8 inches)
- 1½ teaspoons unflavored gelatin
- 2 tablespoons cold water
- ½ cup seedless raspberry jam
- 1 cup heavy whipping cream
- 2 tablespoons confectioners' sugar

1. In a large bowl, beat the cream cheese, sugar and vanilla until smooth. Add eggs; beat on low speed just until combined. Pour into crust. Bake at 325° for 25-30 minutes or until the center is almost set. Cool on a wire rack for 1 hour. Refrigerate overnight.

2. In a small saucepan, sprinkle gelatin over cold water; let stand for 1 minute. Cook over low heat, stirring until gelatin is completely dissolved. Stir in jam. Refrigerate for 10 minutes.

3. In small bowl, beat cream until it begins to thicken. Gradually add confectioners' sugar; beat until stiff peaks form. Remove ½ cup for garnish; cover and refrigerate.

4. Gently stir ¾ cup whipped cream into raspberry mixture just until blended. Fold in the remaining whipped cream; spread over cheesecake. Refrigerate for at least 1 hour. Garnish with reserved whipped cream.

Decadent Brownie Swirl Cheesecake

It may look picture perfect, but this cheesecake is so fast. The secret is the speedy crust—it's from a packaged brownie mix! You don't need to be an experienced cook to make the elegant chocolate swirls on top.

TASTE OF HOME TEST KITCHEN

PREP: 30 MIN. • **BAKE:** 1½ HOURS + CHILLING • **MAKES:** 16 SERVINGS

  1 **package fudge brownie mix (13-inch x 9-inch pan size)**
FILLING:
  4 **packages (8 ounces each) cream cheese, softened**
  1 **cup sugar**

  4 **eggs, lightly beaten**
  3 **teaspoons vanilla extract or 1 teaspoon almond extract and 2 teaspoons vanilla extract**
      Fresh raspberries and chocolate curls, optional

1. Prepare brownie mix according to package directions for chewy fudge brownies. Set aside ⅔ cup brownie batter; spread remaining batter into a greased 9-in. springform pan.

2. Place pan on a double thickness of heavy-duty foil (about 18 in. square). Securely wrap foil around pan. Bake at 350° for 25-28 minutes (brownies will barely test done). Cool for 10 minutes on a wire rack.

3. In a large bowl, beat cream cheese and sugar until smooth. Beat in eggs and vanilla on low speed just until combined. Stir ⅓ cup into reserved brownie batter; set aside. Spoon half of the cheesecake batter into crust; dollop with half of reserved chocolate cheesecake batter. Repeat layers. Cut through batter with a knife to swirl.

4. Place in a larger baking pan; add 1 in. of hot water to larger pan. Bake at 325° for 1½ hours or until surface is no longer shiny and center is almost set.

5. Remove pan from water bath and foil. Cool on a wire rack for 10 minutes. Carefully run a knife around the edge of pan to loosen; cool 1 hour longer. Refrigerate overnight. Remove sides of pan. Garnish with raspberries and chocolate curls if desired.

Bakeshop HOW-TO

Swirling Filling into a Cheesecake

Spoon small amounts of filling to be swirled in a random pattern onto cheesecake batter. Cut through cheesecake batter with a knife to swirl in the filling. Be careful not to draw the blade through the filling too often, or the filling will blend into the rest of the batter and you'll lose the pretty pattern.

Almond Apple Cheesecake

The flavorful apple-cinnamon-nut topping and the raspberry jam layer make this dessert outstanding.

NORMA HARDER, SASKATOON, SASKATCHEWAN

PREP: 20 MIN. • **BAKE:** 55 MIN. + CHILLING • **MAKES:** 12 SERVINGS

- 1 **cup all-purpose flour**
- ⅓ **cup sugar**
- ½ **cup cold butter,cubed**
- ⅓ **cup seedless raspberry jam**

FILLING:

- 2 **packages (8 ounces each) cream cheese, softened**
- ½ **cup sugar**
- 2 **eggs, lightly beaten**
- 2 **teaspoons vanilla extract**

TOPPING:

- ⅓ **cup sugar**
- ½ **teaspoon ground cinnamon**
- 3 **cups thinly sliced peeled tart apples**
- ½ **cup sliced almonds**

1. In a small bowl, combine the flour and sugar; cut in butter until crumbly. Press onto the bottom and 1½ in. up the sides of a greased 9-in. springform pan; prick with a fork. Place on a baking sheet. Bake at 350° for 10 minutes or until soft but set. Cool on a wire rack.

2. Carefully spread jam over crust. For filling, in a large bowl, beat cream cheese and sugar until smooth. Add eggs and vanilla; beat just until blended. Spread over jam. For topping, combine the sugar and cinnamon in a large bowl. Add apples and toss to coat. Spoon over filling. Sprinkle with almonds.

3. Bake at 350° for 55-60 minutes or until center is almost set. Cool on a wire rack for 10 minutes. Carefully run a knife around edge of pan to loosen; cool 1 hour longer. Refrigerate overnight. Remove sides of pan.

Lime Coconut Cheesecake

This refreshing cheesecake's delicate citrus flavor is complemented by a coconut crust.

INGE SCHERMERHORN, EAST KINGSTON, NEW HAMPSHIRE

PREP: 30 MIN. + CHILLING • **MAKES:** 12 SERVINGS

- 1½ **cups flaked coconut**
- 3 **tablespoons ground macadamia nuts or almonds**
- 3 **tablespoons butter, melted**
- 1 **envelope unflavored gelatin**
- ¼ **cup cold water**
- ¾ **cup sugar**
- 2 **packages (8 ounces each) cream cheese, softened**
- ¼ **cup lime juice**
- 1 **tablespoon grated lime peel**
  Green food coloring

- 1½ **cups heavy whipping cream, whipped**
  Toasted coconut and additional whipped cream, optional

1. In a bowl, combine coconut and nuts; stir in butter. Press onto the bottom of a greased 9-in. springform pan. Bake at 350° for 10-15 minutes or until crust is golden brown around the edges. Cool on a wire rack.

2. In a saucepan, sprinkle gelatin over cold water; let stand for 1 minute. Stir in sugar; cook over low heat until sugar and gelatin are dissolved. Remove from the heat. In a bowl, beat cream cheese until smooth. Gradually beat in gelatin mixture. Add lime juice and peel; beat until blended. Tint pale green with food coloring. Fold in whipped cream. Pour over crust. Refrigerate for 5 hours or overnight.

3. Carefully run a knife around the edge of pan to loosen. Remove sides of pan. Garnish with coconut and additional whipped cream if desired.

tasteofhome.com

Cheesecake Squares

These tempting bites are sure to steal top billing at any summer meal or social. Let family and friends choose from a warm drizzle of caramel and almonds, a dollop of fresh fruit and jam or a chocolate-dipped strawberry to top off their cheesecake.

TASTE OF HOME TEST KITCHEN

PREP: 30 MIN. • **BAKE:** 30 MIN. + CHILLING • **MAKES:** 9 SERVINGS

- 1¼ cups chocolate wafer crumbs
- ¼ cup butter, melted
- 2 packages (8 ounces each) cream cheese, softened
- ⅔ cup plus 2 tablespoons sugar, divided
- 2 eggs, lightly beaten
- 1½ teaspoons vanilla extract, divided
- ¼ teaspoon almond extract
- 1 cup (8 ounces) sour cream

CHOCOLATE STRAWBERRIES:
- 2 ounces dark chocolate candy bar, chopped
- 3 fresh strawberries
- 1 ounce white baking chocolate, chopped

CARAMEL TOPPING:
- 6 caramels
- 1 tablespoon heavy whipping cream
  Whipped cream
- 1 tablespoon sliced almonds, toasted

BERRY TOPPING:
- ¼ cup seedless raspberry jam
- 6 fresh raspberries
- 6 fresh blackberries
- 6 fresh blueberries

1. In a small bowl, combine crumbs and butter. Press firmly onto the bottom of an 8-in. square baking dish.

2. In a small bowl, beat cream cheese and ⅔ cup sugar until smooth. Add eggs; beat on low speed just until combined. Stir in ½ teaspoon vanilla and the almond extract.

3. Pour over crust. Bake at 325° for 45-55 minutes or until set. Cool for 5 minutes.

4. Meanwhile, in a small bowl, combine sour cream with remaining sugar and vanilla. Spread over filling; bake 5 minutes longer. Cool on a wire rack for 1 hour. Refrigerate for at least 5 hours or overnight.

5. In a microwave, melt candy bar; stir until smooth. Dip strawberries in chocolate; allow excess to drip off. Place on a waxed paper-lined baking sheet; let stand until set. Melt white chocolate; stir until smooth. Drizzle over strawberries. Refrigerate until serving.

6. Just before serving, cut cheesecake into nine squares. Place chocolate strawberries on three cheesecake squares.

7. For caramel topping, in a small microwave-safe bowl, combine caramels and cream. Microwave, uncovered, on high for 45 seconds, stirring once. Spoon over three cheesecake squares. Top with a dollop of whipped cream; sprinkle with almonds.

8. For berry topping, in a small microwave-safe bowl, combine jam and berries. Microwave, uncovered, on high for 45 seconds, stirring once. Spoon over remaining squares.

Editor's Note: *This recipe was tested in a 1,100-watt microwave.*

Pistachio Cheesecake

Here's an appealing dessert with a pretty pistachio filling and chocolate drizzle. I created it one Christmas Eve and my family raved about it. I've never seen cheesecake disappear so quickly!

KAREN ANKERSON, MANISTEE, MICHIGAN

PREP: 15 MIN. • **BAKE:** 65 MIN. + COOLING • **MAKES:** 12 SERVINGS

- 2 **cups all-purpose flour**
- ½ **cup ground almonds**
- ½ **cup cold butter**
- 6 **packages (8 ounces each) cream cheese, softened**
- 1 **can (14 ounces) sweetened condensed milk**
- 2 **packages (3.4 ounces each) instant pistachio pudding mix**
- 5 **eggs, lightly beaten**
  Chocolate syrup
  Whipped cream and chopped pistachios, optional

1. In a small bowl, combine the flour and almonds; cut in butter until crumbly. Press onto the bottom and 1¼ in. up the sides of a greased 10-in. springform pan. Bake at 400° for 10 minutes.

2. Meanwhile, in a large bowl, beat cream cheese, milk and pudding mixes until smooth. Add eggs; beat on low speed just until combined. Pour over crust.

3. Place pan on a baking sheet. Reduce heat to 350°. Bake for 55-60 minutes or until the center is almost set. Cool on a wire rack for 10 minutes. Carefully run a knife around edge of pan to loosen; cool 1 hour longer. Refrigerate overnight.

4. Slice cheesecake; drizzle slices with chocolate syrup. Garnish with whipped cream and pistachios if desired.

Coffee Toffee Cheesecake

My husband and I host both sides of our families on Thanksgiving every year. I came up with this candy-topped cheesecake a few years ago, and everybody went nuts over it.

TAMMY BAKER, BOWLING GREEN, KENTUCKY

PREP: 45 MIN. • **BAKE:** 55 MIN. + CHILLING • **MAKES:** 12 SERVINGS

- 2½ **cups chocolate wafer crumbs**
- ½ **cup butter, melted**
- 2 **tablespoons sugar**
FILLING:
- 1 **cup (6 ounces) semisweet chocolate chips**
- ¼ **cup heavy whipping cream**
- 4 **teaspoons instant coffee granules**
- 3 **packages (8 ounces each) cream cheese, softened**
- 1⅓ **cups sugar**
- 1½ **cups (12 ounces) sour cream**
- 1 **tablespoon vanilla extract**
- ⅛ **teaspoon salt**
- 3 **eggs, lightly beaten**
- 4 **Heath candy bars (1.4 ounces each), chopped**
- 1 **dark chocolate candy bar (1.45 ounces)**

1. Place a greased 9-in. springform pan on a double thickness of heavy-duty foil (about 18 in. square). Securely wrap foil around pan. In a small bowl, combine wafer crumbs, butter and sugar. Press onto the bottom and 1 in. up the sides of prepared pan. Place pan on a baking sheet. Bake at 350° for 10 minutes. Cool on a wire rack.

2. In a microwave-safe bowl, melt chips and cream; stir until smooth. Stir in coffee granules until dissolved. Set aside.

3. In a large bowl, beat cream cheese and sugar until smooth. Beat in the sour cream, vanilla and salt; gradually beat in chocolate mixture. Add eggs; beat on low speed just until combined. Pour into crust. Place springform pan in a large baking pan; add 1½ in. of hot water to larger pan.

4. Bake at 350° for 55-65 minutes or until center is just set and top appears dull. Remove springform pan from water bath. Cool on a wire rack for 10 minutes. Sprinkle with Heath bars.

5. Carefully run a knife around edge of pan to loosen; cool 1 hour longer. Refrigerate overnight. Chop the dark chocolate candy bar; melt in a microwave and stir until smooth. Drizzle over top of cheesecake.

Cranberry Orange Cheesecake

I can't go to any Christmas gathering without this showstopping dessert in tow. The combination of cranberries, chocolate and orange is a winner.

LAURIE LUFKIN, ESSEX, MASSACHUSETTS

PREP: 45 MIN. • **BAKE:** 1 HOUR + CHILLING • **MAKES:** 12 SERVINGS

- 1 **cup finely chopped pecans**
- ⅔ **cup chocolate wafer crumbs**
- ¼ **cup butter, melted**
- 3 **tablespoons brown sugar**
- 2 **packages (8 ounces each) cream cheese, softened**
- 2 **cartons (8 ounces each) Mascarpone cheese**
- 1¼ **cups sugar**
- 2 **tablespoons cornstarch**
- 2 **teaspoons orange juice**
- 1 **teaspoon orange extract**
- 4 **eggs, lightly beaten**
- ¾ **cup whole-berry cranberry sauce**
- ¼ **cup dried cranberries**
- 1 **tablespoon water**
- ¼ **cup chocolate ice cream topping, warmed**

1. Place a greased 9-in. springform pan on a double thickness of heavy-duty foil (about 18 in. square). Securely wrap foil around pan.

2. Combine the pecans, wafer crumbs, butter and brown sugar. Press onto the bottom and 1 in. up the sides of prepared pan. Place on a baking sheet. Bake at 325° for 8-10 minutes or until lightly browned. Cool on a wire rack.

3. In a large bowl, beat the cheeses, sugar, cornstarch, orange juice and extract until smooth. Add eggs; beat on low speed just until combined. Pour half of the batter over crust.

4. Place the cranberry sauce, cranberries and water in a food processor; cover and process until blended. Gently spread over batter in pan; top with remaining batter.

5. Place springform pan in a large baking pan; add 1 in. of hot water to larger pan. Bake at 325° for 60-70 minutes or until center is just set and top appears dull.

6. Remove pan from water bath. Cool on a wire rack for 10 minutes. Carefully run a knife around edge of pan to loosen; cool 1 hour longer. Refrigerate overnight. Just before serving, drizzle with chocolate topping.

Tropical Cheesecake

This recipe has been a favorite of mine for years because of its simple preparation. It makes a sweet and light dessert.

DELORES MASON, JACKSONVILLE, ILLINOIS

PREP: 20 MIN. + CHILLING • **MAKES:** 8-10 SERVINGS

- 1 package (8 ounces) cream cheese, softened
- ½ cup confectioners' sugar
- 1 can (8 ounces) crushed pineapple, drained
- 2 envelopes whipped topping mix (Dream Whip)
- ½ cup cold milk
- ½ teaspoon vanilla extract
- 1 graham cracker crust (9 inches)

1. In a large bowl, beat cream cheese and confectioners' sugar until fluffy. Stir in pineapple.

2. In another bowl, combine dessert topping mix with milk and vanilla; beat until stiff. Fold into pineapple mixture. Spread evenly into crust. Chill.

Bakeshop HOW-TO

Making a Cheesecake Crumb Crust

Place cookies or crackers in a heavy-duty resealable plastic bag. Seal bag, pushing out as much air as possible. Press a rolling pin over the bag, crushing the cookies or crackers into fine crumbs. Or process cookies and crackers in a food processor.

Use a small glass or flat-bottomed measuring cup to firmly press the crumb mixture onto the bottom (and up the sides if directed in the recipe) of a springform pan.

Gingersnap Berry Torte

This cheesecake-like dessert is loaded with fresh fruit, making it perfect for a small summertime gathering.

SUSAN PETTY-BAILER, WEST HARTFORD, CONNECTICUT

PREP: 25 MIN. + CHILLING • **MAKES:** 4 SERVINGS

- ½ cup finely crushed gingersnap cookies (about 9 cookies)
- ⅓ cup finely crushed vanilla wafers (about 10 wafers)
- 2 tablespoons finely chopped walnuts
- 2 tablespoons butter, melted

FILLING:
- 2 packages (3 ounces each) cream cheese, softened
- ¼ cup sugar
- 1 teaspoon vanilla extract
- 1½ cups fresh blueberries, divided
- ¾ cup sliced fresh strawberries

1. In a bowl, combine the gingersnap crumbs, wafer crumbs, walnuts and butter. Press onto the bottom and 1½ in. up the sides of a greased 6-in. springform pan. Bake at 375° for 5-7 minutes or until crust is set. Cool on a wire rack.

2. In a small bowl, beat cream cheese and sugar until smooth. Beat in vanilla. Gently spread about ⅓ cup mixture over crust. Top with half of the blueberries. Layer with about ⅓ cup cream cheese mixture and the strawberries. Spread with remaining cream cheese mixture; top with remaining blueberries. Chill for at least 4 hours.

Mocha Chip Cheesecake

The chocolate crust and miniature chocolate chips are a great contrast to the creamy coffee filling in this cheesecake.

RENEE GASTINEAU, SEATTLE, WASHINGTON

PREP: 20 MIN. • **BAKE:** 50 MIN. + CHILLING • **MAKES:** 12 SERVINGS

CRUST:
- 2 **cups chocolate wafer crumbs (about 32 wafers)**
- ½ **cup sugar**
- ½ **cup butter, melted**

FILLING:
- 3 **packages (8 ounces each) cream cheese, softened**
- 1 **cup sugar**
- 3 **tablespoons all-purpose flour**
- 4 **eggs, lightly beaten**
- ⅓ **cup heavy whipping cream**
- 1 **tablespoon instant coffee granules**
- 1 **teaspoon vanilla extract**
- 1 **cup (6 ounces) miniature semisweet chocolate chips, divided**

1. In a large bowl, combine crumbs and sugar; stir in butter. Press onto the bottom and 2 in. up the sides of a greased 9-in. springform pan; set aside.

2. In a large bowl, beat cream cheese and sugar until smooth. Add flour and beat well. Add eggs, beating on low speed just until combined.

3. In a small bowl, combine cream and coffee granules; let stand for 1 minute. Add to cream cheese mixture with vanilla; beat just until combined. Stir in ¾ cup chocolate chips. Pour into crust. Sprinkle with remaining chocolate chips.

4. Bake at 325° for 50-55 minutes or until center is almost set. Cool on a wire rack for 10 minutes.

5. Carefully run a knife around edge of pan to loosen; cool 1 hour longer. Refrigerate overnight. Remove sides of pan.

Pumpkin Cheesecake

My wife and I think this is a perfect ending to a good meal. The cheesecake is smooth and creamy.

DEWHITT SIZEMORE, WOODLAWN, VIRGINIA

PREP: 20 MIN. • **BAKE:** 1 HOUR + CHILLING • **MAKES:** 12 SERVINGS

- 1½ **cups graham cracker crumbs**
- 1 **tablespoon sugar**
- 5 **tablespoons butter, melted**

FILLING:
- 3 **packages (8 ounces each) cream cheese, softened**
- 1 **cup sugar**
- 1 **teaspoon vanilla extract**
- 3 **eggs, lightly beaten**
- 1 **cup canned pumpkin**
- ½ **teaspoon ground cinnamon**
- ¼ **teaspoon ground nutmeg**
- ¼ **teaspoon ground allspice**
  Whipped cream

1. In a small bowl, combine cracker crumbs and sugar; stir in butter. Press onto the bottom and 2 in. up the sides of a greased 9-in. springform pan. Bake at 350° for 5 minutes. Cool on a wire rack.

2. In a large bowl, beat the cream cheese, sugar and vanilla until smooth. Beat in eggs on low speed just until combined. Combine the pumpkin, cinnamon, nutmeg and allspice; fold into cheese mixture. Pour into crust.

3. Bake at 350° for 1 hour or until center is almost set. Cool on a wire rack for 10 minutes.

4. Carefully run a knife around edge of pan to loosen; cool 1 hour longer. Refrigerate overnight. Remove sides of pan. Garnish with whipped cream.

Chocolate-Covered Cheesecake Bites

Satisfy your cheesecake craving with these bite-size delights! They're party favorites and perfect for the holidays.

ESTHER NEUSTAETER, LA CRETE, ALBERTA

PREP: 1½ HOURS + FREEZING • **MAKES:** 49 SQUARES

- 1 **cup graham cracker crumbs**
- ¼ **cup finely chopped pecans**
- ¼ **cup butter, melted**

FILLING:
- 2 **packages (8 ounces each) cream cheese, softened**
- ½ **cup sugar**
- ¼ **cup sour cream**
- 2 **eggs, lightly beaten**
- ½ **teaspoon vanilla extract**

COATING:
- 24 **ounces semisweet chocolate, chopped**
- 3 **tablespoons shortening**

1. Line a 9-in. square baking pan with foil and grease the foil. In a small bowl, combine the graham cracker crumbs, pecans and butter. Press into prepared pan; set aside.

2. In a large bowl, beat the cream cheese, sugar and sour cream until smooth. Add eggs and vanilla; beat on low speed just until combined. Pour over crust.

3. Bake at 325° for 35-40 minutes or until center is almost set. Cool on a wire rack. Freeze overnight.

4. In a microwave, melt chocolate and shortening; stir until smooth. Cool slightly.

5. Using foil, lift cheesecake out of pan. Gently peel off foil; cut cheesecake into 1¼-in. squares. Work with a few pieces at a time; keep remaining squares refrigerated until ready to dip.

6. Using a toothpick, completely dip squares, one at a time, in melted chocolate; allow excess to drip off. Place on waxed paper-lined baking sheets. Spoon additional chocolate over the tops if necessary to coat. (Reheat chocolate if needed to finish dipping.) Let stand for 20 minutes or until set. Store in an airtight container in the refrigerator or freezer.

Lemon Dream Cheesecake

Light and lemony, this creamy dessert is just the thing for a spring or summer's day.

BONNIE JOST, MANITOWOC, WISCONSIN

PREP: 30 MIN. • **BAKE:** 55 MIN. + CHILLING • **MAKES:** 16 SERVINGS

- 2 cups graham cracker crumbs
- 6 tablespoons butter, melted
- ¼ cup sugar

FILLING:
- 4 packages (8 ounces each) cream cheese, softened
- 1 cup sugar
- ½ cup heavy whipping cream
- ¼ cup lemon juice
- 2 tablespoons all-purpose flour
- 1 tablespoon grated lemon peel
- 2½ teaspoons vanilla extract
- 1 teaspoon lemon extract
- 10 drops yellow food coloring, optional
- 5 eggs, lightly beaten

1. In a small bowl, combine the cracker crumbs, butter and sugar. Press onto the bottom and 2 in. up the sides of a greased 10-in. springform pan. Place pan on a baking sheet. Bake at 325° for 10 minutes. Cool on a wire rack.

2. In a large bowl, beat cream cheese and sugar until smooth. Beat in the cream, lemon juice, flour, lemon peel, extracts and food coloring if desired. Add eggs; beat on low speed just until combined. Pour into crust. Return pan to baking sheet.

3. Bake for 55-65 minutes or until center is almost set. Cool on a wire rack for 10 minutes. Carefully run a knife around edge of pan to loosen; cool 1 hour longer. Refrigerate overnight. Remove sides of pan.

Cheesecake Pops

These cute, lollipop-like bites will make any occasion memorable. The topping possibilities are endless.

EVELYN MOORE, ELK GROVE, CALIFORNIA

PREP: 2 HOURS + FREEZING • **MAKES:** 45 CHEESECAKE POPS

- 3 packages (8 ounces each) cream cheese, softened
- 1 cup sugar
- 1 cup (8 ounces) sour cream
- 1 teaspoon vanilla extract
- 3 eggs, lightly beaten
- 1 cup graham cracker crumbs
- 45 lollipop sticks (4 inches long)
- 3 packages (10 to 12 ounces each) white baking chips
- 3 tablespoons shortening
  Toppings: grated coconut, grated chocolate, assorted sprinkles and chopped nuts

1. Line the bottom of a 9-in. springform pan with parchment paper; coat paper and sides of pan with cooking spray.

2. In a large bowl, beat cream cheese and sugar until smooth. Beat in sour cream and vanilla until blended. Add eggs; beat on low speed just until combined. Pour into prepared pan.

3. Place pan on a baking sheet. Bake at 350° for 45-50 minutes or until center is almost set. Cool on a wire rack for 10 minutes. Carefully run a knife around edge of pan to loosen; cool 1 hour longer. Cover and freeze overnight.

4. Remove from the freezer and let stand for 30 minutes. Place cracker crumbs in a shallow bowl. Working quickly, scoop out 1-in. balls of cheesecake; roll each in cracker crumbs and insert a lollipop stick. Place on waxed paper-lined baking sheets. Freeze for 1 hour or until firm.

5. In a microwave, melt white chips and shortening at 70% power; stir until smooth. Place toppings in shallow bowls. Dip cheesecake pops in white chip mixture; allow excess to drip off. Roll in toppings. Place on waxed paper; let stand until set. Store in the refrigerator.

4. Cool on a wire rack for 10 minutes. Carefully run a knife around edge of pan to loosen; cool 1 hour longer. Meanwhile, place chopped chocolate in a small bowl.

5. In a small saucepan, bring cream just to a boil. Pour over chocolate; whisk until smooth. Cool slightly; gently pour over cheesecake. Cover and chill overnight. Remove sides of pan.

Blueberry Swirl Cheesecake

My wife, Gail, and I host an annual cheesecake party. For the event's 10th anniversary, we prepared 10 family favorites, including this fruity creation.

SCOTT FOX, FERGUS FALLS, MINNESOTA

PREP: 20 MIN. • **BAKE:** 40 MIN. + CHILLING • **MAKES:** 12 SERVINGS

- 1 **package (12 ounces) frozen blueberries, thawed**
- 1 **tablespoon sugar**
- 1 **tablespoon water**
- 1½ **teaspoons cornstarch**

CRUST:
- 1¼ **cups graham cracker crumbs**
- ¼ **cup sugar**
- ⅓ **cup butter, melted**

FILLING:
- 3 **packages (8 ounces each) cream cheese, softened**
- 1 **can (14 ounces) sweetened condensed milk**
- ¼ **cup lemon juice**
- 3 **eggs, lightly beaten**

1. In a food processor, process the blueberries, sugar, water and cornstarch until blended. Transfer to a heavy saucepan; bring to a boil. Reduce heat; cook and stir over medium heat for 2 minutes or until thickened. Set aside ⅓ cup for filling. Refrigerate remaining sauce for topping.

2. Combine crust ingredients. Press onto the bottom of a greased 9-in. springform pan; set aside. In a large bowl, beat cream cheese and milk until smooth; beat in lemon juice. Add eggs; beat on low speed just until combined. Pour half of the filling over crust; top with half of the reserved blueberry mixture. Repeat layers. Cut through filling with a knife to swirl. Place pan on a baking sheet.

3. Bake at 325° for 40-45 minutes or until center is almost set. Cool 10 minutes. Carefully run a knife around the edge of pan to loosen; cool 1 hour longer. Refrigerate overnight. Remove sides of pan. Serve with blueberry sauce.

Two-Tone Cheesecake

Looking to create an original for the Alaska State Fair contest, I came up with my eye-catching layered cheesecake. It won Grand Champion!

CINDI PAULSON, ANCHORAGE, ALASKA

PREP: 25 MIN. • **BAKE:** 1 HOUR + COOLING • **MAKES:** 12 SERVINGS

- 1½ **cups chocolate graham cracker crumbs**
- 6 **tablespoons sugar**
- 6 **tablespoons butter, melted**

FILLING:
- 4 **packages (8 ounces each) cream cheese, softened**
- 1¾ **cups sugar**
- ¾ **cup heavy whipping cream**
- 4 **eggs, lightly beaten**
- 6 **ounces semisweet chocolate, melted and cooled**

TOPPING:
- 4 **ounces semisweet chocolate, finely chopped**
- ½ **cup heavy whipping cream**

1. In a large bowl, combine cracker crumbs, sugar and butter. Press onto the bottom of a greased 10-in. springform pan. Place on a baking sheet. Bake at 325° for 10 minutes. Cool on a wire rack.

2. In a large bowl, beat cream cheese and sugar until smooth. Gradually beat in cream. Add eggs; beat on low speed just until combined.

3. Remove 3½ cups to a small bowl; gently stir in melted chocolate. Pour filling over crust. Gently pour remaining filling over chocolate layer. Bake at 325° for 1 to 1¼ hours or until center is almost set.

Tiramisu Cheesecake Dessert

I wasn't a big fan of tiramisu until I tried this recipe with its distinctive cheesecake- and coffee-flavored layers. It's one of my favorite desserts to make during the fall.

CHRISTIE NELSON, TAYLORVILLE, ILLINOIS

PREP: 20 MIN. • **BAKE:** 40 MIN. + CHILLING • **MAKES:** 12 SERVINGS

- 1 **package (12 ounces) vanilla wafers**
- 5 **teaspoons instant coffee granules, divided**
- 3 **tablespoons hot water, divided**
- 4 **packages (8 ounces each) cream cheese, softened**
- 1 **cup sugar**
- 1 **cup (8 ounces) sour cream**
- 4 **eggs, lightly beaten**
- 1 **cup whipped topping**
- 1 **tablespoon baking cocoa**

1. Layer half of wafers in a greased 13-in. x 9-in. baking dish. In a small bowl, dissolve 2 teaspoons coffee granules in 2 tablespoons hot water. Brush wafers with half of coffee; set remaining mixture aside.

2. In a large bowl, beat cream cheese and sugar until smooth. Beat in sour cream. Add eggs; beat on low speed just until combined. Divide batter in half. Dissolve remaining coffee granules in remaining hot water; stir into one portion of batter. Spread over wafers. Layer with remaining wafers; brush with reserved coffee. Top with remaining batter.

3. Bake at 325° for 40-45 minutes or until center is almost set. Cool on a wire rack for 10 minutes. Carefully run a knife around edge of dish to loosen; cool 1 hour longer. Refrigerate overnight.

4. Spread with the whipped topping; dust with cocoa. Refrigerate leftovers.

White Chocolate Pumpkin Cheesecake

You'll want to put this delectable cheesecake on a pedestal! The crunchy almond topping is a delightful finishing touch.

PHYLLIS SCHMALZ, KANSAS CITY, KANSAS

PREP: 30 MIN. • **BAKE:** 55 MIN. + CHILLING • **MAKES:** 12 SERVINGS

- 1½ **cups crushed gingersnap cookies (about 32 cookies)**
- ¼ **cup butter, melted**
- 3 **packages (8 ounces each) cream cheese, softened**
- 1 **cup sugar**
- 3 **eggs, lightly beaten**
- 1 **teaspoon vanilla extract**
- 5 **ounces white baking chocolate, melted and cooled**
- ¾ **cup canned pumpkin**
- 1 **teaspoon ground cinnamon**
- ¼ **teaspoon ground nutmeg**

ALMOND TOPPING:
- ½ **cup chopped almonds**
- 2 **tablespoons butter, melted**
- 1 **teaspoon sugar**

1. In a small bowl, combine gingersnap crumbs and butter. Press onto the bottom of a greased 9-in. springform pan; set aside.

2. In a large bowl, beat cream cheese and sugar until smooth. Add eggs and vanilla; beat on low speed just until combined. Stir in melted white chocolate.

3. Combine pumpkin and spices; gently fold into cream cheese mixture. Pour over crust. Place pan on a baking sheet.

4. Bake at 350° for 55-60 minutes or until center is just set. Cool on a wire rack for 10 minutes. Meanwhile, combine the topping ingredients; spread in a shallow baking pan. Bake for 10 minutes or until golden brown, stirring twice. Cool.

5. Carefully run a knife around edge of springform pan to loosen cheesecake; cool 1 hour longer. Refrigerate overnight. Transfer topping to an airtight container; store in the refrigerator. Remove sides of pan. Just before serving, sprinkle topping over cheesecake.

No-Bake Cherry Cheesecakes

My husband and I both work full-time, and taxiing our two teenagers around town leaves me little time in the kitchen. Using ready-to-go crust and pie filling, I can extend a no-bake mix to make two light, fancy-looking pies in just 15 minutes!

PAM NOFFKE, TYLER, TEXAS

PREP: 15 MIN. + CHILLING • **MAKES:** 2 PIES (6-8 SERVINGS EACH)

- 1 package (11.1 ounces) no-bake cheesecake mix
- ½ cup butter, melted
- 2 tablespoons sugar
- 1½ cups cold milk
- 1 package (8 ounces) cream cheese, softened
- 1 cup confectioners' sugar
- 2 cups whipped topping
- 1 graham cracker crust (9 inches)
- 2 cans (21 ounces each) cherry pie filling

1. In a large bowl, combine the cheesecake crust mix, butter and sugar. Press onto the bottom and up the sides of an ungreased 9-in. pie plate. Refrigerate.

2. In another large bowl, beat cheesecake filling mix and milk on medium speed for 3 minutes. In a small bowl, beat cream cheese and confectioners' sugar until smooth. Add to cheesecake mixture and beat well. Fold in whipped topping.

3. Spoon half of cheesecake mixture into chilled crust; spoon the remaining half into the purchased crust. Refrigerate for at least 1 hour. Top each with pie filling.

Chocolate Almond Cheesecake

This cheesecake is easy to make but it's definitely not easy to wait until the next day to eat it! It's a spectacular make-ahead party dessert.

DARLENE BRENDEN, SALEM, OREGON

PREP: 25 MIN. + CHILLING • **BAKE:** 50 MIN. + CHILLING
MAKES: 16 SERVINGS

CRUST:
- 1 package (9 ounces) chocolate wafer cookies, crushed (about 2 cups)
- ¼ cup sugar
- ¼ teaspoon ground cinnamon
- ¼ cup butter, melted

FILLING:
- 2 packages (8 ounces each) cream cheese, softened
- 1 cup sugar
- 1 cup (8 ounces) sour cream
- 8 ounces semisweet chocolate, melted and cooled
- ½ teaspoon almond extract
- 2 eggs, lightly beaten

TOPPING:
- 1 cup (8 ounces) sour cream
- ¼ teaspoon baking cocoa
- 2 tablespoons sugar
- ½ teaspoon almond extract

1. In a small bowl, combine crust ingredients; reserve 2 tablespoons for garnish. Press remaining crumbs evenly onto the bottom and 2 in. up the sides of a 9-in. springform pan. Chill.

2. For filling, in a large bowl, beat cream cheese and sugar until smooth. Beat in the sour cream, chocolate and extract. Add the eggs; beat on low speed just until combined. Pour into crust.

3. Place pan on a baking sheet. Bake at 350° for 40 minutes (filling will not be set). Remove from oven and let stand for 5 minutes.

4. Meanwhile, combine topping ingredients. Gently spread over filling. Sprinkle with reserved crumbs. Bake 10 minutes longer.

5. Cool on a wire rack for 10 minutes. Carefully run a knife around edge of pan to loosen; cool 1 hour longer. Refrigerate overnight.

1. In a large bowl, beat cream cheese and sugar until smooth. Beat in sour cream and vanilla. Fold in whipped topping. Spread half of the mixture evenly into crust. Fold cocoa and confectioners' sugar into remaining mixture; gently spread over cream cheese layer. Refrigerate for at least 4 hours.

2. Cut into slices; top each slice with cherry pie filling.

Peanut Butter Cheese Torte

This dessert has long been a favorite with my family. I especially like the fact that it requires no baking—and who doesn't melt for the combination of peanut butter and chocolate?

RUTH BLAIR, WAUKESHA, WISCONSIN

PREP: 20 MIN. + CHILLING • **MAKES:** 16 SERVINGS

CRUST:
- 1 cup graham cracker crumbs
- ¼ cup packed brown sugar
- ¼ cup butter, melted
- ½ cup finely chopped peanuts

FILLING:
- 2 cups creamy peanut butter
- 2 packages (8 ounces each) cream cheese, softened
- 2 cups sugar
- 2 tablespoons butter, softened
- 2 teaspoons vanilla extract
- 1½ cups heavy whipping cream, whipped

CHOCOLATE TOPPING:
- 4 ounces semisweet chocolate chips
- 3 tablespoons plus 2 teaspoons brewed coffee
  Chopped peanuts, optional

1. Combine all crust ingredients. Press onto the bottom and halfway up the sides of a 10-in. springform pan. Chill.

2. For filling, beat peanut butter, cream cheese, sugar, butter and vanilla in a large bowl on high until smooth, about 2 minutes. Fold in whipped cream. Gently spoon into crust; refrigerate 6 hours or overnight.

3. For topping, in a microwave, melt chocolate with coffee; stir until smooth. Spread over chilled torte. Refrigerate until firm, about 30 minutes. Garnish the top with chopped peanuts if desired.

Black Forest Cheesecake

I take this popular cheesecake to every gathering. I created the recipe about 15 years ago and my family has been asking for it ever since.

CHRISTINE OOYEN, WINNEBAGO, ILLINOIS

PREP: 20 MIN. + CHILLING • **MAKES:** 6-8 SERVINGS

- 1 package (8 ounces) cream cheese, softened
- ⅓ cup sugar
- 1 cup (8 ounces) sour cream
- 2 teaspoons vanilla extract
- 1 carton (8 ounces) frozen whipped topping, thawed
- 1 chocolate crumb crust (8 inches)
- ¼ cup baking cocoa
- 1 tablespoon confectioners' sugar
- 1 can (21 ounces) cherry pie filling

Chocolate Heaven

Chocolate Mallow Pie

This rich and fudgy cream cheese pie should serve eight, but it never does because so many folks request a second slice! I've been cooking for more than 60 years and this is the best chocolate pie recipe I've found.

LOUISE GENN, COSMOPOLIS, WASHINGTON

PREP: 25 MIN. + CHILLING • **MAKES:** 8 SERVINGS

- 1¼ cups Oreo cookie crumbs
- ¼ cup butter, melted
- 2 tablespoons sugar
- 2 packages (one 8 ounces, one 3 ounces) cream cheese, softened
- ½ cup chocolate syrup
- 1⅓ cups semisweet chocolate chips, melted
- 1 carton (8 ounces) frozen whipped topping, thawed
- 2 cups miniature marshmallows
  Chocolate curls, optional

1. In a large bowl, combine the cookie crumbs, butter and sugar. Press into a 9-in. pie plate. Bake at 375° for 8-10 minutes or until set; cool completely on a wire rack.

2. In a large bowl, beat cream cheese and chocolate syrup until blended. Beat in melted chips. Set aside ¼ cup of whipped topping. Fold marshmallows and remaining whipped topping into chocolate mixture.

3. Spoon filling into crust. Refrigerate for at least 8 hours or overnight. Top with reserved whipped topping. Garnish with chocolate curls if desired.

Raspberry Truffle Brownies

On the outside, these look like traditional brownies. But when people bite in, they are pleasantly surprised! It's almost like eating a filled chocolate candy.

LESLIE KNICL, MAHOMET, ILLINOIS

PREP: 30 MIN. • **BAKE:** 30 MIN. + CHILLING • **MAKES:** ABOUT 2½ DOZEN

- ½ cup butter, cubed
- 1¼ cups semisweet chocolate chips
- 2 eggs
- ¾ cup packed brown sugar
- 1 teaspoon instant coffee granules
- 2 tablespoons hot water
- ¾ cup all-purpose flour
- ½ teaspoon baking powder

FILLING:
- 1 cup (6 ounces) semisweet chocolate chips
- 1 package (8 ounces) cream cheese, softened
- ¼ cup confectioners' sugar
- ⅓ cup seedless red raspberry jam

GLAZE:
- ¼ cup semisweet chocolate chips
- 1 teaspoon shortening

1. In a microwave, melt butter and chocolate chips; stir until smooth. Cool slightly. In a large bowl, beat eggs and brown sugar until blended. Dissolve coffee granules in water; add to egg mixture. Beat in chocolate until well blended. Combine flour and baking powder; stir into chocolate mixture just until blended.

2. Spread in a greased 9-in. square baking pan. Bake at 350° for 30-35 minutes or until brownies test done. Cool on a wire rack.

3. For filling, in a microwave, melt chocolate chips; stir until smooth. Cool. In a small bowl, beat cream cheese and confectioners' sugar until smooth. Beat in jam; stir in melted chocolate. Spread over cooled brownies.

4. For glaze, in a microwave, melt chocolate chips and shortening; stir until smooth. Drizzle over filling. Chill before cutting. Store in the refrigerator.

Raspberry Sachertorte

It may look like this torte took hours to make, but it has a surprisingly short list of ingredients. A small slice splendidly satisfies a sweet tooth.

ROSE HOCKETT, COLORADO SPRINGS, COLORADO

PREP: 50 MIN. • **BAKE:** 25 MIN. + STANDING • **MAKES:** 12 SERVINGS

- 4 eggs, separated
- 5 tablespoons butter
- ⅔ cup sugar
- 9 ounces bittersweet chocolate, melted
- ¾ cup ground almonds
- ¼ cup all-purpose flour
- ¼ cup seedless raspberry jam

GLAZE:
- 3 ounces bittersweet chocolate, chopped
- 2 tablespoons butter

1. Place egg whites in a large bowl, let stand at room temperature for 30 minutes. In another bowl, beat butter and sugar until crumbly, about 2 minutes. Add egg yolks and melted chocolate; beat on low speed until combined. Combine almonds and flour; stir into butter mixture just until blended.

2. In another bowl with clean beaters, beat egg whites until stiff peaks form; fold into batter. Transfer to a greased 9-in. springform pan. Bake at 350° for 25-30 minutes or until a toothpick inserted near the center comes out clean. Cool on a wire rack for 10 minutes. Carefully run a knife around edge of pan to loosen; remove sides of pan. Cool completely.

3. Spread jam over top of cake. For glaze, in a small saucepan, melt chocolate and butter; spread over jam. Let stand at room temperature for 1 hour or until set.

Cream-Filled Chocolate Supreme Muffins

Because of her reputation for baking up yummy things, Mom used to sell muffins at my dad's workplace. Among my favorites were these cupcake-like treats.

SUSANNE SPICKER, NORTH OGDEN, UTAH

PREP: 30 MIN. • **BAKE:** 25 MIN. + COOLING • **MAKES:** 1 DOZEN

- 3 cups all-purpose flour
- 2 cups sugar
- ½ cup baking cocoa
- 2 teaspoons baking soda
- 1 teaspoon salt
- 2 cups cold water
- ¾ cup canola oil
- 1 egg
- 2 tablespoons white vinegar
- 2 teaspoons vanilla extract

FILLING:
- 4 ounces cream cheese, softened
- ¼ cup sugar
- ⅛ teaspoon salt
- 2 tablespoons beaten egg
- ½ teaspoon vanilla extract
- ¾ cup milk chocolate chips
  Confectioners' sugar, optional

1. In a large bowl, combine the flour, sugar, cocoa, baking soda and salt. In another bowl, combine the water, oil, egg, vinegar and vanilla. Stir into dry ingredients just until moistened.

2. For filling, beat the cream cheese, sugar and salt until smooth. Beat in egg and vanilla. Fold in chips.

3. Fill 12 paper-lined jumbo muffin cups half full with batter. Drop a rounded tablespoonful of cream cheese mixture into center of each; cover with remaining batter.

4. Bake at 350° for 25-30 minutes or until a toothpick inserted in muffin comes out clean. Cool for 5 minutes before removing from pans to wire racks to cool completely. Sprinkle with confectioners' sugar if desired.

Sour Cream Chocolate Cupcakes

My husband and I often enjoy these moist, chocolaty cupcakes. The sour cream is definitely the ingredient that gives them their distinction.

ALICSA MAYER, ALTA VISTA, KANSAS

PREP: 30 MIN. • **BAKE:** 20 MIN. + COOLING • **MAKES:** 2 DOZEN

- ¼ cup butter, cubed
- 4 ounces unsweetened chocolate, chopped
- 2 eggs
- 2 cups sugar
- 1 cup water
- ¾ cup sour cream
- 1 teaspoon vanilla extract
- 2 cups all-purpose flour
- 1 teaspoon baking soda

FROSTING:
- ½ cup butter, cubed
- 4 ounces unsweetened chocolate, chopped
- 4 cups confectioners' sugar
- ½ cup sour cream
- 2 teaspoons vanilla extract

1. In a microwave, melt butter and chocolate; stir until smooth. Cool for 10 minutes. In a large bowl, beat the eggs, sugar, water, sour cream and vanilla. Combine flour and baking soda; add to the egg mixture and mix well. Add chocolate mixture; beat on high speed for 2-3 minutes.

2. Fill paper-lined muffin cups two-thirds full. Bake at 350° for 18-20 minutes or until a toothpick inserted near the center comes out clean. Cool for 10 minutes before removing from pans to wire racks to cool completely.

3. For frosting, in a large microwave-safe bowl, melt butter and chocolate; stir until smooth. Cool for 10 minutes. With a portable mixer, beat in the confectioners' sugar, sour cream and vanilla on low until smooth. Frost cupcakes. Store in the refrigerator.

Melty Microwave Brownies

These rich, fudgy brownies can't be beat for a quick dessert.

SUE GRONHOLZ, BEAVER DAM, WISCONSIN

PREP: 10 MIN. • **COOK:** 5 MIN. + COOLING • **MAKES:** 1 DOZEN

- ½ cup butter, cubed
- 2 ounces unsweetened chocolate, chopped
- 2 eggs
- ¾ cup sugar
- ½ cup all-purpose flour
- 1 teaspoon baking powder
- 1 teaspoon vanilla extract
- ½ cup semisweet chocolate chips
  Confectioners' sugar

1. In a microwave, melt butter and chocolate; stir until smooth. Cool slightly. In a large bowl, beat eggs for 2 minutes. Gradually add sugar, beating until thick and pale yellow. Combine flour and baking powder; add to egg mixture. Stir in the melted chocolate mixture, vanilla and chips.

2. Pour into a greased 8-in. square microwave-safe dish. Cook on high for 3½ to 4 minutes or until a toothpick inserted near the center comes out clean. Place on a wire rack; cool for 10 minutes. Dust with confectioners' sugar.

Editor's Note: *This recipe was tested in a 1,100-watt microwave.*

Chocolate Velvet Dessert

This extra-speical creation is the result of several attempts to duplicate a dessert I enjoyed on vacation. It looks so beautiful on a buffet table that many folks are tempted to forgo the main course in favor of it.

MOLLY SEIDEL, EDGEWOOD, NEW MEXICO

PREP: 20 MIN. • **BAKE:** 45 MIN. + CHILLING • **MAKES:** 16 SERVINGS

- 1½ cups chocolate wafer crumbs
- 2 tablespoons sugar
- ¼ cup butter, melted
- 2 cups (12 ounces) semisweet chocolate chips
- 6 egg yolks
- 1¾ cups heavy whipping cream
- 1 teaspoon vanilla extract

CHOCOLATE BUTTERCREAM FROSTING:
- ½ cup butter, softened
- 3 cups confectioners' sugar
- 3 tablespoons baking cocoa
- 3 to 4 tablespoons 2% milk

1. In a small bowl, combine wafer crumbs and sugar; stir in butter. Press onto the bottom and 1½ in. up the sides of a greased 9-in. springform pan. Place on a baking sheet. Bake at 350° for 10 minutes. Cool on a wire rack.

2. In a large microwave-safe bowl, melt chocolate chips; stir until smooth. Cool. In a small bowl, combine the egg yolks, cream and vanilla. Gradually stir a small amount of mixture into melted chocolate until blended; gradually stir in remaining mixture. Pour into crust.

3. Place pan on a baking sheet. Bake at 350° for 45-50 minutes or until center is almost set. Cool on a wire rack for 10 minutes. Carefully run a knife around edge of pan to loosen; cool 1 hour longer. Refrigerate overnight.

4. In a large bowl, combine the butter, confectioners' sugar, cocoa and enough milk to achieve a piping consistency. Using a large star tip, pipe frosting on dessert.

Mud Pie

Having grown up in the South, we naturally fell in love with chocolate pie filled with pecans. It could take all day to put one together, but my version takes only 15 minutes. Oh, yeah!

DEBORAH WOOLARD, LAS VEGAS, NEVADA

PREP: 15 MIN. + CHILLING • **MAKES:** 8 SERVINGS

- 3 ounces semisweet chocolate, chopped
- ¼ cup sweetened condensed milk
- 1 chocolate crumb crust (8 inches)
- ½ cup chopped pecans
- 2 cups cold 2% milk
- 2 packages (3.9 ounces each) instant chocolate pudding mix
- 1 carton (8 ounces) frozen whipped topping, thawed, divided

1. In a microwave, melt chocolate; stir in condensed milk until smooth. Pour into crust; sprinkle with pecans.

2. In a small bowl, whisk milk and pudding mixes for 2 minutes (mixture will be thick). Carefully spread 1½ cups of pudding mixture over pecans.

3. Fold ½ cup whipped topping into the remaining pudding mixture; spoon over pudding layer. Top with remaining whipped topping. Chill until set.

Cookie Dough Brownies

When I take these rich brownies to a get-together, I carry the recipe, too, because it always gets requested. Children of all ages love the tempting "cookie dough" filling. These brownies are typically the first to be gone from the buffet table—even before the entrees!

WENDY BAILEY, ELIDA, OHIO

PREP: 20 MIN. + CHILLING • **BAKE:** 30 MIN. + COOLING • **MAKES:** 3 DOZEN

- 4 eggs
- 1 cup canola oil
- 2 cups sugar
- 2 teaspoons vanilla extract
- 1½ cups all-purpose flour
- ½ cup baking cocoa
- ½ teaspoon salt
- ½ cup chopped walnuts, optional

FILLING:
- ½ cup butter, softened
- ½ cup packed brown sugar
- ¼ cup sugar
- 2 tablespoons 2% milk
- 1 teaspoon vanilla extract
- 1 cup all-purpose flour

GLAZE:
- 1 cup (6 ounces) semisweet chocolate chips
- 1 tablespoon shortening
- ¾ cup chopped walnuts

1. In a large bowl, beat the eggs, oil, sugar and vanilla until well blended. Combine the flour, cocoa and salt; gradually beat into egg mixture. Stir in walnuts if desired.

2. Pour into a greased 13-in. x 9-in. baking pan. Bake at 350° for 30 minutes or until brownies test done. Cool completely.

3. For filling, in a large bowl, cream butter and sugars until light and fluffy. Beat in milk and vanilla. Gradually beat in flour. Spread over the brownies; chill until firm.

4. For glaze, in a microwave, melt chocolate chips and shortening; stir until smooth. Spread over filling. Immediately sprinkle with nuts, pressing down slightly. Let stand until set.

Chocolate Silk Pie

This quick and creamy chocolate pie not only melts in your mouth, it also melts any and all resistance to dessert!

MARY RELYEA, CANASTOTA, NEW YORK

PREP: 30 MIN. + CHILLING • **MAKES:** 6-8 SERVINGS

- 1 **unbaked pastry shell (9 inches)**
- 1 **jar (7 ounces) marshmallow creme**
- 1 **cup (6 ounces) semisweet chocolate chips**
- ¼ **cup butter, cubed**
- 2 **ounces unsweetened chocolate**
- 2 **tablespoons strong brewed coffee**
- 1 **cup heavy whipping cream, whipped**

TOPPING:
- 1 **cup heavy whipping cream**
- 2 **tablespoons confectioners' sugar**
  Chocolate curls, optional

1. Line unpricked pastry shell with a double thickness of heavy-duty foil. Bake at 450° for 8 minutes. Remove foil; bake 5 minutes longer. Cool on a wire rack.

2. Meanwhile, in a heavy saucepan, combine the marshmallow creme, chocolate chips, butter, unsweetened chocolate and coffee; cook and stir over low heat until chocolate is melted and mixture is smooth. Cool. Fold in whipped cream; pour into crust.

3. For topping, in a large bowl, beat cream until it begins to thicken. Add confectioners' sugar; beat until stiff peaks form. Spread over filling. Refrigerate for at least 3 hours before serving. Garnish with chocolate curls if desired.

Bakeshop **HOW-TO**

Making Chocolate Curls

For a pretty garnish to accent any dessert, use a vegetable peeler to "peel" curls from a solid block of chocolate. To keep the strips intact, allow them to fall gently onto a plate or a single layer of waxed paper. If you get only shavings, your chocolate may be too hard. Allow it to warm slightly.

Mocha Truffle Cookies

Crisp on the outside, gooey on the inside, these chocolaty treats are perfect for chasing away the doldrums. Why not invite a friend over to share a plateful?

PAMELA JESSEN, CALGARY, ALBERTA

PREP: 15 MIN. • **BAKE:** 10 MIN. + COOLING • **MAKES:** 15 COOKIES

- ¼ cup butter, cubed
- ¼ cup semisweet chocolate chips
- 1½ teaspoons instant coffee granules
- ⅓ cup sugar
- ⅓ cup packed brown sugar
- 1 egg, lightly beaten
- 1 teaspoon vanilla extract
- 1 cup all-purpose flour
- 2 tablespoons plus 2 teaspoons baking cocoa
- ¼ teaspoon baking powder
- ⅛ teaspoon salt
- ⅓ cup English toffee bits or almond brickle chips
- 1 ounce milk chocolate, melted

1. In a microwave-safe bowl, melt butter and chocolate; stir until smooth. Stir in coffee granules until dissolved; cool for 5 minutes. Transfer to a small bowl. Add the sugars, egg and vanilla.

2. Combine the flour, cocoa, baking powder and salt; add to chocolate mixture and mix well. Stir in toffee bits. Drop by rounded tablespoonfuls 2 in. apart onto a baking sheet lightly coated with cooking spray.

3. Bake at 350° for 8-10 minutes or until set. Cool for 1 minute before removing to a wire rack to cool completely. Drizzle with melted milk chocolate.

Double Chocolate Biscotti

Here's a more moist and tender version of biscotti. With a chocolaty taste and sweet drizzle on top, these irresistible cookies just beg for hot coffee to be served alongside them.

TASTE OF HOME TEST KITCHEN

PREP: 20 MIN. • **BAKE:** 35 MIN. + COOLING • **MAKES:** ABOUT 1 DOZEN

- 2 eggs
- 1 teaspoon vanilla extract
- ¼ teaspoon almond extract
- ½ cup sugar
- 1 cup all-purpose flour
- ½ cup finely chopped pecans
- ¼ cup baking cocoa
- ¼ teaspoon salt
- ½ cup miniature semisweet chocolate chips

ICING:
- 1½ teaspoons miniature semisweet chocolate chips
- 3 teaspoons fat-free milk
- ½ cup confectioners' sugar
- ⅛ teaspoon vanilla extract

1. In a large bowl, beat the eggs and extracts. Beat in sugar. Combine the flour, pecans, cocoa and salt; gradually add to egg mixture and mix well. Stir in chocolate chips.

2. On a baking sheet coated with cooking spray, shape dough into a 14-in. x 3-in. rectangle. Bake at 350° for 20-25 minutes or until lightly browned. Cool for 5 minutes.

3. Transfer to a cutting board; cut with a serrated knife into 1-in. slices. Place cut side down on baking sheets coated with cooking spray. Bake for 15-20 minutes or until firm, turning once. Remove to wire racks to cool.

4. For icing, in a microwave, melt chocolate chips; stir until smooth. Stir in milk, confectioners' sugar and vanilla until smooth. Drizzle over cookies; let stand until hardened.

Chocolate Cinnamon Rolls

Here's a yummy departure from regular cinnamon rolls. When I take them to morning bowling league, they are quickly devoured!

MYRNA SIPPEL, THOMPSON, ILLINOIS

PREP: 30 MIN. + RISING • **BAKE:** 25 MIN. • **MAKES:** 20 ROLLS

- 2 **packages (¼ ounce each) active dry yeast**
- 1½ **cups warm water (110° to 115°), divided**
- ½ **cup butter, softened**
- ½ **cup sugar**
- 1 **teaspoon salt**
- 4½ to 4¾ **cups all-purpose flour**
- ⅔ **cup baking cocoa**

FILLING:
- 2 **tablespoons butter, melted**
- ⅓ **cup sugar**
- ½ **teaspoon ground cinnamon**
- 1 **cup miniature semisweet chocolate chips**
- ⅔ **cup finely chopped nuts, optional**

ICING:
- 2 **cups confectioners' sugar**
- ½ **teaspoon vanilla extract**
- 2 **to 3 tablespoons milk**
   Additional miniature semisweet chocolate chips, optional

1. In a large bowl, dissolve yeast in ½ cup warm water. Add the butter, sugar, salt and remaining water. Stir in 2½ cups flour and cocoa. Beat on medium speed for 3 minutes or until smooth. Stir in enough remaining flour to form a soft dough.

2. Turn onto a lightly floured surface; knead until smooth and elastic, about 6-8 minutes. Place in a greased bowl, turning once to grease the top. Cover and let rise in a warm place until doubled, about 1 hour.

3. Turn onto a lightly floured surface; divide in half. Roll each portion into a 12-in. x 10-in. rectangle; brush with melted butter. Combine the sugar, cinnamon, chocolate chips and nuts if desired; sprinkle over dough to within ½ in. of edges.

4. Roll up each jelly-roll style, starting with a long side; pinch seams to seal. Cut each into 10 slices. Place cut side down in a greased 15-in. x 10-in. x 1-in. baking pan. Cover and let rise until doubled, about 45 minutes.

5. Bake at 375° for 25-30 minutes or until lightly browned. Meanwhile, in a small bowl, combine the confectioners' sugar, vanilla and enough milk to reach desired consistency. Spread over rolls while slightly warm; sprinkle with additional chocolate chips if desired.

Bakeshop TIP

Keep Cocoa on Hand

Cocoa is easy to mix into recipes with flour and other dry ingredients to create genuine chocolate flavor. But because cocoa doesn't contain the natural fats that are found in chocolate, it has a much longer shelf life. Cocoa stays fresh in the pantry for about two years!

Special Pleasure Chocolate Cheesecake

When we have time, we enjoy making cheesecakes. In fact, we've come up with a couple of our own recipes. We like this fail-proof dessert because it's so easy to prepare and has just the right mix of ingredients to make it a special pleasure for any palate.

BENJAMIN & SUE ELLEN CLARK, WARSAW, NEW YORK

PREP: 20 MIN. • **BAKE:** 40 MIN. + CHILLING • **MAKES:** 24 SERVINGS

- 1 package (18 ounces) ready-to-bake refrigerated triple-chocolate cookie dough
- 1 package (8 ounces) milk chocolate toffee bits
- 1 package (9½ ounces) Dove dark chocolate candies
- 3 packages (8 ounces each) cream cheese, softened
- 1 can (14 ounces) sweetened condensed milk
- ¾ cup (6 ounces) vanilla yogurt
- 4 eggs, lightly beaten
- 1 teaspoon vanilla extract
  Whipped cream

1. Let dough stand at room temperature for 5-10 minutes to soften. Press nine portions of dough into an ungreased 13-in. x 9-in. baking dish (save remaining dough for another use). Set aside 2 tablespoons toffee bits for garnish; sprinkle remaining toffee bits over dough.

2. In a microwave, melt chocolate candies; stir until smooth. In a large bowl, beat the cream cheese, milk and yogurt until smooth. Add eggs; beat on low speed just until combined. Stir in vanilla and melted chocolate. Pour over crust.

3. Bake at 350° for 40-45 minutes or until center is almost set. Cool on a wire rack. Refrigerate for 4 hours or overnight. Garnish with whipped cream and reserved toffee bits.

tasteofhome.com

Brownie Truffle Torte

This over-the-top truffle cake tastes like it takes all day to make, but we trimmed steps to give you scrumptious results in less time.

TASTE OF HOME TEST KITCHEN

PREP: 30 MIN. + COOLING • **BAKE:** 25 MIN. + CHILLING
MAKES: 16 SERVINGS

- 1 box fudge brownie mix (8-inch square pan size)
- 3 cups (18 ounces) semisweet chocolate chips
- 2 cups heavy whipping cream, divided
- 6 tablespoons butter, cubed
- 1 tablespoon instant coffee granules
- 3 tablespoons vanilla extract
- 14 to 16 Pirouette cookies, cut into 1½-inch pieces

1. Prepare brownie batter according to package directions. Spread into a greased 9-in. springform pan. Place on a baking sheet. Bake at 350° for 25-30 minutes or until a toothpick inserted near the center comes out clean. Cool on a wire rack.

2. Place chocolate chips in a food processor; cover and process until finely chopped. In a small microwave-safe bowl, combine 1 cup cream, butter and coffee granules. Microwave, uncovered, on high for 1 to 1½ minutes or until butter is melted; stir until smooth. With food processor running, add cream mixture to chocolate chips in a slow, steady stream. Add vanilla; cover and process until smooth.

3. Cut a small hole in the corner of a pastry or plastic bag. Fill with ¼ cup chocolate mixture; set aside for garnish. Transfer remaining chocolate mixture to a large bowl.

4. Remove sides of springform pan. Spread half of the remaining chocolate mixture over brownie layer, spreading evenly over top and sides. In a small bowl, beat remaining cream until soft peaks form; fold into remaining chocolate mixture. Spread over chocolate layer. Gently press cookies into sides of dessert.

5. Pipe reserved chocolate mixture on top. Refrigerate for at least 4 hours or overnight. Remove from the refrigerator 5 minutes before cutting.

Editor's Note: *The amount of vanilla called for in the recipe is correct.*

Brownie Truffle Torte

With a cookie crust and two layers of rich chocolate encasing a yummy brownie, this impressive dessert only looks difficult to make!

Prepare and bake brownie. For chocolate layer, slowly add hot cream mixture to the chocolate chips while the food processor is running.

Spread some of the chocolate mixture over the brownie layer, evenly covering the top and sides.

Fold whipped cream into remaining chocolate mixture to create the chocolate truffle layer. Spread over top and sides of torte.

Add cookies around the perimeter and garnish as desired.

Special-Occasion Chocolate Cake

This recipe won the top prize at my state fair, and with one bite, you'll see why! The decadent chocolate cake boasts a luscious ganache filling and fudge buttercream frosting.

CINDI PAULSON, ANCHORAGE, ALASKA

PREP: 40 MIN. + CHILLING • **BAKE:** 25 MIN. + COOLING
MAKES: 12 SERVINGS

- 1 cup baking cocoa
- 2 cups boiling water
- 1 cup butter, softened
- 2¼ cups sugar
- 4 eggs
- 1½ teaspoons vanilla extract
- 2¾ cups all-purpose flour
- 2 teaspoons baking soda
- ½ teaspoon baking powder
- ½ teaspoon salt

GANACHE:
- 10 ounces semisweet chocolate, chopped
- 1 cup heavy whipping cream
- 2 tablespoons sugar

FROSTING:
- 1 cup butter, softened
- 4 cups confectioners' sugar
- ½ cup baking cocoa
- ¼ cup 2% milk
- 2 teaspoons vanilla extract

GARNISH:
- ¾ cup sliced almonds, toasted

1. In a small bowl, combine cocoa and water; set aside. In a large bowl, cream butter and sugar until light and fluffy. Add eggs, one at a time, beating well after each addition. Beat in vanilla. Combine the flour, baking soda, baking powder and salt; add to creamed mixture alternately with cocoa mixture, beating well after each addition.

2. Pour into three greased and floured 9-in. round baking pans. Bake at 350° for 25-30 minutes or until a toothpick inserted near the center comes out clean. Cool for 10 minutes before removing from pans to wire racks to cool completely.

3. For ganache, place chocolate in a small bowl. In a small heavy saucepan over low heat, bring cream and sugar to a boil. Pour over chocolate; whisk gently until smooth. Refrigerate for 35-45 minutes or until ganache begins to thicken, stirring occasionally.

4. For frosting, in a large bowl, beat butter until fluffy. Add the confectioners' sugar, cocoa, milk and vanilla; beat until smooth.

5. Place one cake layer on a serving plate; spread with 1 cup frosting. Top with second layer and 1 cup ganache; sprinkle with ½ cup almonds. Top with third layer; frost top and sides of cake. Warm ganache until pourable; pour over cake, allowing some to drape down the sides. Sprinkle with remaining almonds. Refrigerate until serving.

Special-Occasion Mocha Cake: Add 2 tablespoons instant coffee granules to the boiling water-cocoa mixture. In the frosting, substitute Kahlua for milk.

Low-Fat Chocolate Mini Chip Cupcakes

These tender little cupcakes are chock-full of sweet flavor, yet each has only 139 calories and 2 grams of fat.

LINDA UTTER, SIDNEY, MONTANA

PREP: 20 MIN. • **BAKE:** 15 MIN. + COOLING • **MAKES:** 14 CUPCAKES

- 2 **tablespoons butter, softened**
- ¾ **cup sugar**
- 1 **egg**
- 1 **egg white**
- ½ **cup plus 2 tablespoons buttermilk**
- ⅓ **cup water**
- 1 **tablespoon white vinegar**
- 1 **teaspoon vanilla extract**
- 1½ **cups all-purpose flour**
- ¼ **cup baking cocoa**
- 1 **teaspoon baking soda**
- ½ **teaspoon salt**
- ⅓ **cup miniature semisweet chocolate chips**

1. In a large bowl, beat butter and sugar until crumbly, about 2 minutes. Add egg, then egg white, beating well after each addition. Beat on high speed until light and fluffy. Beat in the buttermilk, water, vinegar and vanilla. Combine the flour, cocoa, baking soda and salt; beat into batter just until moistened. Stir in chocolate chips.

2. Fill muffin cups coated with cooking spray three-fourths full. Bake at 375° for 15-18 minutes or until a toothpick inserted in the muffin comes out clean. Cool for 5 minutes before removing from pans to wire racks.

Flourless Chocolate Cake

One bite of this and you'll agree it's pure pleasure for confirmed chocoholics! A small slice of this rich, dense dessert goes a long way. Chocolate ganache on top takes it to the next level.

TASTE OF HOME TEST KITCHEN

PREP: 30 MIN. • **BAKE:** 40 MIN. + COOLING • **MAKES:** 16 SERVINGS

- 4 **eggs, separated**
- 10 **tablespoons butter, cubed**
- ½ **cup sugar, divided**
- 6 **ounces semisweet chocolate, chopped**
- 3 **ounces unsweetened chocolate, chopped**
- 2 **teaspoons vanilla extract**
- ¼ **cup finely ground pecans, toasted**
   Chocolate Ganache (recipe at right), optional
   Sliced strawberries and fresh mint, optional

1. Let egg whites stand at room temperature for 30 minutes. In a heavy saucepan, melt butter, ¼ cup sugar and chocolates over low heat, stirring constantly. Cool until the mixture is lukewarm.

2. In a large bowl, beat egg yolks until thick and lemon-colored, about 3 minutes. Beat in vanilla. Gradually beat in pecans and chocolate mixture.

3. In a small bowl and with clean beaters, beat egg whites on medium speed until soft peaks form. Gradually add remaining sugar, 1 tablespoon at a time, beating on high speed until stiff peaks form. Stir a small amount of whites into chocolate mixture. Fold in remaining whites.

4. Pour into a greased 9-in. springform pan. Place on a baking sheet. Bake at 350° for 40-50 minutes or until a toothpick inserted near the center comes out with a few moist crumbs. Cool on a wire rack for 20 minutes.

5. Carefully run a knife around edge of pan to loosen; remove sides of pan and cool completely. Frost with Chocolate Ganache if desired. Garnish with strawberries and mint if desired.

Chocolate Ganache

This satiny smooth chocolate treat will bring a touch of elegance to even the simplest dessert. It's so versatile!

TASTE OF HOME TEST KITCHEN

PREP: 15 MIN. + CHILLING • **MAKES:** 1¼ CUPS

- 1 **cup (6 ounces) semisweet chocolate chips**
- ⅔ **cup heavy whipping cream**

1. Place chocolate chips in a small bowl. In a small saucepan, bring cream just to a boil. Pour over chocolate; whisk until smooth.

2. For a pourable ganache, cool, stirring occasionally, until mixture reaches 85°-90° and is slightly thickened, about 40 minutes. Pour over cake, allowing some to drape down the sides. Spread ganache with a spatula if necessary to evenly coat, working quickly before it thickens. Let stand until set.

3. For spreadable ganache, chill, stirring occasionally, until mixture reaches a spreading consistency. Spread over cake.

White Chocolate Ganache: Substitute 6 ounces chopped white baking chocolate for the chocolate chips. Proceed as directed.

Sandy's Chocolate Cake

This velvety, rich cake won first prize at The Greatest Cocoa Cake Contest in my home state. It's so tall and pretty, it's guaranteed to impress.

SANDY JOHNSON, TIOGA, PENNSYLVANIA

PREP: 30 MIN. • **BAKE:** 35 MIN. + COOLING • **MAKES:** 12 SERVINGS

- 3 **cups packed brown sugar**
- 1 **cup butter, softened**
- 4 **eggs**
- 2 **teaspoons vanilla extract**
- 2⅔ **cups all-purpose flour**
- ¾ **cup baking cocoa**
- 1 **tablespoon baking soda**
- ½ **teaspoon salt**
- 1⅓ **cups sour cream**
- 1⅓ **cups boiling water**

FROSTING:

- ½ **cup butter, cubed**
- 3 **ounces unsweetened chocolate, chopped**
- 3 **ounces semisweet chocolate, chopped**
- 5 **cups confectioners' sugar**
- 1 **cup (8 ounces) sour cream**
- 2 **teaspoons vanilla extract**
    Chocolate curls and decorations, optional

1. In a bowl, cream brown sugar and butter until light and fluffy. Add eggs, one at a time, beating well after each addition. Beat in vanilla. Combine the flour, cocoa, baking soda and salt; add alternately with sour cream to creamed mixture. Mix on low just until combined. Stir in water until blended.

2. Pour into three greased and floured 9-in. round baking pans. Bake at 350° for 35 minutes. Cool in pans 10 minutes; remove to wire racks to cool completely.

3. For frosting, in a small saucepan, melt butter and chocolates over low heat. Cool for several minutes.

4. In a bowl, combine the confectioners' sugar, sour cream and vanilla. Add chocolate mixture and beat until smooth. Spread frosting between layers and over top and sides of cake. Top with chocolate garnishes if desired. Store in the refrigerator.

Chocolate Upside-Down Cake

Here's a dessert that's simply out of this world. All of your guests will agree that it's the best ever. Enjoy it with a scoop of vanilla ice cream.

IOLA EGLE, BELLA VISTA, ARKANSAS

PREP: 15 MIN. • **BAKE:** 55 MIN. + COOLING • **MAKES:** 12-15 SERVINGS

1¼ cups water
¼ cup butter, cubed
1 cup packed brown sugar
1 cup flaked coconut
2 cups (12 ounces) semisweet chocolate chips
1 cup chopped pecans
2 cups miniature marshmallows
1 package (18¼ ounces) German chocolate cake mix

SHORT & SWEET

1. In a small saucepan, heat water and butter until butter is melted. Stir in brown sugar until blended. Pour into a greased 13-in. x 9-in. baking pan. Sprinkle with coconut, chocolate chips, pecans and marshmallows.

2. Prepare cake batter according to package directions; carefully pour over marshmallows. Bake at 325° for 55-60 minutes or until a toothpick inserted near the center comes out clean. Cool for 10 minutes before inverting cake onto a serving plate.

Chocolate Oreo Bars

A friend brought these fudgy bars to tempt me with yet another chocolate treat. They are simple to make, and cleanup is a breeze!

NANCY CLARK, ZEIGLER, ILLINOIS

PREP: 15 MIN. • **BAKE:** 10 MIN. + COOLING • **MAKES:** ABOUT 4 DOZEN

- 1 package (15½ ounces) Oreo cookies, crushed
- ¾ cup butter, melted
- 1 can (14 ounces) sweetened condensed milk
- 2 cups (12 ounces) miniature semisweet chocolate chips, divided

1. Combine cookie crumbs and butter; pat onto the bottom of an ungreased 13-in. x 9-in. baking pan.

2. In a microwave, heat milk and 1 cup chocolate chips; stir until smooth. Pour over crust. Sprinkle with remaining chips.

3. Bake at 350° for 10-12 minutes or until chips begin to melt but do not lose their shape. Cool on a wire rack.

Chocolate Ganache Torte

Here's to that chocolate fix we all need. Cream makes it extra rich.

KATHY KITTELL, LENEXA, KANSAS

PREP: 40 MIN. • **BAKE:** 20 MIN. + COOLING • **MAKES:** 12 SERVINGS

- ¾ cup butter, softened
- 1½ cups sugar
- 1 egg
- 1 teaspoon vanilla extract
- 1 cup buttermilk
- ¾ cup sour cream
- 2 cups all-purpose flour
- ⅔ cup baking cocoa
- 1 teaspoon baking soda
- ¼ teaspoon salt

FILLING:
- 4 ounces semisweet chocolate, chopped
- 1 cup heavy whipping cream
- ½ teaspoon vanilla extract

GANACHE:
- ¾ cup heavy whipping cream
- 8 ounces semisweet chocolate, chopped
- ¼ cup butter, cubed

1. In a large bowl, cream butter and sugar until light and fluffy. Beat in egg and vanilla. Combine buttermilk and sour cream. Combine the flour, cocoa, baking soda and salt; add to creamed mixture alternately with buttermilk mixture, beating well after each addition.

2. Pour into two greased and waxed paper-lined 9-in. round baking pans. Bake at 350° for 20-25 minutes or until a toothpick comes out clean. Cool 10 minutes; remove from pans to wire racks to cool completely.

3. In a heavy saucepan, melt chocolate with cream over low heat. Remove from the heat; stir in vanilla. Transfer to a small mixing bowl; chill until slightly thickened, stirring occasionally. Beat on medium speed until light and fluffy. Chill until mixture achieves spreading consistency.

4. For ganache, in a heavy saucepan, bring cream just to a boil. Remove from the heat; stir in chocolate and butter until melted. Chill until slightly thickened. Place one cake layer on a serving plate; spread with filling. Top with remaining cake layer. Slowly pour ganache over top of cake.

Chocolate Cheesecake

This luscious cheesecake has a hint of almond in the creamy chocolate filling. Just one slice and your sweet tooth will rejoice!

LORI COULTHARD, LARAMIE, WYOMING

PREP: 20 MIN • **BAKE:** 45 MIN. + CHILLING • **MAKES:** 12 SERVINGS

- 1¼ **cups graham cracker crumbs (about 20 squares)**
- ½ **cup sugar**
- ¼ **cup baking cocoa**
- 6 **tablespoons butter, melted**

FILLING:
- 3 **packages (8 ounces each) cream cheese, softened**
- ¾ **cup sugar**
- 3 **eggs, lightly beaten**
- 1 **cup (6 ounces) semisweet chocolate chips, melted**
- 1 **teaspoon almond extract**
- ½ **teaspoon vanilla extract**

TOPPING:
- ¼ **cup semisweet chocolate chips**
- ⅓ **cup heavy whipping cream**
- 1 **tablespoon honey**

1. In a large bowl, combine the cracker crumbs, sugar and cocoa; stir in butter until crumbly. Press onto the bottom and 1-in. up the side of a greased 9-in. springform pan; set aside.

2. In a small bowl, beat cream cheese and sugar until smooth. Add eggs; beat on low speed just until combined. Stir in melted chocolate and extracts just until blended. Pour into crust.

3. Bake at 350° for 45-50 minutes or until center is almost set. Cool on a wire rack for 10 minutes. Carefully run knife around the edge of pan to loosen; cool 1 hour longer. Refrigerate until completely cooled.

4. In a small saucepan over low heat, melt the chocolate chips, cream and honey; stir until smooth. Remove from the heat; cool for 5 minutes. Pour topping over the cheesecake. Chill for at least 4 hours or until topping is set.

Molten Chocolate Cakes

I recently came across this wonderful recipe for little oh-so-chocolaty cakes and I just had to make them. My family loves the melty centers.

DEANNA KYMER, BROOMFIELD, COLORADO

PREP: 25 MIN. • **BAKE:** 15 MIN. • **MAKES:** 8 SERVINGS

  8 **ounces semisweet chocolate, chopped**
  1 **cup butter, cubed**
  5 **eggs**
  4 **egg yolks**
  2 **cups confectioners' sugar**
  ¾ **cup all-purpose flour**

1. In a large microwave-safe bowl, melt chocolate and butter; stir until smooth. Cool slightly. Add the eggs, egg yolks and confectioners' sugar; mix well. Stir in flour until blended. Pour into eight greased 6-oz. custard cups.

2. Place custard cups on a baking sheet. Bake at 425° for 15-16 minutes or until a thermometer inserted near the center reads 160°. Remove from the oven and let stand for 1 minute. Run a knife around edges of cups; invert onto dessert plates. Serve immediately.

Chocolate Mint Crisps

If you like chocolate and mint, you can't help but love these delicious crispy cookies with their creamy icing. We always make them for the holidays and guests can never seem to eat just one!

KAREN ANN BLAND, GOVE, KANSAS

PREP: 20 MIN. + CHILLING • **BAKE:** 15 MIN./BATCH + STANDING
MAKES: 6½ DOZEN

  1½ **cups packed brown sugar**
  ¾ **cup butter, cubed**
  2 **tablespoons plus 1½ teaspoons water**
  2 **cups (12 ounces) semisweet chocolate chips**
  2 **eggs**
  2½ **cups all-purpose flour**
  1¼ **teaspoons baking soda**
  ½ **teaspoon salt**
  3 **packages (4.67 ounces each) mint Andes candies**

1. In a heavy saucepan, combine the brown sugar, butter and water. Cook and stir over low heat until butter is melted and mixture is smooth. Remove from the heat; stir in chocolate chips until melted.

2. Transfer to a bowl. Let stand for 10 minutes. With mixer on high speed, add eggs one at a time, beating well after each addition. Combine the flour, baking soda and salt; add to chocolate mixture, beating on low until blended. Cover and refrigerate for 8 hours or overnight.

3. Roll dough into 1-in. balls. Place 3 in. apart on lightly greased baking sheets. Bake at 350° for 11-13 minutes or until edges are set and tops are puffed and cracked (cookies will become crisp after cooling).

4. Immediately top each cookie with a mint. Let stand for 1-2 minutes; spread over cookie. Remove to wire racks; let stand until chocolate is set and cookies are cooled.

Bakeshop TIP

Customize Your Crisps

If you like a softer cookie, bake the Chocolate Mint Crisps for about 11 minutes. For a crispy texture, stick to the higher end of the range provided. Or try some of both; family members are sure to have their favorites!

Chocolate Mini Loaves

Rich and moist, these special mini breads will remind you of pound cake. Slice them for snacking or to serve as dessert with a cup of coffee or tea.

ELIZABETH DOWNEY, EVART, MICHIGAN

PREP: 15 MIN. • **BAKE:** 30 MIN. + COOLING
MAKES: 5 MINI LOAVES (6 SLICES EACH)

- ½ cup butter, softened
- ⅔ cup packed brown sugar
- 1 cup (6 ounces) semisweet chocolate chips, melted
- 2 eggs
- 2 teaspoons vanilla extract
- 2½ cups all-purpose flour
- 1 teaspoon baking powder
- 1 teaspoon baking soda
- 1½ cups applesauce
- ½ cup miniature semisweet chocolate chips

GLAZE:
- ½ cup semisweet chocolate chips
- 1 tablespoon butter
- 5 teaspoons water
- ½ cup confectioners' sugar
- ¼ teaspoon vanilla extract
- Dash salt

1. In a large bowl, cream butter and brown sugar until light and fluffy. Beat in the melted chocolate chips, eggs and vanilla. Combine the flour, baking powder and baking soda; add to creamed mixture alternately with applesauce just until moistened. Fold in miniature chips.

2. Divide batter among five greased 5¾-in. x 3-in. x 2-in. loaf pans, about 1 cup in each. Bake at 350° for 30-40 minutes or until a toothpick inserted near the center comes out clean. Cool for 10 minutes before removing from pans to wire racks to cool completely.

3. For glaze, combine the chocolate chips, butter and water in a saucepan; cook and stir over low heat until chocolate is melted. Remove from the heat; stir in confectioners' sugar, vanilla and salt until smooth. Drizzle over loaves.

Editor's Note: *Two 8-in. x 4-in. x 2-in. loaf pans may be used; bake for 50-55 minutes.*

Chocolate Truffle Cake

This tender, luxurious layer cake is perfect for chocolate lovers. With a ganache glaze and a fabulous bittersweet filling, the indulgence is so worth it!

JO ANN KOERKENMEIER, DAMIANSVILLE, ILLINOIS

PREP: 35 MIN. + CHILLING • **BAKE:** 25 MIN. + COOLING
MAKES: 16 SERVINGS

- 2½ cups 2% milk
- 1 cup butter, cubed
- 8 ounces semisweet chocolate, chopped
- 3 eggs
- 2 teaspoons vanilla extract
- 2⅔ cups all-purpose flour
- 2 cups sugar
- 1 teaspoon baking soda
- ½ teaspoon salt

FILLING:
- 6 tablespoons butter, cubed
- 4 ounces bittersweet chocolate, chopped
- 2½ cups confectioners' sugar
- ½ cup heavy whipping cream

GANACHE:
- ⅔ cup heavy whipping cream
- 10 ounces semisweet chocolate, chopped

1. In a large saucepan, cook the milk, butter and chocolate over low heat until melted. Remove from the heat; let stand for 10 minutes.

2. In a bowl, beat the eggs, vanilla and chocolate mixture until smooth. Combine flour, sugar, baking soda and salt; gradually beat into chocolate mixture (batter will be thin).

3. Transfer to three greased and floured 9-in. round baking pans. Bake at 325° for 25-30 minutes or until a toothpick inserted near the center comes out clean. Cool for 10 minutes before removing from pans to wire racks to cool completely.

4. For filling, in a small saucepan, melt butter and chocolate. Stir in confectioners' sugar and cream until smooth.

5. For ganache, in a small saucepan, bring cream just to a boil. Add chocolate; whisk until smooth. Cool, stirring occasionally, until ganache reaches a spreading consistency.

6. Place one cake layer on a serving plate; spread with half of the filling. Repeat layers. Top with the remaining cake layer. Spread ganache over top and sides of cake. Store in the refrigerator.

Candy Bar Cheesecake

With this recipe, you can easily create a cheesecake that tastes like a fancy store-bought treat. It's always requested when I'm asked to bring dessert to a function.

JULIE CERVENKA, ST. LOUIS, MISSOURI

PREP: 25 MIN. • **BAKE:** 1¼ HOURS + COOLING • **MAKES:** 12 SERVINGS

1¾ cups crushed chocolate wafers (about 28 wafers)
¼ cup sugar
⅓ cup butter, melted
FILLING:
3 packages (8 ounces each) cream cheese, softened
1 can (14 ounces) sweetened condensed milk
1 cup chocolate syrup
2 teaspoons vanilla extract
3 eggs, lightly beaten
6 Snickers candy bars (2.07 ounces each), coarsely chopped, divided
Additional chocolate syrup

1. In a small bowl, combine wafer crumbs and sugar; stir in butter. Press onto the bottom and 1½ in. up the sides of a greased 9-in. springform pan.

2. Place pan on a double thickness of heavy-duty foil (about 18 in. square); securely wrap foil around pan. Place pan on a baking sheet. Bake at 325° for 12 minutes. Cool on a wire rack.

3. In a large bowl, beat the cream cheese, milk, chocolate syrup and vanilla until smooth. Add eggs; beat just until combined. Stir in 2½ cups chopped candy bars. Pour into crust. Place springform pan in a large baking pan; add 1 in. of hot water to larger pan.

4. Bake at 325° for 75-80 minutes or until center is just set and top appears dull. Remove springform pan from water bath. Cool on a wire rack for 10 minutes. Carefully run a knife around edge of pan to loosen; cool 1 hour longer. Refrigerate overnight.

5. Top with remaining chopped candy bars; drizzle with additional chocolate syrup.

Muffins & Scones

I Want S'more Muffins

These fun muffins feature a fluffy marshmallow creme in the center. The s'more flavors are sure to bring back fond childhood memories.

SALLY SIBTHORPE, SHELBY TOWNSHIP, MICHIGAN

PREP: 20 MIN. • **BAKE:** 15 MIN. • **MAKES:** 6 MUFFINS

- 3 tablespoons butter, softened
- ¼ cup packed brown sugar
- 4 teaspoons sugar
- 1 egg
- ⅓ cup sour cream
- 3 tablespoons 2% milk
- ⅔ cup all-purpose flour
- ½ cup graham cracker crumbs
- ¼ teaspoon salt
- ¼ teaspoon baking powder
- ¼ teaspoon ground cinnamon
- ⅛ teaspoon baking soda
- ⅓ cup milk chocolate chips
- 6 tablespoons marshmallow creme

1. In a small bowl, cream butter and sugars until light and fluffy. Beat in the egg, then the sour cream and milk. Combine the flour, graham cracker crumbs, salt, baking powder, cinnamon and baking soda; beat into creamed mixture just until moistened. Fold in chocolate chips.

2. Coat six muffin cups with cooking spray; fill one-fourth full with batter. Spoon 1 tablespoon marshmallow creme into each muffin cup. Top with remaining batter.

3. Bake at 400° for 14-16 minutes or until a toothpick inserted near the center comes out clean. Cool for 5 minutes before removing from pan to a wire rack. Serve warm.

Cream Cheese Cranberry Muffins

Moist and packed with colorful, nutritious berries, these marvelous muffins are a seasonal specialty. They are light and tasty, and they freeze very well.

LEONARD KESZLER, BISMARCK, NORTH DAKOTA

PREP: 15 MIN. • **BAKE:** 20 MIN. • **MAKES:** 2 DOZEN

- 1 cup butter, softened
- 1 package (8 ounces) cream cheese, softened
- 1½ cups sugar
- 4 eggs
- 1½ teaspoons vanilla extract
- 2 cups all-purpose flour
- 1½ teaspoons baking powder
- ½ teaspoon salt
- 2 cups fresh or frozen cranberries
- ½ cup chopped pecans

DRIZZLE:
- 2 cups confectioners' sugar
- 3 tablespoons 2% milk

1. In a large bowl, cream the butter, cream cheese and sugar until light and fluffy. Add eggs, one at a time, beating well after each addition. Beat in vanilla. Combine the flour, baking powder and salt; stir into creamed mixture just until moistened. Fold in cranberries and pecans.

2. Fill greased or paper-lined muffin cups three-fourths full. Bake at 350° for 20-25 minutes or until a toothpick inserted near the center comes out clean. Cool for 5 minutes before removing from pans to wire racks.

3. Combine confectioners' sugar and milk; drizzle over muffins.

Iced Raspberry Cheesecake Muffins

These moist, cake-like muffins are flavored with raspberries and walnuts. The sweet drizzle of icing makes them pretty enough to serve guests.

PHYLLIS EISMANN SCHMALZ, KANSAS CITY, KANSAS

PREP: 25 MIN. • **BAKE:** 25 MIN. + COOLING • **MAKES:** 8 MUFFINS

- 1 **package (3 ounces) cream cheese, softened**
- 2 **tablespoons butter, softened**
- ½ **cup sugar**
- 1 **egg**
- 1 **egg white**
- 3 **tablespoons buttermilk**
- ½ **teaspoon vanilla extract**
- ¾ **cup all-purpose flour**
- ½ **teaspoon baking powder**
- ⅛ **teaspoon baking soda**
- ⅛ **teaspoon salt**
- ¾ **cup fresh raspberries**
- 2 **tablespoons chopped walnuts, toasted**
- ¼ **cup confectioners' sugar**
- 1 **teaspoon 2% milk**

1. In a small bowl, cream the cream cheese, butter and sugar until smooth. Beat in egg and egg white. Beat in buttermilk and vanilla. Combine the flour, baking powder, baking soda and salt; add to creamed mixture just until moistened. Fold in raspberries and walnuts.

2. Fill paper-lined muffin cups three-fourths full. Bake at 350° for 25-28 minutes or until a toothpick inserted in muffin comes out clean. Cool for 5 minutes before removing from pan to a wire rack to cool completely.

3. Combine confectioners' sugar and milk; drizzle icing over the muffins.

Pecan Pie Mini Muffins

While these are delicious year-round, you could easily turn them into a Christmas gift. They look festive on a tray wrapped in red or green cellophane or tucked into a cookie plate. And don't forget to include the recipe so your recipient can enjoy this treat over and over again!

PAT SCHRAND, ENTERPRISE, ALABAMA

PREP: 10 MIN. • **BAKE:** 25 MIN. • **MAKES:** ABOUT 2½ DOZEN

  1 **cup packed brown sugar**
  ½ **cup all-purpose flour**
  1 **cup chopped pecans**
  ⅔ **cup butter, melted**
  2 **eggs, lightly beaten**

1. In a large bowl, combine the brown sugar, flour and pecans; set aside. Combine butter and eggs. Stir into brown sugar mixture.

2. Fill greased and floured miniature muffin cups two-thirds full. Bake at 350° for 22-25 minutes or until a toothpick inserted near the center comes out clean. Immediately remove from pans to wire racks to cool.

Editor's Note: This recipe uses only ½ cup flour.

Hazelnut Chip Scones

When I made a friend's scone recipe, I didn't have enough milk, so I substituted hazelnut-flavored coffee creamer and added chocolate chips. Everyone loved the results!

ELISA LOCHRIDGE, BEAVERTON, OREGON

PREP: 20 MIN. • **BAKE:** 15 MIN. • **MAKES:** 16 SCONES

  4 **cups all-purpose flour**
  3 **tablespoons sugar**
  4 **teaspoons baking powder**
  ½ **teaspoon salt**
  ½ **teaspoon cream of tartar**
  ¾ **cup cold butter**
  1 **egg, separated**
  1½ **cups refrigerated hazelnut nondairy creamer or half-and-half cream**
  1½ **cups semisweet chocolate chips**
      Additional sugar

SPICED BUTTER:
  ½ **cup butter, softened**
  3 **tablespoons brown sugar**
  ¼ **teaspoon ground cinnamon**
  ¼ **teaspoon ground allspice**
  ⅛ **teaspoon ground nutmeg**

1. In a large bowl, combine the first five ingredients; cut in butter until crumbly. In a small bowl, whisk egg yolk and creamer; add to dry ingredients just until moistened. Fold in chocolate chips.

2. Turn onto a floured surface; knead 10 times. Divide dough in half. Pat each portion into a 7-in. circle; cut into eight wedges. Separate wedges and place on greased baking sheets.

3. Beat egg white; brush over dough. Sprinkle with additional sugar. Bake at 425° for 15-18 minutes or until golden brown. Meanwhile, in a small bowl, combine the spiced butter ingredients; beat until smooth. Serve with warm scones.

Cranberry Gingerbread Muffins

This wonderful treat can be served as a breakfast or brunch bread. The spices and cranberries really put people in the holiday spirit!

LISA VARNER, EL PASO, TEXAS

PREP: 20 MIN. • **BAKE:** 20 MIN. • **MAKES:** 1 DOZEN

  2¼ **cups all-purpose flour**
  ½ **cup packed brown sugar**
  2 **teaspoons ground ginger**
  1 **teaspoon baking powder**
  1 **teaspoon ground cinnamon**
  ¾ **teaspoon salt**
  ½ **teaspoon baking soda**
  1 **egg**
  ¾ **cup water**
  ½ **cup fat-free plain yogurt**
  ⅓ **cup molasses**
  ¼ **cup canola oil**
  1 **cup fresh or frozen cranberries, coarsely chopped**

1. In a large bowl, combine the first seven ingredients. In a small bowl, combine the egg, water, yogurt, molasses and oil. Stir into dry ingredients just until moistened. Fold in cranberries.

2. Coat muffin cups with cooking spray or use paper liners; fill ¾ full with batter. Bake at 350° for 18-22 minutes or until a toothpick comes out clean. Cool for 5 minutes before removing from pan to a wire rack.

Pumpkin Cheesecake Muffins

My mother-in-law came up with these tender treats by combining a few of her favorite muffin recipes. Chock-full of pumpkin, they feature both a sweet cream cheese filling and crunchy praline topping.

LISA POWELSON, SCOTT CITY, KANSAS

PREP: 25 MIN. • **BAKE:** 15 MIN. • **MAKES:** 2 DOZEN

  3 **cups all-purpose flour**
  2 **cups sugar**
  2 **teaspoons baking soda**
  2 **teaspoons baking powder**
  1 **teaspoon salt**
  1 **teaspoon ground cinnamon**
  4 **eggs**
  1 **can (15 ounces) solid-pack pumpkin**
  1½ **cups canola oil**
CREAM CHEESE FILLING:
  1 **package (8 ounces) cream cheese, softened**
  ½ **cup sugar**
  1 **egg**
  1 **tablespoon all-purpose flour**
PRALINE TOPPING:
  ⅔ **cup chopped pecans**
  ⅓ **cup packed brown sugar**
  2 **tablespoons sour cream**

1. In a large bowl, combine the first six ingredients. In another bowl, whisk the eggs, pumpkin and oil. Stir into dry ingredients just until moistened. Fill greased or paper-lined muffin cups one-third full.

2. For filling, beat the cream cheese, sugar, egg and flour until smooth. Drop by tablespoonfuls into center of each muffin. Top with remaining batter.

3. For topping, in a small bowl, combine the pecans, brown sugar and sour cream; spoon over batter. Bake at 400° for 15-18 minutes or until a toothpick inserted in the muffin comes out clean. Cool for 5 minutes before removing from pans to wire racks. Serve warm. Refrigerate leftovers.

Mango Colada Scones

The mango adds a great tropical flavor to these scones. I love to serve these for tea or for breakfast.

CHERYL PERRY, HERTFORD, NORTH CAROLINA

PREP: 20 MIN. • **BAKE:** 15 MIN. • **MAKES:** 10 SCONES

- 2½ **cups biscuit/baking mix**
- 2 **tablespoons brown sugar**
- 3 **tablespoons cold butter**
- ½ **cup thawed non-alcoholic pina colada mix**
- 1 **cup chopped peeled mango**
- 3 **tablespoons flaked coconut**
- ¼ **cup macadamia nuts, chopped**

SHORT & SWEET

1. In a large bowl, combine biscuit mix and brown sugar. Cut in 2 tablespoons butter until mixture resembles coarse crumbs. Stir in pina colada mix just until moistened. Fold in mango.

2. Turn onto a floured surface; knead 10 times. Pat into a 9-in. x 7-in. rectangle. Cut into 10 rectangles; separate rectangles and place on a greased baking sheet. Melt remaining butter; brush over scones.

3. Bake at 400° for 12 minutes. Sprinkle with coconut and nuts; bake 2-4 minutes longer or until golden brown. Serve warm.

Banana Brickle Muffins

Toffee bits add great flavor to these delicious banana muffins. Serve them at breakfast, lunch, dinner or as a special snack.

ANDRA COGAN, GROSSE POINTE PARK, MICHIGAN

PREP: 15 MIN. • **BAKE:** 20 MIN. • **MAKES:** 1 DOZEN

2 cups all-purpose flour
½ cup packed brown sugar
1 tablespoon baking powder
1 cup mashed ripe bananas
½ cup milk
⅓ cup canola oil
1 egg
1 package (8 ounces) brickle toffee bits, divided

1. In a large bowl, combine the flour, brown sugar and baking powder. In a small bowl, combine the bananas, milk, oil and egg. Stir into dry ingredients just until moistened. Fold in 1 cup toffee bits.

2. Fill greased muffin cups three-fourths full. Sprinkle with remaining toffee bits. Bake at 350° for 18-20 minutes or until a toothpick inserted near the center comes out clean. Cool for 5 minutes before removing from pan to a wire rack. Serve warm.

Cherry Almond Muffins

As a kid, I loved doughnuts filled with custard or jelly. So I decided to experiment with fillings in muffins. The result was this terrific recipe. These fancy muffins are almost like pastries with their sweet-tart, rich and creamy centers.

JOHN MONTGOMERY, FORTUNA, CALIFORNIA

PREP: 20 MIN. • **BAKE:** 30 MIN. • **MAKES:** 7 MUFFINS

1¾ cups all-purpose flour
½ cup plus 1 tablespoon sugar
½ teaspoon baking powder
½ teaspoon baking soda
¼ teaspoon salt
½ cup cold butter, cubed
1 egg
¾ cup sour cream
1 teaspoon almond extract

FILLING:
1 package (8 ounces) cream cheese, softened
1 egg
¼ cup sugar
½ teaspoon vanilla extract
¾ cup cherry preserves, warmed

TOPPING:
⅓ cup all-purpose flour
2 tablespoons sugar
2 tablespoons cold butter
⅓ cup chopped sliced almonds

1. In a large bowl, combine flour, sugar, baking powder, baking soda and salt. Cut in butter until the mixture resembles coarse crumbs. Beat the egg, sour cream and extract until smooth; stir into dry ingredients just until moistened (batter will be thick).

2. In a large bowl, beat cream cheese, egg, sugar and vanilla until smooth. In a saucepan over low heat, warm preserves. For topping, combine flour and sugar in a small bowl; cut in butter until crumbly. Stir in almonds.

3. Fill greased jumbo muffin cups half full with batter. Divide cream cheese filling and preserves evenly among muffin cups; swirl gently. Cover with remaining batter. Sprinkle with topping.

4. Bake at 350° for 30-35 minutes or until a toothpick inserted in muffin comes out clean. Cool for 5 minutes before removing from pans to wire racks. Serve warm.

Editor's Note: *Recipe may be prepared in 14 regular-size muffin cups; bake muffins for 20-25 minutes.*

Walnut Orange Muffins

These glazed orange muffins are so moist, butter isn't needed. Serve them warm with mugs of coffee or hot apple cider.

PAT HABIGER, SPEARVILLE, KANSAS

PREP: 20 MIN. • **BAKE:** 20 MIN. • **MAKES:** ABOUT 1 DOZEN

- 1 cup butter, softened
- 1 cup sugar
- 2 eggs
- 1 cup buttermilk
- 4 teaspoons grated orange peel
- 2 cups all-purpose flour
- 1 teaspoon baking soda
- ¼ cup chopped walnuts
- 1 cup orange juice
- ½ cup packed brown sugar

1. In a bowl, cream butter and sugar until light and fluffy. Beat in the eggs, buttermilk and orange peel. Combine flour and baking soda; add to creamed mixture just until blended. Stir in walnuts.

2. Fill greased or paper-lined muffin cups two-thirds full. Bake at 350° for 20 minutes or until a toothpick inserted in the muffin comes out clean.

3. In a bowl, combine the orange juice and brown sugar until dissolved. Spoon over warm muffins. Cool for 5 minutes before removing from pan to a wire rack.

Oatmeal Apricot Scones

Besides farming and raising cattle, our family has a home bakery that serves area restaurants and health food stores. We dry lots of local fruit for use in our recipes, like the apricots in these golden scones that are so popular with our customers.

LINDA SWANSON, RIVERSIDE WASHINGTON

PREP: 25 MIN. • **BAKE:** 15 MIN. • **MAKES:** 6 SCONES

- 1½ cups all-purpose flour
- ½ cup quick-cooking oats
- ¼ cup sugar
- 2½ teaspoons baking powder
- ¼ teaspoon salt
- ⅓ cup cold butter, cubed
- 2 eggs
- ¼ cup sour cream
- 1 tablespoon milk
- ¾ cup finely chopped dried apricots

FILLING:
- 3 tablespoons brown sugar
- 1 tablespoon quick-cooking oats
- 1 tablespoon butter, softened
- Additional sugar

1. In a bowl, combine the dry ingredients; cut in butter until mixture resembles fine crumbs. In a small bowl, beat eggs; set aside 1 tablespoon for glaze. In another bowl, combine sour cream, milk and remaining beaten eggs; add apricots. Stir into crumb mixture until the dough clings together.

2. Turn onto a lightly floured surface; knead 12-15 times. Divide dough in half. Pat one portion into a 7-in. circle on a greased baking sheet. Combine the brown sugar, oats and butter; sprinkle over dough. Roll out remaining dough into a 7-in. circle; place over filling.

3. Brush with reserved egg; sprinkle with additional sugar. Cut into wedges but do not separate. Bake at 400° for 15-20 minutes or until scones are golden brown. Cool slightly; cut again if necessary. Serve warm.

Bakeshop HOW-TO

Making Scones

Most scone recipes suggest patting the dough into a circle. For proper baking, be sure the circle meets the dimensions noted in the recipe.

Cut the dough into wedges with a dough scraper or knife. It may be helpful to flour the utensil's edge between cuts to prevent the dough from sticking to it.

Whole Wheat Blueberry Muffins

Whole wheat flour gives a nutritious boost to these yummy muffins packed with juicy blueberries. Fresh from the oven, they'll warm you up on cold winter days.

SHEILA SIEM, CALUMET, MICHIGAN

PREP: 15 MIN. • **BAKE:** 20 MIN. • **MAKES:** 1½ DOZEN

- 1½ cups all-purpose flour
- 1 cup whole wheat flour
- ½ cup sugar
- 2 teaspoons baking powder
- ½ teaspoon baking soda
- ½ teaspoon salt
- ⅛ teaspoon ground nutmeg
- 2 eggs
- 1 cup buttermilk
- ½ cup canola oil
- 2 cups fresh or frozen blueberries

1. In a large bowl, combine the flours, sugar, baking powder, baking soda, salt and nutmeg. In another bowl, beat the eggs, buttermilk and oil. Stir into dry ingredients just until moistened. Fold in blueberries.

2. Fill greased or paper-lined muffin cups three-fourths full. Bake at 375° for 18-20 minutes or until a toothpick inserted in muffin comes out clean. Cool for 5 minutes before removing from pans to wire racks. Serve warm.

Editor's Note: *If using frozen blueberries, use without thawing to avoid discoloring the batter.*

Chocolate Chip Mini Muffins

I bake a lot of different muffins, but this is the recipe I use the most. Their small size makes them hard to resist!

JOANNE SHEW CHUK, ST. BENEDICT, SASKATCHEWAN

PREP: 15 MIN. • **BAKE:** 10 MIN. • **MAKES:** ABOUT 3 DOZEN

- ½ **cup sugar**
- ¼ **cup shortening**
- 1 **egg**
- ½ **cup 2% milk**
- ½ **teaspoon vanilla extract**
- 1 **cup all-purpose flour**
- ½ **teaspoon baking soda**
- ½ **teaspoon baking powder**
- ¼ **teaspoon salt**
- ⅔ **cup miniature semisweet chocolate chips**

1. In a large bowl, cream sugar and shortening until light and fluffy. Beat in egg, then milk and vanilla. Combine the flour, baking soda, baking powder and salt; add to butter mixture just until combined. Fold in chocolate chips.

2. Spoon about 1 tablespoon of batter into each greased or paper-lined mini-muffin cup. Bake at 375° for 10-13 minutes or until a toothpick inserted near the center comes out clean. Cool in pans for 5 minutes before removing to wire racks. Serve warm.

Apple Streusel Muffins

My husband and children enjoy these tender coffee cake-like muffins as a quick breakfast or snack on the run. Add the drizzle of glaze and they're pretty enough for company.

DULCY GRACE, ROARING SPRING, PENNSYLVANIA

PREP: 20 MIN. • **BAKE:** 15 MIN. + COOLING • **MAKES:** 1 DOZEN

- 2 **cups all-purpose flour**
- 1 **cup sugar**
- 1 **teaspoon baking powder**
- ½ **teaspoon baking soda**
- ½ **teaspoon salt**
- 2 **eggs**
- ½ **cup butter, melted**
- 1¼ **teaspoons vanilla extract**
- 1½ **cups chopped peeled tart apples**

STREUSEL TOPPING:
- ⅓ **cup packed brown sugar**
- 1 **tablespoon all-purpose flour**
- ⅛ **teaspoon ground cinnamon**
- 1 **tablespoon cold butter**

GLAZE:
- 1½ **cups confectioners' sugar**
- 1 **to 2 tablespoons milk**
- 1 **teaspoon butter, melted**
- ¼ **teaspoon vanilla extract**
- ⅛ **teaspoon salt**

1. In a large bowl, combine the flour, sugar, baking powder, baking soda and salt. In another bowl, combine the eggs, butter and vanilla; stir into dry ingredients just until moistened (batter will be stiff). Fold in apples.

2. Fill greased or paper-lined muffin cups three-fourths full. In a small bowl, combine the brown sugar, flour and cinnamon; cut in butter until crumbly. Sprinkle over batter.

3. Bake at 375° for 15-20 minutes or until a toothpick inserted near the center comes out clean. Cool for 5 minutes before removing from pan to a wire rack to cool completely. Combine glaze ingredients; drizzle over muffins.

Sugar Plum Scones

Dried plums and a sprinkling of coarse sugar make these treats delightfully Christmasy. Spread them with butter, cream cheese or preserves and revel in their holiday flavor.

JULIE MCQUISTON, BRADENTON, FLORIDA

PREP: 20 MIN. • **BAKE:** 15 MIN. • **MAKES:** 1 DOZEN

- 3 **cups all-purpose flour**
- ½ **cup sugar**
- 3 **teaspoons baking powder**
- ½ **teaspoon salt**
- ½ **cup cold butter**
- 1 **egg**
- 1 **cup buttermilk**
- 1 **cup pitted dried plums, chopped**
- 1 **tablespoon grated orange peel**

TOPPING:
- 1 **egg**
- 1 **tablespoon 2% milk**
- 2 **tablespoons coarse sugar**

1. In a large bowl, combine the flour, sugar, baking powder and salt. Cut in butter until mixture resembles coarse crumbs. Whisk egg and buttermilk; stir into crumb mixture just until moistened. Stir in plums and orange peel. Turn onto a floured surface; knead 10 times.

2. Divide dough in half; pat each into a 7-in. circle. Cut each into six wedges. Separate wedges and place on a greased baking sheet. Combine egg and milk; brush over scones. Sprinkle with coarse sugar. Bake at 375° for 15-20 minutes or until golden brown. Serve warm.

Raspberry Jam Muffins

I like to linger over a cup of coffee and a warm, sweet treat on weekend mornings. These muffins are perfect because making them ties up so little time in the kitchen. I sometimes serve them with holiday meals for something different (and deceptively easy).

TERESA RAAB, TUSTIN, MICHIGAN

PREP/TOTAL TIME: 30 MIN. • **MAKES:** 1 DOZEN

- 2 **cups biscuit/baking mix**
- 2 **tablespoons sugar**
- ¼ **cup cold butter, cubed**
- ⅔ **cup 2% milk**
- ¼ **cup raspberry jam**

GLAZE:
- ½ **cup confectioners' sugar**
- 2 **teaspoons warm water**
- ¼ **teaspoon vanilla extract**

1. In a large bowl, combine biscuit mix and sugar. Cut in butter until the mixture resembles coarse crumbs. Stir in milk just until moistened (batter will be thick).

2. Spoon about 1 tablespoon of batter into 12 paper-lined muffin cups. Top with 1 teaspoon jam. Spoon the remaining batter (about 1 tablespoon each) over jam.

3. Bake at 425° for 12-14 minutes or until a toothpick inserted near the center comes out clean. Cool in pans for 5 minutes.

4. Meanwhile, in a small bowl, combine glaze ingredients until smooth. Remove muffins to a wire rack. Drizzle glaze over warm muffins. Serve warm.

Bakeshop TIP

Tender Muffins & Scones

To ensure tender muffins and scones, mix all of the dry ingredients well before adding wet ingredients, including already-beaten eggs. Stir in the wet ingredients just until the batter or dough comes together. (Muffin batter may contain some lumps, which is normal.) By taking care to avoid overmixing, you'll ensure a finished product that's tender, not tough or chewy.

Lemon-Yogurt Tea Cakes

Light, soft and tangy, these little lemon cakes will be the belle of the brunch. They're also great for lunch, supper or snacking.

RUTH BURRUS, ZIONSVILLE, INDIANA

PREP: 20 MIN. • **BAKE:** 20 MIN. + COOLING • **MAKES:** ABOUT 1 DOZEN

2¼ cups all-purpose flour
1 cup sugar
¾ teaspoon baking powder
½ teaspoon baking soda
½ teaspoon salt
½ cup cold butter
1 cup (8 ounces) fat-free plain yogurt

3 egg whites
2 tablespoons lemon juice
4 teaspoons grated lemon peel
1 teaspoon lemon extract

1. In a large bowl, combine the flour, sugar, baking powder, baking soda and salt; cut in butter until mixture resembles coarse crumbs. Whisk the yogurt, egg whites, lemon juice, peel and extract; stir into crumb mixture just until moistened.

2. Fill greased or paper-lined muffin cups three-fourths full. Bake at 350° for 18-22 minutes or until a toothpick inserted near the center comes out clean. Cool for 10 minutes before removing from pan to a wire rack to cool completely.

Coffee Cakes & Sweet Rolls

Peach Cobbler Coffee Cake

My family took an immediate liking to this special coffee cake. I sometimes make it with apricots and apricot filling, and it's delicious, too.

VIRGINIA KRITES, CRIDERSVILLE, OHIO

PREP: 25 MIN. • **BAKE:** 70 MIN. + COOLING • **MAKES:** 12 SERVINGS

- 1 cup butter, softened
- 1 cup sugar
- 2 eggs
- 3 teaspoons vanilla extract
- 3 cups all-purpose flour
- 1 teaspoon baking powder
- 1 teaspoon baking soda
- ½ teaspoon salt
- 1¼ cups sour cream
- 1 can (21 ounces) peach pie filling
- 1 can (15¼ ounces) sliced peaches, drained

TOPPING:
- 1 cup packed brown sugar
- 1 cup all-purpose flour
- ½ cup quick-cooking oats
- ¼ teaspoon ground cinnamon
- ½ cup cold butter, cubed

GLAZE:
- 1 cup confectioners' sugar
- 1 to 2 tablespoons 2% milk

1. In a large bowl, cream butter and sugar until light and fluffy. Add eggs, one at a time, beating well after each addition. Beat in vanilla. Combine flour, baking powder, baking soda and salt; add to creamed mixture alternately with sour cream. Beat just until combined.

2. Pour half of the batter into a greased 13-in. x 9-in. baking dish. Combine pie filling and peaches; spread over batter. Drop remaining batter by tablespoonfuls over filling.

3. For topping, combine the brown sugar, flour, oats and cinnamon in a bowl. Cut in butter until mixture is crumbly. Sprinkle over batter.

4. Bake at 350° for 70-75 minutes or until a toothpick inserted near the center comes out clean. Cool on a wire rack. In a small bowl, combine confectioners' sugar and enough milk to achieve desired consistency; drizzle glaze over the coffee cake.

Mini Toffee Rolls

I found this delicious recipe in a magazine years ago and adapted the original to make it my own. The rich, bite-sized treats are full of cinnamon flavor!

CAROL GILLESPIE, CHAMBERSBURG, PENNSYLVANIA

PREP: 20 MIN. • **BAKE:** 15 MIN. • **MAKES:** 4 DOZEN

- 6 tablespoons butter, softened
- ½ cup packed brown sugar
- 1 teaspoon ground cinnamon
- ⅓ cup milk chocolate English toffee bits
- 2 tubes (8 ounces each) refrigerated crescent rolls
- 1 cup confectioners' sugar
- 4½ teaspoons 2% milk
- ¼ teaspoon vanilla extract

1. In a small bowl, cream the butter, brown sugar and cinnamon until light and fluffy. Stir in toffee bits.

2. Separate each tube of crescent dough into four rectangles; seal perforations. Spread evenly with butter mixture. Roll up each rectangle jelly-roll style, starting with a long side.

3. Cut each into six 1-in. slices; place cut side down into two greased 8-in. square baking dishes. Bake at 375° for 14-16 minutes or until golden brown.

4. In a small bowl, combine the confectioners' sugar, milk and vanilla until smooth. Drizzle over warm rolls.

1. In a large bowl, dissolve yeast in warm water. Add the milk, buttermilk, sugar, butter, salt and 4 cups flour. Beat on medium speed until smooth. Stir in enough remaining flour to form a soft dough (dough will be sticky).

2. Turn onto a floured surface; knead until smooth and elastic, about 6-8 minutes. Place in a greased bowl, turning once to grease the top. Cover and let rise in a warm place until doubled, about 1 hour.

3. Punch dough down; turn onto a floured surface. Roll into an 18-in. x 12-in. rectangle; brush with butter. Combine the brown sugar, coffee granules and cinnamon; sprinkle over dough to within 1/2 in. of edges.

4. Roll up jelly-roll style, starting with a long side; pinch seam to seal. Cut into 12 slices. Place rolls, cut side down, in a greased 13-in. x 9-in. baking pan. Cover and let rise until doubled, about 30 minutes.

5. Bake at 350° for 22-28 minutes or until golden brown. Place pan on a wire rack. In a small bowl, beat the icing ingredients until smooth. Spread over rolls. Serve warm.

Cappuccino Cinnamon Rolls

Rich coffee flavor emboldens the filling of these gooey rolls. The icing goes on while they're still warm—and they never last long!

SHERRI COX, LUCASVILLE, OHIO

PREP: 45 MIN. + RISING • **BAKE:** 25 MIN. • **MAKES:** 1 DOZEN

- 1 package (¼ ounce) active dry yeast
- 1 cup warm water (110° to 115°)
- ¾ cup warm milk (110° to 115°)
- ½ cup warm buttermilk (110° to 115°)
- 3 tablespoons sugar
- 2 tablespoons butter, softened
- 1¼ teaspoons salt
- 5½ to 6 cups all-purpose flour

FILLING:
- ¼ cup butter, melted
- 1 cup packed brown sugar
- 4 teaspoons instant coffee granules
- 2 teaspoons ground cinnamon

ICING:
- 1½ cups confectioners' sugar
- 2 tablespoons butter, softened
- 1 to 2 tablespoons milk
- 2 teaspoons cappuccino mix
- ½ teaspoon vanilla extract

Pull-Apart Caramel Coffee Cake

The first time I made this delightful treat for a brunch party, it was a huge hit. Now I get requests every time family or friends do anything around the breakfast hour! I always keep the four simple ingredients on hand.

JAIME KEELING, KEIZER, OREGON

PREP: 10 MIN. • **BAKE:** 25 MIN. • **MAKES:** 12 SERVINGS

- 2 tubes (12 ounces each) refrigerated flaky buttermilk biscuits
- 1 cup packed brown sugar
- ½ cup heavy whipping cream
- 1 teaspoon ground cinnamon

1. Cut each biscuit into four pieces; arrange evenly in a 10-in. fluted tube pan coated with cooking spray. Combine the brown sugar, cream and cinnamon; pour over biscuits.

2. Bake at 350° for 25-30 minutes or until golden brown. Cool for 5 minutes before inverting onto a serving platter.

Maple Twist Coffee Cake

If you like maple, you will love this recipe. It is so pretty with all the twists and is always a hit when I take it to bake sales.

DEANNA RICHTER, ELMORE, MINNESOTA

PREP: 45 MIN. + RISING • **BAKE:** 20 MIN.

MAKES: 16 SERVINGS

- 1 package (¼ ounce) active dry yeast
- ¾ cup warm milk (110° to 115°)
- ¼ cup butter, softened
- 3 tablespoons sugar
- 1 egg
- 1 teaspoon maple flavoring
- ½ teaspoon salt
- 2¾ to 3 cups all-purpose flour

FILLING:
- ½ cup sugar
- ⅓ cup chopped walnuts
- 1 teaspoon ground cinnamon
- 1 teaspoon maple flavoring
- ¼ cup butter, melted

GLAZE:
- 1 cup confectioners' sugar
- 2 tablespoons butter, melted
- 1 to 2 tablespoons milk
- ½ teaspoon maple flavoring

1. In a large bowl, dissolve yeast in warm milk. Add the butter, sugar, egg, maple flavoring, salt and 1½ cups flour. Beat until smooth. Stir in enough remaining flour to form a soft dough.

2. Turn onto a floured surface; knead until smooth and elastic, about 6-8 minutes. Place in a greased bowl, turning once to grease top. Cover and let rise in a warm place until doubled, about 1 hour. Meanwhile, in a small bowl, combine the sugar, walnuts, cinnamon and maple flavoring; set aside.

3. Punch dough down. Turn onto a lightly floured surface; divide into thirds. Roll each portion into a 12-in. circle; place one circle on a greased baking sheet or 12-in. pizza pan. Spread with a third of the butter; sprinkle with a third of the filling. Repeat layers twice. Pinch edges of dough to seal.

4. Carefully place a glass in center of circle. With scissors, cut from outside edge just to the glass, forming 16 wedges. Remove glass; twist each wedge five to six times. Pinch ends to seal and tuck under. Cover and let rise until doubled, about 30 minutes.

5. Bake at 375° for 18-20 minutes or until golden brown. In a small bowl, combine glaze ingredients; set aside.

6. Carefully remove coffee cake from pan by running a metal spatula under it to loosen; transfer to a wire rack. Drizzle with the glaze.

Cranberry Almond Coffee Cake

Cranberries add delightful tartness to a coffee cake that has become a Christmas morning tradition for my family. I make my own almond paste to use when baking up this treat.

ANNE KEENAN, NEVADA CITY, CALIFORNIA

PREP: 20 MIN. • **BAKE:** 45 MIN. + COOLING • **MAKES:** 9 SERVINGS

- ½ cup almond paste (recipe on opposite page)
- 6 tablespoons butter, softened
- ½ cup plus 2 tablespoons sugar, divided
- 3 eggs
- 1⅓ cups all-purpose flour, divided
- 1 teaspoon baking powder
- 1 teaspoon almond extract
- ½ teaspoon vanilla extract
- 2¼ cups fresh or frozen cranberries

1. In a small bowl, cream almond paste, butter and ½ cup sugar until fluffy. Add two eggs, beating well after each addition. Combine 1 cup flour and baking powder; add to creamed mixture. Beat in the remaining egg and flour. Stir in extracts. Gently fold in cranberries.

2. Spread evenly into a greased 8-in. square baking dish; sprinkle with remaining sugar. Bake at 325° for 45-55 minutes or until a toothpick inserted near the center comes out clean. Cool on a wire rack.

Homemade Almond Paste

When a recipe I wanted to try called for almond paste, I decided to make my own. It saves the expense of a store-bought product and results in baked goods that are lighter in texture.

ANNE KEENAN, NEVADA CITY, CALIFORNIA

PREP: 10 MIN. + CHILLING • **MAKES:** 1½ CUPS

- 1½ cups blanched almonds
- 1½ cups confectioners' sugar
- 1 egg white
- 1½ teaspoons almond extract
- ¼ teaspoon salt

1. Place almonds in a food processor; cover and process until smooth. Add the confectioners' sugar, egg white, extract and salt; cover and process until smooth.

2. Divide almond paste into ½-cup portions; place in airtight containers. Refrigerate for up to 1 month or freeze for up to 3 months.

Classic Long Johns

I came across the recipe for these wonderful treats many years ago. You can frost them with maple or chocolate glaze, then top with nuts, jimmies, toasted coconut or sprinkles.

ANN SORGENT, FOND DU LAC, WISCONSIN

PREP: 30 MIN. + RISING • **COOK:** 5 MIN./BATCH + COOLING
MAKES: 2 DOZEN

- 2 packages (¼ ounce each) active dry yeast
- ½ cup warm water (110° to 115°)
- ½ cup half-and-half cream
- ¼ cup sugar
- ¼ cup shortening
- 1 egg
- 1 teaspoon salt
- ½ teaspoon ground nutmeg
- 3 to 3½ cups all-purpose flour
  Oil for deep-fat frying

MAPLE FROSTING:
- ¼ cup packed brown sugar
- 2 tablespoons butter
- 1 tablespoon half-and-half cream
- ⅛ teaspoon maple flavoring
- 1 cup confectioners' sugar

CHOCOLATE FROSTING:
- 2 ounces semisweet chocolate, chopped
- 2 tablespoons butter
- 1 cup confectioners' sugar
- 2 tablespoons boiling water
- 1 teaspoon vanilla extract

1. In a large bowl, dissolve yeast in warm water. Add the cream, sugar, shortening, egg, salt, nutmeg and 3 cups flour. Beat until smooth. Stir in enough remaining flour to form a soft dough (dough will be sticky).

2. Turn onto a floured surface; knead until smooth and elastic, about 6-8 minutes. Place in a greased bowl, turning once to grease the top. Cover and let rise in a warm place until doubled, about 1 hour.

3. Punch dough down; divide in half. Turn onto a lightly floured surface; roll each half into a 12-in. x 6-in. rectangle. Cut into 3-in. x 2-in. rectangles. Place on greased baking sheets. Cover and let rise in a warm place until doubled, about 30 minutes.

4. In an electric skillet or deep fryer, heat oil to 375°. Fry long johns, a few at a time, until golden brown on both sides. Drain on paper towels.

5. For maple frosting, combine brown sugar and butter in a small saucepan. Bring to a boil; cook and stir for 2 minutes or until sugar is dissolved. Remove from the heat; stir in cream and maple flavoring. Add the confectioners' sugar; beat for 1 minute or until smooth. Frost cooled long johns.

6. For chocolate frosting, in a microwave, melt chocolate and butter; stir until smooth. Stir in remaining ingredients. Spread over cooled long johns; let stand until set.

Strawberry Cheesecake Turnovers

When I first served these turnovers, folks thought I bought them from a bakery. Everyone was surprised to hear they start with refrigerated crescent rolls and pie filling.

JOLENE SPRAY, VAN WERT, OHIO

PREP/TOTAL TIME: 25 MIN. • **MAKES:** 8 SERVINGS

- 1 package (3 ounces) cream cheese, softened
- 2 tablespoons confectioners' sugar
- ¼ teaspoon almond extract
- 1 tube (8 ounces) refrigerated crescent rolls
- ⅓ cup strawberry pie filling
- ⅓ cup crushed pineapple, drained
- 2 to 3 tablespoons apricot spreadable fruit

1. In a small bowl, beat the cream cheese, sugar and extract until smooth. Unroll crescent dough and separate into eight triangles. Place 1 heaping teaspoonful of cream cheese mixture in the center of each triangle. Top with 1 teaspoon of pie filling and 1 teaspoon of pineapple.

2. With one long side of pastry facing you, fold right and left corners over filling to top corner, forming a square. Seal edges; tuck ends under. Place on an ungreased baking sheet. Bake at 375° for 15-17 minutes or until lightly browned. Brush with spreadable fruit.

Overnight Cherry Danish

With their cherry-filled centers, these rolls melt in your mouth and put a touch of color on your table. Best of all, they store well, unfrosted, in the freezer.

LEANN SAUDER, TREMONT, ILLINOIS

PREP: 1½ HOURS + CHILLING • **BAKE:** 15 MIN. + COOLING
MAKES: 3 DOZEN

- 2 packages (¼ ounce each) active dry yeast
- ½ cup warm 2% milk (110° to 115°)
- 6 cups all-purpose flour
- ⅓ cup sugar
- 2 teaspoons salt
- 1 cup cold butter, cubed
- 1½ cups warm half-and-half cream (110° to 115°)
- 6 egg yolks, lightly beaten
- 1 can (21 ounces) cherry pie filling

ICING:
- 2 tablespoons butter, softened
- 3 cups confectioners' sugar
- ¼ teaspoon vanilla extract
  Dash salt
- 4 to 5 tablespoons half-and-half cream

1. In a small bowl, dissolve yeast in warm milk. In a large bowl, combine the flour, sugar and salt. Cut in butter until crumbly. Add the yeast mixture, cream and egg yolks; stir until mixture forms a soft dough (dough will be sticky). Cover and refrigerate overnight.

2. Punch down dough; divide into quarters. Roll each portion into an 18-in. x 4-in. rectangle; cut into 1-in. x 4-in. strips.

3. Place two strips side by side; twist together. Shape into a ring; pinch ends together. Repeat with remaining strips. Place 2 in. apart on greased baking sheets. Cover and let rise in a warm place until doubled, about 45 minutes.

4. Using the end of a wooden spoon handle, make a ½-in.-deep indentation in the center of each roll. Fill each with about 1 tablespoon pie filling.

5. Bake at 350° for 14-16 minutes or until lightly browned. Remove from pans to wire racks to cool.

6. For icing, in a large bowl, beat butter until fluffy. Gradually beat in the confectioners' sugar, vanilla, salt and enough cream to achieve a drizzling consistency. Drizzle over rolls.

Carrot Cake Doughnuts

I love carrot cake and wanted to carry its flavor over into a doughnut recipe. My experiments worked and these are now my family's favorite doughnuts. The recipe is easy to make, too.

TAMERA DANFORTH, THE DALLES, OREGON

PREP: 30 MIN. • **COOK:** 5 MIN./BATCH • **MAKES:** 1½ DOZEN

- 2 **tablespoons butter, softened**
- 1 **cup sugar**
- 2 **eggs**
- 1 **teaspoon grated orange peel**
- 3½ **cups all-purpose flour**
- 4 **teaspoons baking powder**
- 1½ **teaspoons ground cinnamon**
- 1 **teaspoon baking soda**
- ¾ **teaspoon each salt, ground nutmeg and cloves**
- ⅓ **cup 2% milk**
- 1 **cup shredded carrots**
  Oil for deep-fat frying

GLAZE:
- 1 **cup confectioners' sugar**
- 2 **tablespoons orange juice**
- 1 **tablespoon finely shredded carrot**
- ½ **teaspoon vanilla extract**
- ¼ **cup finely chopped walnuts**

1. In a large bowl, cream butter and sugar until light and fluffy. Add eggs, one at a time, beating well after each addition. Stir in orange peel. Combine the flour, baking powder, cinnamon, baking soda, salt, nutmeg and cloves; add to creamed mixture alternately with milk. Fold in carrots.

2. Turn dough onto a lightly floured surface; roll out to ½-in. thickness. Cut with a floured 2½-in. doughnut cutter.

3. In an electric skillet or deep-fat fryer, heat oil to 375°. Fry doughnuts, a few at a time, for 1½ to 2 minutes on each side or until golden brown. Drain on paper towels.

4. For glaze, combine the confectioners' sugar, orange juice, carrot and vanilla; drizzle over warm doughnuts. Sprinkle with walnuts.

Cinnamon Swirl Rolls

When you don't have time to make from-scratch cinnamon rolls, rely on this recipe that begins with refrigerated breadsticks. Little helpers will like shaping these sweet treats.

TASTE OF HOME TEST KITCHEN

PREP/TOTAL TIME: 30 MIN. • **MAKES:** 4 SERVINGS

- ⅓ cup packed brown sugar
- ¼ cup sugar
- 1 teaspoon ground cinnamon
- 1 tube (11 ounces) refrigerated breadsticks
- 3 tablespoons butter, melted
- ¾ cup confectioners' sugar
- 4 teaspoons milk
- ¼ teaspoon vanilla extract

1. In a shallow bowl, combine the brown sugar, sugar and cinnamon. Separate dough into 12 breadsticks; brush all sides with some of butter, then coat with sugar mixture.

2. On a greased baking sheet, form three breadsticks into a coil, overlapping ends slightly. Secure with a toothpick through the overlapped ends and at the end of the swirl. Repeat with remaining breadsticks. Drizzle remaining butter over rolls; sprinkle with any remaining sugar mixture.

3. Bake at 375° for 15-17 minutes or until golden brown. Remove to a wire rack. Discard toothpicks. Combine the confectioners' sugar, milk and vanilla; drizzle over rolls. Serve warm.

Nut Roll Coffee Cake

This walnut-swirled coffee cake is a great taste to wake up to. As a finishing touch, drizzle it with glaze or add a dusting of confectioners' sugar.

PATRICIA MELE, LOWER BURRELL, PENNSYLVANIA

PREP: 40 MIN. + CHILLING • **BAKE:** 40 MIN. + COOLING
MAKES: 16 SERVINGS

- 2 packages (¼ ounce each) active dry yeast
- ¼ cup warm water (110° to 115°)
- 1 cup butter, melted
- ½ cup warm 2% milk (110° to 115°)
- 4 egg yolks
- 2 tablespoons sugar
- ¾ teaspoon salt
- 2½ cups all-purpose flour

FILLING:

- 3 egg whites
- 1 cup plus 3 tablespoons sugar, divided
- 2 cups ground walnuts
- 2 tablespoons 2% milk
- 2 teaspoons ground cinnamon

1. In a large bowl, dissolve yeast in warm water. Add the butter, milk, egg yolks, sugar, salt and flour. Beat until smooth (mixture will be sticky). Cover and refrigerate overnight.

2. For filling, in a small bowl, beat egg whites on medium speed until soft peaks form. Gradually beat in 1 cup sugar, about 2 tablespoons at a time, on high until sugar is dissolved. In a large bowl, combine the walnuts, milk, cinnamon and remaining sugar; fold in egg whites.

3. Divide dough in half. On a well-floured surface, roll each portion into an 18-in. x 12-in. rectangle. Spread filling evenly over rectangles to within ½ in. of edges. Roll each up jelly-roll style, starting with a long side; pinch seam to seal.

4. Place one filled roll seam side up in a greased 10-in. tube pan. Top with second roll, seam side down. Bake at 350° for 40-45 minutes or until golden brown. Cool for 10 minutes before removing from pan to a wire rack.

Maple Sticky Buns

My family has a small sugaring operation in our backyard. This recipe makes good use of the maple syrup we make. It's a family tradition to serve these sticky buns on Thanksgiving every year.

PRISCILLA ROSSI, EAST BARRE, VERMONT

PREP: 30 MIN. + CHILLING • **BAKE:** 25 MIN. • **MAKES:** 2½ DOZEN

- 2 **packages (¼ ounce each) active dry yeast**
- 2 **cups warm water (110° to 115°)**
- ¼ **cup shortening**
- ½ **cup sugar**
- 1 **egg**
- 2 **teaspoons salt**
- 6 **to 6½ cups all-purpose flour**
- 6 **tablespoons butter, softened**
- ¾ **cup packed brown sugar**
- 1 **tablespoon ground cinnamon**
- ¾ **cup chopped walnuts**
- 1½ **cups maple syrup**
  Additional brown sugar

1. In a large bowl, dissolve yeast in water. Add the shortening, sugar, egg, salt and 5 cups flour. Beat until smooth. Add enough remaining flour to form a soft dough. Cover and refrigerate or up to 24 hours.

2. Punch dough down. Turn onto a floured surface; knead until smooth and elastic, about 6-8 minutes, adding more flour if needed. Divide into thirds. Roll each portion into a 16-in. x 10-in. rectangle.

3. On each rectangle, spread 2 tablespoons butter; sprinkle each with ¼ cup brown sugar, 1 teaspoon cinnamon and ¼ cup walnuts. Pour syrup into three greased 9-in. round baking pans. Sprinkle with additional brown sugar.

4. Tightly roll up each rectangle, jelly-roll style, starting with a short side. Slice each roll into 10 pieces; place over syrup. Cover and let rise until doubled, about 30 minutes.

5. Bake at 350° for 25-30 minutes or until golden brown. Cool in pans for 5 minutes; invert onto serving plates.

Editor's Note: *11-in. x 7-in. baking pans may be substituted for the 9-in. round pans.*

Bakeshop **HOW-TO**

Shaping Cinnamon Rolls and Sticky Buns

Roll dough into a rectangle. Spread or brush with butter; sprinkle with filling. Roll up, starting from a long end, and pinch seam to seal.

Slice into rolls. Place cut side down in a greased baking pan.

Cover and let rise until doubled. Rolls will begin to touch each other.

After baking, combine glaze ingredients if called for in the recipe; spoon over warm rolls.

Cherry Crescent Coffee Cake

A can of pie filling and a few tubes of crescent rolls help me assemble this sweet treat. It's the perfect addition to hot cups of coffee and good conversation.

VALERIE BELLEY, ST. LOUIS, MISSOURI

PREP: 25 MIN. • **BAKE:** 15 MIN. • **MAKES:** 12 SERVINGS

- 1 **package (8 ounces) cream cheese, softened**
- ¾ **cup confectioners' sugar, divided**
- 1 **egg**
- ½ **teaspoon vanilla extract**
- 2 **tubes (8 ounces each) refrigerated crescent rolls**
- 1 **can (21 ounces) cherry pie filling**
- 2 **to 3 teaspoons milk**

1. In a small bowl, beat cream cheese and ¼ cup confectioners' sugar until smooth. Beat in egg and vanilla just until combined; set aside.

2. Unroll crescent dough and separate into triangles. Set four triangles aside. Place remaining triangles on a greased 14-in. pizza pan, forming a ring with wide ends facing outer edge of pan and pointed ends toward the center; leave a 3-in. hole in the center. Lightly press seams together.

3. Spread cream cheese mixture over dough to within ½ in. of edges. Top with pie filling to within ½ in. of cream cheese edges. Cut reserved triangles into thirds, starting at the wide end and ending at the point. Arrange over pie filling with points facing outer edge of pan, forming spokes. Press ends at center and outer edges to seal.

4. Bake at 375° for 15-20 minutes or until golden brown. Cool on a wire rack. Combine remaining confectioners' sugar and enough milk to achieve drizzling consistency; drizzle over coffee cake.

tasteofhome.com

Fresh Plum Kuchen

In summer when plums are in season, this tender fruit-topped cake is delectable! For variety, you can use fresh pears or apples instead.

ANNA DALEY, MONTAGUE, PRINCE EDWARD ISLAND

PREP: 20 MIN. • **BAKE:** 40 MIN. + COOLING • **MAKES:** 10-12 SERVINGS

- ¼ cup butter, softened
- ¾ cup sugar
- 2 eggs
- 1 cup all-purpose flour
- 1 teaspoon baking powder
- ¼ cup milk
- 1 teaspoon grated lemon peel
- 2 cups sliced fresh plums (about 4 medium)
- ½ cup packed brown sugar
- 1 teaspoon ground cinnamon

1. In a small bowl, cream butter and sugar until light and fluffy. Beat in eggs. Combine flour and baking powder; add to the creamed mixture alternately with milk, beating well after each addition. Add lemon peel. Pour into a greased 10-in. springform pan. Arrange plums on top; gently press into batter. Sprinkle with brown sugar and cinnamon.

2. Place pan on a baking sheet. Bake at 350° for 40-50 minutes or until top is golden and a toothpick inserted near the center comes out clean. Cool for 10 minutes. Run a knife around edge of pan; remove sides. Cool on a wire rack.

Maple-Glazed Long Johns

This is a very old recipe from my aunt that I revamped to use with my bread machine. The pastries are deep-fried, then glazed with a simple maple frosting. They're very good for coffee breaks.

PEGGY BURDICK, BURLINGTON, MICHIGAN

PREP: 30 MIN. • **COOK:** 5 MIN./BATCH • **MAKES:** ABOUT 2½ DOZEN

- 1 cup water (70° to 80°)
- 1 egg
- ½ teaspoon vanilla extract
- ½ cup sugar
- ¼ cup shortening
- ½ teaspoon salt
- 3 cups bread flour
- 2¼ teaspoons active dry yeast
  Oil for deep-fat frying
- **GLAZE:**
- 2 cups confectioners' sugar
- ¼ cup half-and-half cream
- 1 tablespoon maple flavoring

1. In bread machine pan, place the first eight ingredients in order suggested by manufacturer. Select dough setting (check dough after 5 minutes of mixing; add 1 to 2 tablespoons of water or flour if needed).

2. When cycle is completed, turn dough onto a lightly floured surface. Divide into four portions. Roll each into a 12-in. x 5-in. rectangle. Cut each rectangle widthwise into 1½-in. strips.

3. In an electric skillet or deep-fat fryer, heat oil to 375°. Drop dough strips, a few at a time, into hot oil. Turn with a slotted spoon and fry for 1 minute on each side or until golden brown. Drain on paper towels.

4. In a small bowl, combine the glaze ingredients. Place the long johns on a wire rack; drizzle with glaze.

Editor's Note: *We recommend you do not use a bread machine's time-delay feature for this recipe.*

Orange-Hazelnut Spiral Rolls

By switching up a coffee cake recipe that was popular with my family, I came up with these scrumptious rolls. I make them for special occasions throughout the year.

LORAINE MEYER, BEND, OREGON

PREP: 30 MIN. + RISING • **BAKE:** 20 MIN. • **MAKES:** ABOUT 2 DOZEN

- 5 **to 5½ cups all-purpose flour, divided**
- 1 **cup mashed potato flakes**
- ¼ **cup sugar**
- 2 **packages (¼ ounce each) quick-rise yeast**
- 1 **teaspoon salt**
- 2 **teaspoons grated orange peel**
- 1 **cup milk**
- ½ **cup butter, cubed**
- ½ **cup sour cream**
- ¼ **cup water**
- 2 **eggs**

FILLING:
- ⅓ **cup butter, softened**
- 1 **cup confectioners' sugar**
- 1 **cup ground hazelnuts**

GLAZE:
- ½ **cup sugar**
- ¼ **cup thawed orange juice concentrate**
- ¼ **cup sour cream**
- 2 **tablespoons butter**

1. In a large bowl, combine 4 cups flour, potato flakes, sugar, yeast, salt and orange peel. In saucepan, heat the milk, butter, sour cream and water to 120°-130°. Add to dry ingredients; beat just until moistened. Add eggs; beat until smooth. Stir in enough remaining flour to form stiff dough.

2. Turn onto floured surface; knead until smooth and elastic, about 6-8 minutes. Place in greased bowl, turning once to grease top. Cover; let dough rest in a warm place for 20 minutes.

3. Punch dough down. Turn onto a floured surface; roll into a 22-in. x 14-in. rectangle. For filling, combine butter, confectioners' sugar and nuts. Spread lengthwise over half of the dough. Fold dough over filling, forming a 22-in. x 7-in. rectangle. Cut into 7-in. x ¾-in. strips.

4. Twist each strip 4 or 5 times and shape into a ring. Pinch ends together. Place on two greased 15-in. x 10-in. x 1-in. baking pans. Cover and let rise for 30 minutes or until doubled.

5. Bake at 375° for 17-20 minutes or until golden brown. Remove to wire racks. Meanwhile, in a saucepan, combine glaze ingredients over medium heat. Bring to boil; cook and stir for 3 minutes or until thickened. Remove from the heat. Drizzle over warm rolls.

Bakeshop **HOW-TO**

Shaping a Tea Ring

Roll into a rectangle. Spread filling evenly over dough to within 1/2 in. of edges. Roll up jelly-roll style, starting with a long side; pinch seam to seal.

Place seam side down on a pan; pinch ends together to form a ring.

With scissors, cut from outside edge to two-thirds of the way toward center of ring at 1-in. intervals.

Separate the pieces slightly and twist each to allow the filling to show.

Swedish Tea Ring

This showstopper will add a special touch to any holiday spread. It's absolutely spectacular.

ELSIE EPP, NEWTON, KANSAS

PREP: 30 MIN. + RISING • **BAKE:** 20 MIN. + COOLING
MAKES: 1 RING (24 SLICES)

- 1 **tablespoon active dry yeast**
- 1½ **cups warm water (110° to 115°)**
- ¼ **cup sugar**
- ¼ **cup canola oil**
- 2 **egg whites, lightly beaten**
- 1¼ **teaspoons salt**
- 5½ to 6 **cups all-purpose flour**
- ½ **cup chopped walnuts**
- ½ **cup chopped maraschino cherries, patted dry**
- ¼ **cup packed brown sugar**
- 1 **teaspoon ground cinnamon**
- 2 **tablespoons butter, melted**

ICING:
- 1 **cup confectioners' sugar**
- 1 **to 2 tablespoons fat-free milk**

1. In a large bowl, dissolve yeast in warm water. Add the sugar, oil, egg whites, salt and 1 cup flour; beat until smooth. Stir in enough remaining flour to form a soft dough.

2. Turn onto a lightly floured surface; knead until smooth, about 6-8 minutes. Place in a bowl coated with cooking spray, turning once to coat the top. Cover and let rise until doubled, about 1 hour.

3. Combine the walnuts, cherries, brown sugar and cinnamon; set aside. Punch dough down; roll into an 18-in. x 12-in. rectangle. Brush with butter; sprinkle with nut mixture to within ½ in. of edges. Roll up jelly-roll style, starting with a long side; pinch seam to seal.

4. Place seam side down on a 14-in. pizza pan coated with cooking spray; pinch ends together to form a ring. With scissors, cut from outside edge two-thirds of the way toward center of ring at scant 1-in. intervals. Separate strips slightly; twist to allow filling to show. Cover and let rise until doubled, about 40 minutes.

5. Bake at 400° for 20-25 minutes or until golden brown. Remove from pan to a wire rack to cool.

6. In a small bowl, combine confectioners' sugar and enough milk to achieve desired consistency; drizzle icing over the tea ring.

Coffee-Klatch Kolaches

These crowd-pleasing Czech treats are the perfect partner for a cup of joe. They're easy to make with canned cherry pie filling, but the homemade prune filling is a delicious option, too.

CAROL HOUDEK, MINNEAPOLIS, MINNESOTA

PREP: 45 MIN. + RISING • **BAKE:** 10 MIN. + COOLING • **MAKES:** 2 DOZEN

- 1 **package (¼ ounce) active dry yeast**
- ¼ **cup warm water (110° to 115°)**
- ¾ **cup warm 2% milk (110° to 115°)**
- ⅓ **cup sugar**
- ⅓ **cup shortening**
- 1 **teaspoon salt**
- ⅛ **teaspoon ground nutmeg**
- 2 **eggs**
- 4 **cups all-purpose flour**
- 1 **can (21 ounces) cherry pie filling**
- 3 **tablespoons butter, melted**

GLAZE:
- 1 **cup confectioners' sugar**
- 1 **tablespoon butter, melted**
- 5 **teaspoons 2% milk**

1. In a large bowl, dissolve yeast in warm water. Add the milk, sugar, shortening, salt, nutmeg, eggs and 2 cups flour; beat until smooth. Add enough remaining flour to form a soft dough. Turn onto a floured surface; knead until smooth and elastic, about 6-8 minutes.

2. Place in a greased bowl, turning once to grease the top. Cover and let rise in a warm place until doubled, about 1 hour.

3. Punch dough down. Divide in half; shape each half into 12 balls. Place 3 in. apart on greased baking sheets. Flatten each ball to a 3-in. circle. Cover and let rise in a warm place until doubled, about 30 minutes.

4. Make a depression in the center of each roll; add a rounded tablespoonful of filling. Bake at 350° for 10-15 minutes or until golden brown. Brush rolls with butter. Remove from pans to wire racks to cool. Combine glaze ingredients; drizzle over the tops.

Prune Kolaches: For prune filling, in a small saucepan, bring an 18-oz. package of pitted dried plums and 2 cups water to a boil. Reduce heat; simmer, uncovered, for 15 minutes or until plums are tender. Drain. Transfer to blender; add ¼ cup sugar and ½ teaspoon ground cinnamon. Cover and process until pureed; cool. Proceed as directed.

Peachy Cheese Danish

I've prepared these pretty sweet rolls for late-night snacks and for breakfast when we have guests.

CAROLYN KYZER, ALEXANDER, ARKANSAS

PREP: 20 MIN. • **BAKE:** 15 MIN. • **MAKES:** 4 SERVINGS

- 1 tube (8 ounces) refrigerated crescent rolls
- 4 ounces cream cheese, softened
- ¼ cup sugar
- 2 tablespoons lemon juice
- 8 teaspoons peach preserves or flavor of your choice

GLAZE:
- ¼ cup confectioners' sugar
- ½ teaspoon vanilla extract
- 1 to 2 teaspoons milk

1. Separate dough into four rectangles; seal perforations. On a lightly floured surface, roll each into a 7-in. x 3½-in. rectangle. In a small bowl, combine cream cheese, sugar and lemon juice until smooth; spread over rectangles. Roll up from a long side; pinch edges to seal. Holding one end, loosely coil each.

2. Place on an ungreased baking sheet. Top each coil with 2 teaspoons preserves. Bake at 350° for 15-20 minutes or until golden brown. Remove from pan to wire rack.

3. For glaze, in a small bowl, combine confectioners' sugar, vanilla and enough milk to achieve desired consistency. Drizzle over warm rolls.

Petite Sticky Buns

Start your morning on a sweet note with these tender maple sticky buns. They are fantastically light and airy. But be careful not to overbake, or they're difficult to get out of the pan!

LISA NAUGLE, FAYETTEVILLE, PENNSYLVANIA

PREP: 30 MIN. + RISING • **BAKE:** 15 MIN. • **MAKES:** 2 DOZEN

- 3 to 3¼ cups all-purpose flour
- ¼ cup sugar
- 1 package (¼ ounce) active dry yeast
- 1 teaspoon salt
- 1¼ cups milk
- ¼ cup butter, cubed
- 1 egg

TOPPING:
- 1 cup packed brown sugar
- ¾ cup butter, cubed
- ¾ cup chopped pecans, toasted
- 2 tablespoons honey
- 1 teaspoon ground cinnamon
- ½ teaspoon maple flavoring

1. In a large bowl, combine 2 cups flour, sugar, yeast and salt. In a small saucepan, heat the milk and butter to 120°-130°. Add to dry ingredients; beat just until moistened. Add egg; beat until smooth. Stir in enough remaining flour to form a soft dough (dough will be sticky). Do not knead. Cover and let rise in a warm place until doubled, about an hour.

2. In a small saucepan over low heat, cook topping ingredients until butter is melted. Drop by rounded teaspoonfuls into 24 well-greased muffin cups.

3. Stir dough down. Fill greased muffin cups half full. Cover and let rise in a warm place until doubled, about 30 minutes.

4. Place muffin cups on foil-lined baking sheets. Bake at 375° for 12-15 minutes or until golden brown. Cool for 2 minutes before inverting onto baking sheets. Transfer to serving platters. Serve warm.

Jumbo Cinnamon Rolls

I especially like recipes that make just enough for the two of us, and these yummy sweet rolls fit the bill. Because these treats begin with a ready-made dough, they couldn't be more convenient to whip up.

EDNA HOFFMAN, HEBRON, INDIANA

PREP: 15 MIN. + RISING • **BAKE:** 15 MIN. • **MAKES:** 2 SERVINGS

> 4 frozen Texas-size dinner rolls
> 2 tablespoons butter, melted
> ¼ cup coarsely chopped pecans
> 2 tablespoons sugar
> ¾ teaspoon ground cinnamon
> **HONEY BUTTER:**
> 2 tablespoons butter, softened
> 2 teaspoons honey

1. Let rolls rise in a warm place until doubled, about 45 minutes. Punch down. Roll each into a 12-in. rope; brush with butter. In a shallow bowl, combine the pecans, sugar and cinnamon; roll ropes in nut mixture.

2. Twist two ropes together; pinch ends to seal. Place in a greased 10-oz. custard cup. Repeat with remaining ropes. Cover and let rise for 30 minutes or until doubled.

3. Bake at 375° for 15-20 minutes or until golden brown. Meanwhile, combine the honey butter ingredients. Serve with rolls.

Glazed Cinnamon Braids

This recipe has been a tradition in my family for many years. The Red Hot candies give it such a yummy zing.

GEORGIA STULL, HARRISONVILLE, MISSOURI

PREP: 40 MIN. + RISING • **BAKE:** 25 MIN.
MAKES: 2 LOAVES (12 SLICES EACH)

> 2 packages (¼ ounce each) active dry yeast
> ¼ cup warm water (110° to 115°)
> 1 cup warm 2% milk (110° to 115°)
> 2 eggs
> ½ cup sugar
> ¼ cup shortening
> 2 teaspoons salt
> 5 to 5½ cups all-purpose flour
> **FILLING:**
> 1 cup chopped pecans
> ½ cup Red Hot candies
> ¼ cup sugar
> 2 teaspoons ground cinnamon
> 2 tablespoons butter, softened
> **GLAZE:**
> 1 cup confectioners' sugar
> ½ teaspoon vanilla extract
> 1 to 2 tablespoons 2% milk

1. In a large bowl, dissolve yeast in warm water. Add the milk, eggs, sugar, shortening, salt and 3 cups flour. Beat until smooth. Stir in enough remaining flour to form a soft dough.

2. Turn onto a floured surface; knead until smooth and elastic, about 6-8 minutes. Place in a greased bowl, turning once to grease top. Cover and let rise in a warm place until doubled, about 1 hour. Meanwhile, in a small bowl, combine the pecans, Red Hots, sugar and cinnamon; set aside.

3. Punch dough down. Divide in half. On a greased baking sheet, roll out one portion into a 12-in. x 10-in. rectangle. Spread 1 tablespoon butter down the center; sprinkle with half of the pecan mixture.

4. On each long side, cut 1-in.-wide strips about 2½ in. into center. Starting at one end, fold alternating strips at an angle across filling. Pinch ends to seal. Repeat, making second loaf. Cover and let rise until doubled, about 45 minutes.

5. Bake at 350° for 25-30 minutes or until golden brown. Remove from pans to wire racks. Combine the glaze ingredients; drizzle over loaves. Serve warm.

Cranberry-White Chocolate Cinnamon Rolls

A basket of warm cinnamon rolls is a sure way to impress family and friends. Add cranberries and white chocolate to the ingredient mix, and these treats become incredibly memorable.

MEG MARRIOTT, TACOMA, WASHINGTON

PREP: 45 MIN. + CHILLING • **BAKE:** 30 MIN. + COOLING
MAKES: 16 SERVINGS

- 2 **packages (¼ ounce each) active dry yeast**
- 2 **cups warm water (110° to 115°)**
- 1 **cup butter, melted**
- ½ **cup sugar**
- 2 **teaspoons salt**
- 5 **to 6 cups all-purpose flour**

FILLING:
- 1 **cup butter, softened**
- ½ **cup packed brown sugar**
- 2 **teaspoons ground cinnamon**
- 1 **package (10 to 12 ounces) white baking chips**
- 1 **cup dried cranberries**
- ½ **cup chopped pecans**

GLAZE:
- 2 **cups confectioners' sugar**
- 2 **teaspoons vanilla extract**
- 5 **to 6 tablespoons heavy whipping cream**

1. In a large bowl, dissolve yeast in warm water. Add the butter, sugar, salt and 4 cups flour; beat until smooth. Stir in enough remaining flour to form a soft dough.

2. Turn onto a floured surface; knead until smooth and elastic, about 6-8 minutes. Place in a greased bowl, turning once to grease the top. Cover and refrigerate overnight.

3. Punch dough down. On a lightly floured surface, roll into a 24-in. x 12-in. rectangle. For filling, combine the butter, brown sugar and cinnamon; spread over dough to within ½ in. of edges. Sprinkle with chips, cranberries and pecans. Roll up jelly-roll style, starting with a long side; pinch seam to seal.

4. Cut into 16 slices. Place cut side down in two greased 13-in. x 9-in. baking pans. Cover and let rise in a warm place until doubled, about 45 minutes.

5. Bake at 350° for 30-35 minutes or until golden brown. Meanwhile, in a small bowl, combine the confectioners' sugar, vanilla and enough cream to achieve desired consistency; drizzle over warm rolls. Cool on wire racks.

Upside-Down Apple Gingerbread

Don't expect any leftovers when you serve this moist and tender cake. People love its heartwarming seasonal flavor.

FLORENCE PALMER, MARSHALL, ILLINOIS

PREP: 15 MIN. • **BAKE:** 45 MIN. + COOLING • **MAKES:** 9 SERVINGS

- ¼ cup butter, melted
- ⅓ cup packed brown sugar
- 2 large apples, peeled and sliced

GINGERBREAD:
- ½ cup butter, softened
- ½ cup sugar
- ⅓ cup packed brown sugar
- 1 egg
- ½ cup molasses
- 2 cups all-purpose flour
- 1 teaspoon baking soda
- 1 teaspoon ground cinnamon
- 1 teaspoon ground ginger
- ½ teaspoon ground cloves
- ½ teaspoon salt
- ¼ teaspoon ground nutmeg
- ¾ cup brewed tea

1. Pour butter into a 9-in. square baking pan; sprinkle with brown sugar. Arrange apples over sugar; set aside.

2. For gingerbread, in a large bowl, cream butter and sugars until light and fluffy. Beat in egg, then molasses. Combine dry ingredients; add to sugar mixture alternately with tea, beating well after each addition. Pour over apples.

3. Bake at 350° for 45-50 minutes or until a toothpick comes out clean. Cool for 10 minutes before inverting onto a plate.

Swedish Doughnuts

One day, my father got a hankering for doughnuts and asked me to make him some. Dad—and everyone else—loved the results.

LISA BATES, DUNHAM, QUEBEC

PREP: 20 MIN. + CHILLING • **COOK:** 5 MIN./BATCH • **MAKES:** 2½ DOZEN

- 2 eggs
- 1 cup sugar
- 2 cups cold mashed potatoes (mashed with milk and butter)
- ¾ cup buttermilk
- 2 tablespoons butter, melted
- 1 teaspoon vanilla or almond extract
- 4½ cups all-purpose flour
- 4 teaspoons baking powder
- 1 teaspoon baking soda
- 1 teaspoon salt
- 2 teaspoons ground nutmeg
- ⅛ teaspoon ground ginger
  Oil for deep-fat frying
  Additional sugar, optional

1. In a large bowl, beat eggs and sugar. Add the potatoes, buttermilk, butter and vanilla. Combine the flour, baking powder, baking soda, salt, nutmeg and ginger; gradually add to egg mixture and mix well. Cover and refrigerate for 1-2 hours.

2. Turn onto a lightly floured surface; roll to ½-in. thickness. Cut with a floured 2½-in. doughnut cutter. In an electric skillet or deep-fat fryer, heat oil to 375°.

3. Fry doughnuts, a few at a time, until golden brown on both sides, about 2 minutes. Drain on paper towels. Roll warm doughnuts in additional sugar if desired.

Café Beverages

Iced Coffee

When my sister introduced me to iced coffee, I wasn't sure I'd like it. Not only did I love it, I decided to start making my own. This easy version is a refreshing alternative to hot coffee.

JENNY REECE, LOWRY, MINNESOTA

PREP/TOTAL TIME: 5 MIN. • **MAKES:** 2 CUPS

- 4 teaspoons instant coffee granules
- 1 cup boiling water
  Sugar substitute equivalent to 4 teaspoons sugar, optional
- 1 cup fat-free milk
- 4 teaspoons chocolate syrup
- ⅛ teaspoon vanilla extract
  Ice cubes

1. In a large bowl, dissolve coffee in water. Add sweetener if desired. Stir in the milk, chocolate syrup and vanilla; mix well. Serve over ice.

Editor's Note: *This recipe was tested with Splenda no-calorie sweetener.*

Chocolate Cherry Cappuccino

I wanted something that both coffee and non-coffee drinkers would enjoy, so I added cherry flavoring to a cappuccino mix.

JENNIFER WATERS, LUBBOCK, TEXAS

PREP/TOTAL TIME: 20 MIN.
MAKES: 48 SERVINGS (6 CUPS CAPPUCCINO MIX)

- 3 cups sugar
- 2 cups confectioners' sugar
- 1⅓ cups powdered nondairy creamer
- 1⅓ cups instant coffee granules
- 1 cup baking cocoa
- 1 envelope (.13 ounce) unsweetened cherry Kool-Aid mix

EACH SERVING:
- 1 cup 2% milk
- 2 tablespoons miniature marshmallows

1. In a large airtight container, combine the first six ingredients. Store in a cool dry place for up to 2 months.

To prepare cappuccino: Place 2 tablespoons mix in a mug. Stir in hot milk until combined; top with marshmallows.

Maple Cream Coffee

On a crisp winter day, this creamy drink is perfect for after dinner. Its rich java flavor is tempered by the sweetness of maple.

TASTE OF HOME TEST KITCHEN

PREP/TOTAL TIME: 10 MIN. • **MAKES:** 2 SERVINGS

- ¾ cup half-and-half cream
- ¼ cup maple syrup
- 1¼ cups brewed coffee
- ¼ cup whipped cream

1. In a small saucepan, cook and stir cream and syrup over medium heat until heated through. (Do not boil.) Divide evenly between two cups. Stir in coffee. Top with whipped cream.

Caramel Macchiato Floats

I made these creamy caramel-flavored floats for a party, and everyone loved them!

MELISSA HELLER, SANTA MARIA, CALIFORNIA

PREP/TOTAL TIME: 20 MIN. • **MAKES:** 8 SERVINGS

- 6 **cups cold brewed coffee**
- 1 **cup 2% milk**
- ⅓ **cup caramel flavoring syrup**
- ¼ **cup sugar**
- 8 **scoops coffee ice cream**
- 8 **scoops dulce de leche ice cream**
   Whipped cream and caramel sundae syrup

1. In a large pitcher, combine the first four ingredients. Divide ice cream among eight chilled glasses; pour coffee mixture over top. Garnish servings with whipped cream and sundae syrup.

Editor's Note: *This recipe was tested with Torani brand flavoring syrup. Look for it in the coffee section.*

Green Tea Frappes

This delicious frappe captures the delicate flavor of green tea with just a hint of added sweetness. You'll love the refreshing treat at get-togethers or a relaxing family brunch.

TASTE OF HOME TEST KITCHEN

PREP/TOTAL TIME: 20 MIN. • **MAKES:** 4 SERVINGS

- 3 **individual green tea bags**
- 1 **cup boiling water**
- 1½ **cups ice cubes**
- ¾ **cup fat-free sweetened condensed milk**
- ½ **cup fat-free milk**

1. Place tea bags in a small bowl; add boiling water. Let stand for 15 minutes or until lukewarm.

2. Discard tea bags. Pour tea into a blender; add the remaining ingredients. Cover and process for 30-45 seconds or until smooth. Pour into chilled glasses; serve immediately.

Vanilla-Almond Coffee

This recipe is perfect for any coffee connoisseur. Instead of buying flavored coffees, I make my own using extracts for baking. They're ideal for making custom coffee without all the calories.

TINA CHRISTENSEN, ADDISON, ILLINOIS

PREP/TOTAL TIME: 5 MIN. • **MAKES:** 1 POUND

- 1 **pound ground coffee**
- 2 **tablespoons almond extract**
- 2 **tablespoons vanilla extract**

SHORT & SWEET

1. Place coffee in a large jar with tight-fitting lid. Add extracts. Cover and shake well. Store in an airtight container in a cool, dark and dry place or in the freezer. Prepare coffee as usual.

Frothy Mexi-Mocha Coffee

Who needs a gourmet coffeehouse when you can whip up your own delicious treat at home? This will wow your friends.

MARIA REGAKIS, SOMERVILLE, MASSACHUSETTS

PREP/TOTAL TIME: 15 MIN. • **MAKES:** 4 SERVINGS

- 1 **cup packed brown sugar**
- 4 **ounces semisweet chocolate, chopped**
- 2 **orange peel strips (1 to 3 inches)**
- ½ **teaspoon ground cinnamon**
- ¼ **teaspoon ground allspice**
- 3 **cups hot strong brewed coffee**
- ½ **cup half-and-half cream, warmed**

  Optional garnishes: cinnamon sticks, orange peel and whipped cream

1. Place the first five ingredients in a blender; cover and process until chocolate is finely chopped. Add coffee; cover and process for 1-2 minutes or until chocolate is melted. Transfer to a small saucepan; heat through.

2. Return mixture to blender; add cream. Cover and process until frothy. Strain, discarding solids; serve in mugs. Garnish with cinnamon sticks, orange peel and whipped cream if desired.

Chai Tea Mix

I received this recipe from my sister, who got it from a friend in Alaska. This warming drink makes a great Christmas gift. For friends at work, I bought some cute jars with lids. I placed some fabric on top and tied them with ribbon.

DONNA GISH, BLUE SPRINGS, MISSOURI

PREP/TOTAL TIME: 20 MIN. • **MAKES:** 32 SERVINGS (8 CUPS TEA MIX)

- 2 cups sugar
- 2 cups unsweetened instant tea
- 1½ cups powdered French vanilla nondairy creamer
- 1¼ cups powdered nondairy creamer
- 1¼ cups packed brown sugar
- ¾ cup nonfat dry milk powder
- 2½ teaspoons ground cinnamon
- 1½ teaspoons ground nutmeg
- 1¼ teaspoons ground cardamom
- 1¼ teaspoons ground cloves
- 1 teaspoon ground allspice
- ¼ teaspoon white pepper

EACH SERVING:
- 1 cup hot 2% milk

1. In a large bowl, combine the first 12 ingredients. In a blender, cover and process tea mixture in batches until powdery. Store in an airtight container in a cool dry place for up to 6 months.

To prepare chai tea: Place ¼ cup mix in a mug. Add hot milk; stir until combined.

Butterscotch Coffee

Five ingredients are all you'll need for this sweet sipper. Top individual servings of hot butterscotch coffee with whipped cream and fun garnishes for a real coffeehouse-style treat.

TASTE OF HOME TEST KITCHEN

PREP/TOTAL TIME: 20 MIN. • **MAKES:** 8 SERVINGS (2 QUARTS)

- 1 cup butterscotch chips, divided
- 8 cups hot brewed coffee
- ½ cup half-and-half cream
- 5 to 8 tablespoons sugar
  Whipped cream in a can

1. In a microwave, melt ½ cup butterscotch chips; stir until smooth. Cut a small hole in the corner of a pastry or plastic bag; insert a #4 round tip. Fill with melted chips. Pipe eight garnishes onto a waxed paper-lined baking sheet. Refrigerate until set, about 10 minutes.

2. In a large pitcher, stir coffee and remaining butterscotch chips until chips are melted. Stir in cream and sugar. Pour into mugs. Top each serving with whipped cream and a butterscotch garnish.

Bakeshop TIP

Subtle Flavored Coffee

To create just a hint of special flavor in hot brewed coffee, mix three parts of unflavored ground coffee with one part of flavored. This gives your coffee a subtle flavor boost without being overwhelming.

Gingerbread Kiss Coffee

Enjoy the flavor of gingerbread around the clock with this unique recipe. The mix stores in the refrigerator for several weeks, which makes holiday entertaining a breeze.

TASTE OF HOME TEST KITCHEN

PREP/TOTAL TIME: 5 MIN.
MAKES: 15 SERVINGS (⅔ CUP MOLASSES MIXTURE)

- ½ cup molasses
- ¼ cup packed brown sugar
- 1 teaspoon ground ginger
- ¾ teaspoon ground cinnamon

EACH SERVING:
- 1 cup hot brewed coffee
  Milk, whipped cream and additional ground cinnamon, optional

1. In a small bowl, combine the molasses, brown sugar, ginger and cinnamon.

2. For each serving, place 2 teaspoons molasses mixture in a mug. Add 1 cup hot coffee; stir until combined. Serve with milk, whipped cream and cinnamon if desired.

3. Cover and store remaining molasses mixture in the refrigerator for up to 2 weeks.

Open-House Coffee Punch

Guests will gather around the punch bowl when you ladle out this frosty, frothy coffee-spiked drink. Try brewing it with different flavored coffees to create your own signature blend.

DIANE PROPST, DENVER, NORTH CAROLINA

PREP/TOTAL TIME: 15 MIN. • **MAKES:** 13 SERVINGS (2½ QUARTS)

- 4 cups brewed vanilla-flavored coffee, cooled
- 1 can (12 ounces) evaporated milk
- ½ cup sugar
- ½ gallon vanilla ice cream, softened
  Ground cinnamon

1. In a large container, combine the coffee, milk and sugar; stir until sugar is dissolved. Spoon ice cream into a punch bowl; pour coffee mixture over the top. Sprinkle with cinnamon. Serve immediately.

Homemade Cream Soda

When your gang's thirsty, it's time to break out this bubbly refresher. Bright pink and creamy, it's instant happiness in a glass.

SHELLY BEVINGTON-FISHER, HERMISTON, OREGON

PREP/TOTAL TIME: 5 MIN. • **MAKES:** 2 SERVINGS

- ¾ cup grenadine syrup
- ¼ cup half-and-half cream
- 1½ cups club soda, chilled
  Ice cubes

1. In a blender, combine grenadine and cream; cover and process until blended. Stir in club soda; serve immediately over ice.

Editor's Note: *This recipe was tested with Rose's grenadine.*

Pumpkin Pie Coffee Creamer

Anyone who likes a cup of java is sure to enjoy this homemade stir-in. For a quick gift, put the creamer in a festive basket and add a fun mug or package of gourmet coffee.

CAROL FORCUM, MARION, ILLINOIS

PREP/TOTAL TIME: 10 MIN. • **MAKES:** ABOUT 1 CUP

1 **cup powdered nondairy creamer**
4 **teaspoons ground cinnamon**
2 **teaspoons ground ginger**
2 **teaspoons ground nutmeg**
1 **teaspoon ground cloves**
1 **teaspoon ground allspice**

1. In a small bowl, combine all ingredients. Store in an airtight container.

Slow-Cooker Spiced Coffee

Even people who don't usually drink coffee will find this special blend with a hint of chocolate appealing. I keep a big batch ready to serve at parties.

JOANNE HOLT, BOWLING GREEN, OHIO

PREP: 10 MIN. • **COOK:** 2 HOURS • **MAKES:** 8 CUPS

- 8 **cups brewed coffee**
- ⅓ **cup sugar**
- ¼ **cup chocolate syrup**
- ½ **teaspoon anise extract**
- 4 **cinnamon sticks (3 inches)**
- 1½ **teaspoons whole cloves**
  Additional cinnamon sticks, optional

1. In a 3-qt. slow cooker, combine the coffee, sugar, chocolate syrup and anise extract. Place cinnamon sticks and cloves in a double thickness of cheesecloth; bring up corners of cloth and tie with string to form a bag. Add to slow cooker. Cover and cook on low for 2-3 hours.

2. Discard spice bag. Ladle coffee into mugs; garnish each with a cinnamon stick if desired.

Viennese Coffee

This isn't your regular cup of joe! I dress it up with chocolate, whipped cream and more, making it a drink to savor.

SHARON DELANEY-CHRONIS, SOUTH MILWAUKEE, WISCONSIN

PREP: 10 MIN. • **COOK:** 3 HOURS • **MAKES:** 4 SERVINGS

- 3 **cups strong brewed coffee**
- 3 **tablespoons chocolate syrup**
- 1 **teaspoon sugar**
- ⅓ **cup heavy whipping cream**
- ¼ **cup creme de cacao or Irish cream liqueur**
  Whipped cream and chocolate curls, optional

1. In a 1½-qt. slow cooker, combine the coffee, chocolate syrup and sugar. Cover and cook on low for 2½ hours.

2. Stir in heavy cream and creme de cacao. Cover and cook 30 minutes longer or until heated through.

3. Ladle coffee into mugs. Garnish with whipped cream and chocolate curls if desired.

A.M. Rush Espresso Smoothie

Want an early morning pick-me-up that's good for you, too? Fruit and flaxseed give this sweet espresso a nutritious twist.

AIMEE WILSON, CLOVIS, CALIFORNIA

PREP/TOTAL TIME: 10 MIN. • **MAKES:** 1 SERVING

- ½ **cup cold fat-free milk**
- 1 **tablespoon vanilla flavoring syrup**
- 1 **cup ice cubes**
- ½ **medium banana, cut up**
- 1 **to 2 teaspoons instant espresso powder**
- 1 **teaspoon ground flaxseed**
- 1 **teaspoon baking cocoa**

1. In a blender, combine all the ingredients; cover and process for 1-2 minutes or until blended. Pour into a chilled glass; serve immediately.

Editor's Note: *This recipe was tested with Torani brand flavoring syrup. Look for it in the coffee section.*

Chilled Lemon Coffees

A surprising burst of lemon infuses this cool coffee drink. It makes an out-of-the-ordinary refresher on a hot summer day.

TASTE OF HOME TEST KITCHEN

PREP/TOTAL TIME: 10 MIN. • **MAKES:** 3 SERVINGS

- 2 **cups strong brewed coffee (French or other dark roast), chilled**
- 1 **cup lemon sherbet, softened**
- 2 **tablespoons sugar**
- 1 **tablespoon lemon juice**
  Lemon peel, optional

1. Place the coffee, sherbet, sugar and lemon juice in a blender; cover and process until smooth. Pour into chilled glasses; garnish with lemon peel if desired. Serve immediately.

Coffee Stirrer Sticks

As a holiday novelty, it's hard to lick these lollipops for grown-ups! They double as coffee stirrers, and they make great party favors or stocking stuffers.

KELLY PICKERING, MESA, ARIZONA

PREP: 10 MIN. • **COOK:** 15 MIN. + COOLING • **MAKES:** ABOUT 1 DOZEN

- 1 **cup sugar**
- ⅓ **cup brewed coffee**
- 1 **tablespoon light corn syrup**
- ¼ **teaspoon baking cocoa**
- ¼ **teaspoon ground cinnamon**
- ½ **teaspoon vanilla extract**
- 12 **wooden lollipop or craft sticks**
   Plastic wrap
   Red and green ribbons

1. In a large heavy saucepan, combine the sugar, coffee, corn syrup, cocoa and cinnamon. Cook over medium heat until the sugar is dissolved, stirring constantly. Cook over medium heat, without stirring, until a candy thermometer reads 290° (soft-crack stage), about 7 minutes. Remove from the heat.

2. Immediately stir in vanilla, then pour into a greased 2-cup heat-proof glass measuring cup. Working quickly, pour tablespoonfuls into circles on a greased baking sheet and lay a stick in each circle. Allow to cool until hardened. When cooled, wrap with plastic wrap and tie with ribbon. Store in an airtight container.

Editor's Note: *We recommend that you test your candy thermometer before each use by bringing water to a boil; the thermometer should read 212°. Adjust your recipe temperature up or down based on your test.*

Hazelnut Coffee

The blend of flavors—coffee, hazelnut and a bit of chocolate—make this drink absolutely sensational. It is great for breakfast or brunch, but is also wonderful for a quiet moment at the end of the day.

FRIEDA BLIESNER, MCALLEN, TEXAS

PREP/TOTAL TIME: 15 MIN. • **MAKES:** 4 SERVINGS

- 4 **cups brewed coffee**
- ¼ **cup hazelnut flavoring syrup**
- 1 **tablespoon sugar**
- ⅛ **teaspoon ground cinnamon**
- ¼ **cup heavy whipping cream**
- 1 **tablespoon Nutella**

1. In a large saucepan, combine the coffee, flavoring syrup, sugar and cinnamon; heat through. Divide coffee mixture among four mugs.

2. In a small bowl, beat cream and Nutella until thickened. Gently spoon onto tops of drinks. Serve immediately.

Editor's Note: *This recipe was tested with Torani brand flavoring syrup. Look for it in the coffee section.*

Bakeshop HOW-TO

Cinnamon Stick Stirrers

Replace spoons with pretty hand-dipped cinnamon sticks that serve as flavorful coffee stirrers.

Dip each cinnamon stick in melted chocolate.

Coat in your choice of sweet indulgences such as raw sugar or crushed peppermint and melted caramel or white candy coating.

Easy Espresso

Capture the classic taste of espresso without the hassle of expensive brewing equipment! For best flavor, serve espresso immediately. Pour leftover espresso into ice cube trays and freeze to use later in cold drinks.

TASTE OF HOME TEST KITCHEN

PREP/TOTAL TIME: 10 MIN. • **MAKES:** 4 SERVINGS

- ½ **cup ground coffee (French or other dark roast)**
- 1½ **cups cold water**
  Lemon twists, optional

1. Place ground coffee in the filter of a drip coffeemaker. Add water; brew according to manufacturer's instructions. Serve immediately in espresso cups with lemon twists if desired.

Editor's Note: *This recipe was tested with Starbucks French Roast ground coffee.*

Cool Lime Pie Frappes

I love serving this light and luscious drink to guests on hot days. It has the taste and creamy texture of key lime pie without the unwanted calories.

MARIE RIZZIO, INTERLOCHEN, MICHIGAN

PREP/TOTAL TIME: 10 MIN. • **MAKES:** 2 SERVINGS

- ¼ **cup fat-free milk**
- 2 **tablespoons lime juice**
- 2 **cups fat-free vanilla frozen yogurt, softened**
- ½ **teaspoon grated lime peel**
- 2 **teaspoons graham cracker crumbs**

1. In a blender, combine the milk, lime juice, frozen yogurt and lime peel; cover and process until blended. Stir if necessary. Pour into chilled glasses; sprinkle with cracker crumbs. Serve immediately.

French Vanilla Cappuccino Mix

I've had this recipe for many years and actually found it in a cookbook from a craft show. My family enjoys it so much that when I make up a batch it disappears almost immediately. It's a great way to warm up.

TAMMY FLEURY, ESCANABA, MICHIGAN

PREP/TOTAL TIME: 20 MIN. • **MAKES:** 16 SERVINGS (4 CUPS MIX)

- 1½ **cups instant hot cocoa mix**
- 1 **jar (8 ounces) powdered French Vanilla nondairy creamer**
- 1 **cup nonfat dry milk powder**
- 1 **cup confectioners' sugar**
- ½ **cup sugar**
- ½ **cup instant coffee granules**

EACH SERVING:
- 1 **cup hot water**
  Sweetened whipped cream and baking cocoa

1. In a large bowl, combine the first six ingredients. Store in an airtight container in a cool dry place for up to 2 months.

To prepare cappuccino: For a single serving, place ¼ cup mix in a coffee mug. Add 1 cup hot water; stir until combined. Top with whipped cream; sprinkle with baking cocoa.

Heavenly Hot Chocolate Mix

Kids of all ages enjoy this malted milk-flavored hot chocolate. At Christmas, I make several batches packaged in jars with festive homemade labels. Friends will return the jars for refills!

SARA TATHAM, PLYMOUTH, NEW HAMPSHIRE

PREP/TOTAL TIME: 10 MIN. • **MAKES:** 30 SERVINGS (10 CUPS MIX)

- 5 **cups nonfat dry milk powder**
- 2 **cups confectioners' sugar**
- 2 **cups instant chocolate drink mix**
- 1 **cup powdered nondairy creamer**
- 1 **cup malted milk powder**
- 1 **cup chocolate malted milk powder**
- ½ **cup baking cocoa**

1. In a large airtight container, combine all ingredients. Store in a cool dry place for up to 2 months (mixture will settle).

To prepare hot chocolate: Place ⅓ cup mix in a mug; add ¾ cup hot water and stir until blended.

Old-Fashioned Strawberry Soda

With just a quick pulse of the blender, you will have this refreshing sipper. I like to try new recipes for my husband and our three sons. No one can resist this fun, bubbly soda!

GINGER HUBBARD, ANDERSON, MISSOURI

PREP/TOTAL TIME: 10 MIN. • **MAKES:** 2 SERVINGS

- 1 **cup 2% milk**
- ½ **cup fresh or frozen strawberries**
- ½ **cup vanilla ice cream, softened**
- 2 **tablespoons sugar**
- 2 **to 3 drops red food coloring, optional**
- 1 **cup ginger ale, chilled**

1. In a blender, combine the milk, strawberries, ice cream, sugar and food coloring if desired; cover and process until smooth. Pour into chilled glasses. Add ginger ale and serve immediately.

Spring

Welcome the season of renewal with beautiful brunch-worthy
sweets and rolls. Enjoy spring's first fruits.

Jam-Topped Mini Cheesecakes

Presto! With this simple recipe, you can turn cheesecake into
irresistible finger food.

TASTE OF HOME TEST KITCHEN

PREP: 20 MIN. • **BAKE:** 15 MIN. + CHILLING • **MAKES:** 1 DOZEN

- 1   **cup graham cracker crumbs**
- 3   **tablespoons butter, melted**
- 1   **package (8 ounces) cream cheese, softened**
- ⅓   **cup sugar**
- 1   **teaspoon vanilla extract**
- 1   **egg, lightly beaten**
     Assorted jams, warmed

1. In a small bowl, combine graham cracker crumbs and
butter. Press gently onto the bottom of 12 paper-lined muffin
cups. In another small bowl, beat the cream cheese, sugar
and vanilla until smooth. Add egg; beat on low speed just
until combined. Spoon over crusts.

2. Bake at 350° for 15-16 minutes or until centers are set.
Cool for 10 minutes before removing from pan to a wire rack
to cool completely. Refrigerate for at least 1 hour. Remove
paper liners; top each cheesecake with 1 teaspoon jam.

Peeps Sunflower Cake

The inspiration for this cake came from one of my favorite
flowers: the sunflower. The yellow Peeps make eye-catching
flower petals, and I carefully placed chocolate chips in a circular
pattern to resemble the seeds in the middle of a sunflower.

BETHANY ELEDGE, CLEVELAND, TENNESSEE

PREP: 15 MIN. • **BAKE:** 30 MIN. + COOLING • **MAKES:** 12 SERVINGS

- 1   **package (18¼ ounces) yellow cake mix**
- 2   **cans (16 ounces each) chocolate frosting**

- 19   **yellow chick Peeps candies**
- 1½   **cups semisweet chocolate chips**

1. Prepare and bake cake according to package directions,
using two greased and waxed paper-lined 9-in. round baking
pans. Cool for 10 minutes before removing from pans to wire
racks to cool completely; carefully remove waxed paper.

2. Level tops of cakes. Spread frosting between layers and
over the top and sides of cake.

3. Without separating Peeps and curving slightly to fit,
arrange chicks around edge of cake for sunflower petals. For
sunflower seeds, arrange chocolate chips in center of cake.

Strawberry Rhubarb Torte

This airy cake will delight your tastebuds! My children, especially my son, really enjoyed this dessert while they were growing up.

KATHLEEN KOWSKI, TRINITY, NORTH CAROLINA

PREP: 40 MIN. + CHILLING • **MAKES:** 4 SERVINGS

- 2 **cups sliced fresh or frozen rhubarb**
- ⅓ **cup water**
- 2 **tablespoons plus 4½ teaspoons sugar, divided**
- 3 **tablespoons plus 1 teaspoon strawberry gelatin**
- ⅔ **cup heavy whipping cream**
- ¼ **teaspoon vanilla extract**
- 14 **ladyfingers, split**
- 1 **teaspoon cornstarch**
- 1 **teaspoon cold water**
- ½ **cup sliced fresh strawberries**

1. In a small saucepan, bring the rhubarb, water and 2 tablespoons sugar to a boil. Reduce heat; simmer, uncovered, for 6-8 minutes or until rhubarb is tender. Cool slightly. Cover and refrigerate ⅓ cup rhubarb liquid for glaze.

2. Place rhubarb and remaining liquid in a blender; cover and process until pureed. Return to saucepan. Bring to a boil; stir in gelatin until dissolved. Refrigerate for at least 15 minutes or until slightly thickened.

3. Meanwhile, in a large bowl, beat cream until it begins to thicken. Add vanilla; beat until stiff peaks form. Fold whipped cream into rhubarb mixture.

4. Arrange half of the ladyfingers on the bottom of an ungreased 6-in. springform pan. Spread half of the rhubarb mixture into pan. Arrange remaining ladyfingers over rhubarb mixture; carefully spread with remaining rhubarb mixture. Refrigerate for 8 hours or overnight.

5. Transfer reserved rhubarb liquid to a small saucepan; stir in remaining sugar. Bring to a boil. Combine cornstarch and water until smooth; gradually stir into the pan. Bring to a boil; cook and stir for 2 minutes or until thickened. Spread over rhubarb layer. Arrange strawberry slices over glaze. Remove sides of pan.

Pineapple Layer Cake

I often prepare this tender, golden cake at Easter, but it's wonderful just about any time of year. Pineapple frosting provides a fast finishing touch.

LINDA SAKAL, BILOXI, MISSISSIPPI

PREP: 15 MIN. • **BAKE:** 25 MIN. + COOLING • **MAKES:** 12 SERVINGS

- 1 **package (18¼ ounces) yellow cake mix**
- 1 **can (11 ounces) mandarin oranges, drained**
- 1 **can (20 ounces) unsweetened crushed pineapple, drained**
- 1 **package (3.4 ounces) instant vanilla pudding mix**
- 1 **package (12 ounces) frozen whipped topping, thawed**

1. Prepare cake batter according to package directions. Beat in oranges until blended. Pour into two greased and floured 9-in. round baking pans.

2. Bake at 350° for 25-30 minutes or until a toothpick inserted near the center comes out clean. Cool for 10 minutes before removing from pans to wire racks to cool completely.

3. Combine pineapple and dry pudding mix; fold in whipped topping. Spread between layers and over top and sides of cake. Store in the refrigerator.

Orange Bunny Rolls

I make these tender yeast rolls for special occasions. Orange zest and marmalade give them a pleasant citrus flavor. Shape them any way you like for year-round enjoyment.

GERRI BROWN, CANFIELD, OHIO

PREP: 45 MIN. + RISING • **BAKE:** 15 MIN. + COOLING • **MAKES:** 1 DOZEN

- 2 **packages (¼ ounce each) active dry yeast**
- ¼ **cup warm water (110° to 115°)**
- 1 **cup warm 2% milk (110° to 115°)**
- ½ **cup shortening**
- 2 **eggs**
- ⅓ **cup sugar**
- ¼ **cup orange juice**
- 2 **tablespoons grated orange peel**
- 1 **teaspoon salt**
- 5 **to 5½ cups all-purpose flour**

GLAZE:
- 2 **cups confectioners' sugar**
- ¼ **cup water**
- 1 **tablespoon orange marmalade**
- ½ **teaspoon butter, softened**

1. In a large bowl, dissolve yeast in warm water. Add the milk, shortening, eggs, sugar, orange juice, orange peel, salt and 3 cups flour; beat until smooth. Stir in enough remaining flour to form a soft dough.

2. Turn onto a floured surface; knead until smooth and elastic, about 6-8 minutes. Place in a greased bowl, turning once to grease top. Cover and let rise in a warm place until doubled, about 1 hour.

3. Punch dough down; turn on a lightly floured surface. Divide into 13 pieces. Shape 12 pieces into 12-in. ropes. Fold each in half; twist top half of the open end twice to form ears. Place 2 in. apart on greased baking sheets. Shape remaining dough into 12 balls. Place one on the loop end of each roll to form a tail; press into dough. Cover and let rise until doubled, about 30 minutes.

4. Bake at 375° for 12-15 minutes or until golden brown. Cool on wire racks. In a small bowl, combine the glaze ingredients. Spread over rolls.

Mini Pineapple Upside-Down Cakes

These individual pineapple upside-down cakes are an eye-catching addition to my holiday dessert table. A cake mix makes them easy to bake on any special day—whether it is a Wednesday or a holiday!

CINDY COLLEY, OTHELLO, WASHINGTON

PREP: 30 MIN. • **BAKE:** 20 MIN. + COOLING • **MAKES:** 2 DOZEN

- ⅔ **cup packed brown sugar**
- ⅓ **cup butter, melted**
- 1 **can (20 ounces) pineapple tidbits**
- 12 **maraschino cherries, halved**

- 1 **package (18¼ ounces) yellow cake mix**
- 3 **eggs**
- ⅓ **cup canola oil**

1. In a small bowl, combine brown sugar and butter until blended. Spoon into 24 greased muffin cups. Drain pineapple, reserving the juice; spoon pineapple into prepared cups. Place a cherry half cut side down in the center of each.

2. In a large bowl, combine the cake mix, eggs, oil and reserved pineapple juice. Beat on low speed for 30 seconds. Beat on medium for 2 minutes. Spoon over pineapple, filling each cup three-fourths full.

3. Bake at 350° for 18-22 minutes or until a toothpick inserted near the center comes out clean. Immediately invert onto wire racks to cool.

Touch of Spring Muffins

Strawberries and rhubarb are a winning combination, and their sweet-tart pairing makes these lovely muffins delightful as part of a meal or as a snack. Remember this recipe when your backyard rhubarb is ready to cut or you see fresh stalks at the store.

GAIL SYKORA, MENOMONEE FALLS, WISCONSIN

PREP: 10 MIN. • **BAKE:** 25 MIN. • **MAKES:** 1 DOZEN

- 2 **cups all-purpose flour**
- ½ **cup sugar**
- 1 **tablespoon baking powder**
- ½ **teaspoon salt**
- 1 **egg**
- ¾ **cup milk**
- ⅓ **cup canola oil**
- ½ **cup sliced fresh strawberries**
- ½ **cup sliced fresh rhubarb**

TOPPING:
- 6 **small fresh strawberries, halved**
- 2 **teaspoons sugar**

1. In a large bowl, combine the flour, sugar, baking powder and salt. In a small bowl, beat the egg, milk and oil until smooth. Stir into dry ingredients just until moistened. Fold in strawberries and rhubarb.

2. Fill greased or paper-lined muffin cups three-fourths full. Place a strawberry half, cut side down, on each. Sprinkle with sugar.

3. Bake at 375° for 22-25 minutes or until a toothpick inserted near the center comes out clean. Cool for 5 minutes before removing from pan to a wire rack. Serve warm.

Easter Egg Bread

I've made this Easter treat for over 25 years! Easter eggs baked in the dough give this sweet bread such a festive look. Leave them out and it can be enjoyed any time of year. It's wonderful with baked ham.

HEATHER DURANTE, WELLSBURG, VIRGINIA

PREP: 35 MIN. + RISING • **BAKE:** 30 MIN. + COOLING
MAKES: 1 LOAF (16 SLICES)

- 6 **to 6½ cups all-purpose flour**
- ½ **cup sugar**
- 2 **packages (¼ ounce each) active dry yeast**
- 1 **to 2 teaspoons ground cardamom**
- 1 **teaspoon salt**
- 1½ **cups milk**
- 6 **tablespoons butter, cubed**
- 4 **eggs**
- 3 **to 6 hard-cooked eggs**
  Canola oil
- 2 **tablespoons water**

1. In a large bowl, combine 2 cups flour, sugar, yeast, cardamom and salt. In a saucepan, heat milk and butter to 120°-130°. Add to dry ingredients; beat just until moistened. Add 3 eggs; beat until smooth. Stir in enough remaining flour to form a soft dough.

2. Turn onto a floured surface; knead until smooth and elastic, about 6-8 minutes. Place in a greased bowl, turning once to grease top. Cover and let rise in a warm place until doubled, about 45 minutes.

3. Dye hard-cooked eggs; lightly rub with oil. Punch dough down. Turn onto a lightly floured surface; divide dough into thirds. Shape each portion into a 24-in. rope.

4. Place ropes on a greased baking sheet and braid; bring ends together to form a ring. Pinch ends to seal. Gently separate braided ropes and tuck dyed eggs into openings. Cover and let rise until doubled, about 20 minutes.

5. Beat water and remaining egg; gently brush over dough. Bake at 375° for 28-32 or until golden brown. Remove from pan to a wire rack to cool. Refrigerate leftovers.

Florida Citrus Meringue Pie

Why limit a great dessert to just one kind of citrus fruit? Thanks to orange and lemon, this lovely pie packs a bold sweet-tart flavor!

BARBARA CARLUCCI, ORANGE PARK, FLORIDA

PREP: 30 MIN. • **BAKE:** 15 MIN. + CHILLING • **MAKES:** 8 SERVINGS

> **Pastry for single-crust pie (9 inches)**
> 1 **cup sugar**
> 5 **tablespoons cornstarch**
> ½ **teaspoon salt**
> 1 **cup water**
> 1 **cup orange juice**
> 4 **egg yolks, lightly beaten**
> ½ **cup lemon juice**
> 2 **tablespoons butter**
> 1 **teaspoon grated lemon peel**
> 1 **teaspoon grated orange peel**
> **MERINGUE:**
> 3 **egg whites**
> 1 **teaspoon vanilla extract**
> 6 **tablespoons sugar**

1. Roll out pastry to fit a 9-in. pie plate. Transfer pastry to pie plate. Trim pastry to ½ in. beyond edge of plate; flute edges. Line unpricked pastry with a double thickness of heavy-duty foil.

2. Bake at 450° for 8 minutes. Remove foil; bake 5-7 minutes longer or until lightly browned. Cool on a wire rack. Reduce heat to 350°.

3. Meanwhile, in a large saucepan, combine the sugar, cornstarch and salt. Gradually stir in water and orange juice until smooth. Cook and stir over medium-high heat until thickened and bubbly. Reduce heat; cook and stir 2 minutes longer (mixture will be thick).

4. Remove from the heat. Stir a small amount of hot mixture into egg yolks; return all to the pan, stirring constantly. Bring to a gentle boil; cook and stir 2 minutes longer. Remove from the heat. Gently stir in the lemon juice, butter, and lemon and orange peels. Pour into prepared crust.

5. In a large bowl, beat egg whites and vanilla on medium speed until soft peaks form. Gradually beat in sugar, 1 tablespoon at a time, on high until stiff glossy peaks form and sugar is dissolved. Spread over hot filling, sealing edges to crust.

6. Bake at 350° for 12-15 minutes or until meringue is golden brown. Cool on a wire rack for 1 hour. Refrigerate for at least 3 hours before serving. Store leftovers in the refrigerator.

Coconut Kisses

Chewy on the inside and crisp on the outside, these meringue cookies are delicious. They add a light touch to the cookie platter, not only during the holidays but all year round.

DOROTHY BEAUDRY, ALBERTVILLE, MINNESOTA

PREP: 15 MIN. • **BAKE:** 20 MIN. • **YIELD:** 1 DOZEN

> 1 **egg white**
> ½ **cup confectioners' sugar**
> 1 **cup flaked coconut**

1. Place egg white in a small bowl; let stand at room temperature for 30 minutes.

2. Beat on medium speed until soft peaks form. Gradually beat in confectioners' sugar, 1 tablespoon at a time, on high until stiff peaks form. Fold in coconut.

3. Drop meringue by rounded tablespoonfuls 2 in. apart onto a parchment paper-lined baking sheet.

4. Bake at 325° for 18-20 minutes or until firm to the touch. Cool for 1 minute before removing to a wire rack. Store in an airtight container.

Chocolate-Covered Eggs

These chocolaty eggs beat store-bought varieties hands down! The smiles you'll see when you serve these pretty candies make them worth the effort.

LOUISE OBERFOELL, BOWMAN, NORTH DAKOTA

PREP: 1 HOUR + CHILLING • **MAKES:** 2 DOZEN

- ¼ **cup butter, softened**
- 1 **jar (7 ounces) marshmallow creme**
- 1 **teaspoon vanilla extract**
- 3 **cups plus 1 tablespoon confectioners' sugar, divided**
- 3 **to 4 drops yellow food coloring, optional**
- 2 **cups (12 ounces) white baking chips or semisweet chocolate chips**
- 2 **tablespoons shortening**
  Icing of your choice
  Assorted decorating candies

1. In a large bowl, beat the butter, marshmallow creme and vanilla until smooth. Gradually beat in 3 cups confectioners' sugar. Place ¼ cup butter mixture in a bowl; add yellow food coloring if desired and mix well. Shape into 24 small balls; cover and chill for 30 minutes. Wrap plain mixture in plastic wrap; chill for 30 minutes.

2. Dust work surface with remaining confectioners' sugar. Divide plain dough into 24 pieces. Wrap one piece of plain dough around each yellow ball and form into an egg shape. Place on a waxed paper-lined baking sheet; cover with plastic wrap. Freeze for 15 minutes or until firm.

3. In a microwave, melt chips and shortening; stir until smooth. Dip eggs in mixture; allow excess to drip off. Return eggs to waxed paper. Refrigerate for 30 minutes or until set. Decorate with icing and decorating candies as desired. Store in an airtight container in the refrigerator.

Apricot Upside-Down Cake

My Aunt Anne, who is a great cook, gave me a taste of this golden cake and I couldn't believe how delicious it was. Apricots give it a unique and attractive twist.

RUTH ANN STELFOX, RAYMOND, ALBERTA

PREP: 30 MIN. • **BAKE:** 35 MIN. + COOLING • **MAKES:** 9 SERVINGS

- 2 **cans (15 ounces each) apricot halves**
- ¼ **cup butter, cubed**
- ½ **cup packed brown sugar**
- 2 **eggs, separated**
- ⅔ **cup sugar**
- ⅔ **cup cake flour**
- ¾ **teaspoon baking powder**
- ¼ **teaspoon salt**

1. Drain apricots, reserving 3 tablespoons juice (discard remaining juice or save for another use); set aside. Place butter in a greased 9-in. square baking pan; place in a 350° oven for 3-4 minutes or until melted. Stir in the brown sugar. Arrange apricot halves, cut side up, in a single layer over sugar.

2. In a large bowl, beat egg yolks on high speed for 3 minutes or until light and fluffy. Gradually add sugar, beating until thick and lemon-colored. Stir in reserved apricot juice. Combine flour, baking powder and salt; gradually add to egg yolk mixture. In another bowl, beat egg whites until stiff peaks form. Fold into yolk mixture.

3. Carefully spread over apricots. Bake at 350° for 35-40 minutes or until a toothpick inserted near the center comes out clean. Cool for 10 minutes before inverting onto a serving plate.

Hot Cross Buns

I found the handwritten copy of this recipe tucked inside one of my mother's old cookbooks. As a young girl, I used to help her make these buns.

LOUELL FRANKS, EAST PEORIA, ILLINOIS

PREP: 35 MIN. + RISING • **BAKE:** 25 MIN. + COOLING • **MAKES:** 1 DOZEN

- 1 **package (¼ ounce) active dry yeast**
- 1 **tablespoon plus ½ cup sugar, divided**
- 1 **cup warm milk (110° to 115°)**
- ¼ **cup butter, softened**
- ¼ **cup raisins**
- 1 **egg**
- ¼ **teaspoon salt**
- 3½ to 3¾ **cups all-purpose flour**

ICING:
- ⅔ **cup confectioners' sugar**
- 1 **teaspoon butter, softened**
- ¼ **teaspoon vanilla extract**
- 2 **to 3 teaspoons milk**

1. In a large bowl, dissolve yeast and 1 tablespoon sugar in milk. Let stand for 5 minutes. Add the butter, raisins, egg, salt and remaining sugar; beat until smooth. Stir in enough flour to form a soft dough.

2. Turn onto a floured surface; knead until smooth and elastic, about 6-8 minutes. Place in a greased bowl, turning once to grease the top. Cover and let rise in a warm place until doubled, about 1 hour.

3. Punch dough down. Turn onto a lightly floured surface; divide into 12 portions. Shape each into a ball. Place in a greased 13-in. x 9-in. baking pan. Cover and let rise until doubled, about 45 minutes.

4. Bake at 375° for 25-30 minutes or until browned. Remove from the pan to a wire rack to cool.

5. For icing, combine the confectioners' sugar, butter, vanilla and enough milk to achieve a piping consistency. Pipe an "X" on top of each bun.

Swan Cream Puffs

Grandpa's farm was the setting for our serviceman son's wedding to his German bride. The reception included special touches like these impressive little pastries. They look beautiful and taste marvelous.

CAROL DAVIS, KEENE, NEW HAMPSHIRE

PREP: 1½ HOURS + CHILLING • **BAKE:** 35 MIN. + COOLING
MAKES: 3 DOZEN

    1 cup water
    ½ cup butter, cubed
    ¼ teaspoon salt
    1 cup all-purpose flour
    4 eggs
    2 packages (3.4 ounces each) instant vanilla pudding mix
    2 tablespoons seedless raspberry jam, optional
       Confectioners' sugar

1. In a heavy saucepan over medium heat, bring the water, butter and salt to a boil. Add flour all at once; stir until a smooth ball forms. Remove from the heat; let stand for 5 minutes. Add eggs, one at a time, beating well after each addition. Beat until smooth and shiny.

2. Cut a small hole in the corner of pastry bag or heavy-duty resealable plastic bag; insert round pastry tip #7. Fill bag with batter. On a greased baking sheet, pipe 3 dozen 2-in.-long "S" shapes for the swan necks, making a small dollop at the end of each for the head. Bake at 400° for 5-8 minutes or until golden brown. Remove to wire racks to cool.

3. For swan bodies, drop remaining batter by 36 level tablespoonfuls 2 in. apart onto greased baking sheets. With a small icing knife or spatula, shape batter into 2-in. x 1½-in. teardrops. Bake at 400° for 30-35 minutes or until golden brown. Cool on wire racks.

4. Meanwhile, prepare pudding according to package directions for pie filling; chill.

5. Just before serving, cut off top third of swan bodies; set tops aside. Remove any soft dough inside. Spoon filling into bottoms of puffs. Top each with a small amount of jam if desired. Cut reserved tops in half lengthwise to form wings; set wings in filling. Place necks in filling. Dust with confectioners' sugar.

Bakeshop **HOW-TO**

Making Swan Cream Puffs

To make swan necks, pipe batter into 3 dozen 2-in. "S" shapes onto greased baking sheets, making a small dollop at the end of each for the head. Bake as directed.

To assemble cream puffs, cut off the top third of each swan body. Remove any soft dough inside. Cut tops in half lengthwise to form wings. Fill bottoms of puffs with pudding. Arrange necks and wings in filling.

Heavenly Filled Strawberries

Put down the cake balls! These luscious stuffed berries are the perfect bite-size dessert for a party.

STEPHEN MUNRO, BEAVERBANK, NOVA SCOTIA

PREP/TOTAL TIME: 20 MIN. • **MAKES:** 3 DOZEN

- 3 **dozen large fresh strawberries**
- 2 **packages (one 8 ounces, one 3 ounces) cream cheese, softened**
- ½ **cup confectioners' sugar**
- ¼ **teaspoon almond extract**
  Grated chocolate

1. Remove stems from strawberries; cut a deep "X" in the tip of each berry. Gently spread berries open.

2. In a small bowl, beat the cream cheese, confectioners' sugar and extract until light and fluffy. Pipe or spoon about 2 teaspoons into each berry; sprinkle with chocolate. Chill until serving.

Almond Petits Fours

Dainty bite-size cakes are often the highlight of a ladies' luncheon. Serve them on a platter with a small tongs so guests can easily help themselves.

TASTE OF HOME TEST KITCHEN

PREP: 1½ HOURS • **BAKE:** 15 MIN. + COOLING • **MAKES:** 2½ DOZEN

    1   can (8 ounces) almond paste
    ¾   cup butter, softened
    ¾   cup sugar
    4   eggs
    1   cup cake flour
    ¼   cup seedless raspberry spreadable fruit
GLAZE:
    4½ cups sugar
    2¼ cups water
    ¼   teaspoon cream of tartar
    1½ teaspoons clear vanilla extract
    ¼   teaspoon almond extract
    6   cups confectioners' sugar
        Assorted food coloring

1. Line a 15-in. x 10-in. x 1-in. baking pan with parchment paper; coat the paper with cooking spray and set aside.

2. In a large bowl, cream the almond paste, butter and sugar until light and fluffy. Add eggs, one at a time, beating well after each addition. Beat in flour. Spread evenly into prepared pan.

3. Bake at 325° for 12-15 minutes or until a toothpick inserted near the center comes out clean. Cool for 10 minutes before removing from pan to a wire rack to cool completely.

4. Cut cake in half widthwise. Spread jam over one half; top with remaining half. Cut into assorted 1½-in. shapes.

5. In a large saucepan, combine the sugar, water and cream of tartar. Cook over medium-high heat, without stirring, until a candy thermometer reads 226°. Remove from the heat; cool at room temperature to 100°. Stir in extracts. Using a portable mixer, beat in confectioners' sugar until smooth. Tint glaze with food coloring.

6. Gently dip petits fours, one at a time, into warm glaze. Remove with a fork; allow excess glaze to drip off. (If glaze becomes too thick, stir in 1 teaspoon hot water at a time to thin.) Place petits fours on wire racks over waxed paper; let dry completely.

Editor's Note: *We recommend that you test your candy thermometer before each use by bringing water to a boil; the thermometer should read 212°. Adjust your recipe temperature up or down based on your test.*

Carrot Cake

We have enjoyed this cake for years. Whenever there's a gathering of family and friends, my cake is always requested.
MELANIE HABENER, SANTA MARIA, CALIFORNIA

PREP: 20 MIN. • **BAKE:** 50 MIN. + COOLING • **MAKES:** 12-15 SERVINGS

    3   eggs
    ¾   cup canola oil
    ¾   cup buttermilk
    2   cups sugar
    2   teaspoons vanilla extract
    2   cups all-purpose flour
    2   teaspoons ground cinnamon
    2   teaspoons baking soda
    ½   teaspoon salt
    1   can (8 ounces) crushed pineapple, undrained
    2   cups grated carrots
    1   cup raisins
    1   cup chopped walnuts
    1   cup flaked coconut
CREAM CHEESE FROSTING:
    1   package (8 ounces) cream cheese, softened
    ½   cup butter, softened
    3¾ cups confectioners' sugar
    2   tablespoons heavy whipping cream
    1   teaspoon vanilla extract

1. In a large bowl, beat the eggs, oil, buttermilk, sugar and vanilla until well blended. Combine the flour, cinnamon, baking soda and salt; gradually beat into egg mixture until blended. Stir in the pineapple, carrots, raisins, walnuts and coconut.

2. Pour into a greased 13-in. x 9-in. baking dish. Bake at 350° for 50-55 minutes or until a toothpick inserted near the center comes out clean. Cool on a wire rack.

3. In another large bowl, combine frosting ingredients; beat until creamy. Frost cake.

Raspberry Lemon Cake

Want a change from chocolate cake? Try this elegant after-dinner treat packed with refreshing lemon flavor from the cake to the homemade lemon curd and creamy frosting. It won a blue ribbon at the Alaska State Fair and it's definitely a winner with me.

SHIRLEY WARREN, THIENSVILLE, WISCONSIN

PREP: 1¼ HOURS + CHILLING • **BAKE:** 20 MIN. + COOLING
MAKES: 16 SERVINGS

- 3 eggs
- ¾ cup sugar
- ½ cup lemon juice
- ¼ cup butter, cubed
- 1 tablespoon grated lemon peel
CAKE:
- 1 package (3 ounces) lemon gelatin
- ½ cup boiling water
- ½ cup butter, softened
- ½ cup canola oil
- 1¾ cups sugar, divided
- 4 eggs
- ½ cup lemon juice
- 4 teaspoons grated lemon peel
- 1 teaspoon lemon extract
- 1 teaspoon vanilla extract
- 2½ cups all-purpose flour
- 2½ teaspoons baking powder
- ½ teaspoon salt
- ½ cup evaporated milk
- ¾ cup thawed lemonade concentrate
FROSTING:
- 2 packages (3 ounces each) cream cheese, softened
- 6 tablespoons butter, softened
- 3¾ to 4 cups confectioners' sugar
- 4½ teaspoons lemon juice
- 1½ teaspoons grated lemon peel
- ¾ teaspoon vanilla extract
- ¾ cup seedless raspberry jam
  Fresh raspberries, optional

1. For lemon curd, in a heavy saucepan, beat eggs and sugar. Stir in the lemon juice, butter and lemon peel. Cook and stir over medium-low heat for 15 minutes or until mixture is thickened and reaches 160°. Cool for 10 minutes. Cover and chill for 1½ hours or until thickened.

2. For cake, in a small bowl, dissolve gelatin in boiling water; set aside to cool.

3. In a large bowl, beat the butter, oil and 1½ cups sugar until light and fluffy, about 5 minutes. Add eggs, one at a time, beating well after each addition. Beat in the gelatin mixture, lemon juice, lemon peel and extracts. Combine the flour, baking powder and salt; add to the butter mixture alternately with milk, beating well after each addition.

4. Pour into three greased and floured 9-in. round baking pans. Bake at 350° for 20-25 minutes or until a toothpick inserted near the center comes out clean.

5. In a microwave-safe bowl, combine lemonade concentrate and remaining sugar. Microwave, uncovered, on high for 2 minutes or until sugar is dissolved, stirring occasionally. Poke holes in warm cakes with a fork; pour lemonade mixture over cakes. Cool for 10 minutes before removing from pans to wire racks to cool completely.

6. For frosting, in a large bowl, beat cream cheese and butter until fluffy. Add the confectioners' sugar, lemon juice, lemon peel and vanilla; beat until blended.

7. To assemble, place one cake layer on a serving plate; spread with 6 tablespoons raspberry jam. Repeat. Top with remaining cake layer. Spread about ½ cup lemon curd over top of cake (save remaining curd for another use).

8. Spread frosting over sides of cake and pipe a border along the top and bottom edges. Garnish with raspberries if desired. Chill for 1 hour.

Butterhorns

I always have to double the recipe for these buttery rolls because they never last long. You can shape them any way you like, but to me, a crescent shape is so pretty.

KELLY KIRBY, WESTVILLE, NOVA SCOTIA

PREP: 35 MIN. + RISING • **BAKE:** 10 MIN. • **MAKES:** 2 DOZEN

- 1 **tablespoon active dry yeast**
- 1 **teaspoon plus ⅓ cup sugar**
- ½ **cup warm water (110° to 115°)**
- ½ **cup butter, softened**
- ½ **cup warm 2% milk (110° to 115°)**
- 1 **egg**
- ¾ **teaspoon salt**
- 4 **cups all-purpose flour**

1. In a large bowl, dissolve yeast and 1 teaspoon sugar in warm water. Add the butter, milk, egg, salt, remaining sugar and 2 cups flour. Beat until smooth. Stir in enough remaining flour to form a soft dough.

2. Turn onto a floured surface; knead until smooth and elastic, about 6-8 minutes. Place in a greased bowl, turning once to grease the top. Cover and let rise in a warm place until doubled, about 1 hour.

3. Punch dough down. Turn onto a lightly floured surface; divide in half. Roll each portion into a 12-in. circle; cut each circle into 12 wedges. Roll up wedges from the wide end and place point side down 2 in. apart on greased baking sheets. Curve ends to form crescents.

4. Cover and let rise in a warm place until doubled, about 30 minutes. Bake at 350° for 10-12 minutes or until golden brown. Remove from pans to wire racks.

Brunch Beignets

Enjoy breakfast the New Orleans way with these warm, crispy bites. Topped with powdered sugar, they are a delight!

LOIS RUTHERFORD, ELKTON, FLORIDA

PREP: 20 MIN. • **COOK:** 5 MIN./BATCH • **MAKES:** ABOUT 2 DOZEN

- 2 **eggs, separated**
- 1 **cup all-purpose flour**
- 1 **teaspoon baking powder**
- ⅛ **teaspoon salt**
- ½ **cup sugar**
- ¼ **cup water**
- 1 **tablespoon butter, melted**
- 2 **teaspoons grated lemon peel**
- 1 **teaspoon vanilla extract**
- 1 **teaspoon brandy, optional**
  Oil for deep-fat frying
  Confectioners' sugar

1. Place egg whites in a small bowl; let stand at room temperature for 30 minutes.

2. Meanwhile, in a large bowl, combine the flour, baking powder and salt. Combine the egg yolks, sugar, water, butter, lemon peel, vanilla and brandy if desired; stir into dry ingredients just until combined. Beat egg whites on medium speed until soft peaks form; fold into batter.

3. In an electric skillet or deep-fat fryer, heat oil to 375°. Drop batter by teaspoonfuls, a few at a time, into hot oil. Fry until golden brown, about 1½ minutes on each side. Drain on paper towels. Dust with confectioners' sugar. Serve warm.

Layered Lemon Pie

This is a great ending for almost any meal that kids and adults all enjoy. The creamy lemon filling is always a hit with my husband.
ELIZABETH YODER, BELCOURT, NORTH DAKOTA

PREP: 20 MIN. + CHILLING • **MAKES:** 8 SERVINGS

- 1 package (8 ounces) cream cheese, softened
- ½ cup sugar
- 1 can (15¾ ounces) lemon pie filling, divided
- 1 carton (8 ounces) frozen whipped topping, thawed
- 1 graham cracker crust (9 inches)

1. In a small bowl, beat cream cheese and sugar until light and fluffy. Beat in half of the pie filling. Fold in whipped topping. Spoon into crust. Spread remaining pie filling over cream cheese layer. Refrigerate for at least 15 minutes before serving.

Special Rhubarb Cake

The women at church made this special cake with sweet vanilla sauce for my 84th birthday.
BIENA SCHLABACH, MILLERSBURG, OHIO

PREP: 20 MIN. • **BAKE:** 40 MIN. + COOLING
MAKES: 9 SERVINGS (1¼ CUPS SAUCE)

- 2 tablespoons butter, softened
- 1 cup sugar
- 1 egg
- 2 cups all-purpose flour
- 1 teaspoon baking powder
- ½ teaspoon baking soda
- ½ teaspoon salt
- 1 cup buttermilk
- 2 cups chopped fresh or frozen rhubarb

STREUSEL TOPPING:
- ¼ cup all-purpose flour
- ¼ cup sugar
- 2 tablespoons butter, melted

VANILLA SAUCE:
- ½ cup butter, cubed
- ¾ cup sugar
- ½ cup evaporated milk
- 1 teaspoon vanilla extract

1. In a large bowl, cream butter and sugar until light and fluffy. Beat in egg. Combine flour, baking powder, baking soda and salt; add to creamed mixture alternately with buttermilk, beating just until moistened. Fold in the rhubarb. Pour into a greased 9-in. square baking dish.

2. Combine topping ingredients; sprinkle over batter. Bake at 350° for 40-45 minutes or until a toothpick comes out clean. Cool on a wire rack.

3. For sauce, melt butter in a saucepan. Add sugar and milk. Bring to a boil; cook and stir for 2-3 minutes or until thickened. Remove from the heat; stir in vanilla. Serve with the cake.

Editor's Note: *If using frozen rhubarb, measure rhubarb while still frozen, then thaw completely. Drain in a colander, but do not press liquid out.*

Bakeshop TIP

Rhubarb Basics

Look for rhubarb stalks that are crisp and brightly colored. Tightly wrap in a plastic bag and store in the refrigerator for up to 3 days. Wash the stalks and remove the poisonous leaves before using. One pound of rhubarb stalks yields about 3 cups chopped rhubarb.

Summer

Thrill your gang with fun and refreshing treats. Desserts inspired by Creamsicles, root beer floats, even watermelon? We got 'em!

3. Set aside 2 tablespoons frosting for decorating. Place 1¼ cups frosting in a bowl; tint red. Tint remaining frosting green.

4. Place one cake layer on a serving plate; spread with ½ cup red frosting to within ¼ in. of edges. Top with second cake. Frost top with remaining red frosting to within ¾ in. of edges. Frost sides and top edge of cake with green frosting.

5. Cut a ¼-in. hole in the corner of pastry or plastic bag. Fill the bag with reserved white frosting. Pipe around top edge of cake where green and pink frostings meet. For seeds, insert chocolate chips upside down into cake top.

Watermelon Cake

No one will ever guess how simple it is to make this whimsical cake. A package of watermelon gelatin added to the cake batter gives it refreshing flavor while chocolate chips form the sweet seeds. After one bite, kids of all ages will be lining up for a second slice.

TASTE OF HOME TEST KITCHEN

PREP: 20 MIN. • **BAKE:** 30 MIN. + COOLING • **MAKES:** 12 SERVINGS

- 1 **package (18¼ ounces) white cake mix**
- 1 **package (3 ounces) watermelon gelatin**
- 1¼ **cups water**
- 2 **eggs**
- ¼ **cup canola oil**
- 2½ **cups prepared vanilla or cream cheese frosting, divided**
  Red and green gel food coloring
  Chocolate chips

1. In a large bowl, combine the cake mix, gelatin, water, eggs and oil; beat on low speed for 30 seconds. Beat on medium for 2 minutes.

2. Pour into two greased and floured 9-in. round baking pans. Bake at 350° for 30-35 minutes or until a toothpick inserted near the center comes out clean. Cool for 10 minutes before removing from pans to wire racks to cool completely.

Star-Spangled Fruit Tart

This crispy, creamy dessert is perfect for a Fourth of July celebration! With patriotic colors and a light, fluffy filling, this summery delight will be the hit of your get-together.

RENAE MONCUR, BURLEY, IDAHO

PREP: 25 MIN. • **BAKE:** 10 MIN. + COOLING • **MAKES:** 16 SERVINGS

- 1 **tube (18 ounces) refrigerated sugar cookie dough, softened**
- 1 **package (8 ounces) cream cheese, softened**
- ¼ **cup sugar**
- ½ **teaspoon almond extract**
- 1 **cup fresh blueberries**
- 1 **cup fresh raspberries**
- 1 **cup halved fresh strawberries**

1. Press cookie dough onto an ungreased 12-in. pizza pan. Bake at 350° for 10-15 minutes or until golden brown. Cool on a wire rack.

2. In a small bowl, beat the cream cheese, sugar and extract until smooth. Spread over crust. In center of tart, arrange berries in the shape of a star; add a berry border. Refrigerate until serving.

Berry Nectarine Buckle

I found this recipe in a magazine quite a long time ago but have changed it over the years to suit our tastes. We enjoy the combination of three berries plus nectarines, especially with a scoop of low-fat frozen yogurt.

LISA SJURSEN-DARLING, SCOTTSVILLE, NEW YORK

PREP: 25 MIN. • **BAKE:** 35 MIN. • **MAKES:** 20 SERVINGS

- ⅓ cup all-purpose flour
- ⅓ cup packed brown sugar
- 1 teaspoon ground cinnamon
- 3 tablespoons cold butter

BATTER:
- 6 tablespoons butter, softened
- ¾ cup plus 1 tablespoon sugar, divided
- 2 eggs
- 1½ teaspoons vanilla extract
- 2¼ cups all-purpose flour
- 2½ teaspoons baking powder
- ½ teaspoon salt
- ½ cup fat-free milk
- 1 cup fresh blueberries
- 1 pound medium nectarines, peeled, sliced and patted dry or 1 package (16 ounces) frozen unsweetened sliced peaches, thawed and patted dry
- ½ cup fresh raspberries
- ½ cup fresh blackberries

1. For topping, in a small bowl, combine the flour, brown sugar and cinnamon; cut in butter until crumbly. Set aside.

2. In a large bowl, cream the butter and ¾ cup sugar until light and fluffy. Add eggs, one at a time, beating well after each addition. Beat in vanilla. Combine the flour, baking powder and salt; add to creamed mixture alternately with milk, beating well after each addition. Set aside ¾ cup batter. Fold blueberries into remaining batter.

3. Spoon into a 13-in. x 9-in. baking dish coated with cooking spray. Arrange nectarines on top; sprinkle with remaining sugar. Drop reserved batter by teaspoonfuls over nectarines. Sprinkle with raspberries, blackberries and reserved topping.

4. Bake at 350° for 35-40 minutes or until a toothpick inserted near the center comes out clean. Serve warm.

Pink Lemonade Pie

Here's a cool comfort food. On very hot days, I serve it straight from the freezer. That way, it's slightly frosty and extra refreshing.

NELLA PARKER, HERSEY, MICHIGAN

PREP: 10 MIN. + FREEZING • **MAKES:** 6-8 SERVINGS

- 1 package (8 ounces) cream cheese, softened
- ¾ cup thawed pink lemonade concentrate
- 4 drops red food coloring, optional
- 1 carton (8 ounces) frozen whipped topping, thawed
- 1 shortbread pie crust (9 inches)
  Lemon slices and additional whipped topping, optional

1. In a large bowl, beat cream cheese until smooth. Beat in lemonade and food coloring if desired. Fold in whipped topping.

2. Spoon into pie crust. Freeze for at least 20 minutes. Remove from the freezer 10 minutes before serving. Garnish with lemon and additional whipped topping if desired.

Banana Split Cheesecake

This fruity dessert makes a light and festive treat that's sure to dazzle friends and family at the end of any meal. I top the tempting sweet with syrup, caramel and pecans for a fantastic look and mouthwatering taste.

CHERIE SWEET, EVANSVILLE, INDIANA

PREP: 35 MIN. + FREEZING • **MAKES:** 8 SERVINGS

- 1 **can (8 ounces) unsweetened crushed pineapple, divided**
- 2 **medium firm bananas, sliced**
- 1 **graham cracker crust (9 inches)**
- 1 **package (8 ounces) cream cheese**
- 1½ **cups pineapple sherbet, softened**
- 1 **package (3.4 ounces) instant vanilla pudding mix**
- 1 **carton (8 ounces) frozen whipped topping, thawed, divided**
- 4 **maraschino cherries, divided**
- 1 **tablespoon chocolate syrup**
- 1 **tablespoon caramel ice cream topping**
- 1 **tablespoon chopped pecans**

1. Drain pineapple, reserving juice. In a small bowl, combine bananas and 2 tablespoons reserved juice; let stand for 5 minutes. Drain bananas, discarding juice. Arrange bananas over bottom of crust; set aside.

2. In a large bowl, beat cream cheese and 2 tablespoons reserved pineapple juice. Gradually beat in sherbet. Gradually add pudding mix; beat 2 minutes longer. Refrigerate ⅓ cup pineapple until serving; fold remaining pineapple into cream cheese mixture. Fold in 2 cups whipped topping; spread evenly over banana slices. Cover and freeze until firm.

3. Remove from the freezer 10-15 minutes before serving. Chop three maraschino cherries and pat dry; arrange cherries and reserved pineapple around edge of pie. Drizzle with chocolate syrup and caramel topping. Dollop remaining whipped topping onto center of pie. Sprinkle with pecans; top with remaining cherry.

Orange Icebox Cheesecake

I love serving this impressive no-cook cheesecake with its pretty layers and silky texture. It is so light and dreamy!

MADONNA FAUNCE, BOISE, IDAHO

PREP: 25 MIN. + CHILLING • **MAKES:** 10-12 SERVINGS

- **2 cups graham cracker crumbs**
- **1 teaspoon ground cinnamon**
- **1 teaspoon grated orange peel**
- **½ cup butter, melted**

FILLING:
- **1 package (3 ounces) orange gelatin**
- **3 packages (8 ounces each) cream cheese, softened**
- **1¼ cups sugar**
- **1 can (5 ounces) evaporated milk**
- **⅓ cup thawed orange juice concentrate**
- **1 teaspoon lemon juice**
- **1 teaspoon vanilla extract**
- **1 envelope unflavored gelatin**
- **2 tablespoons cold water**
- **2 tablespoons boiling water**
- **1 carton (8 ounces) frozen whipped topping, thawed**

TOPPING:
- **2 cups whipped topping**
- **¼ cup sugar**
- **Citrus fruits and lemon balm, optional**

1. In a large bowl, combine the cracker crumbs, cinnamon, orange peel and butter. Press unto the bottom of a greased 10-in. springform pan. Refrigerate for at least 30 minutes.

2. Prepare orange gelatin according to package directions. Set aside ½ cup at room temperature. Chill remaining gelatin until slightly thickened, 40-60 minutes.

3. In a large bowl, beat cream cheese and sugar until smooth. Beat in the milk, orange juice concentrate, lemon juice and vanilla. Beat on medium-high speed 2 minutes longer.

4. In a small bowl, sprinkle unflavored gelatin over cold water; let stand for 2 minutes. Stir in boiling water until gelatin is completely dissolved. Stir into the room-temperature orange gelatin. Stir into cream cheese mixture, then fold in whipped topping. Pour into crust.

5. For topping, in a large bowl, beat whipped topping and sugar. Beat in refrigerated orange gelatin (mixture will be thin). Chill for 30 minutes. Gently spoon over filling (pan will be full). Refrigerate overnight. Remove sides of pan. Garnish with fruit and lemon balm if desired.

Frozen Oreo Loaf

Frosty slices of this show-stopping treat have a creamy blend of chocolate, coffee and cheesecake that's delightful any time of the year.

CHERYL MARTINETTO, GRAND RAPIDS, MINNESOTA

PREP: 15 MIN. + FREEZING • **MAKES:** 12 SERVINGS

- 2 **cups finely crushed Oreo cookies (about 20 cookies)**
- 3 **tablespoons butter, melted**
- 1 **package (8 ounces) cream cheese, softened**
- 1 **can (14 ounces) sweetened condensed milk**
- 1 **teaspoon vanilla extract**
- 2 **cups heavy whipping cream, whipped**
- 2 **tablespoons instant coffee granules**
- 1 **tablespoon hot water**
- ½ **cup chocolate syrup**

1. Line a 9-in. x 5-in. loaf pan with foil. In a bowl, combine the cookie crumbs and butter. Press firmly onto the bottom and 1½ in. up the sides of prepared pan.

2. In a large bowl, beat cream cheese until light and fluffy. Add milk and vanilla and mix well. Fold in whipped cream. Spoon half of the mixture into another bowl and set aside. Dissolve coffee in hot water; fold into remaining cream cheese mixture. Fold in chocolate syrup.

3. Spoon half of the chocolate mixture over crust. Top with half of the reserved cream cheese mixture. Repeat layers. Cut through layers with a knife to swirl the chocolate (pan will be full). Cover and freeze for 6 hours or overnight.

4. To serve, lift out of the pan; remove foil. Cut into slices.

Cherry Cola Chocolate Cake

For a truly different chocolate cake, think outside the box and inside the slow cooker. This easy dessert comes out warm, moist, fudgy and wonderful. And it won't heat up the kitchen.

ELAINE SWEET, DALLAS, TEXAS

PREP: 30 MIN. + STANDING • **COOK:** 2 HOURS + STANDING
MAKES: 8 SERVINGS

- ½ **cup cola**
- ½ **cup dried tart cherries**
- 1½ **cups all-purpose flour**
- ½ **cup sugar**
- 2 **ounces semisweet chocolate, chopped**
- 2½ **teaspoons baking powder**
- ½ **teaspoon salt**
- 1 **cup chocolate milk**
- ½ **cup butter, melted**
- 2 **teaspoons vanilla extract**

TOPPING:
- 1¼ **cups cola**
- ½ **cup sugar**
- ½ **cup packed brown sugar**
- 2 **ounces semisweet chocolate, chopped**
- ¼ **cup dark rum**
  Vanilla ice cream and maraschino cherries, optional

1. In a small saucepan, bring cola and dried cherries to a boil. Remove from the heat; let stand for 30 minutes.

2. In a large bowl, combine the flour, sugar, chocolate, baking powder and salt. Combine the chocolate milk, butter and vanilla; stir into dry ingredients just until moistened. Fold in cherry mixture. Pour into a 3-qt. slow cooker coated with cooking spray.

3. For topping, in a small saucepan, combine the cola, sugar and brown sugar. Cook and stir until sugar is dissolved. Remove from the heat; stir in chocolate and rum until smooth. Pour over batter; do not stir.

4. Cover and cook on high for 2 to 2½ hours or until set. Turn off heat; let stand, covered, for 30 minutes. Serve warm with ice cream and maraschino cherries if desired.

Editor's Note: *This recipe does not use eggs.*

3. In a small bowl, combine ⅔ cup frosting and blue food coloring. In another bowl, combine 1½ cups frosting and red food coloring. Fill pastry or plastic bag with ¼ cup white frosting; cut a small hole in the corner of the bag and set aside.

4. Frost cake top and sides with remaining white frosting. With blue frosting, frost a 3-in. section in the upper left corner of the cake. Pipe white stars over blue frosting. Fill another pastry or plastic bag with red frosting; cut a large hole in the corner of the bag. Pipe stripes across top of cake.

Strawberry Shortcake Cups

Back when store-bought shortcake was an unheard-of thing, my grandmother passed this recipe down to my mother. Mother later shared it with me, and I've since given it to my daughter.

ALTHEA HEERS, JEWELL, IOWA

PREP: 15 MIN. • **BAKE:** 15 MIN. + COOLING • **MAKES:** 8 SERVINGS

- 1 quart fresh strawberries
- 4 tablespoons sugar, divided
- 1½ cups all-purpose flour
- 1 tablespoon baking powder
- ½ teaspoon salt
- ¼ cup cold butter, cubed
- 1 egg
- ½ cup milk
  Whipped cream

1. Mash or slice the strawberries; place in a large bowl. Add 2 tablespoons sugar and set aside. In another bowl, combine flour, baking powder, salt and remaining sugar; cut in butter until crumbly. In a small bowl, beat egg and milk; stir into flour mixture just until moistened.

2. Fill eight greased muffin cups two-thirds full. Bake at 425° for 12 minutes or until golden. Remove from the pan to cool on a wire rack.

3. Just before serving, split shortcakes in half horizontally. Spoon berries and whipped cream between layers and over tops of shortcakes.

Patriotic Cake

Yes, you can make a decorated cake! This one looks great on a picnic table. It conveniently starts with a boxed cake mix, then is topped with a sweet and simple homemade frosting.

GLENDA JARBOE, OROVILLE, CALIFORNIA

PREP: 20 MIN. • **BAKE:** 20 MIN. + COOLING • **MAKES:** 12 SERVINGS

- 1 package (18¼ ounces) white cake mix
- 1 cup shortening
- 1 package (2 pounds) confectioners' sugar
- ½ cup water
- ½ teaspoon salt
- ½ teaspoon vanilla extract
  Blue and red food coloring

1. Prepare and bake cake according to package directions, using two greased 9-in. round baking pans. Cool for 10 minutes before removing from pans to wire racks.

2. For frosting, in a large bowl, cream the shortening and sugar until light and fluffy. Beat in the water, salt and vanilla until smooth. Place one cake on a serving plate; spread with ⅔ cup frosting. Top with remaining cake.

Italian Spumoni Cookies

These cookies inspired by the frozen treat taste like they were made from scratch. Ready-made cookie dough makes it easy.

TASTE OF HOME TEST KITCHEN

PREP: 30 MIN. + CHILLING • **BAKE:** 10 MIN./BATCH • **MAKES:** 4 DOZEN

- 2 **tubes (16½ ounces each) refrigerated sugar cookie dough**
- 1 **cup all-purpose flour, divided**
- ¼ **cup chopped maraschino cherries**
- 4 **to 6 drops red food coloring, optional**
- 2 **tablespoons baking cocoa**
- 2 **teaspoons hazelnut liqueur**
- ⅓ **cup chopped pistachios**
- 4 **to 6 drops green food coloring, optional**

1. Let cookie dough stand at room temperature for 5-10 minutes to soften. In a large bowl, beat cookie dough and ¾ cup flour until combined. Divide dough into three portions.

2. Add the cherries, red food coloring if desired and remaining flour to one portion. Add cocoa and liqueur to the second portion. Add pistachios and green food coloring to the remaining portion.

3. Roll each portion between two pieces of waxed paper into an 8-in. x 6-in. rectangle. Remove waxed paper. Place cherry rectangle on a piece of plastic wrap. Layer with chocolate and pistachio rectangles; press together lightly. Wrap with plastic wrap and refrigerate overnight.

4. Cut chilled dough in half widthwise. Return one rectangle to the refrigerator. Cut remaining rectangle into ¼-in. slices. Place 1 in. apart on ungreased baking sheets. Repeat with remaining dough.

5. Bake at 375° for 8-10 minutes or until set. Cool for 2 minutes before removing to wire racks. Store in an airtight container.

Root Beer Float Cake

Serve this cake to a bunch of hungry kids and watch it disappear! I put root beer in both the cake portion and the fluffy, irresistible topping. Yum!

KAT THOMPSON, PRINEVILLE, OREGON

PREP: 15 MIN. • **BAKE:** 30 MIN. + COOLING • **MAKES:** 12-15 SERVINGS

- 1 package (18¼ ounces) white cake mix
- 1¾ cups cold root beer, divided
- ¼ cup canola oil
- 2 eggs
- 1 envelope whipped topping mix (Dream Whip)

1. In a large bowl, combine cake mix, 1¼ cups root beer, oil and eggs. Beat on low speed for 2 minutes or stir by hand for 3 minutes.

2. Pour into a greased 13-in. x 9-in. baking pan. Bake at 350° for 30-35 minutes or until a toothpick inserted near the center comes out clean. Cool completely on a wire rack.

3. In a small bowl, combine the whipped topping mix and remaining root beer. Beat until soft peaks form. Frost cake. Store in the refrigerator.

Cocoa Cola Cake

I love this tender cake because I usually have the ingredients on hand and it mixes up in a jiffy. The rich fudge frosting is easy to prepare, and the chopped pecans add nice crunch.

ELLEN CHAMPAGNE, NEW ORLEANS, LOUISIANA

PREP: 15 MIN. + STANDING • **BAKE:** 35 MIN. + COOLING
MAKES: 12-15 SERVINGS

- 1 package (18¼ ounces) white cake mix
- 1 cup cola
- 2 eggs
- ½ cup buttermilk
- ½ cup butter, melted
- ¼ cup baking cocoa
- 1 teaspoon vanilla extract
- 1½ cups miniature marshmallows

FUDGE FROSTING:
- ¼ cup baking cocoa
- ½ cup butter, cubed
- ⅓ cup cola
- 4 cups confectioners' sugar
- 1 cup chopped pecans, toasted

1. In a large bowl, combine the first seven ingredients; beat on low speed for 30 seconds. Beat on medium for 2 minutes. Fold in marshmallows.

2. Pour into a greased 13-in. x 9-in. baking pan. Bake at 350° for 35-40 minutes or until a toothpick inserted near the center comes out clean. Cool on a wire rack for 15 minutes.

3. Meanwhile, for frosting, combine cocoa and butter in a small saucepan. Cook over low heat until butter is melted. Stir in cola until blended. Bring to a boil, stirring constantly. Remove from the heat; stir in confectioners' sugar until smooth. Fold in pecans. Spread over cake. Let stand for 20 minutes before cutting.

Bakeshop TIP

Toasting Nuts

Toasting nuts brings out their natural flavor, which adds richness to your baked goods. To toast, spread nuts in a baking pan and bake at 350° until golden brown, stirring often, for 5-8 minutes. You can also toast small quantities of nuts in a dry skillet on the stovetop.

Strawberry Banana Split Cake

It's nearly impossible to believe this no-bake dessert comes together so easily. You do have to chill the layers individually, but the scrumptious results are well worth the wait.

JOAN PACEY, ENNISMORE, ONTARIO

PREP: 20 MIN. + CHILLING • **MAKES:** 12-15 SERVINGS

 2 **cups graham cracker crumbs**
 ½ **cup butter, melted**
 ¼ **cup sugar**
FILLING:
 ½ **cup butter, softened**
 2 **cups confectioners' sugar**
 1 **tablespoon milk**
 1 **teaspoon vanilla extract**
 3 **large firm bananas, cut into ¼-inch slices**
 2 **cans (8 ounces each) crushed pineapple, drained**
 2 **quarts fresh strawberries, sliced**
TOPPING:
 2 **cups heavy whipping cream**
 ¼ **cup confectioners' sugar**
 1½ **cups chopped walnuts**

1. Combine the crumbs, butter and sugar; press into an ungreased 13-in. x 9-in. dish. Chill for 1 hour.

2. In a bowl, beat the butter, confectioners' sugar, milk and vanilla until smooth. Spread over crust; chill for 30 minutes. Layer with bananas, pineapple and strawberries.

3. In a small bowl, beat cream until soft peaks form. Add confectioners' sugar; beat until stiff peaks form. Spread over fruit. Sprinkle with nuts. Chill until serving.

Orange Dream Angel Food Cake

A basic angel food cake becomes a heavenly indulgence thanks to a hint of orange flavor swirled into every bite. The orange color makes slices of the cake look so pretty.

LAUREN OSBORNE, HOLTWOOD, PENNSYLVANIA

PREP: 25 MIN. • **BAKE:** 30 MIN. + COOLING • **MAKES:** 16 SERVINGS

 12 **egg whites**
 1 **cup all-purpose flour**
 1¾ **cups sugar, divided**
 1½ **teaspoons cream of tartar**
 ½ **teaspoon salt**
 1 **teaspoon almond extract**
 1 **teaspoon vanilla extract**
 1 **teaspoon grated orange peel**
 1 **teaspoon orange extract**
 6 **drops red food coloring, optional**
 6 **drops yellow food coloring, optional**

1. Place egg whites in a large bowl; let stand at room temperature for 30 minutes. Sift flour and ¾ cup sugar together twice; set aside.

2. Add the cream of tartar, salt and almond and vanilla extracts to egg whites; beat on medium speed until soft peaks form. Gradually add remaining sugar, about 2 tablespoons at a time, beating on high until stiff glossy peaks form and sugar is dissolved. Gradually fold in flour mixture, about ½ cup at a time.

3. Gently spoon half of batter into an ungreased 10-in. tube pan. To the remaining batter, stir in the orange peel, orange extract and food colorings if desired. Gently spoon orange batter over white batter. Cut through both layers with a knife to swirl the batter and to remove air pockets.

4. Bake on the lowest oven rack at 375° for 30-35 minutes or until lightly browned and entire top appears dry. Immediately invert pan; cool completely, about 1 hour.

5. Run a knife around side and center tube of pan. Remove cake to a serving plate.

Chocolate Banana Split Cupcakes

My mom often made these cute cupcakes when I was young. They go over just as well now when I bake them for my three children.

LORELIE MILLER, BENITO, MANITOBA

PREP: 20 MIN. • **BAKE:** 20 MIN. + COOLING • **MAKES:** 1 DOZEN

- 1¼ cups all-purpose flour
- ½ cup sugar
- ¼ teaspoon baking soda
- ¼ teaspoon salt
- ½ cup mashed banana (about 1 medium)
- ½ cup butter, melted
- ¼ cup buttermilk
- 1 egg, lightly beaten
- ½ teaspoon vanilla extract
- ½ cup chopped walnuts
- 2 milk chocolate bars (1.55 ounces each), broken into squares, divided

FROSTING:
- 1½ cups confectioners' sugar
- 1 tablespoon butter, melted
- ½ teaspoon vanilla extract
- 1 to 2 tablespoons milk
- 12 maraschino cherries with stems

1. In a large bowl, combine the flour, sugar, baking soda and salt. In another bowl, combine the banana, butter, buttermilk, egg and vanilla. Add to the dry ingredients; stir just until combined. Fold in walnuts. Place 1 tablespoon of batter in each of 12 paper-lined muffin cups. Top each with one candy bar square. Fill cups two-thirds full with batter.

2. Bake at 350° for 20-25 minutes or until a toothpick inserted in the cupcake comes out clean. Cool for 10 minutes before removing from pan to a wire rack to cool completely.

3. In a large bowl, combine the confectioners' sugar, butter, vanilla and enough milk to achieve a spreading consistency. Frost cupcakes. In a microwave, melt the remaining candy bar squares; drizzle chocolate over frosting. Top each cupcake with a cherry.

Root Beer Sandwich Cookies

A hint of good old-fashioned root beer flavors these chewy, soft cookies. They're superb alongside scoops of ice cream!

JIM GORDON, BEECHER, ILLINOIS

PREP: 45 MIN. • **BAKE:** 10 MIN./BATCH + COOLING • **MAKES:** 2½ DOZEN

- ½ cup butter, softened
- 1 cup packed brown sugar
- 1 egg
- 1 teaspoon root beer concentrate
- 1¾ cups all-purpose flour
- ½ teaspoon salt
- ½ teaspoon baking soda

FILLING:
- ¼ cup butter, softened
- 1⅓ cups confectioners' sugar
- 1 teaspoon water
- 1 teaspoon root beer concentrate

1. In a large bowl, cream butter and brown sugar until light and fluffy. Beat in egg and root beer concentrate. Combine the flour, salt and baking soda; gradually add to creamed mixture and mix well.

2. Shape dough into ¾-in. balls. Place 2 in. apart on ungreased baking sheets. Bake at 375° for 6-8 minutes or until lightly browned. Remove cookies to wire racks to cool completely.

3. In a small bowl, beat the filling ingredients until smooth. Spread on the bottoms of half of the cookies; top with remaining cookies.

Editor's Note: *This recipe was tested with McCormick root beer concentrate.*

Bakeshop **HOW-TO**

Shaping Cookie Dough into Balls

Roll the dough between your palms until it forms a ball. A 1-in. ball requires about 2 teaspoons of dough. If the dough is sticky, refrigerate it until easy to handle. Or lightly flour your hands or spray them with cooking spray.

Sugar Cone Pie

This cute pie never seems to last long—especially when our grandchildren visit. We really enjoy it when berries are plentiful.

BERNICE JANOWSKI, STEVENS POINT, WISCONSIN

PREP: 45 MIN. + FREEZING • **MAKES:** 8 SERVINGS

- 1 package (5¼ ounces) ice cream sugar cones, crushed
- ¼ cup ground pecans
- ⅓ cup butter, melted
- 2 cups vanilla ice cream, softened
- 2 medium ripe bananas, mashed
- 2 large firm bananas, cut into ¼-inch slices
- 2 cups strawberry ice cream, softened
- 1 pint fresh strawberries
- 1 carton (8 ounces) frozen whipped topping, thawed

1. In a large bowl, combine the crushed ice cream cones, pecans and butter. Press into a greased 10-in. pie plate. Refrigerate for at least 30 minutes.

2. In another large bowl, combine vanilla ice cream and mashed bananas. Spread into crust; cover and freeze for 30 minutes.

3. Arrange sliced bananas over ice cream mixture; freeze 30 minutes longer. Top with strawberry ice cream; freeze for about 45 minutes.

4. Hull and halve strawberries; place around edge of pie. Mound or pipe whipped topping in center of pie. Cover and freeze for up to 1 month. Remove from the freezer 20 minutes before serving.

Fall

Put the crowning jewel on your next holiday feast with
one or more of these best-loved showstoppers.

Cranberry Pear Pie

When our family is invited to holiday gatherings, this pie usually comes with us. The recipe is very versatile. You can make it with a double crust or replace the pears with baking apples. Serve it with ice cream or whipped topping.

HELEN TOULANTIS, WANTAGH, NEW YORK

PREP: 20 MIN. • **BAKE:** 50 MIN. + COOLING • **MAKES:** 6-8 SERVINGS

      Pastry for single-crust pie (9 inches)
  2 tablespoons all-purpose flour
  ½ cup maple syrup
  2 tablespoons butter, melted
  5 cups sliced peeled fresh pears
  1 cup fresh or frozen cranberries
TOPPING:
  ½ cup all-purpose flour
  ¼ cup packed brown sugar
  1 teaspoon ground cinnamon
  ⅓ cup cold butter, cubed
  ½ cup chopped walnuts

1. Line a 9-in. pie plate with pastry; trim and flute edges. Set aside. In a large bowl, combine the flour, syrup and butter until smooth. Add pears and cranberries; toss to coat. Spoon into crust.

2. For topping, combine the flour, brown sugar and cinnamon; cut in butter until crumbly. Stir in walnuts. Sprinkle over filling.

3. Cover edges of crust loosely with foil to prevent overbrowning. Bake at 400° for 15 minutes. Reduce heat to 350°. Remove foil; bake 35-40 minutes longer or until crust is golden brown and filling is bubbly. Cool on a wire rack.

Pumpkin Torte

This beautiful layered cake has a creamy filling with a mild pumpkin flavor and a little spice. It's quick and always turns out so well. The nuts and caramel topping add a nice finishing touch.

TRIXIE FISHER, PIQUA, OHIO

PREP: 30 MIN. • **BAKE:** 25 MIN. + COOLING • **MAKES:** 10-12 SERVINGS

  1 package (18¼ ounces) yellow cake mix
  1 can (15 ounces) solid-pack pumpkin, divided
  ½ cup milk
  4 eggs
  ⅓ cup canola oil
  1½ teaspoons pumpkin pie spice, divided
  1 package (8 ounces) cream cheese, softened
  1 cup confectioners' sugar
  1 carton (16 ounces) frozen whipped topping, thawed
  ¼ cup caramel ice cream topping
  ⅓ cup chopped pecans, toasted

1. In a large bowl, combine the cake mix, 1 cup pumpkin, milk, eggs, oil and 1 teaspoon pumpkin pie spice; beat on low speed for 30 seconds. Beat on medium for 2 minutes. Pour into two greased and floured 9-in. round baking pans.

2. Bake at 350° for 25-30 minutes or until a toothpick inserted near the center comes out clean. Cool for 10 minutes before removing from pans to wire racks to cool completely.

3. In a large bowl, beat the cream cheese until light and fluffy. Add the confectioners' sugar and remaining pumpkin and pumpkin pie spice; beat until smooth. Fold in whipped topping.

4. Cut each cake horizontally into two layers. Place bottom layer on a serving plate; spread with a fourth of the filling. Repeat layers three times. Drizzle with caramel topping; sprinkle with pecans. Store in the refrigerator.

Mark's Praline Cheesecake

I wowed my wife, Carla, and a group of her friends with this luscious dessert, the finale to a meal I catered at church.

MARK JONES, CLOVIS, CALIFORNIA

PREP: 40 MIN. • **BAKE:** 1¼ HOURS + CHILLING
MAKES: 12 SERVINGS

- 7 **whole graham crackers**
- ½ **cup chopped pecans, toasted**
- 6 **tablespoons butter, melted**

FILLING:
- 4 **packages (8 ounces each) cream cheese, softened**
- 1½ **cups sugar**
- 2 **cups (16 ounces) sour cream**
- ¼ **cup all-purpose flour**
- ¼ **cup milk**
- 1 **tablespoon vanilla extract**
- 5 **eggs, lightly beaten**

TOPPING:
- 1 **cup sugar**
- ¼ **cup water**
- 1 **cup heavy whipping cream**
- 1 **tablespoon butter**
- 1 **teaspoon vanilla extract**
- ½ **cup pecan halves, toasted**

1. Place a greased 10-in. springform pan on a double thickness of heavy-duty foil (about 18 in. square). Securely wrap foil around pan.

2. In a food processor, combine graham crackers and pecans; cover and process until fine and crumbly. Stir in butter. Press onto the bottom of prepared pan. Chill for 30 minutes.

3. In a large bowl, beat cream cheese and sugar until smooth. Beat in the sour cream, flour, milk and vanilla. Add eggs, beating on low speed just until combined. Pour over crust. Place springform pan in a large baking pan; add 1 in. of hot water to larger pan.

4. Bake at 325° for 75-80 minutes or until center is just set and top appears dull. Remove springform pan from water bath. Cool on a wire rack for 10 minutes. Carefully run a knife around edge of pan to loosen; cool 1 hour longer. Chill.

5. For topping, in a small heavy pan over medium-low heat, combine sugar and water. Cook, stirring occasionally, until sugar begins to melt. Cook without stirring until dark reddish brown, about 15 minutes.

6. Reduce heat to low; gradually whisk in cream. Cook and stir over medium heat until a candy thermometer reads 225°. Remove from the heat; stir in butter and vanilla. Cool to room temperature.

7. Spread topping evenly over cheesecake (do not scrape sides of pan). Garnish with pecan halves. Refrigerate overnight. Remove sides of pan.

Bakeshop **TIP**

Perfect Caramel

Gritty sugar crystals can be the undoing of an otherwise good caramel. To ensure a perfectly smooth caramel, gently stir the sugar mixture until it comes to a boil, then remove the spoon and let it continue to cook untouched.

For added insurance, use a pastry or basting brush dipped in cold water to gently wash down the sides of the pot after you've removed the spoon. This prevents sugar crystals from forming on the pan's walls.

When pouring out the cooked caramel, don't scrape down the pan's walls, and avoid re-introducing the spoon you previously used.

Apple Dumplings with Sauce

Covered in a luscious caramel sauce, these dumplings are great served alone or with a generous scoop of vanilla ice cream. Kids of all ages love the warm and spicy apple flavor.

ROBIN LENDON, CINCINNATI, OHIO

PREP: 1 HOUR + CHILLING • **BAKE:** 50 MIN. • **MAKES:** 8 SERVINGS

- 3 **cups all-purpose flour**
- 1 **teaspoon salt**
- 1 **cup shortening**
- ⅓ **cup cold water**
- 8 **medium tart apples, peeled and cored**
- 8 **teaspoons butter**
- 9 **teaspoons cinnamon sugar, divided**

SAUCE:
- 1½ **cups packed brown sugar**
- 1 **cup water**
- ½ **cup butter, cubed**

1. In a large bowl, combine flour and salt; cut in shortening until crumbly. Gradually add water, tossing with a fork until dough forms a ball. Divide into eight portions. Cover and refrigerate for at least 30 minutes or until easy to handle.

2. Roll each portion of dough between two lightly floured sheets of waxed paper into a 7-in. square. Place an apple on each square. Place 1 teaspoon butter and 1 teaspoon cinnamon sugar in the center of each apple.

3. Gently bring up corners of pastry to each center; pinch edges to seal. If desired, cut out apple leaves and stems from dough scraps; attach to dumplings with water. Place in a greased 13-in. x 9-in. baking dish. Sprinkle with remaining cinnamon sugar.

4. In a large saucepan, combine sauce ingredients. Bring just to a boil, stirring until blended. Pour over apples.

5. Bake at 350° for 50-55 minutes or until apples are tender and pastry is golden brown, basting occasionally with sauce. Serve warm.

Apple Cranberry Crumble

When I first took this fruity dessert to my family's Thanksgiving dinner, it quickly became a tradition. We enjoy it for breakfast, lunch, dinner and snack time!

TERI ROBERTS, HILLIARD, OHIO

PREP: 15 MIN. • **BAKE:** 55 MIN. • **MAKES:** 6 SERVINGS

- 3 **cups chopped peeled apples**
- 2 **cups fresh or frozen cranberries, thawed**
- ¾ **cup sugar**
- 1 **cup old-fashioned or quick-cooking oats**

SHORT & SWEET

- ¾ **cup packed brown sugar**
- ⅓ **cup all-purpose flour**
- ½ **cup butter, melted**
- ½ **cup chopped pecans, optional**

1. In a greased 8-in. square baking dish, combine apples and cranberries; sprinkle with sugar.

2. In another bowl, combine the oats, brown sugar, flour and butter; sprinkle over cranberry mixture. Top with pecans if desired.

3. Bake, uncovered, at 350° for 55-60 minutes or until browned and bubbly. Serve warm.

Mixed Nut 'n' Fig Pie

A hint of orange enhances this sweet, crunchy pie.

BARBARA ESTABROOK, RHINELANDER, WISCONSIN

PREP: 30 MIN. • **BAKE:** 1 HOUR + COOLING • **MAKES:** 8 SERVINGS

 Pastry for single-crust pie (9 inches)
 ½ cup chopped dried figs
 3 tablespoons water
 2 tablespoons orange marmalade
 ¾ cup packed brown sugar
 1 tablespoon cornstarch
 1 cup corn syrup
 3 eggs
 6 tablespoons butter, melted
 2 teaspoons vanilla extract
 1½ cups deluxe mixed nuts
TOPPING:
 1 cup heavy whipping cream
 2 tablespoons sugar
 1 tablespoon orange marmalade

1. Line a 9-in. pie plate with pastry; trim and flute edges. Line pastry with a double thickness of heavy-duty foil. Bake at 450° for 8 minutes. Remove foil; bake 5 minutes longer. Cool on a wire rack. Reduce heat to 300°.

2. In a small saucepan, combine figs and water. Cook and stir over low heat until water is absorbed. Remove from heat; stir in marmalade. In a large bowl, combine brown sugar and cornstarch. Add the corn syrup, eggs, butter, vanilla and fig mixture; stir in nuts. Pour into crust.

3. Bake for 1 to 1¼ hours or until set. Cover edges with foil during last 30 minutes to prevent overbrowning if necessary. Cool on a wire rack. Beat cream until thickened. Add sugar and marmalade; beat until soft peaks form. Serve with pie.

Caramel Stripe Cheesecake

I love to bake cheesecakes, and this recipe is one of the best I've tried. It really stands out on a buffet.

BRENDA LABRIE, CLARK, SOUTH DAKOTA

PREP: 35 MIN. + CHILLING • **BAKE:** 40 MIN. + CHILLING
MAKES: 12 SERVINGS

 2 cups crushed vanilla wafers (about 60 wafers)
 ⅓ cup butter, melted

FILLING:
 3 packages (8 ounces each) cream cheese, softened
 1 cup sugar
 2 tablespoons all-purpose flour
 2 tablespoons heavy whipping cream
 1 teaspoon vanilla extract
 3 eggs, lightly beaten
CARAMEL TOPPING:
 12 caramels
 2 tablespoons heavy whipping cream
CHOCOLATE TOPPING:
 ½ cup semisweet chocolate chips
 2 teaspoons butter
 4 teaspoons heavy whipping cream
 Whipped cream and coarsely chopped pecans, optional

1. In a small bowl, combine wafer crumbs and butter. Press onto the bottom and 1½ in. up the sides of an ungreased 9-in. springform pan. Place on a baking sheet. Bake at 400° for 10 minutes. Cool on a wire rack. Reduce heat to 350°.

2. In a large bowl, beat cream cheese and sugar until smooth. Beat in the flour, cream and vanilla. Add eggs; beat on low speed just until combined. Pour into crust.

3. Bake for 40-45 minutes or until center is almost set. Cool on a wire rack for 10 minutes. Carefully run a knife around edge of pan to loosen; cool 1 hour longer. Chill while preparing toppings.

4. In a saucepan, melt caramels with cream over medium heat, stirring constantly. In another pan, melt chips and butter with cream over low heat, stirring until smooth. Drizzle toppings over cheesecake. Refrigerate overnight.

5. Remove sides of pan. Garnish with whipped cream and pecans if desired.

Low-Fat Fruit & Carrot Cake

This is the best carrot cake I've ever made. It has all the texture, taste and density of regular carrot cake, but is much lower in fat.

ELLIE RAUSCH, GOODSOIL, SASKATCHEWAN

PREP: 35 MIN. • **BAKE:** 40 MIN. + COOLING • **MAKES:** 16 SERVINGS

⅔ cup sugar
⅔ cup packed brown sugar
2 eggs
⅓ cup unsweetened applesauce
¼ cup canola oil
3 teaspoons vanilla extract
3 cups all-purpose flour
3 teaspoons baking powder
1½ teaspoons ground cinnamon
½ teaspoon salt
3 cups shredded carrots
⅓ cup finely chopped dried apricots
⅓ cup dried currants
3 tablespoons chopped crystallized ginger
GLAZE:
1 can (6 ounces) unsweetened pineapple juice
½ cup orange juice
2 tablespoons honey
2 tablespoons finely chopped dried apricots
1 tablespoon dried currants
4 teaspoons chopped pecans, toasted

1. In a large bowl, beat the first six ingredients until well blended. Combine the flour, baking powder, cinnamon and salt; gradually beat into sugar mixture until blended (batter will be thick). Stir in the carrots, apricots, currants and ginger.

2. Coat a 10-in. fluted tube pan with cooking spray and sprinkle with flour; pour batter into pan. Bake at 350° for 40-50 minutes or until a toothpick inserted near the center comes out clean. Cool for 10 minutes before removing from pan to a wire rack to cool completely.

3. For glaze, in a small saucepan, combine the pineapple juice, orange juice and honey. Bring to a boil. Reduce heat; simmer, uncovered, for 25-30 minutes or until mixture is reduced to ⅓ cup. Remove from the heat; cool for 15 minutes. Stir in apricots and currants. Spoon over cake. Sprinkle with pecans.

Triple-Apple Pie

My apple pie won the blue ribbon in the Double Crust Apple Pie class at the Iowa State Fair. It's my original recipe, plus I used my homemade apple jelly in the pie.

LOUISE PIPER, GARNER, IOWA

PREP: 30 MIN. + STANDING • **BAKE:** 50 MIN. + COOLING
MAKES: 6-8 SERVINGS

5½ cups thinly sliced peeled tart apples
¼ cup apple cider or juice
⅓ cup apple jelly, melted
1 cup sugar
3 tablespoons all-purpose flour
1 tablespoon quick-cooking tapioca
⅛ teaspoon salt
Pastry for double-crust pie (9 inches)
2 tablespoons butter

1. In a large bowl, combine the apples, cider and jelly. Combine the sugar, flour, tapioca and salt; add to apple mixture and toss gently to coat. Let stand for 15 minutes.

2. Meanwhile, line a 9-in. pie plate with bottom pastry; trim pastry even with edge of plate. Add filling; dot with butter. Roll out remaining pastry to fit top of pie; place over filling. Trim, seal and flute edges. Cut slits in top. Cover edges loosely with foil.

3. Bake at 400° for 20 minutes. Remove foil; bake 30-35 minutes longer or until crust is golden brown and filling is bubbly. Cool on a wire rack.

Maple Pumpkin Pie

Tired of traditional pumpkin pie? The maple syrup in this special pie provides a subtle but terrific enhancer.

LISA VARNER, EL PASO, TEXAS

PREP: 25 MIN. • **BAKE:** 1 HOUR + CHILLING • **MAKES:** 8 SERVINGS

- 2 **eggs**
- 1 **can (15 ounces) solid-pack pumpkin**
- 1 **cup evaporated milk**
- ¾ **cup sugar**
- ½ **cup maple syrup**
- 1 **teaspoon pumpkin pie spice**
- ¼ **teaspoon salt**
  Pastry for single-crust pie (9 inches)

MAPLE WHIPPED CREAM:
- 1 **cup heavy whipping cream**
- 2 **tablespoons confectioners' sugar**
- 1 **tablespoon maple syrup**
- ¼ **teaspoon pumpkin pie spice**
  Chopped pecans, optional

1. In a large bowl, combine the first seven ingredients; beat until smooth. Line a 9-in. pie plate with pastry; trim and flute edges. Pour filling into crust.

2. Bake at 425° for 15 minutes. Reduce heat to 350°. Bake 45-50 minutes longer or until crust is golden brown and top of pie is set (cover edges with foil during the last 15 minutes to prevent overbrowning if necessary). Cool on a wire rack for 1 hour. Refrigerate overnight or until set.

3. In a small bowl, beat the cream, confectioners' sugar, syrup and pumpkin pie spice until stiff peaks form. Pipe or dollop onto pie. Sprinkle with pecans if desired.

Raspberry Pear Tart

Here's a festive tart that looks and smells as delightful as it tastes. It's destined to become a holiday favorite. If you'd like, substitute cranberries, blueberries or even cherries for the raspberries called for in the recipe.

BERNICE JANOWSKI, STEVENS POINT, WISCONSIN

PREP: 30 MIN. • **BAKE:** 40 MIN. + COOLING • **MAKES:** 16 SERVINGS

- 1⅔ cups all-purpose flour
- ⅔ cup sugar
- ⅔ cup cold butter, cubed
- ⅓ cup chopped macadamia nuts

FILLING:
- 3 medium pears, peeled and thinly sliced
- ½ cup sugar
- 2 tablespoons cornstarch
- 1 teaspoon ground cinnamon
- 1 teaspoon grated lemon peel
- 2 cups fresh or frozen raspberries

TOPPING:
- ½ cup all-purpose flour
- ½ cup packed brown sugar
- 1 teaspoon grated lemon peel
- ¼ cup cold butter, cubed
- ⅓ cup chopped macadamia nuts

1. In a large bowl, combine flour and sugar; cut in butter until mixture resembles coarse crumbs. Stir in nuts. Press onto the bottom and up the sides of an ungreased 11-in. fluted tart pan with removable bottom.

2. In a large bowl, combine the pears, sugar, cornstarch, cinnamon and lemon peel. Add raspberries; toss gently. Pour into crust. Bake at 425° for 25 minutes.

3. For topping, in a small bowl, combine the flour, brown sugar and lemon peel; cut in butter until crumbly. Stir in nuts. Sprinkle over filling.

4. Bake 15-20 minutes longer or until filling is bubbly and topping is golden brown. Cool on a wire rack. Refrigerate leftovers.

Fruits of the Forest Pie

Five kinds of nuts are squirreled away in this deliciously sweet pie. There's crunch in every bite.

MARY LOU TIMPSON, COLORADO CITY, ARIZONA

PREP: 30 MIN. • **BAKE:** 45 MIN. + COOLING • **MAKES:** 8 SERVINGS

- Pastry for single-crust pie (9 inches)
- ⅓ cup coarsely chopped macadamia nuts
- ⅓ cup chopped hazelnuts
- ½ cup salted cashew halves
- ½ cup pecan halves
- ⅓ cup slivered almonds
- 4 eggs
- 1 cup light corn syrup
- ½ cup sugar
- ¼ cup packed brown sugar
- 2 tablespoons butter, melted
- 1 teaspoon vanilla extract
- ¼ teaspoon salt

1. Line a 9-in. pie plate with pastry; trim pastry to ½ in. beyond edge of plate and flute edges. Sprinkle macadamia nuts and hazelnuts into the pastry shell. Arrange cashews, pecans and almonds over the chopped nuts.

2. In a small bowl, beat the eggs, corn syrup, sugars, butter, vanilla and salt until well blended. Pour over nuts.

3. Bake at 350° for 45-50 minutes or until a knife inserted near the center comes out clean. (Cover edges with foil during the last 10 minutes to prevent overbrowning if necessary.) Cool on a wire rack. Store in the refrigerator.

Upside-Down Apple Pie

I combined two of my favorite recipes to come up with this sensational pie. It won the local apple pie contest a few years ago. I usually make two pies because we always end up wanting more.

BECKY BERGER, DEERFIELD, ILLINOIS

PREP: 1 HOUR + CHILLING • **BAKE:** 1 HOUR + COOLING
MAKES: 8 SERVINGS

- 3 **cups all-purpose flour**
- 1 **tablespoon sugar**
- 1 **teaspoon salt**
- ¾ **cup cold butter, cubed**
- ⅓ **cup shortening, cubed**
- 4 **to 6 tablespoons cold water**

PECANS:
- ½ **cup packed brown sugar**
- ¼ **cup butter, melted**
- 1 **cup pecan halves**

FILLING:
- 1 **cup sugar**
- ⅓ **cup all-purpose flour**
- 2 **tablespoons butter, melted**
- ¼ **teaspoon ground cinnamon**
- 8 **cups thinly sliced peeled tart apples**

1. In a food processor, combine the flour, sugar and salt; cover and pulse until blended. Add butter and shortening; pulse until mixture resembles coarse crumbs. While processing, gradually add water until dough forms a ball.

2. Divide dough in half so that one portion is slightly larger than the other; wrap each in plastic wrap. Refrigerate for 45 minutes or until easy to handle.

3. Coat a 9-in. deep-dish pie plate with cooking spray. Line bottom and sides of plate with parchment paper; coat paper with cooking spray and set aside.

4. In a small bowl, combine brown sugar and butter; stir in pecans. Arrange in the bottom of prepared pie plate with rounded sides of pecans facing down.

5. On a lightly floured surface, roll out larger portion of dough to fit bottom and sides of pie plate. Transfer to plate; press the crust firmly against pecans and sides of pie plate. Trim edges.

6. In a large bowl, combine the sugar, flour, butter and cinnamon. Add apples; toss to coat. Fill crust. Roll out remaining pastry to fit top of pie; place over filling. Trim and seal edges. Cut slits in pastry.

7. Place a foil-lined baking sheet on a rack below the pie to catch any spills. Bake pie at 375° for 60-70 minutes or until golden brown.

8. Carefully loosen the parchment paper around edge of pie; invert hot pie onto a serving plate. Remove paper. Cool for at least 15 minutes before serving.

Praline Pumpkin Pie

A rich, crispy pecan topping and maple syrup give this creamy pumpkin pie a mouthwatering twist. Yum!

DEBORAH WHITLEY, NASHVILLE, TENNESSEE

PREP: 10 MIN. • **BAKE:** 55 MIN. + CHILLING • **MAKES:** 8 SERVINGS

> Pastry for single-crust pie (9 inches)
2 eggs
1 can (15 ounces) solid-pack pumpkin
½ cup maple syrup
¼ cup sugar
¼ cup heavy whipping cream
1 teaspoon ground cinnamon
½ teaspoon ground nutmeg

TOPPING:
2 eggs, lightly beaten
1 cup chopped pecans
½ cup sugar
½ cup maple syrup
Whipped topping, optional

1. Line a 9-in. pie plate with pastry; trim and flute edges. In a large bowl, beat the eggs, pumpkin, syrup, sugar, cream, cinnamon and nutmeg until smooth; pour into pastry.

2. For the topping, in a large bowl, combine the eggs, pecans, sugar and syrup; spoon over top.

3. Bake at 425° for 15 minutes. Reduce heat to 350°. Bake 40-45 minutes longer or until crust is golden brown and top of pie is set.

4. Cool on a wire rack for 1 hour. Refrigerate overnight. Serve with whipped topping if desired.

Pumpkin Cheesecake with Sour Cream Topping

Why not surprise Thanksgiving guests with this delectable cheesecake instead of the traditional pie?

DOROTHY SMITH, EL DORADO, ARKANSAS

PREP: 15 MIN. + COOLING • **BAKE:** 55 MIN. + CHILLING
MAKES: 12 SERVINGS

1½ cups graham cracker crumbs
¼ cup sugar
⅓ cup butter, melted
FILLING:
3 packages (8 ounces each) cream cheese, softened
1 cup packed brown sugar
1 can (15 ounces) solid-pack pumpkin
1 can (5 ounces) evaporated milk
2 tablespoons cornstarch
1¼ teaspoons ground cinnamon
½ teaspoon ground nutmeg
2 eggs, lightly beaten

TOPPING:
2 cups (16 ounces) sour cream
⅓ cup sugar
1 teaspoon vanilla extract
Additional ground cinnamon

1. In a small bowl, combine crumbs and sugar; stir in butter. Press onto the bottom and 1½ in. up the sides of a greased 9-in. springform pan. Bake at 350° for 5-7 minutes or until set. Cool for 10 minutes.

2. In a large bowl, beat cream cheese and brown sugar until smooth. Beat in the pumpkin, milk, cornstarch, cinnamon and nutmeg. Add eggs; beat on low speed just until combined. Pour into crust.

3. Place pan on a baking sheet. Bake at 350° for 55-60 minutes or until center is almost set.

4. In a small bowl, combine the sour cream, sugar and vanilla; spread over filling. Bake 5 minutes longer. Cool on a wire rack for 10 minutes. Carefully run a knife around edge of pan to loosen; cool 1 hour longer. Chill overnight.

5. Remove sides of pan. Let stand at room temperature 30 minutes before slicing. Sprinkle with cinnamon.

Dixie Pie

When Mom baked this old-fashioned sugar pie, family members would clamor for second servings. We love the combination of cinnamon, coconut, nuts and raisins. She'd sometimes toss in a few chocolate chips for variety. Thanksgiving and Christmas dinners were not complete without this dessert.

SANDRA PICHON, MEMPHIS, TENNESSEE

PREP: 20 MIN. • **BAKE:** 30 MIN. + COOLING
MAKES: 2 PIES (6-8 SERVINGS EACH)

    Pastry for two single-crust pies (9 inches)
1½ cups raisins
1   cup butter, softened
1   cup sugar
1   cup packed brown sugar
6   eggs
2   teaspoons vanilla extract
2   to 4 teaspoons ground cinnamon
1   cup chopped pecans or walnuts
1   cup flaked coconut
    Whipped topping and additional chopped nuts, optional

1. Line two 9-in. pie plates with pastry. Trim pastry to ½ in. beyond edge of plates; flute edges. Line crusts with a double thickness of heavy-duty foil. Bake at 450° for 10 minutes. Place on wire racks to cool; discard foil.

2. Place raisins in a saucepan and cover with water; bring to a boil. Remove from heat; set aside. In a large bowl, cream butter and sugars until light and fluffy. Beat in eggs, vanilla and cinnamon until blended.

3. Drain raisins. Stir the raisins, nuts and coconut into creamed mixture (mixture will appear curdled). Pour into the crusts. Bake at 350° for 30-35 minutes or until set. Cool on wire racks. Garnish with whipped topping and additional nuts if desired.

Bakeshop HOW-TO

Creating A Decorative Pie Crust

Fluted Edge
Trim pastry ½ in. beyond edge of pie plate. Turn overhanging pastry under to form a rolled edge. Position your thumb and index finger about 1 in. apart on the edge of the crust, pointing out. Position the index finger of your other hand between the two fingers and gently push the pastry toward the center in an upward direction. Continue around the edge.

Braided Edge
Trim pastry even with edge of pie plate. With a sharp knife, cut additional pastry into twelve ¼-in.-wide strips; braid three strips. Brush edge of crust with water; place braid on edge and press lightly to secure. Repeat with remaining strips, attaching braids until entire edge is covered. Cover with foil to protect edges from overbrowning.

Mayan Chocolate Pecan Pie

This started off as a regular pecan pie for Thanksgiving Day, but it evolved into something even tastier and more special!

CHRIS MICHALOWSKI, DALLAS, TEXAS

PREP: 20 MIN. • **BAKE:** 55 MIN. + COOLING • **MAKES:** 8 SERVINGS

- ½ **cup chopped pecans**
- ½ **cup dark chocolate chips**
- 1 **frozen pie shell (9 inches)**
- 3 **eggs**
- 1 **cup sugar**
- 1 **cup dark corn syrup**
- 2 **tablespoons butter, melted**
- 1 **tablespoon coffee liqueur**
- 1 **teaspoon ground ancho chili pepper**
- 1 **teaspoon vanilla extract**
- 1 **cup pecan halves**

1. Sprinkle chopped pecans and chocolate chips into pastry shell. In a small bowl, whisk the eggs, sugar, corn syrup, butter, liqueur, pepper and vanilla. Pour into pastry; arrange pecan halves over filling.

2. Bake at 350° for 55-60 minutes or until set. Cool on a wire rack. Refrigerate leftovers.

Festive Cranberry-Topped Cheesecake

When my daughter was 4 months old, my husband and I hosted both our families for Christmas dinner. I served this beautiful cheesecake for dessert. It was thoroughly enjoyed by everyone.

STACY DUTKA, BIENFAIT, SASKATCHEWAN

PREP: 40 MIN. • **BAKE:** 45 MIN. + CHILLING • **MAKES:** 12 SERVINGS

- 2 **cups crushed shortbread cookies**
- 2 **tablespoons sugar**
- ¼ **cup butter, melted**

FILLING:
- 3 **packages (8 ounces each) cream cheese, softened**
- ¾ **cup sugar**
- 2 **tablespoons orange juice**
- 1 **tablespoon grated orange peel**
- 2 **teaspoons vanilla extract**
- ½ **teaspoon ground cinnamon**
- 3 **eggs, lightly beaten**

TOPPING:
- 3 **cups fresh or frozen cranberries, coarsely chopped**
- 1¼ **cups sugar**
- 1 **cup water**
- 2 **tablespoons cornstarch**
- ¼ **cup orange juice**
- ½ **cup coarsely chopped pecans, toasted**

1. Combine cookie crumbs and sugar; stir in butter. Press onto bottom of a greased 9-in. springform pan. Place pan on a baking sheet. Bake at 325° for 6-8 minutes or until set. Cool.

2. In a large bowl, beat cream cheese and sugar until smooth. Beat in the orange juice and peel, vanilla and cinnamon. Add eggs; beat on low speed just until combined. Pour over crust.

3. Return pan to baking sheet. Bake at 325° for 45-50 minutes or until center is almost set. Cool on a wire rack for 10 minutes. Carefully run a knife around edge of pan to loosen; cool 1 hour longer. Refrigerate overnight.

4. In a large saucepan, bring the cranberries, sugar and water to a boil. Reduce heat; simmer, uncovered, for 3 minutes. Combine cornstarch and orange juice; stir into cranberry mixture. Bring to a boil; cook and stir for 2 minutes or until thickened. Cool to room temperature; stir in pecans. Spoon over cheesecake. Refrigerate until chilled.

Caramel Apple Cheesecake

This cheesecake won the grand prize in an apple recipe contest. With caramel both on the bottom and over the top, it's ooey-gooey good.

LISA MORMAN, MINOT, NORTH DAKOTA

PREP: 45 MIN. • **BAKE:** 50 MIN. + CHILLING • **MAKES:** 12 SERVINGS

- 1½ **cups cinnamon graham cracker crumbs (about 8 whole crackers)**
- ¾ **cup sugar, divided**
- ¼ **cup butter, melted**
- 1 **package (14 ounces) caramels**
- ⅔ **cup evaporated milk**
- ½ **cup chopped pecans, divided**
- 2 **packages (8 ounces each) cream cheese, softened**
- 2 **tablespoons all-purpose flour, divided**
- 2 **eggs, lightly beaten**
- 1½ **cups chopped peeled apples**
- ½ **teaspoon ground cinnamon**

1. Place a greased 9-in. springform pan on a double thickness of heavy-duty foil (about 18 in. square). Securely wrap foil around pan.

2. In a small bowl, combine the cracker crumbs, ¼ cup sugar and butter. Press onto the bottom and 1 in. up the sides of prepared pan. Place on a baking sheet. Bake at 350° for 10 minutes or until lightly browned. Cool on a wire rack.

3. In a heavy saucepan over medium-low heat, cook and stir caramels and milk until melted and smooth. Pour 1 cup over crust; sprinkle with ¼ cup pecans. Set remaining caramel mixture aside.

4. In a large bowl, beat the cream cheese, 1 tablespoon flour and remaining sugar until smooth. Add eggs; beat on low speed just until combined. Combine the apples, cinnamon and remaining flour; fold into cream cheese mixture. Pour into crust.

5. Place springform pan in a large baking pan; add 1 in. of hot water to larger pan. Bake for 40 minutes. Reheat reserved caramel mixture if necessary; gently spoon over cheesecake. Sprinkle with remaining pecans.

6. Bake 10-15 minutes longer or until center is just set. Remove pan from water bath. Cool on a wire rack for 10 minutes. Carefully run a knife around edge of pan to loosen; cool 1 hour longer. Refrigerate overnight. Remove sides of pan.

Pecan Pumpkin Dessert

I always fix this recipe for Thanksgiving. It was given to me by a friend and I haven't stopped sharing it since.

SUE WILLIAMS, MT. HOLLY, NORTH CAROLINA

PREP: 15 MIN. • **BAKE:** 1 HOUR + COOLING • **MAKES:** 16 SERVINGS

- 2 cans (15 ounces each) solid-pack pumpkin
- 1 can (12 ounces) evaporated milk
- 1 cup sugar
- 3 eggs
- 1 teaspoon vanilla extract
- 1 package (18¼ ounces) yellow cake mix
- 1 cup butter, melted
- 1½ cups chopped pecans

FROSTING:
- 1 package (8 ounces) cream cheese, softened
- 1½ cups confectioners' sugar
- 1 teaspoon vanilla extract
- 1 carton (12 ounces) frozen whipped topping, thawed

1. Line a 13-in. x 9-in. baking dish with waxed paper and coat the paper with cooking spray; set aside.

2. In a large bowl, beat the pumpkin, milk, sugar, eggs and vanilla until well blended. Pour into prepared pan. Sprinkle with cake mix and drizzle with butter. Sprinkle with pecans.

3. Bake at 350° for 1 hour or until golden brown. Cool completely in pan on a wire rack. Invert onto a large serving platter; carefully remove waxed paper.

4. In a large bowl, beat the cream cheese, confectioners' sugar and vanilla until smooth. Fold in whipped topping. Frost dessert. Store in the refrigerator.

Pumpkin Cake Roll

This lovely cake is delicious—especially if you like cream cheese and pumpkin. It tastes so good in fall and makes a fancy dessert for holidays, too.

ELIZABETH MONTGOMERY, ALLSTON, MASSACHUSETTS

PREP: 25 MIN. • **BAKE:** 15 MIN. + CHILLING • **MAKES:** 8-10 SERVINGS

- 3 eggs
- 1 cup sugar
- ⅔ cup canned pumpkin
- 1 teaspoon lemon juice
- ¾ cup all-purpose flour
- 2 teaspoons ground cinnamon
- 1 teaspoon baking powder
- ½ teaspoon salt
- ¼ teaspoon ground nutmeg
- 1 cup finely chopped walnuts

CREAM CHEESE FILLING:
- 2 packages (3 ounces each) cream cheese, softened
- 1 cup confectioners' sugar
- ¼ cup butter, softened
- ½ teaspoon vanilla extract
  Additional confectioners' sugar

1. In a large bowl, beat eggs on high for 5 minutes. Gradually beat in sugar until thick and lemon-colored. Add pumpkin and lemon juice. Combine the flour, cinnamon, baking powder, salt and nutmeg; fold into the pumpkin mixture.

2. Grease a 15-in. x 10-in. x 1-in. baking pan and line with waxed paper. Grease and flour the paper. Spread batter into pan; sprinkle with walnuts. Bake at 375° for 15 minutes or until cake springs back when lightly touched.

3. Immediately turn out onto a clean dish towel dusted with confectioners' sugar. Peel off paper and roll cake up in towel, starting with a short end. Cool.

4. Meanwhile, in a large bowl, beat the cream cheese, sugar, butter and vanilla until fluffy. Carefully unroll the cake. Spread filling over cake to within 1 in. of edges. Roll up again. Cover and chill until serving. Dust with confectioners' sugar.

Winter

Bake gift-worthy cookies and craft whimsical breads. Discover
Old World favorites. Make your own traditions. Steal hearts!

Chocolate Cherry Cheesecake

I started cooking when I was 11 years old. I fell in love with it,
and I have enjoyed creating many recipes since then. Everyone
says this cheesecake has the best flavor combination. I love how
simple it is!

SHELLY KLINGER, BLOOMINGTON, ILLINOIS

PREP: 15 MIN. • **BAKE:** 30 MIN. + CHILLING • **MAKES:** 6 SERVINGS

- 1 jar (12 ounces) maraschino cherries
- 2 packages (8 ounces each) cream cheese, softened
- ½ cup sugar
- 2 eggs, lightly beaten
- ½ cup miniature semisweet chocolate chips
- 1 chocolate cookie crust (9 inches)
- 6 chocolate-covered cherries

SHORT & SWEET

1. Drain maraschino cherries, reserving 2 teaspoons juice.
Cut cherries into quarters; set aside.

2. In a small bowl, beat the cream cheese, sugar and reserved
cherry juice until smooth. Add eggs; beat just until combined.
Fold in chocolate chips and reserved cherries.

3. Pour into crust (crust will be full). Bake at 350°
for 30-35 minutes or until center is almost set. Cool
on a wire rack. Refrigerate until chilled. Serve with
chocolate-covered cherries.

Hot Chocolate Gingerbread Boys

This is like having hot chocolate in a cookie. These adorable
cookies are filled with marshmallow creme to make them taste
even more authentic.

TASTE OF HOME TEST KITCHEN

PREP: 30 MIN. + CHILLING • **BAKE:** 10 MIN./BATCH + COOLING
MAKES: 20 COOKIES

- 1 cup butter, softened
- 1 cup sugar
- ½ cup packed brown sugar
- 1 egg
- 1 teaspoon vanilla extract
- 2 cups all-purpose flour
- ¾ cup ground almonds
- ½ cup baking cocoa
- 1 teaspoon baking soda
- 1¼ cups marshmallow creme

1. In a large bowl, cream butter and sugars until light and
fluffy. Beat in egg and vanilla. Combine the flour, ground
almonds, cocoa and baking soda; gradually add to creamed
mixture and mix well. Cover and refrigerate for 2 hours or
until easy to handle.

2. On a lightly floured surface, roll out dough to 1/16-in.
thickness. Cut with a floured 3-in. gingerbread man cookie
cutter. Using a floured ¾-in. heart-shaped cookie cutter, cut
a heart from half of the cookies.

3. Place on greased baking sheets. Bake at 375° for 7-9
minutes or until set. Remove to wire racks to cool completely.

4. Just before serving, spread the bottom of each solid
cookie with 1 tablespoon marshmallow creme; gently place
cutout cookies over creme.

1. Line four greased and floured 5¾-in. x 3-in. x 2-in. loaf pans with waxed paper and grease the paper; set aside.

2. In a large bowl, combine the dates, nuts, cherries and coconut. Combine the flour, sugar, baking powder and salt; stir into fruit mixture until well coated.

3. In a small bowl, beat eggs and vanilla until foamy. Fold into fruit mixture and mix well. Pour into prepared pans.

4. Bake at 300° for 60-70 minutes or until a toothpick inserted near the center comes out clean. Cool for 10 minutes before removing from pans to wire racks to cool completely. Wrap tightly and store in a cool dry place. Cut with a serrated knife.

EDITOR'S NOTE: *Fruitcake may be baked in two greased and floured 8-in. x 4-in. loaf pans lined with waxed paper at 300° for 70-80 minutes or until a toothpick inserted near the center comes out clean.*

Jeweled Fruitcake

I promise that this fruitcake is simply fantastic. Even my friends and family members who would ordinarily avoid fruitcake say they love it!

SHARON HOFFMAN, DONNA, TEXAS

PREP: 30 MIN. • **BAKE:** 1 HOUR + COOLING
MAKES: 4 MINI LOAVES (6 SLICES EACH)

- 2 packages (8 ounces each) pitted dates, chopped
- ½ pound pecan halves
- ½ pound Brazil nuts
- 1 jar (10 ounces) red maraschino cherries, well drained
- 1 jar (10 ounces) green maraschino cherries, well drained
- ½ cup flaked coconut
- 1½ cups all-purpose flour
- 1½ cups sugar
- 1 teaspoon baking powder
- 1 teaspoon salt
- 3 eggs
- 2 teaspoons vanilla extract

Italian Pignoli Cookies

Cookies are the crown jewels of Italian sweets. I can't let a holiday go by without baking these traditional treats. You could substitute slivered almonds if you would like, but pignoli are classic.

MARIA REGAKIS, SOMERVILLE, MASSACHUSETTS

PREP: 30 MIN. • **BAKE:** 15 MIN./BATCH • **MAKES:** 2½ DOZEN

- 1¼ cups (12 ounces) almond paste
- ½ cup sugar
- 4 egg whites, divided
- 1 cup confectioners' sugar
- 1½ cups pine nuts

1. In a small bowl, beat almond paste and sugar until crumbly. Beat in 2 egg whites. Gradually add confectioners' sugar; mix well.

2. Whisk remaining egg whites in a shallow bowl. Place pine nuts in another shallow bowl. Shape dough into 1-in. balls. Roll in egg whites and coat with pine nuts. Place 2 in. apart on parchment paper-lined baking sheets. Flatten slightly.

3. Bake at 325° for 15-18 minutes or until lightly browned. Cool for 1 minute before removing from pans to wire racks. Store in an airtight container.

Hazelnut Shortbread

We have several acres of hazelnut trees here in the Willamette Valley, where the climate is perfect for this crop. Harvesttime is a big family event with everyone pitching in to help. I try to incorporate this wonderful nut into many recipes, and this cookie is always a hit.

KAREN MORRELL, CANBY, OREGON

PREP: 15 MIN. + CHILLING • **BAKE:** 15 MIN./BATCH + COOLING
MAKES: 6 DOZEN

- 1 **cup butter, softened**
- ½ **cup sugar**
- 2 **tablespoons maple syrup or honey**
- 2 **teaspoons vanilla extract**
- 2 **cups all-purpose flour**
- 1¼ **cups finely chopped hazelnuts**
- ½ **cup each white, red, green, yellow and dark chocolate candy coating disks**

1. In a large bowl, cream butter and sugar until light and fluffy. Add syrup and vanilla. Beat in flour just until combined; fold in nuts. Shape into two 1½-in. rolls; wrap tightly in waxed paper. Chill for 2 hours or until firm.

2. Cut into ¼-in. slices and place 2 in. apart on ungreased baking sheets. Bake at 325° for 14-16 minutes or until edges begin to brown. Remove to wire racks to cool.

3. In separate microwave-safe bowls, melt candy coating disks; stir until smooth. Drizzle over cookies. Let stand until set.

Gigantic Cinnamon Rolls

These luscious, over-the-top cinnamon rolls are always a hit at my parents' Christmas brunch.

KATHY WELLS, BRODHEAD, WISCONSIN

PREP: 20 MIN. + RISING • **BAKE:** 20 MIN.
MAKES: 2 ROLLS (6-8 SERVINGS EACH)

- ½ cup sugar
- ½ cup packed brown sugar
- 2 teaspoons ground cinnamon
- 2 loaves (1 pound each) frozen bread dough, thawed
- ½ cup butter, melted
- ½ cup chopped pecans
- 1¼ cups confectioners' sugar
- 6 teaspoons milk
- ½ teaspoon vanilla extract

1. In a shallow bowl, combine sugars and cinnamon; set aside. On a lightly floured surface, roll each loaf of dough into a 12-in. x 4-in. rectangle. Cut each rectangle lengthwise into four 1-in. strips. Roll each into an 18-in.-long rope. Dip in butter, then roll in sugar mixture.

2. Coil one rope in the center of a greased 12-in. pizza pan. Add three more ropes, pinching ends together to fill one pan. Repeat with remaining ropes on a second pizza pan. Sprinkle with pecans and remaining cinnamon-sugar. Cover and let rise in a warm place until doubled, about 45 minutes.

3. Bake at 350° for 20-30 minutes or until golden brown. In a small bowl, combine the confectioners' sugar, milk and vanilla until smooth. Drizzle over warm rolls.

Cherry Almond Wreath

I usually serve this spectacular coffee cake on a silver tray with a small artificial poinsettia blossoms in the center. My daughter and I enjoy making specialty breads like this one and find they make excellent Christmas gifts for family and friends.

GWEN ROFFLER, GRASSY BUTTE, NORTH DAKOTA

PREP: 30 MIN. + RISING • **BAKE:** 35 MIN. + COOLING
MAKES: 20 SERVINGS

- 1 package (¼ ounce) active dry yeast
- ½ cup warm milk (110° to 115°)
- ¼ cup warm water (110° to 115°)
- 2 eggs
- ¼ cup butter, softened
- 3 tablespoons sugar
- 1½ teaspoons salt
- 1 teaspoon grated lemon peel
- ½ teaspoon ground cardamom
- 3 to 4½ cups all-purpose flour

FILLING:
- ¼ cup butter, softened
- ¼ cup all-purpose flour
- 2 tablespoons sugar
- 1 teaspoon almond extract
- ½ teaspoon grated lemon peel
- ⅔ cup finely chopped blanched almonds
- ½ cup chopped red and green candied cherries

GLAZE:
- ⅔ cup confectioners' sugar
- 2 teaspoons lemon juice
- 1 teaspoon water

1. In a large bowl, dissolve yeast in warm milk and water. Add the eggs, butter, sugar, salt, lemon peel, cardamom and 2 cups flour; beat until smooth. Add enough remaining flour to form a soft dough.

2. Turn onto a floured surface; knead until smooth and elastic, about 6 to 8 minutes. Place in a greased bowl, turning once to grease the top. Cover and let rise in a warm place until doubled, about 1 hour.

3. In a small bowl, beat butter, flour, sugar, extract and lemon peel. Stir in almonds and cherries. Refrigerate.

4. Punch dough down. Turn on a lightly floured surface. Roll into a 30-in. x 9-in. rectangle. Crumble filling over rectangle to within ½ in. of edges.

5. Roll up jelly-roll style, starting with a long side; pinch seam to seal. Place seam side down on a greased baking sheet. With scissors, cut lengthwise down the middle of the roll; carefully turn cut sides up. Loosely twist dough portions together, keeping cut sides up. Shape into a ring and pinch ends together. Cover and let rise for 1 hour.

6. Bake at 350° for 35-40 minutes or until browned. Cool for 15 minutes on a wire rack. Combine glaze ingredients; drizzle over warm coffee cake. Cool completely.

Mint Chocolate Torte

This recipe is a combination of two different ones—the chocolate cake from my childhood and the filling from a pie I saw in a cookbook. The flavor is reminiscent of an after-dinner chocolate mint.

NADINE TAYLOR, DURHAM, NORTH CAROLINA

PREP: 30 MIN. + CHILLING • **BAKE:** 15 MIN. + COOLING
MAKES: 16 SERVINGS

- ¾ **cup baking cocoa**
- ½ **cup hot water**
- 2 **cups sugar**
- 1¾ **cups all-purpose flour**
- 1 **teaspoon baking soda**
- 1 **teaspoon salt**
- ¼ **teaspoon baking powder**
- 1 **cup milk**
- ½ **cup mayonnaise**
- 2 **eggs**
- 2 **teaspoons vanilla extract**

FILLING:
- 2 **cups miniature marshmallows**
- ¼ **cup milk**
  Dash salt
- ⅛ **to ¼ teaspoon peppermint extract**
- 2 **to 3 drops green food coloring, optional**
- 1 **cup heavy whipping cream, whipped**

TOPPING:
- 1 **cup (6 ounces) semisweet chocolate chips**
- ⅓ **cup heavy whipping cream**

1. Combine cocoa and water until smooth; set aside. In a large bowl, combine the sugar, flour, baking soda, salt and baking powder. Add the milk, mayonnaise, eggs, vanilla and cocoa mixture; beat on medium speed for 2 minutes.

2. Pour into three greased and floured 9-in. round baking pans. Bake at 350° for 15-20 minutes or until a toothpick inserted near the center comes out clean. Cool for 10 minutes before removing from pans to wire racks to cool completely.

3. In a small saucepan, cook and stir the marshmallows, milk and salt over low heat until smooth. Remove from the heat; stir in peppermint extract and food coloring if desired. Transfer to a bowl; refrigerate until chilled.

4. Fold in whipped cream. Place bottom cake layer on a serving plate; spread with a third of the filling. Repeat layers twice.

5. For topping, combine chocolate chips and cream in a small saucepan; cook and stir over low heat until chips are melted. Drizzle over top of cake. Store in the refrigerator.

Bakeshop TIP

Achieve the Fluffiest Whipped Cream Fillings

To ensure that whipped cream is light and airy, begin with a cold (preferably metal) bowl and beaters. You may wish to pour the cream into a bowl, then chill the bowl and beaters before use. If folding whipped cream into a cooked preparation, as with Mint Chocolate Torte, be sure the preparation is chilled but not so cold that it is stiff. Too much heat will deflate the whipped cream, as will overmixing a filling that has already begun to set.

Pecan Kringle Sticks

My family loves the kringle's flakiness and that it's not too sweet; it just melts in your mouth. It makes a beautiful presentation on a cookie platter along with other holiday sweets.

CONNIE VJESTICA, BROOKFIELD, ILLINOIS

PREP: 40 MIN. + CHILLING • **BAKE:** 20 MIN.
MAKES: 4 KRINGLES (6 SERVINGS EACH)

> 2 **cups all-purpose flour**
> 1 **cup cold butter, cubed**
> 1 **cup sour cream**

FILLING:

> 1 **egg white**
> 1 **teaspoon vanilla extract**
> ½ **cup sugar**
> 1 **cup chopped pecans**

ICING:

> 1¼ **cups confectioners' sugar**
> 2 **tablespoons 2% milk**

1. Place flour in a large bowl; cut in butter until crumbly. Stir in sour cream. Wrap in plastic wrap. Refrigerate for 1 to 1½ hours or until easy to handle.

2. In a small bowl, beat egg white and vanilla on medium speed until soft peaks form. Gradually beat in sugar on high until stiff peaks form. Fold in pecans.

3. Divide dough into four portions. Roll one portion into a 12-in. x 6-in. rectangle; place on an ungreased baking sheet. Spread a fourth of the egg white mixture lengthwise down the center. Fold in sides of pastry to meet in the center; pinch seam to seal. Repeat.

4. Bake at 375° for 18-22 minutes or until lightly browned. Combine confectioners' sugar and milk; drizzle over warm pastries.

Chocolate Yule Log

For many years, this impressive rolled cake has been a favorite Christmas dessert for our family— everyone just loves it! I'm also asked to bring it to our annual church Christmas function.

BERNADETTE COLVIN, TOMBALL, TEXAS

PREP: 50 MIN. • **BAKE:** 10 MIN. + COOLING • **MAKES:** 14-16 SERVINGS

- 4 **eggs, separated**
- ⅔ **cup sugar, divided**
- ½ **cup all-purpose flour**
- 2 **tablespoons baking cocoa**
- 1 **teaspoon baking powder**
- ¼ **teaspoon salt**

FILLING:
- 1 **cup heavy whipping cream**
- 2 **tablespoons sugar**
- ¼ **teaspoon almond extract**

FROSTING:
- ½ **cup butter, softened**
- 2 **cups confectioners' sugar**
- 2 **ounces unsweetened chocolate, melted**
- 2 **tablespoons milk**
- 2 **teaspoons vanilla extract**

1. Place egg whites in large bowl; let stand at room temperature for 30 minutes. Line a greased 15-in. x 10-in. x 1-in. baking pan with waxed paper; grease the paper and set aside.

2. In a large bowl, beat egg yolks on high speed for 5 minutes or until thick and lemon-colored. Gradually beat in ⅓ cup sugar. Sift flour, baking cocoa, baking powder and salt together twice; gradually add to yolk mixture and mix well (batter will be very thick).

3. With clean beaters, beat egg whites on medium speed until soft peaks form. Gradually beat in remaining sugar, 1 tablespoon at a time, on high until stiff peaks form. Gradually fold into batter. Spread evenly into prepared pan.

4. Bake at 375° for 10-12 minutes or until cake springs back when lightly touched. Cool for 5 minutes. Turn cake onto a kitchen towel dusted with cocoa powder. Gently peel off waxed paper. Roll up cake in the towel, jelly-roll style, starting with a short side; cool completely on a wire rack.

5. Meanwhile, for the filling, beat the cream in a large bowl until soft peaks form. Gradually add sugar and almond extract, beating until stiff peaks form. Unroll the cake; spread the filling to within 1 in. of edges. Roll up again.

6. In a large bowl, cream the butter and confectioners' sugar until light and fluffy. Beat in the chocolate, milk and vanilla until smooth. Frost the cake, using a metal spatula to create a bark-like effect.

Stollen

My family and friends agree that the holidays just wouldn't be the same without this traditional German bread.

VALERIA MAUIK, ELKHART LAKE, WISCONSIN

PREP: 1½ HOURS + RISING • **BAKE:** 25 MIN. + COOLING
MAKES: 2 LOAVES (14 SLICES EACH)

- ¾ cup raisins
- ½ cup chopped mixed candied fruit
- ¼ cup dried currants
- ¾ cup apple juice
- 4½ to 5 cups all-purpose flour
- 2 packages (¼ ounce each) active dry yeast
- ¼ cup sugar
- 1 teaspoon salt
- 1 cup milk
- ½ cup butter, cubed
- 2 eggs
- 2 tablespoons grated orange peel
- 1 tablespoon grated lemon peel
- ½ teaspoon almond extract
- ½ cup chopped almonds
   Confectioners' sugar, optional

GLAZE:
- 1 cup confectioners' sugar
- 3 to 4 tablespoons milk

1. In a large bowl, soak raisins, fruit and currants in apple juice for 1 hour; drain and set aside.

2. In a large bowl, combine 1-½ cups of flour, yeast, sugar and salt. In a small saucepan, heat milk and butter to 120°-130°. Add to dry ingredients; beat just until moistened. Add the eggs, grated peels and extract; beat until smooth. Stir in the almond, fruit mixture and enough remaining flour to form a soft dough.

3. Turn onto a floured surface; knead until smooth and elastic, about 6-8 minutes. Place in a greased bowl, turning once to grease the top. Cover and let rise in a warm place until doubled, about 1 hour.

4. Punch dough down; divide in half. Cover and let rest for 10 minutes. On a lightly floured surface, roll each half into a 12-in. x 8-in. oval. Fold one of the long sides over to within 1 in. of the opposite side; press edges lightly to seal. Place on greased baking sheets. Cover and let rise until almost doubled, about 30 minutes.

5. Bake at 350° for 25-30 minutes or until golden brown. Cool on wire racks. Dush with confectioners' sugar or combine glaze ingredients and drizzle over loaves.

Gingerbread Cookies with Buttercream Icing

These holiday-spiced cookies are the first ones I make in December. The recipe came from my mother-in-law. If you like, tint the buttery icing a cheery pink or green and pipe it on with a decorating tip.

ANN SCHERZER, ANACORTES, WASHINGTON

PREP: 30 MIN. + CHILLING • **BAKE:** 10 MIN./BATCH + COOLING
MAKES: ABOUT 3½ DOZEN

- ⅔ cup shortening
- 1 cup sugar
- 1 egg
- ¼ cup molasses
- 2 cups all-purpose flour
- 1 teaspoon baking soda
- 1 teaspoon salt
- 1 teaspoon each ground cinnamon, cloves and ginger

ICING:
- 3 cups confectioners' sugar
- ⅓ cup butter, softened
- 1 teaspoon vanilla extract
- ¼ teaspoon lemon extract
- ¼ teaspoon butter flavoring
- 3 to 4 tablespoons milk

1. In a large bowl, cream shortening and sugar until light and fluffy. Beat in egg and molasses. Combine flour, baking soda, salt and spices; gradually add to the creamed mixture and mix well. Refrigerate for 2 hours or overnight.

2. On a lightly floured surface, roll dough to ¼-in. thickness. Cut into desired shapes. Place on ungreased baking sheets. Bake at 350° for 8-10 minutes or until edges begin to brown. Remove from pans to cool on wire racks.

3. For icing, beat sugar, butter and flavorings in a bowl. Gradually stir in enough milk to achieve desired consistency. Frost cookies.

Kris Kringle Star Bread

I make this recipe for family and friends every holiday season. Its pretty shape was unexpected the first time and is fun every time!

EVELYN FISHER, HAINES, OREGON

PREP: 30 MIN. + RISING • **BAKE:** 25 MIN.
MAKES: 2 BREADS (18 SLICES EACH)

FILLING:
- 2 **cups chopped walnuts or hazelnuts**
- 1 **cup chopped maraschino cherries, patted dry**
- ⅔ **cup honey**
- ½ **cup sugar**

BREAD:
- 2 **packages (¼ ounce each) active dry yeast**
- 1 **cup warm water (110° to 115°)**
- ½ **cup butter, softened**
- ½ **cup sugar**
- 2 **eggs**
- 1 **teaspoon salt**
- 4½ **to 5 cups all-purpose flour**
  Confectioners' sugar icing

1. In a small bowl, combine filling ingredients; set aside. In a small bowl, dissolve yeast in water. In a large bowl, combine the butter, sugar, eggs, salt, yeast mixture and 2 cups flour; beat until smooth. Stir in enough remaining flour to form a soft dough.

2. Turn onto a floured surface; knead until smooth and elastic, about 6-8 minutes. Place in a greased bowl, turning once to grease the top. Cover with plastic wrap and let rise in a warm place until doubled, about 1 hour.

3. Punch dough down. Divide in half; roll each half into a 14-in. circle. Transfer to two greased baking sheets. Cut five 4-in.-long slits into each circle equal distance apart. Set aside half of filling for garnish; spoon remaining filling into the center of each section.

4. Fold the two outer edges of each section over each other to enclose filling, forming star points. Pinch edges together to seal. Cover and let rise in a warm place until doubled, about 30 minutes. Bake at 350° for 25 minutes or until golden brown. Drizzle with confectioners' sugar icing. Spoon reserved filling into the centers.

Candy Cane Coffee Cakes

Dotted with dried apricots and maraschino cherries, this tender coffee cake has a festive flavor and look. I love to serve it at Christmastime to my family, students and fellow teachers. It makes a welcome holiday gift, too.

LINDA HOLLINGSWORTH, QUITMAN, MISSISSIPPI

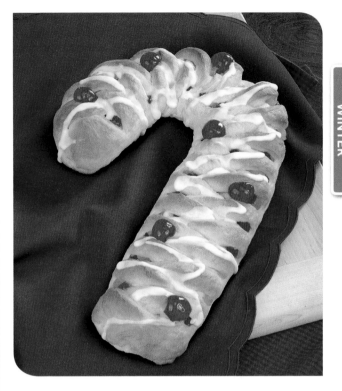

PREP: 35 MIN. + RISING • **BAKE:** 20 MIN.
MAKES: 3 LOAVES (12 SLICES EACH)

2 packages (¼ ounce each) active dry yeast
½ cup warm water (110° to 115°)
2 cups warm sour cream (110° to 115°)
6 tablespoons butter, divided
⅓ cup sugar
2 eggs
2 teaspoons salt
5¾ to 6¼ cups all-purpose flour
1½ cups finely chopped dried apricots
1½ cups finely chopped maraschino cherries
2 cups confectioners' sugar
2 tablespoons cold water
   Additional cherries, halved

1. In a large bowl, dissolve yeast in warm water. Add the sour cream, 4 tablespoons butter, sugar, eggs, salt and 2 cups flour; beat until smooth. Stir in enough remaining flour to form a soft dough.

2. Turn onto a floured surface; knead until smooth and elastic, about 6-8 minutes. Place in a greased bowl, turning once to grease the top. Cover and let rise in a warm place until doubled, about 1 hour.

3. Punch dough down. Turn onto a lightly floured surface; divide into thirds. Roll each portion into a 14-in. x 7-in. rectangle on a greased baking sheet.

4. Combine apricots and cherries; spoon down the center of each rectangle. On each long side, cut ¾-in.-wide strips about 2 in. into center. Starting at one end, fold alternating strips at an angle across filling. Pinch ends to seal. Curve top.

5. Bake at 375° for 18-20 minutes or until golden brown. Melt the remaining butter and brush over warm coffee cakes.

6. In a small bowl, combine confectioners' sugar and cold water until smooth; drizzle over the tops. Arrange cherries on top of each coffee cake.

Bakeshop HOW-TO

Shaping Candy Cane Coffee Cakes

Starting at one end, fold strips alternately at an angle across the filling. Seal ends.

Curve one end to form a candy cane.

1. In a large bowl, cream butter and confectioners' sugar until light and fluffy. Beat in egg and extract. Combine flour and salt; gradually add to creamed mixture and mix well.

2. Using a cookie press fitted with the disk of your choice, press cookies 1 in. apart onto ungreased baking sheets. Sprinkle with colored sugar.

3. Bake at 375° for 6-9 minutes or until lightly browned. Cool for 2 minutes before removing from pans to wire racks.

Finnish Cardamom Braids

Every Finn I know often serves Nissua, a sweet bread with cardamom. I believe my mom's recipe beats all others, hands down! Her bread is soft and fluffy while others can be dry. No matter how many Nissua braids she makes for a popular annual craft fair, they're all gone by noon!

ANNE HEINONEN, HOWELL, MICHIGAN

PREP: 25 MIN. + RISING • **BAKE:** 25 MIN. + COOLING
MAKES: 2 LOAVES (16 SLICES EACH)

2 **packages (¼ ounce each) active dry yeast**
¼ **cup warm water (110° to 115°)**
2 **cups warm milk (110° to 115°)**
¾ **cup sugar**
½ **cup butter, softened**
1½ **teaspoons salt**
¾ **teaspoon ground cardamom**
2 **eggs**
7 **to 8 cups all-purpose flour**

1. In a bowl, dissolve yeast in warm water. Add milk, sugar, butter, salt, cardamom, eggs and 3 cups flour; beat until smooth. Stir in enough remaining flour to form a soft dough.

2. Turn onto a floured surface; knead until smooth and elastic, about 6-8 minutes. Place in a greased bowl, turning once to grease the top. Cover and let rise in a warm place until doubled, about 1 hour.

3. Punch dough down. Turn onto a lightly floured surface; divide in half. Divide each half into thirds. Shape each piece into a 13-in. rope. Place three ropes on a greased baking sheet. Braid ropes; pinch ends to seal and tuck under. Repeat. Cover and let rise until doubled, about 45 minutes.

4. Bake at 350° for 25-30 minutes or until golden brown. Remove from pans to wire racks to cool.

Holiday Spritz

I tried subbing rum extract for vanilla in a classic Christmas recipe, and the end result was a cookie that tasted a lot like my favorite seasonal specialty—eggnog!

LISA VARNER, CHARLESTON, SOUTH CAROLINA

PREP: 30 MIN. **BAKE:** 10 MIN./BATCH • **YIELD:** 7 DOZEN

1 **cup butter, softened**
1 **cup confectioners' sugar**
1 **egg**
1-½ **teaspoons rum extract**
2-½ **cups all-purpose flour**
¼ **teaspoon salt**
Colored sugar

Cranberry Rugalach

These traditional Polish treats will keep for a long time in an airtight container. One Christmas, I sent a batch to my sister, but the box got lost. She received it 12 days later and the cookies still tasted fresh and yummy!

JEAN DOXON, OMAHA, NEBRASKA

PREP: 25 MIN. + CHILLING • **BAKE:** 20 MIN./BATCH
MAKES: 64 COOKIES

- 1 **cup butter, softened**
- 1 **package (8 ounces) cream cheese, softened**
- ½ **cup sugar**
- 2¾ **cups all-purpose flour**
- 1 **teaspoon salt**

FILLING:
- ¾ **cup sugar**
- ⅔ **cup dried cranberries, finely chopped**
- ½ **cup finely chopped walnuts, toasted**
- ⅓ **cup butter, melted**
- 2 **teaspoons ground cinnamon**
- 1 **teaspoon ground allspice**
- 1 **egg, lightly beaten**
  Additional sugar

1. In a large bowl, cream the butter, cream cheese and sugar until light and fluffy. Combine flour and salt; gradually add to creamed mixture and mix well.

2. Turn onto a lightly floured surface; knead for 3 minutes or until smooth. Divide into eight portions. Roll each portion into a ball; flatten into a 4-in. circle. Wrap in plastic wrap and refrigerate for at least 1 hour.

3. In a small bowl, combine the sugar, cranberries, walnuts, butter, cinnamon and allspice. On a lightly floured surface, roll one portion of dough into an 8-in. circle. Sprinkle with 3 tablespoons of filling to within ½ in. of edges. Cut into eight wedges.

4. Roll up wedges from the wide end and place point side down 2 in. apart on foil-lined baking sheets. Curve ends down to form a crescent shape. Brush with egg and sprinkle with additional sugar.

5. Repeat with remaining dough and filling. Bake at 350° for 18-20 minutes or until golden brown. Remove to wire racks.

2. Fill paper-lined muffin cups two-thirds full. Press a chocolate kiss into the center of each cupcake until batter completely covers candy.

3. Bake at 375° for 20-25 minutes or until a toothpick inserted into the cakes comes out clean. Cool for 10 minutes before removing from pans to wire racks to cool completely. Frost cupcakes.

Chocolate-Mint Hearts

This is one of my favorite holiday cookies. Dipping in the chocolate mint glaze really makes these cookies a special treat.

SHERI LIVERMORE, WAUKESHA, WISCONSIN

PREP: 25 MIN. + CHILLING • **BAKE:** 10 MIN./BATCH + COOLING
MAKES: 2 DOZEN

  1 **package (10 ounces) mint chocolate chips, divided**
  ¼ **cup butter, softened**
  ⅓ **cup sugar**
  1 **egg**
  ½ **teaspoon vanilla extract**
1¼ **cups all-purpose flour**
  ¾ **teaspoon baking powder**
  ¼ **teaspoon salt**
  ¼ **teaspoon baking soda**
  ¼ **cup shortening**
      Colored sprinkles, optional

1. In a microwave-safe bowl, melt ½ cup chocolate chips; stir. Cool slightly. In a small bowl, cream butter and sugar. Beat in the egg, vanilla and melted chocolate. Combine the flour, baking powder, salt and baking soda; gradually add to creamed mixture and mix well.

2. Cover and refrigerate for 1-2 hours or until easy to handle. On a lightly floured surface, roll out dough to ¼-in. thickness. Cut with a floured 2½-in. heart-shaped cookie cutter. Place 2 in. apart on ungreased baking sheets. Bake at 350° for 7-10 minutes or until set. Remove to wire racks to cool completely.

3. In a microwave, melt shortening and remaining chocolate chips; stir until smooth. Dip each cookie halfway into chocolate mixture; allow excess to drip off. Sprinkle chocolate with sprinkles if desired. Place on waxed paper; refrigerate until set.

Secret Kiss Cupcakes

I came up with these cupcakes for a Cub Scouts meeting. You should have seen the adorable grins when the kids bit into the chocolate kisses in the middle.

CAROL HILLEBRENNER, FOWLER, ILLINOIS

PREP: 20 MIN. • **BAKE:** 20 MIN. + COOLING • **MAKES:** ABOUT 2½ DOZEN

3⅓ **cups all-purpose flour**
  2 **cups sugar**
  1 **cup baking cocoa**
  2 **teaspoons baking soda**
  1 **teaspoon salt**
  2 **cups buttermilk**
  1 **cup butter, melted**
  2 **eggs, lightly beaten**
  2 **teaspoons vanilla extract**
 30 **milk chocolate kisses**
  1 **can (16 ounces) fudge frosting**

1. In a large bowl, combine the flour, sugar, cocoa, baking soda and salt. Combine the buttermilk, butter, eggs and vanilla. Add to the dry ingredients until blended.

Lollipop Cookies

Cookie "lollipops" are always a hit with kids (and their parents). Use your imagination with this recipe to create treats for any season—the possibilities are endless!

JEAN EDWARDS, INDIANAPOLIS, INDIANA

PREP: 20 MIN. + CHILLING • **BAKE:** 10 MIN./BATCH + COOLING
MAKES: 3 DOZEN

  1 **cup butter, softened**
1½ **cups confectioners' sugar**
  1 **egg**
  1 **teaspoon vanilla extract**
 ¼ **to ½ teaspoon almond extract**
2½ **cups all-purpose flour**
  1 **teaspoon baking soda**
  1 **teaspoon cream of tartar**
  2 **ounces semisweet chocolate, melted**
FROSTING:
  1 **cup confectioners' sugar**
 ¼ **to ½ teaspoon almond extract**
 ¼ **teaspoon salt**
  1 **to 2 teaspoons milk**
    Red-hot candies and red sprinkles

1. In a large bowl, cream butter and confectioners' sugar until light and fluffy. Beat in egg and extracts. Combine the flour, baking soda and cream of tartar; gradually add to the creamed mixture and mix well. Divide dough in half; stir chocolate into one half. Refrigerate for 2 hours or until easy to handle.

2. On a lightly floured surface, roll out each portion to ⅛-in. thickness. Cut with a 2½-in. cookie cutter. Place 1 in. apart on lightly greased baking sheets.

3. Bake at 375° for 7-8 minutes or until lightly browned. Remove to wire racks to cool.

4. For frosting, combine the confectioners' sugar, extract, salt and enough milk to achieve spreading consistency. Frost bottoms of chocolate cookies. Place a wooden stick on each cookie, leaving 3 in. for handle. Top each with a plain cookie. Frost tops; add candies and sprinkles.

Glittering Cutout Cookies

The dessert table really sparkles with these crispy cookies.

GRACE VAN TIMMEREN, GRAND RAPIDS, MICHIGAN

PREP: 50 MIN. + CHILLING • **BAKE:** 10 MIN./BATCH + COOLING

MAKES: ABOUT 4 DOZEN

- ¾ cup butter, softened
- 1 cup sugar
- 2 eggs
- 1 teaspoon almond extract
- 2½ cups all-purpose flour
- 1 teaspoon baking powder
- 1 teaspoon salt

FROSTING:

- ½ cup butter, softened
- 4½ cups confectioners' sugar
- 1½ teaspoons vanilla extract
- 5 to 6 tablespoons 2% milk
  Paste food coloring of your choice
  Edible glitter and colored sugar

1. Cream butter and sugar. Beat in eggs and extract. Combine flour, baking powder and salt; add to creamed mixture and mix well. Chill 1 hour or until easy to handle.

2. On a floured surface, roll dough to ¼-in. thickness. Cut with floured love-themed cookie cutters. Place on greased baking sheets. Bake at 400° for 6-8 minutes or until set. Remove to wire racks to cool completely.

3. Beat butter until fluffy. Beat in confectioners' sugar, vanilla and enough milk to achieve desired consistency. Tint as desired; frost cookies. Combine equal amounts of edible glitter and colored sugar; sprinkle over cookies.

Editor's Note: *Edible glitter is available from Wilton Industries. Call 800-794-5866 or visit wilton.com.*

Conversation Brownie

I like to make this special heart on Valentine's Day, which is also my daughter's birthday!

ANGIE POWELL, OREM, UTAH

PREP: 25 MIN. • **BAKE:** 15 MIN. + COOLING • **MAKES:** 8-10 SERVINGS

- ⅓ cup butter-flavored shortening
- ¾ cup packed brown sugar
- 1 egg
- 1½ teaspoons water
- ½ teaspoon vanilla extract
- ¾ cup all-purpose flour
- 3 tablespoons baking cocoa
- ¼ teaspoon salt
- ⅛ teaspoon baking soda
- 1 cup milk chocolate chips

FROSTING:

- 3½ cups confectioners' sugar, divided
- 3 tablespoons butter, softened
- 1 tablespoon shortening
- ½ teaspoon vanilla extract
- 3 to 4 tablespoons milk, divided
  Red paste food coloring

1. In a large bowl, cream shortening and brown sugar. Beat in egg, water and vanilla. Combine the flour, cocoa, salt and baking soda; gradually add to creamed mixture until combined. Stir in chocolate chips. Pour into a greased and floured 9-in. heart-shaped baking pan.

2. Bake at 375° for 15-20 minutes or until center is set (do not overbake). Cool for 10 minutes before removing from pan to a wire rack.

3. In a large bowl, combine 1½ cups confectioners' sugar, butter, shortening, vanilla and 3 tablespoons milk; beat until smooth. Gradually add remaining confectioners' sugar; beat until light and fluffy, about 3 minutes. Add enough remaining milk to achieve a frosting consistency. Frost brownie with ¾ cup frosting. Using food coloring, tint remaining frosting and decorate as desired.

Daily Breads

Cranberry Orange Bagels

These scrumptious morning treats have a bright, sweet-tart taste. Switch up the flavor, if you'd like, by using raisins and cinnamon.

KRISTY REEVES, LEROY, KANSAS

PREP: 30 MIN. + STANDING • **BAKE:** 20 MIN. + COOLING
MAKES: 9 BAGELS

- 1 cup plus 4 tablespoons water (70° to 80°), divided
- ½ cup dried cranberries
- ⅓ cup packed brown sugar
- 4½ teaspoons grated orange peel
- 1 teaspoon salt
- ¼ teaspoon ground cloves
- 3 cups bread flour
- 1 package (¼ ounce) active dry yeast
- 1 tablespoon sugar
- 1 egg white
- 1 tablespoon cornmeal

1. In bread machine, place 1 cup plus 2 tablespoons water and the next seven ingredients in order suggested by manufacturer. Select dough setting (check after 5 minutes of mixing; add 1 to 2 tablespoons of water or flour if needed).

2. When cycle is completed, turn dough onto a lightly floured surface. Shape into nine balls. Push thumb through centers to form a 1-in. hole. Stretch and shape dough to form an even ring. Cover and let rest for 10 minutes; flatten rings slightly.

3. Fill a Dutch oven two-thirds full with water; add sugar and bring to a boil. Drop bagels, two at a time, into boiling water. Cook for 45 seconds; turn and cook 45 seconds longer. Remove with a slotted spoon; drain on paper towels.

4. Whisk egg white and remaining water; brush over bagels. Grease a baking sheet; sprinkle with cornmeal. Place bagels on pan 2 in. apart. Bake at 400° for 18-22 minutes or until golden brown.

Caramelized Onion Flatbread

I top pizza crust with sweet, buttery onions and grated cheese for easy homemade bread in one hour!

DEIRDRE DEE COX, MILWAUKEE, WISCONSIN

PREP: 45 MIN. • **BAKE:** 15 MIN. • **MAKES:** 15 SERVINGS

- 3 large sweet onions, thinly sliced
- 2 tablespoons brown sugar
- 1 tablespoon Marsala wine or apple juice
- ¼ teaspoon salt
- ¼ teaspoon pepper
- 2 tablespoons butter
- 1 tube (13.8 ounces) refrigerated pizza crust
- 1 tablespoon olive oil
- ¼ cup shredded Parmesan cheese

SHORT & SWEET

1. In a large skillet, cook the onions, brown sugar, wine, salt and pepper in butter over medium-low heat for 30-40 minutes or until onions are caramelized, stirring frequently.

2. On a greased baking sheet, roll out pizza crust into a 13-in. x 10-in. rectangle. Brush the crust with oil. Top with onions and cheese.

3. Bake at 400° for 15-18 minutes or until lightly browned. Serve warm.

2. Turn onto a floured surface; knead until smooth and elastic, about 6-8 minutes. Place in a greased bowl, turning once to grease the top. Cover and let rise in a warm place until doubled, about 1 hour.

3. Punch dough down. Turn onto a lightly floured surface; divide into 24 pieces. Shape each into a ball. Place in a greased 13-in. x 9-in. baking pan. Cover and let rise until doubled, about 30 minutes.

4. Bake at 375° for 20-22 minutes or until golden brown. Melt remaining butter; brush over rolls. Remove from pan to a wire rack.

Pumpernickel Muffins

These savory muffins are a perfect accompaniment to a hearty entree. Molasses, chocolate and dried cherries add just the right hint of sweetness to a rich rye dough.

NANCY MUELLER, HIGHLANDS RANCH, COLORADO

PREP: 20 MIN. • **BAKE:** 15 MIN. • **MAKES:** 6 MUFFINS

- ¾ **cup rye flour**
- ⅔ **cup all-purpose flour**
- 3 **tablespoons sugar**
- 1 **teaspoon baking powder**
- ½ **teaspoon ground cinnamon**
- ¼ **teaspoon baking soda**
- ¼ **teaspoon salt**
- 1 **egg**
- ⅔ **cup buttermilk**
- ¼ **cup canola oil**
- 1 **tablespoon molasses**
- ½ **ounce unsweetened chocolate, melted and cooled**
- ¼ **cup dried cherries**

1. In a large bowl, combine the flours, sugar, baking powder, cinnamon, baking soda and salt.

2. In another bowl, combine the egg, buttermilk, oil, molasses and chocolate. Stir into dry ingredients just until moistened. Fold in cherries.

3. Fill greased or paper-lined muffin cups three-fourths full. Bake at 400° for 15-20 minutes or until a toothpick inserted in the muffin comes out clean. Cool for 5 minutes before removing from pan to a wire rack. Serve warm.

Honey-Oat Pan Rolls

These tender rolls are a welcome addition to any meal. Whole wheat flour and oats make them nutritious, too.

ARLENE BUTLER, OGDEN, UTAH

PREP: 45 MIN. + RISING • **BAKE:** 20 MIN. • **MAKES:** 2 DOZEN

- 2½ to 2¾ **cups all-purpose flour**
- ¾ **cup whole wheat flour**
- ½ **cup old-fashioned oats**
- 2 **packages (¼ ounce each) active dry yeast**
- 1 **teaspoon salt**
- 1 **cup water**
- ¼ **cup honey**
- 5 **tablespoons butter, divided**
- 1 **egg**

1. In a large bowl, combine 1 cup all-purpose flour, whole wheat flour, oats, yeast and salt. In a small saucepan, heat the water, honey and 4 tablespoons butter to 120°-130°. Add to dry ingredients; beat just until moistened. Add egg; beat until well combined. Stir in enough remaining all-purpose flour to form a soft dough.

Ezekiel Bread

This bread bakes up tender and chewy with a hint of sweetness. It's great to give as a gift or to accompany your Sunday dinner.

ROGER HAWLEY, VALLEY PARK, MISSOURI

PREP: 45 MIN. + RISING • **BAKE:** 30 MIN. + COOLING
MAKES: 4 LOAVES (16 SLICES EACH)

- 3 **packages (¼ ounce each) active dry yeast**
- 5 **cups warm water (110° to 115°), divided**
- 1 **tablespoon plus ⅔ cup honey, divided**
- ⅔ **cup canola oil**
- ½ **cup sugar**
- 2 **teaspoons salt**
- 4 **cups whole wheat flour**
- 1 **cup toasted wheat germ**
- 6 **to 8 cups bread flour**

1. In a large bowl, dissolve yeast in ¾ cup warm water and 1 tablespoon honey. Add the remaining water and honey, oil, sugar, salt, whole wheat flour, wheat germ and 3 cups bread flour. Beat until smooth. Stir in enough remaining bread flour to form a soft dough (dough will be sticky).

2. Turn onto a lightly floured surface; knead until smooth and elastic, about 6-8 minutes. Place in a bowl coated with cooking spray, turning once to coat the top. Cover and let rise in a warm place until doubled, about 1 hour.

3. Punch dough down. Shape into loaves. Place in four 9-in. x 5-in. loaf pans coated with cooking spray. Cover and let rise until nearly doubled, about 30 minutes.

4. Bake at 350° for 30-35 minutes or until golden brown. Remove from pans to wire racks to cool.

Honey White Loaves

When I was searching for a moist bread that wouldn't crumble when thinly sliced, a friend recommended her grandmother's cherished recipe. It slices perfectly.

LOIS KAMPS, HUDSONVILLE, MICHIGAN

PREP: 20 MIN. + RISING • **BAKE:** 25 MIN. + COOLING
MAKES: 3 LOAVES (12 SLICES EACH)

- 2 packages (¼ ounce each) active dry yeast
- 2½ cups warm water (110° to 115°)
- ½ cup butter, melted
- ½ cup honey
- 2 eggs
- 3 teaspoons salt
- 8 to 9 cups all-purpose flour

1. In a large bowl, dissolve yeast in warm water. Add the butter, honey, eggs, salt and 4 cups flour. Beat on medium for 3 minutes. Stir in enough remaining flour to form a soft dough.

2. Turn onto a floured surface; knead until smooth and elastic, about 6-8 minutes. Place in a greased bowl, turning once to grease top. Cover and let rise in a warm place until doubled, about 1 hour.

3. Punch dough down; shape into loaves. Place in three greased 8-in. x 4-in. loaf pans. Cover and let rise until doubled, about 30 minutes.

4. Bake at 375° for 25-30 minutes or until golden brown. Remove from pans to wire racks to cool.

Rosemary Olive Focaccia

These are so delicious! For a thinner, crispier focaccia, try using three 10-inch rounds instead of two to bake up this recipe. Just remember to adjust the bake time accordingly.

TASTE OF HOME TEST KITCHEN

PREP: 35 MIN. + RISING • **BAKE:** 25 MIN.
MAKES: 2 LOAVES (8 SLICES EACH)

- 3 cups all-purpose flour
- 1 package (¼ ounce) active dry yeast
- 1 teaspoon sugar
- 1 teaspoon dried rosemary, crushed, divided
- ¾ teaspoon salt
- ⅛ teaspoon coarsely ground pepper
- 1 cup warm water (120° to 130°)
- 4 tablespoons olive oil, divided
- ⅓ cup sliced ripe olives
- 2 tablespoons yellow cornmeal
- 2 tablespoons grated Parmesan cheese
  Additional coarsely ground black pepper and rosemary

1. In a large bowl, combine flour, yeast, sugar, ½ teaspoon rosemary, salt and pepper. Stir in warm water and 2 tablespoons oil. Turn out onto a lightly floured surface; knead 3 minutes. Add olives and remaining rosemary; knead 1 minute longer. Place in a greased bowl, turning once to grease the top. Cover and let rise until doubled, about 45 minutes.

2. Punch dough down and divide in half. Cover and let rest for 5 minutes. Sprinkle cornmeal on greased baking sheets. Roll each piece of dough into a 10-in. circle; place on baking sheets. Cover and let rise until doubled, about 30 minutes. With fingertips, make several dimples over top of dough.

3. Brush dough with remaining oil. Sprinkle with cheese and additional pepper and rosemary. Bake at 375° for 25-30 minutes or until golden brown. Serve warm.

Golden Oat Bread

This wholesome bread incorporates grains that my sons, Tim and Jon, wouldn't normally touch. But even they can't resist these beautiful loaves!

KAY KRAUSE, SIOUX FALLS, SOUTH DAKOTA

PREP: 30 MIN. + RISING • **BAKE:** 20 MIN. + COOLING
MAKES: 2 LOAVES (16 SLICES EACH)

- 3 to 4 cups all-purpose flour
- 1 cup old-fashioned oats, divided
- ¼ cup sugar
- 3 tablespoons chopped walnuts
- 2 tablespoons sunflower kernels
- 2 teaspoons active dry yeast
- ¾ teaspoon salt
- ¾ cup water
- ⅓ cup canola oil
- ¼ cup buttermilk
- ¼ cup honey
- 2 eggs
- ¾ cup whole wheat flour
- 1 tablespoon cold water

1. In a large bowl, combine 2 cups all-purpose flour, ¾ cup oats, sugar, walnuts, sunflower kernels, yeast and salt. In a small saucepan, heat the water, oil, buttermilk and honey to 120°-130°. Add to dry ingredients; beat until well blended. Beat in 1 egg until smooth. Stir in whole wheat flour and enough remaining all-purpose flour to form a soft dough.

2. Turn onto a floured surface; knead until smooth and elastic, about 6-8 minutes. Place in a greased bowl, turning once to grease the top. Cover and let rise in a warm place until doubled, about 1 hour.

3. Punch dough down; turn onto a lightly floured surface. Divide in half; shape into round loaves. Sprinkle 2 tablespoons oats on a greased baking sheet; place loaves over oats. Cover and let rise until doubled, about 45 minutes.

4. Beat remaining egg and cold water; brush over loaves. Sprinkle with remaining oats. Bake at 350° for 20-25 minutes or until golden brown. Cool on wire racks.

Irish Soda Bread

I've been making bread since I was a young girl, and this is one of my favorites. It's moist with a wonderful texture and flavor. Golden raisins peek out of every slice.

ANN LAUVER, LITITZ, PENNSYLVANIA

PREP: 30 MIN. + RISING • **BAKE:** 30 MIN. + COOLING
MAKES: 1 LOAF (12 SLICES)

- 1 package (¼ ounce) active dry yeast
- ½ cup warm water (110° to 115°)
- 3 tablespoons sugar, divided
- 1 cup warm buttermilk (110° to 115°)
- 2 tablespoons butter, softened
- ½ teaspoon salt
- ½ teaspoon baking soda
- 3½ to 4 cups all-purpose flour
- ¾ cup golden raisins

1. In a large bowl, dissolve yeast in warm water. Add 1 tablespoon sugar; let stand for 5 minutes. Beat in the buttermilk, butter, salt, baking soda, 1 cup flour and remaining sugar until smooth. Stir in raisins and enough remaining flour to form a soft dough.

2. Turn onto a floured surface; knead until smooth and elastic, about 6-8 minutes. Place in a greased bowl, turning once to grease the top. Cover and let rise in a warm place until doubled, about 40 minutes.

3. Punch dough down. Turn onto a lightly floured surface; knead for 2 minutes. Shape into a round loaf. Place on a greased baking sheet. Cover and let rise until doubled, about 30 minutes. With a sharp knife, cut a ¼-in.-deep cross on top of loaf.

4. Bake at 350° for 30-35 minutes or until golden brown. Remove from pan to cool on a wire rack.

Editor's Note: *Warmed buttermilk will appear curdled.*

Baker's Dozen Yeast Rolls

A yummy honey-garlic topping turns these easy dinner rolls into something extra special. Try 'em with soups and chili.

TASTE OF HOME TEST KITCHEN

PREP: 25 MIN. + RISING • **BAKE:** 15 MIN. + COOLING • **MAKES:** 13 ROLLS

- 2 **to 2½ cups all-purpose flour**
- 2 **tablespoons sugar**
- 1 **package (¼ ounce) quick-rise yeast**
- ½ **teaspoon salt**
- ¾ **cup warm water (120° to 130°)**
- 2 **tablespoons plus 4 teaspoons butter, melted, divided**
- ¾ **cup shredded sharp cheddar cheese**
- 2 **teaspoons honey**
- ⅛ **teaspoon garlic salt**

1. In a large bowl, combine 1½ cups flour, sugar, yeast and salt. Add water and 2 tablespoons butter; beat on medium speed for 3 minutes or until smooth. Stir in cheese and enough remaining flour to form a soft dough.

2. Turn onto a lightly floured surface; knead until smooth and elastic, about 4-6 minutes. Cover and let rest for 10 minutes. Divide into 13 pieces. Shape each into a ball. Place in a greased 9-in. round baking pan. Cover and let rise in a warm place until doubled, about 30 minutes.

3. Bake at 375° for 11-14 minutes or until lightly browned. Combine the honey, garlic salt and remaining butter; brush over rolls. Cool on a wire rack.

Tomato-Herb Focaccia

With its medley of herbs and tomatoes, this rustic bread will liven up any occasion, from a family meal to a game-day get-together. And it won't stick around long.

JANET MILLER, INDIANAPOLIS, INDIANA

PREP: 30 MIN. + RISING • **BAKE:** 20 MIN. • **MAKES:** 1 LOAF (12 PIECES)

- 1 package (¼ ounce) active dry yeast
- 1 cup warm water (110° to 115°)
- 2 tablespoons olive oil, divided
- 1½ teaspoons salt
- 1 teaspoon sugar
- 1 teaspoon garlic powder
- 1 teaspoon each dried oregano, thyme and rosemary, crushed
- ½ teaspoon dried basil
  Dash pepper
- 2 to 2½ cups all-purpose flour
- 2 plum tomatoes, thinly sliced
- ¼ cup shredded part-skim mozzarella cheese
- 1 tablespoon grated Parmesan cheese

1. In a large bowl, dissolve yeast in warm water. Add 1 tablespoon oil, salt, sugar, garlic powder, herbs, pepper and 1½ cups flour. Beat until smooth. Stir in enough remaining flour to form a soft dough (dough will be sticky).

2. Turn onto a floured surface; knead until smooth and elastic, about 6-8 minutes. Place in a greased bowl, turning once to grease the top. Cover and let rise in a warm place until doubled, about 1 hour.

3. Punch dough down. Cover and let rest for 10 minutes. Shape into a 13-in. x 9-in. rectangle; place on a greased baking sheet. Cover and let rise until doubled, about 30 minutes. With fingertips, make several dimples over top of dough.

4. Brush dough with remaining oil; arrange tomatoes over the top. Sprinkle with cheeses. Bake at 400° for 20-25 minutes or until golden brown. Remove to a wire rack.

Buttery Whole Wheat Dinner Rolls

These whole grain rolls are tender and delicious just eaten plain; they don't even need butter. I adapted the recipe from one my mom made after she sampled a similar roll at a restaurant.

ANGELA COFFMAN, KANSAS CITY, MISSOURI

PREP: 30 MIN. + RISING • **BAKE:** 10 MIN. • **MAKES:** 16 ROLLS

- 1 tablespoon active dry yeast
- ¾ cup warm water (110° to 115°)
- ⅓ cup sugar
- ⅓ cup nonfat dry milk powder
- 4 tablespoons butter, softened, divided
- 1 egg
- 1 teaspoon salt
- 2 cups whole wheat flour
- ½ to 1 cup bread flour

1. In a small bowl, dissolve yeast in warm water. Add the sugar, milk powder, 2 tablespoons butter, egg, salt and whole wheat flour. Beat until smooth. Stir in enough bread flour to form a soft dough (dough will be sticky).

2. Turn onto a floured surface; knead until smooth and elastic, about 6-8 minutes. Place in a greased bowl, turning once to grease the top. Cover and let rise in a warm place until doubled, about 1 hour.

3. In a shallow microwave-safe bowl, melt remaining butter. Punch dough down. Turn onto a lightly floured surface; divide into 16 pieces. Shape each into a ball; roll in melted butter. Place 2 in. apart on greased baking sheets. Cover and let rise until doubled, about 30 minutes.

4. Bake at 375° for 8-10 minutes or until golden brown. Remove from pans to wire racks.

English Batter Buns

Since receiving this easy-to-prepare recipe from a dear friend, I've made these rolls often for the holidays.

GERALDINE WEST, OGDEN, UTAH

PREP: 15 MIN. + RISING • **BAKE:** 10 MIN. • **MAKES:** 1 DOZEN

- 2 packages (¼ ounces each) active dry yeast
- 1 cup warm milk (110° to 115°)
- ½ cup shortening
- 2 tablespoons sugar
- 1 teaspoon salt
- 2 eggs
- 3½ cups all-purpose flour
  Melted butter

1. In a large bowl, dissolve yeast in warm milk. Add the shortening, sugar, salt, eggs and 2 cups flour; beat on medium speed for 3 minutes. Stir in remaining flour until smooth. Cover and let rise in a warm place until doubled, about 30 minutes.

2. Stir batter vigorously for 25 strokes (dough will be slightly sticky). Spoon into greased muffin cups. Tap pans to settle the batter. Cover and let rise until batter reaches tops of cups, about 20 minutes.

3. Bake at 400° for 10-15 minutes or until golden brown. Brush with butter.

Bakeshop TIP

Batter Up!

Easy batter bread lets you enjoy homemade yeast bread without the work of kneading. It dirties fewer dishes and leaves your counter clean, since the dough stays in its mixing bowl for the first rise. Since beating the batter with a mixer takes the place of kneading, be sure to beat for the time specified in the recipe. Batter bread dough is more loose and sticky than traditional kneaded doughs.

Cheddar Herb Rings

These impressive cheese loaves are great sliced into thin wedges to go with soup, salads or casseroles. I've served this recipe to large crowds and received many compliments. One year, I gave a loaf to our neighbor for Christmas.

EVELYN BEAR, KINGSTON, IDAHO

PREP: 35 MIN. + CHILLING • **BAKE:** 20 MIN. + COOLING
MAKES: 2 LOAVES (12 SLICES EACH)

- 1 package (¼ ounce) active dry yeast
- ¼ cup warm water (110° to 115°)
- 1 cup warm milk (110° to 115°)
- ¼ cup canola oil
- 2 tablespoons honey
- 1 egg
- 1 teaspoon salt
- 1 cup whole wheat flour
- 2½ cups all-purpose flour
- 1 teaspoon each dried oregano, basil and rosemary, crushed

FILLING:
- 1½ cups (6 ounces) shredded cheddar cheese
- ½ teaspoon dried parsley flakes
- ¼ teaspoon garlic powder
- ¼ teaspoon paprika

TOPPING:
- 1 egg, lightly beaten
- 2 teaspoons sesame seeds
- 4 teaspoons grated Parmesan cheese

1. In a large bowl, dissolve yeast in warm water. Add the milk, oil, honey, egg, salt, whole wheat flour, 1 cup all-purpose flour and herbs. Beat until blended. Stir in enough remaining all-purpose flour to form a soft dough. Cover and refrigerate overnight.

2. Punch dough down and turn onto a floured surface; divide in half. Roll one portion into a 15-in. x 10-in. rectangle. Combine filling ingredients; sprinkle half over dough. Roll up jelly-roll style, starting with a long side; pinch seams to seal.

3. Place seam side down on a greased baking sheet; pinch ends together to form a ring. With a sharp knife, cut ½-in. slashes at 2-in. intervals. Repeat with remaining dough and filling. Cover and let rise in a warm place until doubled, about 30 minutes.

4. Brush each ring with egg; sprinkle with sesame seeds and cheese. Bake at 350° for 20-25 minutes or until golden brown. Remove from pans to wire racks to cool.

Garlic Knots

Here's a handy bread that can be made in no time flat. Refrigerated biscuits make preparation simple. The Italian flavors complement a variety of meals.

JANE PASCHKE, UNIVERSITY PARK, FLORIDA

PREP/TOTAL TIME: 30 MIN. • **MAKES:** 2½ DOZEN

- 1 tube (12 ounces) refrigerated buttermilk biscuits
- ¼ cup canola oil
- 3 tablespoons grated Parmesan cheese
- 1 teaspoon garlic powder
- 1 teaspoon dried oregano
- 1 teaspoon dried parsley flakes

1. Cut each biscuit into thirds. Roll each piece into a 3-in. rope and tie into a knot; tuck ends under. Place 2 in. apart on greased baking sheets. Bake at 400° for 8-10 minutes or until golden brown.

2. In a large bowl, combine the remaining ingredients; add the warm knots and gently toss to coat.

Bakeshop HOW-TO

Shaping Knot Rolls

Divide dough as directed; roll each portion into a rope. Tie into a knot. Tuck and pinch ends under.

Sunflower Seed & Honey Wheat Bread

I've tried other bread recipes, but this one is a staple in our home. I won $50 in a baking contest with a loaf that I had stored in the freezer.

MICKEY TURNER, GRANTS PASS, OREGON

PREP: 40 MIN. + RISING • **BAKE:** 35 MIN. + COOLING
MAKES: 3 LOAVES (12 SLICES EACH)

> 2 **packages (¼ ounce each) active dry yeast**
> 3¼ **cups warm water (110° to 115°)**
> ¼ **cup bread flour**
> ⅓ **cup canola oil**
> ⅓ **cup honey**
> 3 **teaspoons salt**
> 6½ **to 7½ cups whole wheat flour**
> ½ **cup sunflower kernels**
> 3 **tablespoons butter, melted**

1. In a large bowl, dissolve yeast in warm water. Add the bread flour, oil, honey, salt and 4 cups whole wheat flour. Beat until smooth. Stir in sunflower kernels and enough remaining flour to form a firm dough.

2. Turn onto a floured surface; knead until smooth and elastic, about 6-8 minutes. Place in a greased bowl, turning once to grease the top. Cover and let rise in a warm place until doubled, about 1 hour.

3. Punch dough down; divide into three portions. Shape into loaves; place in three greased 8-in. x 4-in. loaf pans. Cover and let rise until doubled, about 30 minutes.

4. Bake at 350° for 35-40 minutes or until golden brown. Brush with melted butter. Remove from pans to wire racks to cool.

Mini White Breads

These small and tender loaves have wonderful flavor and texture. I've found them to be the perfect size when cooking for a smaller number or when preparing them for gifts around the holidays.

NILA TOWLER, BAIRD, TEXAS

PREP: 20 MIN. + RISING • **BAKE:** 20 MIN. + COOLING
MAKES: 2 LOAVES (4 SLICES EACH)

- 1 package (¼ ounce) active dry yeast
- 1 tablespoon sugar
- ⅓ cup warm water (110° to 115°)
- 2¼ to 2½ cups all-purpose flour
- 1 teaspoon salt
- ½ cup milk
- 2 teaspoons butter, melted
  Additional melted butter

1. Combine yeast, sugar and water in a large bowl. Add 1½ cups of flour, salt, milk and butter. Mix for 3 minutes on medium speed. Stir in enough remaining flour to form a soft dough.

2. Turn onto a floured surface; knead until smooth and elastic, 6-8 minutes. Place in a greased bowl, turning once to grease the top. Cover and let rise in a warm place until doubled, about 45 minutes.

3. Punch dough down; shape into loaves. Place in two greased 5¾-in. x 3-in. x 2-in. pans. Cover and let rise until doubled, about 30 minutes.

4. Bake at 375° for 20-25 minutes or until golden brown. Remove from pans to wire racks to cool. Brush tops with melted butter.

From-Scratch Bagels

Instead of going to a baker, head to the kitchen and surprise your family with homemade bagels. For variation and flavor, sprinkle the tops with cinnamon-sugar instead of sesame and poppy seeds.

REBECCA PHILLIPS, BURLINGTON, CONNECTICUT

PREP: 30 MIN. + RISING • **BAKE:** 20 MIN. + COOLING • **MAKES:** 1 DOZEN

- 1 teaspoon active dry yeast
- 1¼ cups warm milk (110° to 115°)
- ½ cup butter, softened
- 2 tablespoons sugar
- 1 teaspoon salt
- 1 egg yolk
- 3¾ to 4¼ cups all-purpose flour
  Sesame or poppy seeds, optional

1. In a large bowl, dissolve yeast in warm milk. Add the butter, sugar, salt and egg yolk; mix well. Stir in enough flour to form a soft dough.

2. Turn onto a floured surface; knead until smooth and elastic, about 6-8 minutes. Place in a greased bowl, turning once to grease the top. Cover and let rise in a warm place until doubled, about 1 hour.

3. Punch dough down. Shape into 12 balls. Push thumb through centers to form a 1½-in. hole. Stretch and shape dough to form an even ring. Place on a floured surface. Cover and let rest for 10 minutes; flatten bagels slightly.

4. Fill a Dutch oven two-thirds full with water; bring to a boil. Drop bagels, two at a time, into boiling water. Cook for 45 seconds; turn and cook 45 seconds longer. Remove with a slotted spoon; drain well on paper towels.

5. Sprinkle with sesame or poppy seeds if desired. Place 2 in. apart on greased baking sheets. Bake at 400° for 20-25 minutes or until golden brown. Remove from pans to wire racks to cool.

Pizza Pan Bread

People are astounded to learn that I make this yummy bread from scratch in less than an hour. With this recipe from my brother-in-law, hot homemade bread is an easy alternative to garlic toast. I sometimes serve it as a snack or appetizer.

SANDRA WINGERT, STAR CITY, SASKATCHEWAN

PREP: 20 MIN. + RISING • **BAKE:** 15 MIN. • **MAKES:** 1 LOAF (16 PIECES)

> 2½ cups all-purpose flour
> 1 tablespoon quick-rise yeast
> 1 teaspoon sugar
> 1 teaspoon salt
> 1 cup warm water (120° to 130°)
> 1 tablespoon canola oil
> **TOPPING:**
> ¼ to ⅓ cup prepared Italian salad dressing
> ¼ teaspoon salt
> ¼ teaspoon garlic powder
> ¼ teaspoon dried oregano
> ¼ teaspoon dried thyme
> Dash pepper
> 1 tablespoon grated Parmesan cheese
> ½ cup shredded part-skim mozzarella cheese

1. In a large bowl, combine 2 cups flour, yeast, sugar and salt. Beat in water and oil until blended. Stir in enough remaining flour to form a soft dough.

2. Turn onto a floured surface; knead for 1-2 minutes or until smooth and elastic. Place in a greased bowl, turning once to grease the top. Cover and let rise in a warm place for 20 minutes.

3. Punch the dough down; place on a greased 12-in. pizza pan and pat into a 12-in. circle. Brush with salad dressing. Combine the seasonings; sprinkle over top. Sprinkle with cheeses.

4. Bake at 450° for 15 minutes or until golden brown. Serve warm.

Swedish Rye

This recipe came from my mother, and it's long been a family favorite. You can make a meal of it with soup and a salad.

MARY ANN ROSS, CROWN POINT, INDIANA

PREP: 25 MIN. + RISING • **BAKE:** 30 MIN.
MAKES: 4 LOAVES (10 SLICES EACH)

> 1 package (¼ ounce) active dry yeast
> 1¾ cups warm water (110° to 115°), divided
> ¼ cup packed brown sugar
> ¼ cup molasses
> 2 tablespoons shortening
> 2 teaspoons salt
> 2½ cups rye flour
> 3¾ to 4¼ cups all-purpose flour
> 2 tablespoons butter, melted

1. In a large bowl, dissolve yeast in ¼ cup water. Add sugar, molasses, shortening, salt and remaining water; stir well. Add rye flour; beat until smooth. Add enough all-purpose flour to form a soft dough.

2. Turn onto a floured surface; knead until smooth and elastic, about 6-8 minutes. Place in a greased bowl, turning once to grease the top. Cover and let rise in a warm place until doubled, about 1½ hours. Punch dough down.

3. Shape into four round loaves. Place on greased baking sheets. Cover and let rise until doubled, about 45-60 minutes. Bake at 350° for 30-35 minutes or until golden brown. Brush with butter.

Cloverleaf Bran Rolls

These tender and delicious rolls are great for a gathering. They're especially good served warm.

MARVEL HERRIMAN, HAYESVILLE, NORTH CAROLINA

PREP: 40 MIN. + RISING • **BAKE:** 15 MIN. • **MAKES:** 2 DOZEN

- 1 cup All-Bran
- 1 cup boiling water
- 2 packages (¼ ounce each) active dry yeast
- 1 cup warm water (110° to 115°)
- 1 cup shortening
- ¾ cup sugar
- 1 teaspoon salt
- 2 eggs, beaten
- 6 cups all-purpose flour

1. In a small bowl, combine bran and boiling water; set aside. In another bowl, dissolve yeast in warm water.

2. In a large bowl, cream shortening, sugar and salt. Add eggs and yeast mixture; mix well. Add bran mixture and 2 cups flour; beat well. Gradually add enough remaining flour to form a soft dough.

3. Turn onto a floured surface; knead until smooth, about 6-8 minutes. Place in a greased bowl, turning once to grease top. Cover and let rise until doubled, about 1 hour.

4. Punch dough down. Turn onto a lightly floured surface. Divide into six portions; divide each into 12 pieces. Shape each into a ball; place three balls in each greased muffin cup. Cover and let rise until doubled, about 1 hour.

5. Bake at 350° for 15-18 minutes or until lightly browned. Remove from pans to wire racks.

Bakeshop HOW-TO

Shaping Cloverleafs

Divide dough into balls. Make balls smooth by pulling the edges under. Place smooth side up in greased muffin cups.

Challah

This traditional Jewish bread uses more eggs than most, which give it a rich flavor and attractive golden color.

TASTE OF HOME TEST KITCHEN

PREP: 30 MIN. + RISING • **BAKE:** 30 MIN. + COOLING
MAKES: 2 LOAVES (16 SLICES EACH)

- 2 packages (¼ ounce each) active dry yeast
- 1 cup warm water (110° to 115°)
- ½ cup canola oil
- ⅓ cup sugar
- 1 tablespoon salt
- 4 eggs
- 6 to 6½ cups all-purpose flour

EGG WASH:

- 1 egg
- 1 teaspoon cold water

1. Dissolve yeast in warm water. Add oil, sugar, salt, eggs and 4 cups flour. Beat until smooth. Stir in enough remaining flour to form a firm dough. Turn onto a floured surface; knead until smooth, 6-8 minutes. Place in a greased bowl, turning once to grease the top. Cover and let rise until doubled, about 1 hour.

2. Punch down. Turn onto a floured surface; divide in half. Divide each portion into thirds; shape each into a 15-in. rope.

3. Place three ropes on a greased baking sheet and braid; pinch ends and tuck under. Repeat. Cover and let rise until doubled, about 1 hour.

4. Beat egg and cold water; brush over braids. Bake at 350° for 30-35 minutes or until golden brown. Cool on wire racks.

Rustic Rye Bread

This gorgeous rye bread has just a touch of sweetness and the perfect amount of caraway seeds. With a crusty top and firm texture, it holds up well to sandwiches...but a pat of butter will do the job, too.

HOLLY WADE, HARRISONBURG, VIRGINIA

PREP: 20 MIN. + RISING • **BAKE:** 30 MIN. + COOLING
MAKES: 2 LOAVES (12 SLICES EACH)

- 1 package (¼ ounce) active dry yeast
- 1¾ cups warm water (110° to 115°), divided
- ¼ cup packed brown sugar
- ¼ cup light molasses
- 3 tablespoons caraway seeds
- 2 tablespoons canola oil
- 3 teaspoons salt
- 1¾ cups rye flour
- ¾ cup whole wheat flour
- 1¾ to 2¼ cups all-purpose flour

1. In a large bowl, dissolve yeast in ¼ cup warm water. Add the brown sugar, molasses, caraway seeds, oil, salt and remaining water; mix well. Add the rye flour, whole wheat flour and 1¾ cups all-purpose flour. Beat until smooth. Stir in enough remaining all-purpose flour to form a firm dough.

2. Turn onto a lightly floured surface; knead until smooth and elastic, about 6-8 minutes. Place in a bowl coated with cooking spray, turning once to coat the top. Cover and let rise in a warm place until doubled, about 1 hour.

3. Punch dough down; shape into two round loaves. Place on a baking sheet coated with cooking spray. Cover and let rise until doubled, about 1 hour.

4. Bake at 350° for 30-35 minutes or until golden brown. Remove from pan to wire rack to cool.

tasteofhome.com

Alphabetical Index